EXPLORERS

EXPLORERS

GREAT TALES OF ADVENTURE AND ENDURANCE

ROYAL GEOGRAPHICAL SOCIETY

 Smithsonian Institution

LONDON, NEW YORK, MUNICH,
MELBOURNE, AND DELHI

Project Editor Bob Bridle
Senior Art Editor Michael Duffy
Jacket Designer Duncan Turner
US Editor Margaret Parrish
Production Editor Ben Marcus
Production Controller Sophie Argyris
Managing Editor Stephanie Farrow
Managing Art Editor Lee Griffiths

Produced for DK by
TALL TREE LTD.

Managing Editor David John
Senior Editor Rob Colson
Editors Richard Gilbert, Deirdre Headon
Designers Ben Ruocco, Peter Laws,
Jonathan Vipond
Picture Researcher Louise Thomas

Written by Alasdair Macleod
Additional writing Philip Parker, Eugene Rae

Smithsonian
Institution

Smithsonian Project Coordinator
Ellen Nanney

Smithsonian Consultant David Buisseret,
Scholar-in-residence, Newberry Library, Chicago

First American Edition, 2010

Published in the United States by
DK Publishing
375 Hudson Street
New York, New York 10014

10 11 12 13 14 10 9 8 7 6 5 4 3 2 1

RD174—September 2010

Published in Great Britain by
Dorling Kindersley Limited.

A catalog record for this book is
available from the Library of Congress.

ISBN 978-0-7566-6737-5

DK books are available at special discounts when
purchased in bulk for sales promotions, premiums,
fund-raising, or educational use. For details, contact:
DK Publishing Special Markets, 375 Hudson Street,
New York, New York 10014 or SpecialSales@dk.com.

Reproduced by MDP, Bath, UK
Printed and bound by Star Standard, Singapore

Discover more at
www.dk.com

CONTENTS

FOREWORD

Over thousands of years and throughout the world, journeys into the unknown have been undertaken by explorers, scholars, travelers, merchants, diplomats, and others. Many have returned from their travels to document and record their experiences, from the personal diary of an explorer focused on the practicalities of survival and progress, to the scientific documentation of the sample record, chart position, or satellite data reading. Whatever the motivation behind each journey of exploration, these accounts reflect the personal feats of human skill and endurance that made them possible and the extraordinary changes that have taken place, as a result, in our understanding of the planet.

Drawn for the most part from the rich historical collections of the Royal Geographical Society (with IBG), their stories are illustrated here through maps, journals, archive material, and other records covering a span of some 500 years—confirming the passion, skills, and spirit required to achieve individual goals. The sharp realities of each journey and the punishing physical extremes experienced by men and women in often alien environments are so often shown to be exceeded by an explorer's courage and ingenuity. The desire of these diverse figures to describe, understand, and extend geographical knowledge is common to all. From the starkness of conditions faced by such heroic figures as Scott and Shackleton

in Antarctica, to the skills of adaptation and cultural immersion displayed by the likes of Richard Francis Burton traveling in 19th-century Africa and Arabia, personal and public stories are told here, accompanied by a wealth of visual material including unique early photography by some of the earliest practitioners of this art: Frank Hurley and Herbert Ponting.

In addition to those names that are familiar to all, this book also provides an ideal opportunity to understand the interconnection between figures involved with exploration across centuries and cultures, from Alexander von Humboldt's key role in inspiring later generations of scientific exploration in South America to the role of early Arabists such as Bertram Thomas, whose empathy for local indigenous life and culture would do much to improve European understanding of Bedouin life. The contribution of the many indigenous porters, translators, guides, and diplomats to the process of exploration is also of key importance, for without their local geographical knowledge, often invested over thousands of years, little could be achieved. Exploration continues to evolve as the scientific skills that first enabled us to understand new landscapes and people are now employed in the investigation of the cause and process that bring about changes in the environment; passion and determination will remain at the heart of future exploratory endeavor.

SIR RANULPH FIENNES
May 2010

INTRODUCTION

In my lifetime, the world seems to have become smaller. Distant lands have been made accessible. Thanks to modern transportation, satellite, and computer, the mysterious has become the mainstream and the exotic has become the everyday. Not that I'm complaining. I've done my fair share of bringing the world closer to home, and as President of the Royal Geographical Society (with IBG), I'm delighted that more people than ever are interested in discovering for themselves the remarkable beauty and diversity of our planet.

What we should not forget is how quickly this new technology has changed things, and how recently these new opportunities have become available. In my childhood, traveling outside Britain was the privilege of a very few and someone as fascinated by the world as I was had to rely on a certain

breed of men and women to do the hard traveling for them. We called them explorers, and I wanted to be one.

As an island nation, exploration is very much part of British history and tradition. From the late 15th century onward, the British, along with the Dutch and the Portuguese, were one of the more restless nations, always looking to extend their knowledge of the world and the potential of new routes and new markets. Later, in the 18th and 19th centuries, science and religion became an added motive for people to set aside the comforts of home for the trials and tribulations of difficult and often dangerous lands.

Though it might seem hard to comprehend in our safety-conscious times, death, disease, and constant hardship did nothing to dampen the

urge to explore. Where one traveler fell, there was another prepared to pick up his bag and keep moving on into the unknown. It is because so little is "unknown" today that a book like this is important. With vivid illustrations and much use of maps and personal accounts (many from our RGS-IBG archive), we can learn a lot more of what motivated men and women to take such risks.

We who set out armed with maps, guide books, immunizations, and GPS trackers can easily forget what it must have been like to enter a land that no one had ever seen and for which no map existed. To experience extremes of heat and cold that nothing had prepared you for, to suffer illness and disease for which there was no precedent and very often, no treatment. Exploration was rarely heroic. The failure rate was high, progress often a frustrating business of trial and error. All this is captured in the book, but so is the other side of the story: the feeling of achievement, the huge thrill of seeing mountains, rivers, deserts, gorges, waterfalls, and civilizations that no Western eye had ever seen before, the enormous relief at risks resolved and instinct triumphant.

While being full of new information and fresh detail on the great explorers, this book is, most of all, a celebration of the perverse, obsessive, often destructive urge to go beyond the boundaries of human experience. It's an urge that still exists, and although the outlets are few these days, there are still places on Earth that are fierce, desolate, remote, and irresistible. The story of exploration is not over yet.

MICHAEL PALIN
President, Royal Geographical Society
(with the Institute of British Geographers)
May 2010

THE EARLY EXPLORERS

THE EARLY EXPLORERS

2500BCE	700BCE	300BCE	1CE

c. 670BCE
Pharaoh Necho dispatches an expedition from Egypt that attempts to circumnavigate Africa

c. 563BCE
Siddhartha Gautama, the Buddha, is born in Lumbini in northern India

▲ **2500BCE**
Sumerian tablets record trading routes between Syria and Anatolia (present-day Turkey)

▶ **500BCE**
Hanno departs from the Phoenician city of Carthage and voyages to West Africa, possibly reaching as far as Cameroon (see pp.18–19)

▲ **334BCE**
Alexander the Great begins his career as conqueror of Asia Minor and the Persian Empire, reaching Egypt in 332BCE and India in 324BCE (see pp.22–25)

▼ **330BCE**
Persepolis, capital of the Persian Empire, is captured by the army of Alexander the Great and destroyed, possibly in revenge for the destruction of the Acropolis during the Greco–Persian War

▲ **2300BCE**
Harkhuf makes three expeditions from Egypt to Nubia; his last journey is made in the name of Pharaoh Pepi II, whose name is inscribed on this stone vessel (see pp.16–17)

500BCE
Greek cartographer **Hecataeus** produces the first known world map, portrayed as a flat disk surrounded by "Ocean"

82CE
Roman emperor **Domitian** dispatches an expedition across the Sahara to the lands of the Aramantes; they possibly reach as far as Ethiopia

▲ **130CE**
Claudius Ptolemy of Alexandria maps the coordinates for all parts of the known world, with latitude measured from the equator, as it is today

◀ **1500BCE**
A lavish trading expedition is sent by Queen Hatshepsut from Egypt to the land of Punt, thought to be in the Horn of Africa

▶ **5TH CENTURY** BCE
Phoenicians colonize as far west as Mogador in present-day Morocco, where they establish a trade in purple dye made from murex shells

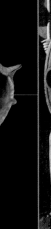

▶ **1ST CENTURY** CE
Nabatean city Palmyra acts as a link between Rome to the west and Parthia to the east, and becomes wealthy through trade

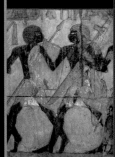

▶ **1000BCE**
Polynesians arrive in Tonga and Samoa from southern China; during the next 2,000 years, they spread east across the Pacific

5TH CENTURY BCE
Bantus begin to spread from the Niger area to colonize the region around the African Great Lakes

330BCE
Pytheas sails from Greek Marseilles, reaching the Hebrides and possibly as far as Iceland, and describes pack-ice and the northern lights for the first time (see pp.20–21)

138BCE
Zhang Qian is sent by Chinese emperor Wu of Han on an expedition to Central Asia, where he establishes the trade routes that will become the Silk Road (see pp.30–31)

148CE
Parthian prince **An Shigao** arrives in Luoyang, the Han Chinese capital, and makes the first Chinese translations of Buddhist texts

166CE
A **Roman embassy** reaches as far as the Chinese court, establishing trade links with East Asia

◀ PP. 10–11 Wall paintings surround a statue of the Buddha in the Ajanta Caves, India, where temples were carved from the rock between 200BCE and 700CE

FROM THE VERY EARLIEST TIMES, travelers have ventured beyond the borders of their territory as traders, conquerors, or simply as visitors. Before the Common Era, Phoenician navigators reached West Africa, and Greek voyager Pytheas sailed to the British Isles. Later, Vikings made landfall in North America. However, the accounts of ancient travelers often interweaved the fantastic with the practical, so a real sense of the geography of the globe was still not possible. The advanced cultures of the Americas remained isolated from the rest of the ancient world. China's contacts with European civilizations were sporadic, and even those with India and Persia were dependent on a very tenuous route down the Silk Road. Africa, too, aside from its northern shores, was largely unknown to the outside world.

300CE

▶ 399
Fa Xian the Monk
sets off from China
on his epic pilgrimage
to India and Sri
Lanka in search of
Buddhist scriptures
(see pp.44–45)

512–530
Irish monk
St. Brendan makes
his legendary journey
north to the mythical
Isle of the Blessed

▼ 600
**Chinese luxury
goods,** such as this
terra-cotta horse, are
traded as far west
as Egypt

▲ 629
Xuanzang, a Chinese
Buddhist monk, sets
off on his epic journey
across Central Asia,
visiting the colossal
Buddhas at Bamyan,
Afghanistan, en route
to India (see pp.46–47)

700CE

700
Arab merchants
reach Canton
(Guangdong) in China

▲ 850
**Suleiman the
Merchant** sets out
from Baghdad and
visits the Maldives,
Malacca, Vietnam,
and Canton

635
The first **Christian
missionaries,** led by
Alopen, arrive in
China, setting up
places of worship in
Xian and spreading
the Nestorian doctrine
of Christianity

◀ 860
The **Vikings** land
on Iceland; the first
recorded permanent
settler, Ingólfur
Arnarson, builds a
home on the site
of present-day
Reykjavik in 874

900–1000CE

c. 900
Arab dhows start to
sail routes along the
coast of East Africa,
reaching as far south
as Sofala

914
Al-Masudi, an
Arab historian and
geographer, sets off
on his travels; he
reaches as far south
as East Africa, and as
far east as India and
possibly China

950
Erik the Red is exiled
from Sweden and sent
to Iceland; in 982, he
discovers Greenland
and encourages others
to follow him there
(see p.39)

▼ 1003
Leif Eriksson sails
from Iceland and
reaches the Labrador
Coast, where he
makes an unsuccessful
attempt to establish
a colony he
names "Vinland"
(see pp.36–39)

◀ 922
Ibn Fadlan sets
out north from the
Abbasid caliphate,
which boasts the
largest mosque in the
world at Samarra, on a
mission to convert the
Volga Bulgars to Islam
(see pp.32–33)

▼ 11TH CENTURY
Vikings conquer and
settle lands as far
south as Sicily

EXPANDING THE ANCIENT WORLD

T HE PROSPERITY OF ANCIENT CIVILIZATIONS DEPENDED ON SECURING SUPPLIES OF COMMODITIES SUCH AS GOLD, PRECIOUS STONES, AND SLAVES. TRADE ROUTES WERE ESTABLISHED TO ACQUIRE THEM AND MILITARY EXPEDITIONS WERE DESPATCHED TO CONTROL THEIR SOURCES.

TRIBUTE BEARERS
Natives from the land of Kush (the Egyptian name for Nubia) bear typical produce of their country as tribute to the Egyptian pharaoh.

Civilizations were first made possible by the coming of agriculture 10,000 years ago. Trade between the first civilizations was established very early on. The mining of the semiprecious stone lapis lazuli in Afghanistan for transport to Egypt began as far back as 6000BCE, while objects from civilizations around the Indus Valley have been found in archeological layers in Mesopotamia dating to about 2500BCE.

SEA CROWS
The Romans copied the design of Carthaginian warships and added a vicious spike known as a *corvus* (Latin for "crow"), which smashed into the decks of enemy vessels and rendered them unable to move.

The most ancient evidence of cartographic representations (of settlements) have been found at sites such as Tepe Gawra in Iraq and Mont Bégo in France. These date from Neolithic times (the final stage of the Stone Age, from about 9500–3500BCE).

However, it was Sumerian scribes in about 2500BCE who first transcribed lists of place names. A few cuneiform tablets of the 19th century BCE describe what appear to be trading itineraries along routes from Assyria into central Anatolia (in present-day Turkey).

The first records of organized exploration come from the Old Kingdom of Egypt in the 6th Dynasty (2323-2150BCE).

ALEXANDER THE GREAT
Depicted here entering the city of Babylon in
Mesopotamia, the Macedonian king Alexander
the Great established an enormous empire
that extended east to India and south to Egypt.

PTOLEMAIC WORLD
None of Ptolemy's original maps survive,
but the coordinates he provided enabled
reconstructions of them to be made, such
as this one showing India, dating from 1482.

WAR AT SEA
The Greek city-state of
Athens depended on the
strength of its navy for its
power. This vase depicts a
large Athenian warship.

The land of Nubia,
to Egypt's south, lay
astride a trade route
that brought precious
commodities such as
ivory, ebony, incense, and
wild animal skins to the Nile.
The Egyptians made strenuous
efforts to control this trade route and
during the 6th Dynasty, Harkhuf, the
Egyptian governor of the city of Aswan,
made four expeditions into the land of "Yam"
(see pp. 16–17). By the reign of Hatshepsut
(1473–1458BCE), Egypt possessed a fleet on
the Red Sea that carried out frequent trading
and diplomatic missions to a land the Egyptians
called Punt, which has been variously identified
as Eritrea or the southwestern coast of Arabia.
During the 26th Dynasty, another feat of
Egyptian navigation was recorded by the
Greek historian Herodotus, who relates that
the pharaoh Necho (672–664BCE) despatched
an expedition to circumnavigate Africa.

SPREAD OF THE PHOENICIANS

The sailors Necho employed for his bid to round
Africa were Phoenicians, members of a group
that, from the late 1st millennium BCE, had
expanded from their homelands in present-day
Lebanon to establish a series of colonies along
western Mediterranean coastlines. Typically
siting their settlements on offshore coastal
islands, the Phoenicians founded colonies at
Gadir (near present-day Cadiz in Spain), Lixus
(in Morocco), and Utica (in Tunisia), all in about
1100BCE. By the 8th century BCE, they controlled

parts of Sicily, Sardinia, and
eastern Spain (with its access to
the rich silver mines of the interior).
With the foundation of the city of
Carthage (traditionally held to be in 814BCE),
the Phoenicians had a stranglehold on the
western Mediterranean. Not content with such
dominance, Phoenician explorers ventured even
farther afield with the African voyage of Hanno
in the late 5th century BCE (see pp. 18–19) and
Himilco, who, in the 5th century BCE, sailed
northwest, possibly reaching as far as Ireland.

THE RISE OF GREECE

By the time of the voyage of Hanno, the
Phoenicians faced competition from the Greeks,
who in the 8th century BCE had themselves
begun to send waves of colonists to the west.
The Greeks expanded into
Sicily and Sardinia, south
to the African coastlines of
Cyrenaica and Tripolitania
and northward along the
coastlines of the Black Sea.
This expansion of the Greek
world combined with the
flowering of Greek science
and philosophy. In the 6th
century BCE, they produced
the first world maps,

including that of Hecataeus (c. 500BCE), who
portrayed a flat world surrounded by "Ocean,"
though with a reasonable representation of the
shapes of India and Arabia. By the 5th century
BCE, Herodotus disputed this traditional view,
basing his own accounts on direct experience
and travel, which involved, in the compilation
of his *Histories*, a visit to Egypt to quiz priests
there about their religious rituals.

COLLECTING DATA

As time went on, ancient Greek scientists began
to collect empirical evidence to support their
ideas. Alexander the Great (see pp. 22–25) took
an entourage of scholars with him on his great
campaign of conquest eastward, including
two, Baito and Diognetus, who kept a log of
distances, geographical features, fauna, and flora.

This tradition culminated in
the work of Ptolemy of
Alexandria (c. 90-168CE),
who mapped coordinates for
all parts of the known world,
discussed the merits of
various map projections in
approximating to a sphere,
and established principles for
mapping the globe that
remained influential until
the late Middle Ages.

After the fall of the western
Roman Empire in the 5th
century CE, waves of invaders
migrated into Europe: in the
west, Huns, Goths, Franks,
and, in the 9th century,
Vikings; in the east, Arab
Muslims, who captured
the whole of North Africa.

HARKHUF

ANCIENT EGYPTIAN EXPLORER OF NUBIA

EGYPT

C. 2300 BCE

HARKHUF IS THE earliest recorded explorer. He was born into a noble family on Elephantine, an island on the Nile River close to Egypt's border with Nubia (present-day northern Sudan) and served as a court official to two pharaohs of Egypt's 6th Dynasty: Merenra and Pepi II. All that is known of his life and his four expeditions to Nubia during the 24th century BCE comes from the inscriptions on the walls of his tomb at Aswan, southern Egypt. These proudly record his titles, exploits, and the royal favors he received.

Ancient Egypt's relations with its southern neighbor were important. Nubia was rich in natural resources that were much coveted in Egypt, including gold and natron (a salt-ash mix used in mummification). As it also controlled access to trade routes south and west into the African continent, Nubia was a strategic focus for Egyptian exploration.

The records from Harkhuf's tomb show that he first traveled to Nubia on a mission from the pharaoh with his father, Iri, whose title was "Overseer of Interpreters." Describing the journey, Harkhuf recorded that: "The Majesty of Merenra, my Lord, sent me, together with my father, the Sole Companion and Lector-Priest, Iri, to Yam … I did it within seven months … I brought back all the beautiful and exotic

products therefrom. I was praised on account of it greatly." Archeologists believe that the location of Yam, or Iyam, was the fertile plain south of present-day Khartoum, where the Blue and White Niles join.

A DONKEY CARAVAN

For security, Harkhuf's party did not travel by river, where they risked being attacked by Nubian warlords, but on foot over the desert roads with a caravan of donkeys and soldiers. The donkeys were laden with gifts from the pharaoh to the rulers of Yam, together with food and water for the animals and men. This suggests that the desert at that time was not as

barren as it is today and was able to sustain animal grazing. It was not until the Persians introduced the camel to Egypt nearly a thousand years later, that an effective method of desert transportation could be guaranteed.

The royal approval Harkhuf so proudly recorded led to Merenra requesting that the explorer carry out a second and a third expedition. Egypt's rulers wanted to forge trade links with their southern neighbor. "His Majesty sent me a second time alone; I went forth

DESERT GOLD
Harkhuf's destination, Nubia, was among the richest gold-producing regions of the ancient world.

AN EGYPTIAN MODEL DEPICTS NUBIAN ARCHERS, HIRED AS MERCENARIES IN EGYPT DURING THE 11TH DYNASTY

A LIFE'S WORK

- Promotes Egyptian trade with **Nubia** by bringing back incense, ebony, leopard skins, ivory, gold, and spears

- Trades with **Central Africa** by accessing Nubian-controlled trade routes

- Increases **Egypt's knowledge** of her only near neighbor

- **Mediates** between warring Nubian rulers to secure the stability of the region and protect the trade routes south

- Prepares for the eventual **expansion of Egypt** into Nubia under later pharaohs

IN HIS FOOTSTEPS

→ **First and second expeditions to Yam**
Harkhuf makes a goodwill mission with gifts from Egypt; he befriends local Nubian chiefs

○ **Third expedition to Yam**
Is sent by the pharaoh to pacify warring Nubian chiefs; successfully makes peace

○ **Fourth expedition to Yam**
Harkhuf brings back a pygmy for the boy pharaoh, Pepi II

→ **Hatshepsut's expedition to Punt**
Boats carried across the Eastern Desert sail to what is thought to be present-day Somalia

○ Not shown on map

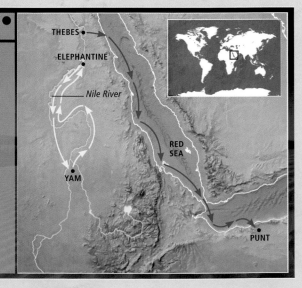

THEBES

ELEPHANTINE

Nile River

YAM

RED SEA

PUNT

upon the Elephantine road … being an affair of eight months. When I descended I brought gifts from this country in very great quantity … I descended from the dwelling of the chief of Sethu and Irthet after I had explored these countries."

On the way back, the caravan was so loaded down with Nubian goods that it had to travel along the Nile (so that the donkeys did not need to carry water). Because of the danger of attack, he hired troops from Yam for protection.

TRUSTED ADVISER

Harkhuf's third expedition was a diplomatic mission to pacify warring Nubian rulers. By his own account he was successful, and the royal gifts he brought helped to heal local rifts.

SLAVES OF THE PHARAOH
Harkhuf lived during the 6th Dynasty, when the pharaohs of the day wanted friendly relations with Nubia. Later dynasties, however, would view Nubia as a target for plunder. These tiles from the 20th Dynasty show the pharaoh's Nubian slaves.

THE PEPI CENTURY
Harkhuf served Pepi II, shown as a boy on his mother's knee. He was the longest reigning monarch in history, becoming pharaoh aged six and living to 100 years.

Following Merenra's death, Harkhuf was once more asked to travel south, and it is the record of this expedition that offers an insight into his role as a trusted royal official. The new boy pharaoh, Pepi II, dictated a letter with enthusiasm for the explorer's latest spoils, and the text of it was carved on Harkhuf's tomb wall: "You said in your dispatch that you have brought a pygmy … Hurry, bring with you this pygmy … If he goes down into a boat with you, choose trusty men to be beside him on both sides of the boat in case he falls into the water … My Majesty longs to see this pygmy more than the spoils of the mining country and of Punt."

Harkhuf's travels provide an insight into a far-off time when the world was vast. Most Egyptians never left their villages, and even neighboring civilizations seemed remote.

HATSHEPSUT

EGYPT	REIGNED 1479–58BCE

Harkhuf returned home with great riches, but no further Egyptian journey south is recorded until about 800 years later.

The next great expedition took place during the 18th Dynasty. The temple of Queen Hatshepsut near Luxor commemorates a lavish trading expedition to Punt, thought to be in the Horn of Africa. Boats were carried from Thebes in pieces across the Eastern Desert and reassembled on the Red Sea coast to sail south.

HANNO THE NAVIGATOR

EARLY EXPLORER OF THE WEST AFRICAN COAST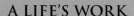

CARTHAGE, NORTH AFRICA   C. 500BCE

HANNO OF CARTHAGE made the earliest recorded journey down the west coast of Africa. Carthage, a great port city that once stood in present-day Tunisia, was founded by the Phoenicians, a seafaring people whose civilization spread along the coast of North Africa. There is fragmentary evidence for several early feats of Phoenician navigation and exploration, of which Hanno's is probably the greatest.

A LIFE'S WORK

- A **stone tablet** hung in the **Temple of Ba'al Hammon** in Carthage tells of his voyage; the tablet is later translated into Greek; we know of his journey through these Greek accounts

- Establishes **new colonies** along the coast just beyond the Strait of Gibraltar

- After dropping off the colonists, he continues south along the coast of Africa, possibly sailing as far as **Mount Cameroon**

- Describes an encounter with a group of **hairy, savage people**, who were probably gorillas or another species of great ape

- **May have traveled farther** than Mount Cameroon but the full truth is still shrouded in mystery; it is likely that the account on the tablet did not tell the whole story, and that the details of many of his discoveries were kept secret

The original story of Hanno's adventures was carved on a stone tablet in Phoenician, but this was lost when the Romans razed Carthage to the ground in 146BCE. Luckily, a Greek translation, known as *The Periplus of Hanno,* survived. This account describes an expedition to colonize the coast to the west of the Strait of Gibraltar and a voyage that was made to what is probably the Senegal River. But the expedition may also have been driven by a search for new sources of the murex shellfish, from which a costly purple dye used in clothing was made. A longer voyage south remains the subject of speculation, and various locations have been suggested for those described in the account.

FOUNDING COLONIES

Hanno's expedition was a huge undertaking. The account describes a fleet of 60 ships, each with 50 oarsmen and carrying some 500 men and women, as well as supplies. The fleet sailed out beyond the "Pillars of Hercules" (the Strait of Gibraltar), and on to lands then little known

TROPICAL RAINFOREST
The landscape Hanno saw along the Gulf of Guinea was alien to the Phoenicians, who had never before entered a tropical region.

to the people of the Mediterranean. Phoenician mariners sailed within sight of land, so Hanno would have kept close to the African coast as he headed west, allowing groups of settlers to disembark at regular intervals of every two days. Eight colonies were established, the first at Lixus and the last at Mogador, both on the present-day Moroccan coast. Sailing up a great river, probably the Senegal, Hanno describes elephants, crocodiles, and "river horses" (or hippopotamuses). Within weeks, the expedition reached "an immense opening of the sea," thought to have been the Gambia estuary.

MEETING GORILLAS?

Following a particular landing, Hanno's concerns for his ships is clear: "we were then afraid, and our diviners induced us to abandon the island. Sailing quickly thence, we went past a country burning with fires and perfumes, and streams of fire supplied by it fell into the sea … we discovered at night a country full of fire." Based on estimates of

the fleet's position, this could place Hanno close to Mount Kakoulima, in present-day Guinea. Hanno continued, "On the third day after our departure thence, having sailed by those streams of fire, we arrived at a bay … at the bottom of which was an island full of savage people, the greater part of whom were women, whose bodies were hairy and whom our interpreters called Gorillae. Though we pursued the men, we could not seize any of them, but all fled from us, escaping over the precipices and defending themselves with stones. Three women, however, were taken, but they attacked

BOAT OF TARSUS
A Phoenician trading ship is depicted on this 1st-century sarcophagus known as the *Boat of Tarsus.* These ships were broad, sturdy craft with a single square sail.

PHOENICIAN TRADERS

At the height of their civilization in the 10th century BCE, the warships and merchant vessels of the Phoenicians were, according to contemporary accounts, without parallel in the Mediterranean. This is clearly seen in the bas-reliefs and other records of the time. By the 6th century BCE, in addition to coastal dominance, Phoenician traders had developed a network of overland trade routes, stretching into western Asia. In addition to carrying goods, the caravans that plied these routes brought back information about distant peoples and places.

their conductors with their teeth and hands, and could not be prevailed upon to accompany us. Having killed them, we flayed them and brought their skins to Carthage." Debate continues as to whether this passage describes contact with humans or with apes. In *The Periplus*, the narrative ends abruptly at this point, with a decision to abandon further exploration "because victuals failed us."

HOW FAR DID HE GET?

Later theories that Hanno sailed right around Africa derive from the title of the Greek work, *Periplus*, meaning "circumnavigation." Hanno was credited with having continued on a journey around the Cape of Good Hope, returning to Carthage from the east, a notion that may have arisen because he did, in fact, sail east, into the Gulf of Guinea. This story was disputed by the Greek historian Herodotus, and today it is generally thought highly unlikely.

IN HIS FOOTSTEPS

→ *c.* 500BCE—**Hanno sails from Carthage down the west coast of Africa**
The date and route of the voyage are both uncertain, but it appears that he traveled as far as the equator; nothing at all is known of Hanno's return journey

○ **4th century BCE—*The Periplus of Hanno* is mentioned by the historian Herodotus**
In his book *The Histories,* the Greek historian dismisses the possibility that Hanno had sailed right around Africa

○ Not shown on map

PILLARS OF HERCULES
CARTHAGE
MOGADOR
ISLAND OF HERNE
MOUTH OF RIVER GAMBIA
MOUNT KAKOULIMA
MOUNT CAMEROON
ATLANTIC OCEAN

THE LANDING OF HANNO
Hanno tells of an encounter with "hairy" people on an island. These could have been gorillas but are more likely to have been another of the great apes, since gorillas cannot swim. The Roman author Pliny the Elder later wrote that the furs of the "gorillas" were exhibited at the Temple of Tanit in Carthage.

PYTHEAS OF MASSALIA

"DISCOVERER" OF THE BRITISH ISLES

GREEK MASSALIA   C. 380–310BCE

PYTHEAS WAS A GREEK MATHEMATICIAN, astronomer, and explorer living in the colony of Massalia (present-day Marseilles, France). In about 330BCE, he undertook an expedition to search for a sea route for the transportation of tin from northern Europe. On this journey, he is believed to have "discovered" the British Isles, reaching as far as the Shetland Islands. He also established the existence of "Thule," the mysterious end of the known world according to Greek and Roman geographers and scholars.

TO THE FAR NORTH

As he sailed north along the coast of Britain, Pytheas's recorded observations place him at Flamborough Head, Yorkshire, England, and then later at Tarbat Ness, Scotland. Along the way, he noted the disappearance of cultivated grains and fruits and the dependence of people in the far north on millet, herbs, and roots. He continued along the coast of Caithness and the Orkney Islands, arriving at Burra Fjord, on Unst Island, the most northerly of the Shetland Islands. Pytheas recorded this as "Orcas," the most extreme point of the British Isles and undoubtedly a local native name.

THE CLIFFS OF UNST, SHETLAND ISLANDS, THE SIGHT THAT GREETED PYTHEAS'S CREW AS THEY HEADED NORTH

No direct evidence exists for Pytheas's voyages, and the texts that record his travels are often critical and unreliable in their presentation of his achievements. According to the later Greek geographer Strabo (c. 64BCE–24CE), Pytheas lived in relatively difficult financial circumstances and would not have been able to pay for the expedition himself. It is likely that the funding was given by the governing body of the colony, or possibly by a wealthy patron eager to obtain access to supplies of tin and other goods, which until that time were received from northern Europe by a long overland route, descending through the Rhône valley. The nearest approximation that can be established for the date of the voyage is 330BCE.

PLANNING THE VOYAGE

Before he sailed, Pytheas worked out the latitude of his point of departure. This was vital in order to make navigational calculations during the voyage. The earliest method of calculating the distance of a location from the equator was by observing the length of the longest and shortest days. To do this, he erected a large gnomon, or sundial, and from his measurements was able to establish the latitude of Massalia, which is almost exactly that of the present-day observatory at Marseilles. He then fixed his instruments on the nearest star to the North Star to determine his course. Both these preparations mark Pytheas as one of the earliest known navigators.

His trireme, a vessel named for its three rows of oars, was 150–170 ft (45–50 m) in length and weighed about 400–500 tons. It is interesting to compare the scale of this warship to later vessels of exploration, such as Columbus's *Santa Maria*, which was only about 70 ft (20 m) in length. The main mast of Pytheas's ship was equipped with square sails, and fore- and aftermasts. Most of the ship's power, however, came from the galley, where 174 men were positioned on three levels. The oars were 7½ ft (2.3m) in length, with an increase of 3 ft (90 cm) in length for each ascending row. The distance covered by ancient Greek ships of this kind would have been on average 500 stadia (56 miles/90 km) in a day; the stadium (295 ft/ 90 m) being the ancient Greek unit of measurement for all geographical distances.

A LIFE'S WORK

- After setting sail from Massalia (Marseilles), Pytheas passes **beyond the limits of the known world** at Cape St. Vincent in present-day Portugal

- Sails to Unst Island, the most **northerly inhabited point** of the British Isles

- Reported to have reached Thule, which may lie in present-day Norway within the **Arctic Circle**; he is the first person on record to describe the midnight Sun and drift ice

- Discovers that the people in Britain drink **beer**, an alcoholic beverage made from fermented barley then **unknown in the Mediterranean**

OAR-POWERED WARSHIP
The sturdiness of Pytheas's ship, with its crossbeams and swan-necked bow and stern, was enhanced by a wooden ledge around the waterline. On the poop deck, there was a tentlike structure to house the pilot and helmsman.

**DISCOVERY
OF AMBER**
During a voyage to the
mouths of the Rhine and
Elbe rivers, Pytheas recorded
the existence of amber,
known then as electrum.

Pytheas and his crew sailed within sight of land,
like all ancient mariners, toward the Sacred
Promontory (present-day Cape St. Vincent in
Portugal), which was then the western limit of
the known world. They then continued north
as far as Oestrymnis (Cape Finisterre) and then
eastward along the north coast of Iberia.

LANDFALL IN BRITAIN

Pytheas's first landing in Britain is recorded as
being on the coast of Cantion (Kent), where
he continued his travels on foot to Belerion
(present-day Cornwall), gathering key
information on the supply of tin.

After returning to his ship, he continued
his journey northward, with his observations
placing him on the Shetland Islands in Scotland.
It was here that he learned of the existence of an
Arctic land, Thule (ancient Saxon for "limit"),
which was estimated at a six-day sail and near
the frozen oceans of the north. Thule, as
described, might have been Iceland or the coast
of Norway. There is no evidence to support
claims that he visited this area, although he did
receive information and reports on the region
and described floating pancake ice.

Pytheas then returned to Kent via the east
coast of Britain, before setting out on a voyage
to the mouths of the Rhine and Elbe rivers
(in present-day Germany). On finally returning
to his colony, it is recorded that Pytheas wrote
two books describing his expeditions: *On the
Ocean*, believed to have been his record of the
expedition to the British Isles, and *The Periplus
of Pytheas*, describing his second journey to the
Elbe and the Rhine. Both accounts were lost in
antiquity but had a major impact on the Greeks'
knowledge of northern Europe and the Arctic.

BRITISH BEER

In Britain, Pytheas recorded observations of the
people and their farming methods. He noted that,
in the absence of Sun, the people threshed their
grain in large barns rather than in the open air, as
in the Mediterranean. He also discovered a drink
made from fermented barley called *curmi*, which
was consumed instead of wine. As Columbus
discovered tobacco in the New World, so Pytheas
can be said to have discovered beer in Britain.

ALEXANDER THE GREAT

ALEXANDER OF MACEDONIA: WARRIOR CONQUEROR

MACEDONIA

356–323 BCE

BY THE END OF HIS SHORT LIFE, the empire of Alexander the Great stretched from the Balkans to the Indian subcontinent. An exceptionally driven and ruthless individual, conscious of his own greatness, he brought Hellenistic culture to the civilizations he conquered, but also showed a willingness to learn, often adopting regional customs to the chagrin of his troops. His curiosity for the world took him deep into Asia and he might even have continued to China had his homesick armies not forced him to turn back.

A LIFE'S WORK

- Taught as a child by the Greek **philosopher Aristotle**, who inspires in him the urge to emulate the heroes of Homer's epics

- Conquers Egypt and is named **Pharaoh of all Egypt**

- Establishes **the city of Alexandria** in the Nile Delta, which becomes the second most important city in the ancient world after Rome

- Conquers **the Persian Empire** to establish the most powerful empire ever seen and extend Greek culture into Asia

- Extends his empire **into India**, leaving conquered chiefs to rule in his name

- **Studies the cultures and traditions** of the peoples he conquers and adopts their customs

- **Inspires future explorers** to follow his footsteps from Europe into Persia and India

ALEXANDER IN CULTURE
This Greek bust of Alexander, dating from the 2nd century BCE, shows him in an idealized form as a Homeric hero. Over the centuries, the style of representing him has reflected the culture of the sculptor, be it Roman, Renaissance, and so on.

Alexander's father, Philip of Macedonia, employed the philosopher Aristotle to tutor his son. The philosopher gave his young charge a specially prepared edition of Homer's epic poems, *The Iliad* and *The Odyssey*, an inspired gift the future conqueror would carry with him on all his adventures. From an early age, Alexander was determined to emulate the exploits of the poems' heroes Achilles and Odysseus. His chance came at age 19, when he ascended the throne following his father's murder. His inheritance was the Greek Empire.

NORTH TO THE DANUBE
Following his initial journey around Greece to quell rebellions sparked by the news of his father's death, Alexander's first military expedition as king was to quash an uprising in the Danube Valley to the north of

Macedonia. On reaching the region, he realized that to defeat the local chief he would be forced to steal an advantage by crossing the river to the other bank. He therefore directed the construction of rafts buoyed up with inflated animal skins, and transferred his army, horses, baggage, and weapons overnight. His strategy, based on a reading of the landscape, was a success. At the age of 22, he had proved himself a brilliant

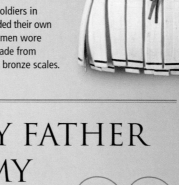

BATTLE DRESS
The hoplites, citizen-soldiers in ancient Greece, provided their own equipment. Wealthier men wore armor such as this, made from fabric reinforced with bronze scales.

tactician. With his European empire secured, Alexander turned his attention toward Persia, which his father had long planned to conquer.

TAKING PERSIA
Alexander set off through the Cilician Gate (the Gülek Pass) in southern Turkey at the head of an army of 32,000 men. He made his way down through Syria and confronted the army of the Persian king, Darius, across a river on the plain of Issus. Alexander's earlier tactic in crossing the Danube was reemployed as he forced the Persians into a weak position, and Darius fled east. Writing two centuries later, the Greek historian Plutarch records how, when he saw the opulence of the Persian king's apartments, Alexander turned to his men and said, "This, it seems, is royalty."

After crossing Syria and Palestine, Alexander traveled to Egypt, at that time part of the Persian Empire. Interpreting a passage from Homer's *Odyssey*, he identified a small fishing village as the site on which to build a city in 331 BCE. Named Alexandria, this city became a center for trade between Europe and the East. Within a century of its foundation, it was to become the largest city in the ancient world.

I AM INDEBTED TO MY FATHER FOR LIVING, BUT TO MY TEACHER FOR LIVING WELL 99

ALEXANDER THE GREAT

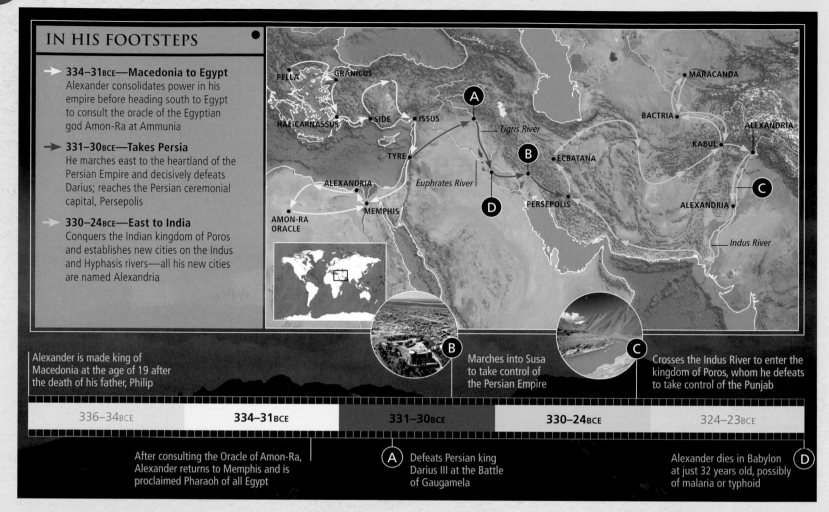

IN HIS FOOTSTEPS

➤ **334–31BCE—Macedonia to Egypt**
Alexander consolidates power in his empire before heading south to Egypt to consult the oracle of the Egyptian god Amon-Ra at Ammunia

➤ **331–30BCE—Takes Persia**
He marches east to the heartland of the Persian Empire and decisively defeats Darius; reaches the Persian ceremonial capital, Persepolis

➤ **330–24BCE—East to India**
Conquers the Indian kingdom of Poros and establishes new cities on the Indus and Hyphasis rivers—all his new cities are named Alexandria

Alexander is made king of Macedonia at the age of 19 after the death of his father, Philip

B Marches into Susa to take control of the Persian Empire

C Crosses the Indus River to enter the kingdom of Poros, whom he defeats to take control of the Punjab

| 336–34BCE | 334–31BCE | 331–30BCE | 330–24BCE | 324–23BCE |

After consulting the Oracle of Amon-Ra, Alexander returns to Memphis and is proclaimed Pharaoh of all Egypt

A Defeats Persian king Darius III at the Battle of Gaugamela

D Alexander dies in Babylon at just 32 years old, possibly of malaria or typhoid

MAN OF DESTINY

During his time in Egypt, Alexander made an expedition to the temple of Amon-Ra, the Egyptian god of the Sun who was identified by the Greeks with their god of the sky, Zeus. The temple was located at the oasis of Siwah in the Libyan Desert. According to Aritobulus, one of his biographers, the journey to the temple took Alexander along the coast to Ammunia (present-day Mersa Matruh) and then inland for about 497 miles (800 km). Alexander consulted with an oracle at the temple, reporting afterward that he had received the answer "that my heart desired." On his return to Memphis, he was proclaimed Pharaoh of all Egypt.

Alexander next marched eastward across the Euphrates to the Tigris. He engaged Darius in battle once more, and this time decisively

CONQUEST OF PERSEPOLIS

Persepolis was the official residence of the Persian kings. The city was built in a remote alpine region, however, and the empire's most important trading cities were Susa and Babylon. In fact, the Greeks did not know of Persepolis at all until Alexander conquered it. The Roman historian Diodorus describes it as "the richest city under the Sun." Alexander destroyed the great palaces and gave the rest of the city over to his troops to plunder.

THE STAIRWAY OF THE PALACE OF DARIUS, IN THE CITY OF PERSEPOLIS

defeated him, capturing Babylon. From there, he took Susa before marching on Persepolis, the Persian ceremonial capital. Soon, the whole Persian Empire was his, and the spoils of war from Persepolis alone "were so great that 20,000 mules and 5,000 camels could hardly have carried them." Alexander was aware of the need to mesh together the Greek and Persian traditions and made the farsighted decision to integrate officers from the defeated army into his own. It was a dangerous and unprecedented step, the first in recorded history to give the values and knowledge of the defeated equal status to those of the conqueror.

EAST TO INDIA

In 327BCE, having successfully incorporated the Persian Empire into his realm, Alexander placed his sights on the kingdoms of India, to reach "the ends of the world and the great outer sea." His was the first recorded invasion to enter the subcontinent from the northwest, a route of great interest to later explorers such as Marc Aurel Stein (see pp. 234–37). Alexander crossed the Indus River, and learned that the great ruler of the region was Poros, whose kingdom lay in the Punjab. Marching across the salt ranges to

LIVING GOD
This silver coin shows Alexander as the semidivine Greek hero Herakles, distinguished by his lionskin cap. On other coins he bears the horns of Amon-Ra, the Egyptian deity.

reach the Hydaspes River must have been a grueling experience for such a large body of men. They went unchallenged until, as the Roman historian Arrian records, "Alexander encamped on the banks of the river and Poros was seen on the opposite side, with all his army and array of elephants around him." Alexander split his army into sections and chose a smaller party to cross with him under cover of night, using a combination of rafts and boats. Poros was defeated by Alexander's superior cavalry and strategy, but accepted an offer to continue ruling his territory under his conqueror. At the site of the battle, Alexander ordered the construction of two new Greek cities.

In addition to founding cities in the conquered territories, Alexander sent collections of plants and animals back to Greece. The observations of the landscape made by his generals and officers greatly enriched Greek knowledge. Alexander ruled for just 13 years, but his reign had a profound impact on all aspects of language, culture, and society within his vast empire.

THE EMPIRE COLLAPSES

When Alexander died in 323BCE, his son and heir, Alexander IV, was as yet unborn. Alexander's bodyguard, Perdiccas, proposed that the empire should be ruled jointly by Alexander's half-brother Philip and his baby son. In the background, Perdiccas would wield the real power, dividing up the empire among Alexander's former generals. But when Perdiccas was assassinated in 321BCE, this arrangement immediately fell apart, leading to 40 years of conflict. In the end, four stable regions emerged: Macedonia, Ptolomaic Egypt, the Seleucid Empire in the east, and Pergamon in Turkey.

RECONSTRUCTION OF THE ISHTAR GATE, IN BABYLON. THE ORIGINAL STOOD MORE THAN 38 FT (12 M) HIGH AND WAS COVERED WITH GLAZED BRICK RELIEFS

HEROIC AGE
The Alexander Sarcophagus, found in Lebanon, dates from the 4th century BCE. Macedonian horsemen ride without saddles to hunt a lion alongside their former enemies, the Persians. The sarcophagus may have been made for one of the rulers Alexander appointed after the conquest of Persia.

EXPERIENCING LIFE IN THE...

DESERT REGIONS

THESE ARID, UNFORGIVING lands present explorers with some of their toughest challenges. The wise explorers learn the ways of the nomadic tribes who live there, the people who can show them how to navigate the ever-shifting sands, how to dress for protection, where to shelter, and most importantly, where water might be found. Many explorers have become enchanted with the hardy peoples who inhabit the world's wastes, echoing the sentiment of the English wanderer of Arabia, Wilfred Thesiger, who considered that "the harder the way, the more worthwhile the journey."

BANDITS, SANDSTORMS, AND STINGS

In the 19th century, exploring desert regions was perilous. Deserts are sparsely populated, making them ideal hideaways for outlaws. The Takla Makan Desert had long harbored bandits who preyed on the caravans passing along the Silk Road. The Sahara, too, was dangerous: Heinrich Barth (see pp. 202–03) was attacked by robbers while crossing it in the 1840s. In the great sandy deserts,

sandstorms can make travel impossible. If caught without shelter, travelers can only sit with their backs to the wind and cover their heads. Rocks may also conceal danger, such as scorpions, and, in the Sahara, the cerastes—a venomous viper. In the deserts of the southwestern US, the black widow spider can deliver a deadly bite, as can the Gila Monster lizard.

SMALL BUT DEADLY
Scorpions can deliver a nasty sting to bare ankles and may climb into footwear at night. All scorpions are poisonous, and 25 species have potentially deadly stings.

SHIPS OF THE DESERT

The traditional method of desert travel, the camel, was widely used by explorers even after the advent of motorized transportation, and Ahmed Hassanein and Rosita Forbes used them when they located the "lost" oasis of Kufra in Libya in

1921. The first motorized crossing of the Sahara was made in 1922–23 in a French expedition led by Georges Marie Haardt and Louis Audouin-Dubreuil, who drove from Touggourt in Algeria to Timbuktu in Mali in Citroën Kégresse half-tracked

vehicles. Camels were preferred by Wilfred Thesiger in Arabia in the 1940s (see pp. 250–51). For him, a sense of communion with the desert was important—something he thought traveling by jeep made impossible.

MONGOLIAN CONVOY
In four expeditions between 1922–25, American Roy Chapman Andrews led a fleet of Dodge cars across the Gobi Desert.

FINDING FOOD AND PRECIOUS WATER

Before the age of motorized transportation, water had to be either carried by camel or located along the way at oases or, more elusively, desert wells. Harry St. John Philby (see pp. 238–39) described how in the Rub' al Khali the Bedouin knew the location of the desert wells from memory, and avoided those of rival tribes. Often, wells were hard to find, since their entrances were blocked to prevent them from becoming clogged with sand. Without reliable guides to locate the wells, desert travel could be hazardous. Sven Hedin, explorer of China's Takla Makan Desert in the 1890s (see pp. 228–31), described how, after the water ran out, he struck out alone, hoping to reach a source of water before he died. Eventually, he found a river and was able to carry back water for his companions in his leather boot.

DESERT DIET

Dates, rice, coffee, and camel milk were the staples of the Bedouin diet. The desert was not entirely devoid of food, however, and Philby described the excitement among his Bedouin companions when a hare was spotted, resulting in a lengthy chase before it was shot. On occasion, baby camels, yak, and sheep were killed for their meat.

NIGHT AND DAY

In the Arabian Desert, Philby noted how "Each night the water in our skins froze hard and had to be thawed by the fire before we could make our morning tea..." By day, excessive heat coupled with a lack of water can cause heatstroke, especially during the first few days of exposure. Its symptoms include headache, nausea, diarrhea, convulsions, hyperventilation, and loss of consciousness. The temperature in the Takla Makan Desert can reach as low as -4°F (-20°C) in winter, and hypothermia is a real danger in such cold deserts if adequate shelter is not found.

MAKING CAMP

In the harsh environment of the desert, a simple tent can help to keep the heat at bay during the day and the cold out during the night. In the past, tents were bulky items, so a desert journey would involve a baggage train of camels, which followed the expedition party, catching up with them in the early evening when it was time to make camp for the night. This was how Bertram Thomas crossed the Rub' al Khali (see pp. 248–49). The Bedouin of Arabia, being a nomadic people, are expert in the construction and erection of tents. In the Takla Makan Desert, the nomadic Uyghur build yurts, shelters made from light wooden frames with thick felt coverings, to protect them from the extremes of temperature. In recent decades, many formerly nomadic desert peoples have abandoned this traditional way of life.

DESERT DRIVING

During World War I, Model T Fords were adapted for the desert because horses were not suitable for transportation over sand. With oversized tires, a higher clearance between ground and chasis, and endless maintenance, the cars were described by British officer Claude Williams as having "more lives than a cat." The Model T's gear box was suited to quick gear changes—essential to avoid getting stuck in sand. One way of avoiding the daytime heat was to travel at night, but British explorer Ralph Bagnold could not do so because he needed to see that the sand ahead was not so soft that it would sink the vehicle. During World War II, Bagnold used a simple sun compass to navigate by day. Mounted on the vehicle's dashboard, it comprised a gnomon (vertical pin) that cast a noon shadow that fell due north or south of the pin depending on the geographical position. Its advantage over a magnetic compass was that it was not disturbed by the vehicle's metal body.

STUCK IN THE SAND

Driving across the desert is a risky enterprise even today, as cars can become stuck in the sand or axles can break. In many ways, the camel, supremely adapted to the conditions, is still a traveler's best option.

I LONG ONLY FOR A NIGHT CAMP IN THE DESERT, THAT IMMEASURABLE OPEN SPACE, WITHOUT AMBITION AND WITHOUT CARES

HEINRICH BARTH

BEDOUIN LIFE

Many European explorers have survived through the hospitality of the Bedouin in the Arabian Desert. Some, such as Wilfred Thesiger, developed a profound respect for their way of life.

GOING NATIVE

In the 19th century, explorers approached desert tribes with caution. The robbing of Heinrich Barth served to illustrate what could happen to a European traveling without local guides in the wilderness. Some European explorers adopted a disguise to avoid attracting the attention of the local people. Johann Ludwig Burckhardt, who "discovered" Petra in 1812 (see pp. 240–41), went to elaborate lengths to back up his false identity, learning Arabic and Islamic law before beginning his travels. The German desert explorer Gerhard Rohlfs also tried to disguise himself as a Muslim, but he was nonetheless robbed by his guides

and left for dead after visiting Tafilet in the Moroccan Sahara in the 1860s. In Arabia, Wilfred Thesiger encountered a tribe that determined a man's status by how many men he had killed and castrated. Philby relished the spartan desert ways. He converted to Islam in 1930 before making his crossing of the Rub' al Khali. His conversion was genuine, but it also won the respect of the Bedouin. During Ramadan, he joined his guides in their fasting, and for 55 days eschewed water, drinking only tea and freshly drawn camel milk, once at dawn with a bowl of rice, and again at dusk. At the journey's end, his guides killed a camel and feasted.

TRADE AND DIPLOMACY

F OLLOWING THE RAPID BREAK-UP OF ALEXANDER THE GREAT'S EMPIRE IN THE 3RD CENTURY BCE, CONTACT BETWEEN EAST AND WEST DECLINED. WITH THE RISE OF NEW POWERS—ROME IN THE WEST AND CHINA IN THE EAST—NEW TRADE AND DIPLOMATIC LINKS WERE FORGED.

INCENSE KING
The Egyptian pharaoh Rameses II (1290–24BCE) carries a lamp burning incense, a commodity much in demand for the elaborate rituals in Egypt's temples.

Once ancient Rome came to dominate the Mediterranean from the mid-2nd century BCE, its borders began to reach the limits of the world as previously explored by the ancient Greeks. Roman exploration generally accompanied military expeditions: for example, Roman forces advanced as far as Marib in the Yemen during an abortive invasion of the country in 24BCE, the furthest point south the Roman army ever reached. There was some civilian exploration, too: in 82CE, a mission despatched by Emperor Domitian crossed the Sahara through the lands of the Garamantes—a tribe implacably hostile to Rome—and reached "Agysimba" (possibly near the Ethiopian border) where they were the first Romans to see a rhinoceros.

Just as important were the contacts beyond Rome's borders carried out by merchants, particularly those bearing goods by ship across the Red Sea, or taking the caravan routes that led across the desert to rich trading posts such as the Nabataean city of Petra or Palmyra on the fringes of the Syrian Desert. Petra, in particular, grew rich from its dominance of the Mediterranean end of the Spice Route, which began in the Hadhramaut and over which precious goods such as frankincense and myrrh had been traded since the 2nd millennium BCE.

Handbooks were compiled for merchants, such as the *Periplus of the Erythrean Sea*, a guide by an anonymous Egyptian Greek of the 1st century CE, which lists the commodities that might most profitably be traded on various routes, and gives an account of the major ports from Egypt's Red Sea coast as far as those of western India. The tradition continued as late as the 6th century CE, with the work of Cosmas Indicopleustes, an Alexandrian monk who settled in Sinai, but who gave an account of the Persian Gulf, India, and Ceylon (present-day Sri Lanka). By then, guides for Christian pilgrims visiting the sites of the Holy Land had become as common as merchants' manuals, while Christianity, in its early version, had reached the borders of China, creating the first cultural links along the Silk Road for many centuries.

ANCIENT SILK ROAD

A trading route of great antiquity, the Silk Road was not one trail, but a network of routes that carried silk and other goods from China to the West. Chinese interest in the possibilities offered

SILK WORKERS
Elegantly dressed Chinese ladies pound silk with wooden pestles, a scene of domestic life that traditionally also expressed the longing of wives for their husbands away on military expeditions.

SPICE TRADE
The insatiable demand for spices in the countries of the Middle East and the Mediterranean led to the development of a major trade route from southwestern Arabia.

MERCHANT RICHES
The Syrian city of Palmyra grew rich from exacting tolls on trade that passed through its territory, allowing the civic authorities to build lavish public buildings, such as this theatre.

SETTING THE SCENE

- In the ancient world, trade overland is risky and expensive; it is far cheaper and safer to carry goods by ship. The development of the **Silk Road** across Asia and the **caravan routes** across the deserts from Arabia show that for the right money, merchants will travel across even these **dangerous terrains**.

- The Chinese **Zhou emperor Mu Wang** travels west along the future Silk Road in the 5th century BCE, possibly reaching as far as present-day Iran, but it is not for another four centuries that the route is fully exploited for trade.

- The Parthian Persians **act as middlemen**, controlling the central part of the Silk Route and trying to monopolize both trading and diplomatic contacts between East and West. Direct **contact between Europe and China is very intermittent** until the 13th century.

- In Syria and Arabia, cities such as **Petra, Palmyra** and, later, **Mecca**, grow rich on imposing taxes on traders carrying spices and other goods from the Red Sea ports. Each one, though, ultimately loses its independence to a larger power.

- When Muslim armies conquer Arabia and most of the Middle East in the 7th and 8th centuries, they, too, seek to dominate the trade routes, sending **merchants, explorers, and ambassadors** as far as China, Sri Lanka, East Africa and Germany.

by the Silk Road began in earnest with the despatch of the general Zhang Qian (see pp. 30–31) on several expeditions from 138BCE to recruit allies against the nomadic Xiongnu, whose hostility blocked the exploitation of the route. His success opened the way to regular trade with Persia. The first Chinese ambassador to reach there (in 105BCE) is said to have laid out a spread of luxurious silks in front of the Parthian ruler Mithridates II, who in turn sent back an ostrich egg and a troupe of magicians to the Chinese court.

> After centuries with few ties between East and West, trade and cultural contacts slowly resumed in the 13th century with the journeys of William of Rubruck, Marco Polo, Zheng He, and Ibn Battuta.

CHINA AND THE WEST

Chinese attempts to extend their diplomatic and trading links further west and make direct contact with the Romans were blocked, however, by the Parthians. A Chinese envoy, Kan Ying, who was sent to Rome in 98CE, only reached as far as Najaf in present-day Iraq, where the Parthians persuaded him that the journey to the Roman empire was so arduous—taking up to three years—that he might just as well return home. There are accounts of a Roman "embassy" to the Chinese court in 166CE, but it was probably just a small group of merchants with no official backing and did not lead to any lasting diplomatic or trading ties.

With the fall of the Han dynasty in 220CE, China fragmented and unity was not restored until the time of the Sui dynasty in 588. Sixty

years later, the enfeebled Sassanid rulers of Persia were overthrown by the advancing armies of a new force, the Muslim Arabs. Initial hostility between China and the Arabs subsided after the Arab defeat of a Chinese army at the River Talas in 751.

ARAB EXPLORATION

Arab merchants may have reached Canton (present-day Guangdong, China) as early as 700. From 800 the tempo of trade links quickened, anchored, at the Arab end, on the great political and trading centre of Baghdad. Explorers such as Suleiman the Merchant visited the Maldives, Malacca, present-day Vietnam, and Canton in the early 850s, while a decade earlier, Sallam the Interpreter had been despatched from Baghdad to chart the lands to the north and west of the Caspian Sea. It was the exploits of men such as these that gave rise to the legendary stories of Sinbad the Sailor. Equally well traveled was the great al-Masudi (896–956), whose three decades of travel from 914 encompassed the Caspian Sea, India, Sri Lanka, the east coast of Africa, and Egypt. Among the groups he described were Swedish Vikings, as they sailed across the Sea of Azov in 914. A similar group of Viking settlers

(the Rus) was encountered by the diplomat Ibn Fadlan (see pp. 32–33), who traveled as part of an embassy sent by the Abbasid ruler of Baghdad to the king of the Volga Bulgars in 922. That trading ties of a sort were established between Baghdad and the Rus is demonstrated by the many thousands of silver Arab dirhams found in hoards in eastern Sweden. However, by the late 10th century, with the firm establishment of Christianity in the Rus principality of Kiev, both trading and diplomatic links between East and West began to diminish. By the time Marco Polo came to discover the old routes again (see pp. 56–59), the Silk Road was largely forgotten in the medieval West—and China was a place impossibly exotic and remote.

BLUE BOTTLE
The Roman world paid for the luxuries it imported largely in silver and gold, but it did produce some luxury goods of its own, such as beautifully crafted glassware, which was in great demand elsewhere.

ZHANG QIAN

PIONEER OF THE SILK ROAD

CHINA   C.195–114BCE

As the envoy for the Han emperor, Zhang Qian's journeys opened up new lands for Chinese trade. He pioneered the trails of the Silk Road by forging new routes to the West through the deserts and mountains of Central Asia. Zhang's account of his explorations is laid out in the *Shiji*, a chronicle compiled by historian Sima Qian a few years after Zhang Qian's death, which tells the story of 2,000 years of Chinese history.

A LIFE'S WORK

- Travels west to **lands previously unknown to the Chinese** to open up new trade routes for Chinese goods, particularly silk

- Spends 10 years as **a captive of the Xiongnu**, a nomadic people hostile to the Han

- Brings back intelligence of **the empires of Mesopotamia and Persia**

- His exploits are recorded in the *Shiji*, also called *Records of the Grand Historian*

- Is celebrated as **a national hero in China** today for his role in opening up routes to the West, which helped Han China to become one of the most powerful empires in the world

Born in the 2nd century BCE in the province of Shaanxi, Zhang Qian entered the service of the Chinese Han emperor in around 140BCE. The Han were eager to create trade links with the peoples of Central Asia, but bordering Han lands in present-day Inner Mongolia lived a hostile people called the Xiongnu, who blocked their progress. Zhang had some experience of the Xiongnu and was chosen to lead a mission beyond their territory to the Yuezhi people, who were known to be hostile to the Xiongnu. The Chinese hoped an alliance with the Yuezhi would break the power of the Xiongnu.

CAPTURE BY THE XIONGNU

Zhang headed west but was soon captured by the Xiongnu. He was held captive for 10 years, during which time he married and fathered a child, but he never forgot his mission and, when the opportunity arose, he escaped and resumed his westward progress.

Zhang was to be disappointed upon reaching the Yuezhi, finding a king who "thought only of his own enjoyment" and was not interested in an alliance with the Han. He returned home without having achieved his goal. However, he did bring back intelligence on the lands to the west. In his report, he noted that, "When I was in Daxia [Bactria, in present-day Iran] I saw bamboo canes from Qiong and cloth from Shu. When I asked the people how they had obtained such articles, they replied, 'Our merchants go to buy them in the markets of Shendu' [India]." The Han emperor was impressed with Zhang's news and sent him on a new mission to reach Daxia via Shu, but his way was blocked by a number of hostile tribes, including the Kunming "who devote themselves to plunder and robbery."

CHINESE EXPORTS
In addition to silk, the Han Chinese exported finely crafted goods such as this jade plaque dating from the 3rd century BCE.

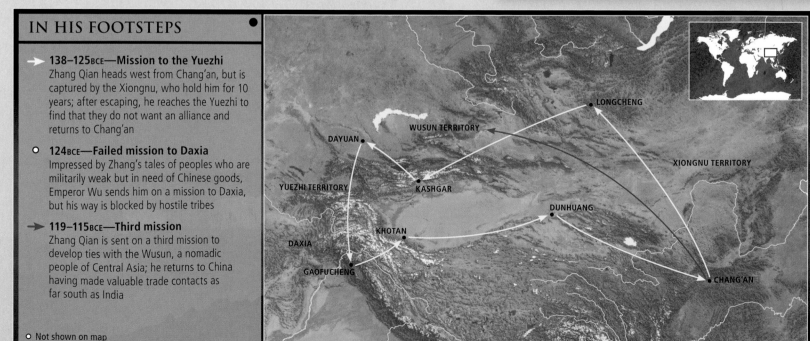

IN HIS FOOTSTEPS

→ **138–125BCE—Mission to the Yuezhi**
Zhang Qian heads west from Chang'an, but is captured by the Xiongnu, who hold him for 10 years; after escaping, he reaches the Yuezhi to find that they do not want an alliance and returns to Chang'an

○ **124BCE—Failed mission to Daxia**
Impressed by Zhang's tales of peoples who are militarily weak but in need of Chinese goods, Emperor Wu sends him on a mission to Daxia, but his way is blocked by hostile tribes

→ **119–115BCE—Third mission**
Zhang Qian is sent on a third mission to develop ties with the Wusun, a nomadic people of Central Asia; he returns to China having made valuable trade contacts as far south as India

○ Not shown on map

LONGCHENG

WUSUN TERRITORY

DAYUAN

XIONGNU TERRITORY

YUEZHI TERRITORY

KASHGAR

DUNHUANG

KHOTAN

DAXIA

CHANG'AN

GAOFUCHENG

THE PEOPLE ARE AFRAID OF BATTLE, BUT THEY ARE CLEVER AT COMMERCE

ZHANG QIAN

BUDDHIST INFLUENCE
The opening of the Silk Road allowed Buddhism to reach China from India. Although Emperor Wu did not convert, there is evidence that he received Buddhist statues. This carving of the Buddha was made along the Silk Road in present-day Pakistan around the time of Zhang Qian.

In 123BCE, Zhang was ennobled for his successful participation in a campaign against the Xiongnu, but the following year he was sentenced to death for his part in a disastrous battle against the same enemies. He escaped execution by paying a large fine. Although in disgrace, he was still consulted by the emperor, who continued to dream of the lands to the west. When Zhang told him of the Wusan, who had thrown off the yoke of the Xiongnu, he was sent to try to forge an alliance with the Wusan, which it was hoped would "cut off the right arm of the Xiongnu."

SPREADING THE WORD

Zhang was unable to persuade the Wusan to migrate east and threaten the Xiongnu, but he did manage to send envoys to every neighboring state requesting that they visit the Han court to see for themselves the wealth and power of the Han emperor. Zhang returned home in 115BCE and, according to Sima Qian, he was "honored with the post of grand messenger, ranking him among the nine highest ministers of the government." Zhang died the following year. Although the immediate goals of his missions had not been achieved, the seeds of communication sowed during his travels were to bear bounteous fruit. Many of the countries visited by Zhang did send envoys to the Han court, where, as he had promised, they were greatly impressed and eager to start trading. The route pioneered by Zhang became the main avenue by which the Chinese exported silk to Central Asia and the West.

CHINA'S FIRST GREAT HISTORIAN
Zhang Qian's journeys form just a small part of Sima Qian's great 130-chapter work *Shiji*, which gives a complete history of China from the legendary Yellow Emperor to his own time.

EMPEROR WU OF HAN

Zhang Qian's missions were sponsored by Emperor Wu, whose long reign from 141–87BCE saw the Han extend their empire from Korea in the north to Vietnam in the south. Wu established a strong government based on Confucian principles that encouraged the self-improvement of his subjects, a political system that is still influential in China today.

EMPEROR WU SENDS ZHANG QIAN OFF ON HIS FIRST MISSION, A WALL-PAINTING IN THE MOGAO CAVES

IBN FADLAN

ARAB WHO TRAVELED TO EASTERN EUROPE

PERSIA   C. 900

ISLAMIC SCHOLAR IBN FADLAN is known for the remarkable journey he made from Baghdad to the Volga River in Eastern Europe. His mission was to teach the Volga Bulgars about Islam. As his party traveled from the Caspian Sea to the East European Plain, Fadlan recorded the customs of the different peoples he encountered, including a fair-skinned group he called "the Rus," who may have been descendants of Vikings.

A LIFE'S WORK

- Travels to the **Volga Bulgars**, and as a Muslim scholar, is charged with guiding their religious instruction

- Keeps a **detailed journal** of the journey, recording the customs of the various tribes they meet, paying particular attention to their **funeral rites**

- Leaves a journal of his travels that is discovered inside a **medieval document** in 1923

- Meets with a people on the Volga he calls **the Rus**, who may have been descendants of Vikings who traveled there from Scandinavia

- **Historians still debate** which tribes Ibn Fadlan actually met

In about 920, in Baghdad (present-day Iraq), the Caliph al-Muqtadir received a letter from the king of the Volga Bulgars, a people who lived in the north of present-day Kazan, Russia. The king's tribal followers included Muslim converts and it is reasonable to assume that his request was for Islamic teaching and guidance, in addition to funds to construct a fortress against the Khazars. The caliph agreed to his request and, in June 921, despatched Nadhir al-Harami as his ambassador, with scholar Ibn Fadlan in his party.

ASTROLABE
Fadlan carried an astrolabe similar to this one, called the Qibla, with the direction of Mecca marked on it.

Fadlan kept a detailed journal on the expedition, which covered 2,500 miles (4,000 km), and wrote of a series of encounters with people whose origins remain a matter of hot debate among historians to this day. Evidence of the journey comes mainly from a 13th-century manuscript that lay undiscovered until 1923. It contains four accounts of medieval Arab geographical thinking, one of which is Ibn Fadlan's report of his journey.

The expedition set out from Baghdad, following the age-old route of the Silk Road through Central Asia, and then turning north to trace

the Fur Route, which traders dealing in fur, silver, and amber used to travel between Central Asia and Northern Europe.

INTO THE NORTH

The expedition stayed three months at a place Fadlan called "al-Jurjaniya" close to the Aral Sea. For the Arab party, conditions were starkly different from the hot climate of the Persian capital. Fadlan records how "leaving the hammam [steam bath] and going back to my dwelling, I looked at my beard. It was a single lump of ice and I had to thaw it in front of the fire." He also noted how a group of camels froze to death in the subzero temperatures. By

CHIEF'S CREMATION
Ibn Fadlan witnessed a dramatic funeral rite on the Volga when a dead chief was cremated in a longship alongside sacrificed slaves.

I SAW PEOPLE WHO OWNED 10,000 HORSES AND 100,000 SHEEP

IBN FADLAN

GREAT MOSQUE OF XIAN
Arab merchants took Islam along the Silk Road as far as western China, where the Great Mosque was built at Xian. Ibn Fadlan may have visited the mosque on his way to the Volga.

February 922, the weather conditions had improved and, despite the warnings of the local people that they would never return, the expedition departed, taking with them three months' supplies and a group of Bactrian camels. They also carried with them several small boats covered in camel skin, to cross the rivers they expected to encounter en route.

As predicted, the conditions deteriorated as the party pushed north. When they reached an area to the north of the Caspian Sea, the camels floundered in snow so deep that it reached up to their knees. Fadlan looked back on the cold he had experienced earlier in the journey that seemed "like days of summer" in comparison

with the conditions he now encountered. He also made detailed descriptions of the tribes he met, including the nomadic Turkish tribe, the Oghuz. He marveled at their huge herds of sheep and horses, and made some of the earliest written descriptions of nomadic burial practices. The bodies of Oghuz chiefs would be buried in pits and covered by a mud dome. The noble's horses would then all be slaughtered and eaten, and their heads, hooves, hides, and tails used to decorate the grave.

COURT OF THE BULGAR KING

Some 70 days from al-Jurjaniya, the expedition arrived at the court of the Volga Bulgars, where Fadlan records the reading of letters from Caliph al-Muqtadir and the handing over of gifts to King Yiltawr and his consort. By Fadlan's own account he was treated by the king as something of a favorite, which may explain the freedom he

AL-BIRUNI

PERSIA   973–C. 1050

Born in Katy in northern Persia, al-Biruni was a brilliant scholar who made major contributions to a wide range of subjects, from mathematics to history and medicine. He traveled extensively as a young man in the company of Sultan Mahmood Ghaznawi, who was touring his new conquests in northern India.

Al-Biruni spent 20 years traveling around India, learning Hindu philosophy and mathematics, and teaching Greek and Arabic philosophy and science. On his return to his homeland, he wrote a vivid account of his travels in the book *Kitab-al-Hind* (A History of India), which contributed toward the acceptance of the Hindu culture of India by its new Muslim rulers. He made major contributions to astronomy, too, figuring out that the Earth orbits the Sun and studying the phases of the Moon (see below).

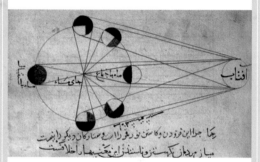

THE PHASES OF THE MOON, DRAWN BY AL-BIRUNI IN HIS ENCYCLOPEDIA OF SCIENTIFIC OBSERVATIONS

was given to explore and note the sights of the landscape around him, including the bones of a "giant," which could be interpreted as the remains of a mammoth or other skeletal fossil.

During this period, the medieval manuscript records Fadlan's impression of a people he describes as "the Rus." One interpretation is that these were tribes of Scandinavian origin, possibly part of a Viking expansion into present-day Russia. Fadlan described these Volga-Russian fur traders as men "like palm trees. They are fair and their skin white and red … Each of them has an ax, a broadsword, and a knife and they are never without these things." The account also details a burial ritual in which a dead chieftain was laid out in a long ship and burned with grave goods and sacrificed slaves before a barrow was built over the remains. His journal ends there so we do not know how the expedition ended. Despite its fragmentary nature, however, Ibn Fadlan's account gives a unique insight into the cultures of Eastern Europe in the early medieval period, and it is an essential source of information about the Rus.

IN HIS FOOTSTEPS

→ 921—Ibn Fadlan's party leaves Baghdad for Eastern Europe
Ibn Fadlan joins the mission to provide Islamic guidance to the Bulgars; his detailed journal describes the different peoples he encounters on the way and their customs

○ 11th century—al-Biruni travels around India
The Persian scholar spends 20 years in India and writes a book about his experiences; he extends knowledge in many fields, including astronomy, mathematics, and geography

○ Not shown on map

BULGAR

SAMARA
Volga River

ARAL SEA

AL-JURJANIYA

CASPIAN SEA

BUKHARA

GORGAN

BAGHDAD

IN SEARCH OF NEW LAND

F ROM THE LATE 8TH CENTURY CE, A NEW GROUP, THE VIKINGS, EMERGED FROM SCANDINAVIA. THEY BEGAN BY RAIDING, BUT SOON SET UP INDEPENDENT STATES. ACROSS THE NORTH ATLANTIC, THEY SETTLED A STRING OF ISLANDS, ULTIMATELY LANDING IN NORTH AMERICA.

RUNIC WRITING
Across the Viking world, some 3,000 inscriptions in the angular futhark, the Scandinavian runic alphabet, commemorate the lives of those who died on Viking expeditions.

The reasons for the sudden onset of the Viking raids, heralded by the sack of the English monastery of Lindisfarne in 793, are unclear. They may have started because of the pressure of overpopulation at home in Scandinavia, and the beginnings of political centralization that pushed those unwilling to obey the law to seek adventure overseas. Whatever the explanation, advances in naval technology in the 7th and 8th centuries, leading to the development of the longship, assisted the Viking raiders.

Sleek and shallow-draughted, these ships could travel rapidly, venture up rivers, and were not dependent on deep anchorages. Traveling in these vessels and in sturdier ships more adapted for ocean crossings, the Vikings terrorized a vast swathe of northern Europe.

STAYING FOR THE WINTER

It was not long before the Vikings sought bases in which to overwinter, rather than returning to Scandinavia after each raid. Scotland had been an early target of Viking attacks, with the first recorded raid coming against the monastic community on Iona in 795. The Scottish islands, particularly the Orkneys, Shetlands, and Hebrides, offered ideal havens for the Vikings

RAIDER'S SWORD
Although traditionally depicted wielding great axes, the Vikings carried a variety of weapons, including, for the nobility, longswords such as this one, which could deliver vicious slashing blows.

to establish more permanent bases. By the middle of the 9th century, these places were subject to the overlordship of a variety of Scandinavian jarls (earls). In Scotland the Vikings displaced or assimilated the native population, while farther afield their ships encountered islands that were nearly or entirely uninhabited. In about 800, a Viking expedition under Grim Kamban came across the Faroes (or "sheep islands"), which soon became the first of the Viking North Atlantic colonies. The Faroes acted as a natural stepping stone for the next great Viking expansion across the Atlantic—on to Iceland. There had long been rumors of an island called Thule in the frozen wastes of the north and its name had been included by the 1st-century Roman geographer Ptolemy in his world map. The Irish monk Dicuil wrote in about 825 of an island visited by monks where the summer nights were so bright that they could pick the lice from their shirts.

ICELAND AND GREENLAND

In about 860, the first Viking to land on Iceland, one Nadodd, who had been driven off course from the Faroes, climbed the nearest mountain and, seeing the icy waste of the interior, dubbed the place

> The Americas were first settled from Asia at least 12,000 years ago. After Leif Eriksson, this new land was forgotten by Europe until Christopher Columbus's voyage in 1492, which paved the way for European conquest and colonization.

Snaeland ("snow-land"). He was followed a few years later by the Swede Gardar Svarsson, similarly storm-tossed on his way to the Hebrides, who circumnavigated the island and named it Gardarsholm. The first real effort at settlement came in about 865 when Floki Vilgedarsson sailed to Iceland. Not knowing quite where he would find the island, he took to releasing two ravens, and when they did not return to the ship, he knew that land was nearby. Floki's name for the place, Iceland, stuck, but his settlement only lasted two years. It was only the expeditions of Ingolf Herjolfsson in 870, and 874, which founded a settlement near present-day Reykjavik, that marked the true beginnings of Viking Iceland.

Within 50 years, the Landnam ("land-taking") saw almost all the best land in Iceland secured by new settlers, with the fiercely independent colony dotted with small farmsteads, ruled over by a popular assembly, the Thing, which met annually on a plain near Reykjavik. The sometimes lawless early days of Iceland were later recounted in sagas, originally tales transmitted orally, but later set down in writing during the 12th and early 13th centuries. Some of them tell the story of Viking expeditions yet further afield. The Saga of Erik the Red relates the career of a fiery young

ICELANDIC HOME
As protection against the bitter cold of the north Atlantic islands, the Vikings adapted their architecture, creating turf-covered farmsteads such as this one in Iceland.

VIKING FUNERAL
In Scotland's Shetland Islands, the festival of Up-Helly-Aa features the ceremonial burning of a longship, an echo of the ritual ship burials of the pagan Scandinavians.

SETTING THE SCENE

- Viking **raids against northern Europe** begin in the late 8th century. By the 860s, Vikings have conquered northern England (the Danelaw), much of the north of Scotland and its Isles, and founded Dublin (in about 840) along with ports on the coast of Ireland.

- After the settlement of Iceland in the 870s, many refugees travel there, fleeing from the political centralization of Norwegian **King Harald Finehair** in the late 9th century.

- As Scandinavia **converts to Christianity** in the late 10th and early 11th centuries, and the kings there grow more powerful, the Viking raids cease. Iceland loses its independence in 1262 and becomes subject to the Norwegian crown. Greenland accepts Norwegian control at about the same time, but as the climate grows colder at the end of the **"Medieval Warm Period"**, and fewer ships sail there, the colony dies out.

Viking whose family settled in western Iceland (see p.39). He became involved in a feud, and, during a quarrel, killed two of his neighbour's sons. As a result, in 982 he was banished from Iceland for three years. Taking his family, Erik set sail west, searching for a land that had been sighted by Gunnbjörn Ulfsson some

60 years earlier. Initially making landfall on the east coast of Greenland, Erik then sailed round the island's southern tip where he found a series of sheltered harbours. When his term of banishment expired, Erik returned to Iceland with glowing accounts of the new land's bounty,

calling it "Greenland" to entice settlers. When Erik returned in 986, it was with a fleet of some 25 ships, carrying almost 500 people to Greenland, including his wife Thjodhild and son Leif (see pp.36–39). Erik built a farm at Brattahlid in what became Greenland's Eastern Settlement, the hub of a Viking colony that lasted more than 300 years and eventually had its own bishop.

VIKING AMERICA

Greenland's Viking population only ever reached about 4,000 people and the Scandinavian colonists failed to adapt their way of life to the harsh environment. It was hardly surprising, then, that the idea of lands to the west of Greenland that were richer in resources was an enticing one. So it was that Erik's son Leif set out in about 1001 in search of a coastline spotted a few years earlier by a mariner, Bjarni Herjolfsson. When this new Viking venture to the coastline of North America failed, after several attempts at settlement, Greenland found itself ever more isolated. A ship that was driven there from Iceland in about 1400 found the Eastern Settlement still functioning, but another ship that landed in 1541 found the houses abandoned and only a solitary corpse.

VIKING-AGE ICELAND
This map of Iceland by the 17th-century Flemish cartographer Ortelius gives a vivid depiction of the fjord-studded land that Ingolf Herjolfsson settled in the 870s.

LEIF ERIKSSON

VIKING DISCOVERER OF NORTH AMERICA

ICELAND   C. 970–1020

ACCORDING TO THE VIKING SAGAS, Leif Eriksson sailed westward from Iceland into unknown seas and found a land described as fruitful with mild winters that he called "Vinland." He had probably reached Newfoundland, in present-day Canada, and was the first European ever to set foot in the New World, nearly five centuries before Christopher Columbus. The sagas record at least three attempts to establish a Viking colony in America, but these all failed due to the hostility of the native peoples and the sheer distance from home.

Leif Eriksson was born in about 970, in Iceland, but probably grew up in Greenland. His father was Erik the Red, an outlaw and explorer who was credited with discovering Greenland. As a child, Leif was inspired by his father's tales of exploration, and those of Bjarni Herjolfsson, the son of Erik's friend Herjolf.

Bjarni was a trader, and often sailed between Iceland and Norway. One winter, returning to Iceland, he found that Herjolf and Eric had left for Greenland to establish a new Viking settlement. A skilled seaman, Bjarni had not previously voyaged to Greenland but decided to join them. Sailing west, his ship was blown off course in dense fog. When he sighted land, it did not match Herjolf's descriptions of Greenland's grassy hills—instead it was covered in dense forests. Bjarni chose not to land. Instead he headed north, but found the same forested terrain twice more before losing sight of land. Finally, some seven days later, he sighted Greenland, at last reaching his father's settlement.

DISCOVERY OF AMERICA
The mysterious land described by Bjarni intrigued the young Leif. As he grew up, he resolved that he, too, would explore the unknown world to the west. In about 1002 or 1003, he was ready to begin his voyage. He had purchased Bjarni's ship and selected a crew of 35 Icelanders. Erik the Red was

invited to accompany his son, but the old man refused, saying his exploring days were over. En route to visit the ship, Erik was thrown from his horse and injured, and this was seen as an omen that he should not join the expedition.

Leif and his crew set off, retracing Bjarni's earlier route in reverse. However, the first terrain they encountered was not Bjarni's forested landscape, but a bleak land of large, slab-like stones and icy mountains. The crew landed a boat and explored, but found the barren place worthless as a location for settlement, naming it Helluland, or "slab land" (this may have been present-day Baffin Island).

On Leif sailed, and next sighted a land that matched Bjarni's description of low-lying coastal forest and sandy beaches. He called this Markland, or "forest land" (probably Labrador Island). Eventually, the explorers reached another small island where, according to the sagas, the men tasted the dew from the grass and were astounded by its sweet taste. This landing point was probably Nantucket, Massachusetts.

Sailing around a nearby promontory, which may have been Cape Cod, the Vikings next landed at the mouth of a river. They set up a camp, using animal-skin cots brought from their

THOR IN AMERICA
Most Vikings were still pagans at the time of Leif's expedition. His men would have carried talismans, such as this one of the Viking god Thor, to Vinland.

OCEAN-GOING SHIP
The Vikings were superb seamen, skilled in handling vessels on rough Arctic seas. Wherever possible they sailed within sight of land, lowering the sail and rowing when they neared the shore. Explorers sailed in sturdy, wide-bodied ships with overlapping strakes (planks), a keel and matching prow and stern. There was room on deck for livestock and supplies.

WITS ARE NEEDED FOR THOSE WHO TRAVEL WIDELY—ANYTHING WILL DO AT HOME

HAVAMAL, "SAYINGS OF THE HIGH ONE"

ship, and built rudimentary shelters from wooden posts covered with branches and turf. The men marveled at the quality of the grasslands for grazing livestock, and the plentiful large salmon in the river. A crew member named Tyrkir went missing during the first weeks of exploration inland, but later returned with wild grapes taken from vines. This inspired Leif to call his new settlement Vinland, or "Vine Land," and it was here that they spent the winter. After Greenland and Iceland the climate seemed mild; the grass was green all year round and there was little frost. Eventually the men gathered a crop of grapes, along with vines and substantial amounts of timber before setting sail for home.

Within the first few days at sea, still in sight of Vinland, Leif spotted a shape off the coastline. Sailing closer to the shore, he came

VIKING SETTLEMENT

The Vikings were notorious raiders, but they were also great explorers and colonizers. Between 870 and 930, for example, about 10,000 settlers arrived in Iceland from Scandinavia in search of farmland, which was in short supply in Norway. From Iceland, they migrated to Greenland, although the population there never exceeded about 4,000. There are several reasons why the settlements in Vinland did not succeed—the settlers were very far from home, the winters were long, and the native peoples persistently hostile.

VIKING SETTLERS CONSTRUCTED SHELTERS UPON ARRIVAL IN VINLAND, USING LUMBER CUT FROM NEARBY WOODS

DRAGON SHIP
The medieval written accounts of the Viking sagas feature fanciful depictions. Here, a Viking warship carries with it the cities its crew of warriors have conquered.

upon a partially wrecked Viking ship. Its captain, Thorer, his 15 men, and their cargo were taken on board Leif's ship, which then set course for Eriksfjord in Greenland. The rescue of Thorer and his men earned their saviour a new nickname—"Leif the Lucky."

VINLAND COLONIES

About two years after the expedition, Leif's brother, Thorvald, set out for Vinland. He and his crew reached the location of the settlement and spent the winter there, gathering wood and catching fish. Thorvald took a longboat to explore the coastline to the west, but found no sign of native people. However, during his second winter on Vinland, the sagas record that the crew were attacked by "Skraelings"

(a Viking word meaning "screechers"), presumably the Inuit people of the region. Thorvald was fatally wounded, the first known European to die and be buried in the Americas. His men returned to Greenland, taking back a cargo of wood and wineberries. Leif's half-sister, Freydis, also led a party of settlers to Vinland, but she, too, suffered attacks from the Skraelings. Over the winter at the settlement, a disagreement arose between the Greenlanders and the Icelanders in the party. Freydis was a ferocious, strongwilled woman, whose solution to the dispute was to have the Icelanders murdered. Driven from Vinland by the

THE START OF ERIKSSON'S VOYAGE
A statue of Leif Eriksson stands today at Brattahlid, South Greenland, from where he is believed to have embarked on his voyage to Newfoundland.

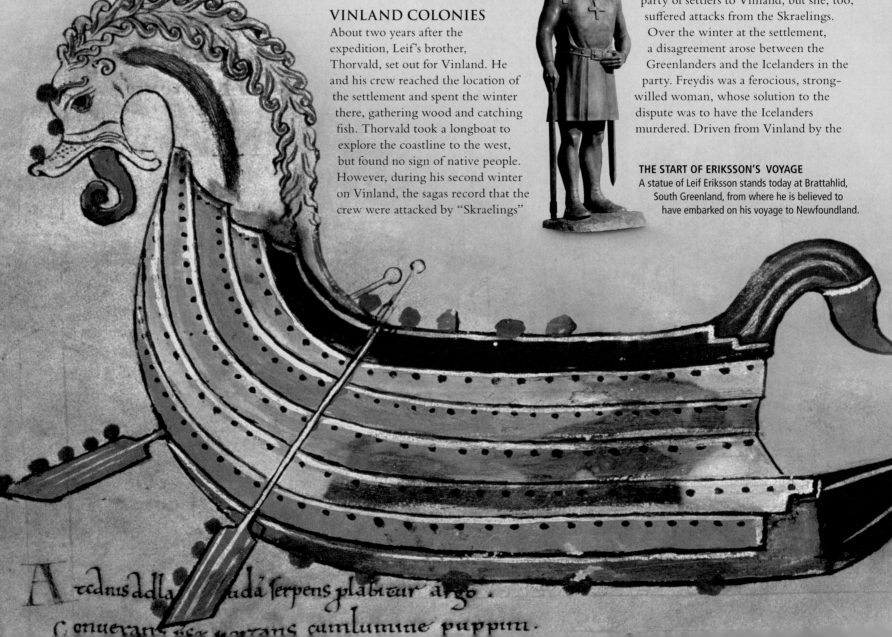

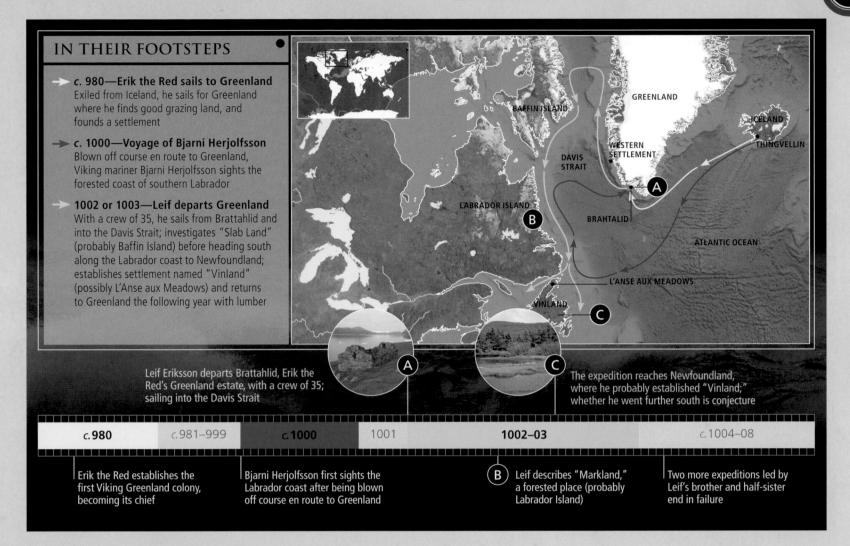

IN THEIR FOOTSTEPS

c. 980—Erik the Red sails to Greenland
Exiled from Iceland, he sails for Greenland where he finds good grazing land, and founds a settlement

c. 1000—Voyage of Bjarni Herjolfsson
Blown off course en route to Greenland, Viking mariner Bjarni Herjolfsson sights the forested coast of southern Labrador

1002 or 1003—Leif departs Greenland
With a crew of 35, he sails from Brattahlid and into the Davis Strait; investigates "Slab Land" (probably Baffin Island) before heading south along the Labrador coast to Newfoundland; establishes settlement named "Vinland" (possibly L'Anse aux Meadows) and returns to Greenland the following year with lumber

Leif Eriksson departs Brattahlid, Erik the Red's Greenland estate, with a crew of 35; sailing into the Davis Strait

The expedition reaches Newfoundland, where he probably established "Vinland;" whether he went further south is conjecture

c. 980	c. 981–999	c. 1000	1001	1002–03	c. 1004–08

Erik the Red establishes the first Viking Greenland colony, becoming its chief

Bjarni Herjolfsson first sights the Labrador coast after being blown off course en route to Greenland

B Leif describes "Markland," a forested place (probably Labrador Island)

Two more expeditions led by Leif's brother and half-sister end in failure

---

Skraelings, Freydis and her party returned to Greenland where she was shunned when Leif learnt of her crime.

LOST IN THE MISTS OF TIME

It appears likely that no more attempts at settlement were made after Freydis's return to Greenland and the Vinland settlement was abandoned. Icelandic records also suggest that knowledge of the colony's location was already lost by the early 12th century. Even though the precise location of Vinland still remains a mystery, a Viking settlement was discovered in 1963 at L'Anse aux Meadows in northern Newfoundland. However, references in the sagas to mild winters and wild grapes would suggest that the site was a more southerly location, possibly to the south side of the St. Lawrence estuary.

Some historians point out that Leif's voyage took place during the Medieval Warm Period, when temperatures were higher on average than they are today, and that the types of flora described in the sagas may indeed have grown in Newfoundland. Others suggest that he did not find grapes at all, but the abundant blueberries that grow in the region.

TURF HOME
The remains of large Viking-style "longhouses" have been found at L'Anse aux Meadows, Newfoundland. The houses were built with thick turf walls, which insulated the inhabitants during the long winter months and could withstand high winds.

ERIK THE RED
NORWAY   *C. 950–1003*

Leif's father, Erik "the Red" Thorvaldson, probably got his nickname because of his hair color.

Born in Norway, Erik was just a child when his father was exiled to Iceland (along with his family) on account of "some killings." It was from Iceland in 982 that Erik was in turn exiled for similar crimes. On returning after the banishment had ended, he brought with him tales of a land he had discovered called "Greenland," a name he chose to make the harsh land appealing to migrants. Taking with him some 500 colonists, he established settlements, becoming a wealthy and respected chieftain. He remained a pagan, unlike his son, Leif, who converted to Christianity and helped to spread the religion in Iceland. Erik died in an epidemic brought by one group of settlers.

SEA-GOING RAIDER OF THE 9TH CENTURY

VIKING LONGSHIP

LIGHT AND SLENDER, the longship evolved from early Stone Age craft in Scandinavia and culminated in the fast, elegant vessels of the 9th century. The Vikings were superb mariners. In open seas they relied on a large, rectangular sail. To maneuver in coastal waters and rivers they dropped mast and rowed the ship. Wherever possible, they sailed within sight of land. Used for trade, migration, and war, longships had such a shallow keel that they could glide directly onto beaches without the need for a jetty or quay, even when fully loaded. Once beached, animals and men could wade ashore.

▼ BATTLE SHIP
Warriors' shields were attached to a rack along the gunwales of the longship, ready to be used in surprise raids on foreign shores.

▲ SETTING THE MAST
When not in use, the mast was lowered into a grooved timber called the keelson that was laid parallel to the keel and locked in place by a piece called the "mast fish." The deck boards were loose, so the sailors could store cargo beneath them.

▼ OAR POWER
Depending on its size, the longship needed 24–50 oars or more when the sail was not in use. On long voyages, Viking sailors rowed in shifts.

◄ SCALE SHINGLES
Wooden shingles demonstrate the craftsmanship of the Viking shipbuilders. Running from prow to stern, they help create the longship's serpent theme.

► IN FULL SAIL
This replica longship is seen sailing along the coast of Norway. With the wind behind it, a longship could reach 7–12 knots. This was fast by the standards of the time—it would take about 28 days to sail from Sweden to Newfoundland. A ship built for Atlantic voyages was known as a "knarr."

▲ KEEL CARVING
A close-up of a longship's keel shows the finely fitted strakes (planks) that made the vessel so aquadynamic. The gaps between the strakes were stuffed with tarred wool to keep out the water—a technique known as caulking.

▲ SERPENT ON BOARD
This serpent's head adorns the 70-ft (21.5-m) long Oseberg ship, found in a burial mound near Oslo, Norway, in 1903. The soggy clay preserved the ship's superb animal carvings.

◄ ENIGMATIC CARVINGS
A detail from the Oseberg ship's stern shows strange bearded figures in flowing gowns. Their significance is not known.

▼ MONSTER'S HEAD
Some longships sported carved monsters on their prows. Denizens of Europe's coasts were terrified at the sight of the "dragon ships."

▲ SHIP'S INTERIOR
Cross beams were used to add strength to the hull. The crosswise timbers could support a deck and were secured to planks at the side with curved "knees."

▼ WIND VANE
Weather vanes were attached to the prow of the ship and used to tell the direction of the wind. They may also have been used to display the rank of those on board. This is a replica of a vane found at Söderala, Sweden.

▲ SHIP'S PAIL
This wood and ceramic figure adorns an intricately made pail, found with the Oseberg ship. It was made in England and may have been taken in a raid.

EXPLORING THE BUDDHIST WORLD

FROM EARLY IN ITS HISTORY, BUDDHISM WAS CHARACTERIZED BY A MISSIONARY EFFORT THAT SPREAD FROM INDIA TO IRAN, SRI LANKA, CHINA, AND JAPAN. BUDDHIST PILGRIMS SEARCHING FOR SCRIPTURES OR SPREADING THEIR FAITH MADE JOURNEYS ALONG THE LENGTH OF THE SILK ROAD.

"JOURNEY TO THE WEST"
Known as *Monkey* in its popular Western translation, this Chinese classic celebrates the adventures of the Buddhist monk Xuanzang during his pilgrimage to India (see pp. 46–47).

For the first two centuries after the death of the Buddha in about 483BCE, the religion that grew up around his teachings remained confined largely to the Ganges Valley in India. It was the adoption of Buddhism by Ashoka the Great, (*c.* 274–236BCE), ruler of the powerful Mauryan Empire of India, that led to an upsurge in missionary activity. Buddhist teachers were despatched to neighboring countries to spread the faith, while within the Mauryan realm itself, the king ordered the erection of numerous rocks and pillars on which were inscribed edicts that proclaimed his adherence to Buddhism. Initially, the faith was able to spread to the west, encouraged by the presence of an Indo-Greek kingdom that had expanded into present-day Pakistan in 180BCE. Its ruler, Menander (*c.* 160-135BCE), converted to Buddhism and under his successors the region acted as a conduit for Buddhism to spread west into Parthia (in present-day Iran) and north and east into Central Asia.

> From the early 13th century, Western travelers (such as Marco Polo) began to arrive in China, enabling information on the country to begin to flow westward along the Silk Road for the first time.

BUDDHISM SPREADS
Knowledge of Buddhism reached as far west as the city of Alexandria in Egypt, where the Christian theologian Clement (*c.* 150-215CE) made a reference in one of his works to the veneration accorded to the Buddha in India. Buddhism gained a firmer foothold in the Parthian Empire, so much so that the first translation of Buddhist scriptures into Chinese was undertaken by An Shigao (or Arsaces), a Parthian prince who arrived in the Han capital of Lo-yang in about 150CE.

The earliest reference to Buddhism in Chinese writings had come half a century earlier, but the religion did not make serious inroads into China until the period of disunity that followed the collapse of the Han dynasty in 220.

By the late 4th century, Buddhism was well established in China, and in 399 the first in a series of Chinese Buddhist monks set out in search of scripture. Fa Xian (see pp. 44–45) returned to China in 414, having visited most of the Buddhist centers in India, a region where before long the religion would be in headlong retreat in the face of a Hindu resurgence. He was followed a century later by Sung Yin, who was sent in 518 by an empress of the Northern Wei dynasty. Sung Yin succeeded in collecting some 170 books of scripture, but found to his horror that the Buddhist kingdom of Gandhara (in present-day Pakistan) had been conquered by the non-believing White Huns, a nomadic people of Central Asia.

CHINESE PILGRIMS
Under the Tang dynasty, the flow of Chinese travelers to India increased. The *Record and Memoir of I-Tsing*—who himself traveled to India and reached the kingdom of Srivijaya in the Malay Arcipelago in 687—lists at least 56 Buddhist travelers between 650 and 700 alone. In about 650, one pilgrim, Xuanzhao, traveled to India, Nepal, and Tibet, but found his way back blocked by the Arabs who had by then occupied Bactria in Central Asia and he was never able to return home. Although from the early 8th century, conditions were not so auspicious for Chinese Buddhist travelers, contacts with the greater Buddhist world continued, with Korea having been converted at the end of the 4th century and Buddhism reaching Japan in 552. The religion continued to flourish, too, in Central Asia, with the complex of cave-monasteries at Tunhuang remaining a center of Buddhist art and scholarship into the Song dynasty of the 10th century.

From the 8th century onward, most traces of contacts with the West are from travelers visiting China, beginning with Christian missionaries who may have arrived as early as 635, and continuing with the efforts by European powers to

BUDDHIST LION
This is the lion-headed capital from one of the columns Ashoka put up to commemorate his support for Buddhism and his promotion of *dharma* ("righteous living").

OASIS IN THE SANDS
The Crescent Moon Lake oasis near Tunhuang, in Central Asia, is surrounded by sand dunes, which show the terrible conditions travelers had to endure to reach the sanctuary there.

BUDDHA'S BIRTHPLACE
Lumbini, in Nepal, the birthplace of the Buddha, is one of the holiest places of Buddhism; among the earliest pilgrims was the emperor Ashoka in around 249BCE.

SETTING THE SCENE

- **Gautama Siddhartha, the founder of Buddhism**, is born into a royal family in about 560BCE, but **rejects his privileged background** for the life of a religious mendicant and preacher.

- As time goes on, Buddhism splits into **two principal schools**: Theravada (or "canonical") Buddhists are predominant today in Sri Lanka and most of Southeast Asia; Mahayana (or "great vehicle") Buddhists form the majority in China, Japan, and Korea.

- Ashoka the Great is said to have converted to Buddhism **out of a sense of remorse** at the sight of burned homes and corpses during his brutal conquest of the state of Kalinga, India, in 263–262BCE. Buddhism, a relatively new religion, becomes the **state religion** of the Mauryan Empire in about 260BCE and quickly acquires a new sophistication.

- In 401CE, just two years after Fa Xian the monk left China for India, the **Indian monk Kumarajiva** arrives in the Chinese capital of Chang'an, where he settles and **translates many Buddhist scriptures into Chinese**.

- The Chinese Buddhist traveler Ch'ang Te, who undertook an embassy from the Mongol ruler Mangu Khan to his brother Hulagu in 1259, leaves an account of the **Ismaili Muslim sect of Assassins**, who specialize in the covert killing of their enemies.

enlist the help of the Mongol rulers of China against the Muslim Arabs in the 13th century. But the Mongol era also saw fresh accounts by Chinese travelers of the lands to their west. In 1219, Yeh'lu Ch'u ts'ai, one of Genghis Khan's ministers, accompanied his master on campaign in Persia, and his account of that journey, the *Si yu lu* ("Account of a Journey to the West"), is replete with detailed descriptions of the land, such as the enormous size of the local

watermelons. Such missions continued while the Mongols retained a hold over Persia, culminating in the journey of the Christian monk Rabban Bar Sauma, born in northern China, who in 1287 traveled west to broker an alliance with European powers against the Muslim rulers of Egypt, visiting Rome, Paris, and Constantinople (present-day Istanbul).

BUDDHIST STUPA
The northern gateway of the stupa at Sanchi, a complex originally established by Ashoka and one of the oldest Buddhist sanctuaries still in existence.

FA XIAN THE MONK

PILGRIM WHO TRAVELED THE BUDDHIST WORLD

CHINA   C. 350–C. 422CE

DURING AN EXTENSIVE PILGRIMAGE through India, Sri Lanka, and Java, the Chinese monk Fa Xian went in search of Buddhist teachings not then available in China, known as the "Books of Discipline." In doing so, he created one of the earliest written accounts of Central Asia and India. Fa Xian's book, *A Record of the Buddhist Countries*, provides a unique insight into early Buddhism and the geography, cultures, and history of the various lands he visited on his 15-year odyssey.

SUPREME BUDDHA
This silk banner found in the Mogao Caves near Dunhuang depicts the Buddha (enlightened one), who lived in about 400BCE. On his travels, Fa Xian searched for sutras—works containing the Buddha's original teachings.

In 399CE, Fa Xian and other members of his order departed from Chang'an, capital of Han China, along the southern route of the Silk Road. The monks paused at various places along their pilgrimage, often for months at a time, as they undertook their traditional summer monastic retreats.

CROSSING THE GOBI DESERT
As they approached the Gobi Desert, which Fa Xian called the "River of Sand," he was warned of the rigors that were to come by the District Prefect Le Hâo: "There is not a bird to be seen in the air nor an animal on the ground

CHANDRAGUPTA II
Fa Xian visited India during the reign of Chandragupta II, sometimes referred to as India's Golden Age. The ruler's head appears on this coin.

below. Though you look all around to find where you can cross … the only indication being the dry bones of the dead left upon the sand."

The monks crossed the treacherous desert in 17 days. At the city of Khotan, they found residence at the Gomati Monastery, home to 3,000 monks. There they received hospitality and food from the common store. Fa Xian witnessed a major Buddhist festival, including a four-wheeled float "more than thirty cubits

[45 ft/13 m] high, which looked like the great hall [of a monastery] moving along … with silken streamers and canopies hanging all around." The procession took four months to complete, after which the party continued to Kashgar.

INTO INDIA
It took more than a month for the party to traverse what the local people described as the "snow mountains" (the Karakorums) and cross into northern India. Traveling southwest, they began a hazardous descent, dropping 15,000 ft (4,500 m) into the Indus Valley. They crossed the Indus River east to west on a suspension bridge. Fa Xian noted that this must have been the original point of crossing for the Buddhist faith into China, and that holy men from India "had crossed this river carrying with them Sutras and Books of Discipline." The monks passed through Gandhara province to reach the Buddha's birthplace at Lumbini. As they proceeded south to Kohat, one of Fa

A LIFE'S WORK

- **Makes a 15-year pilgrimage** across Asia in search of texts with the teachings of the Buddha

- Provides a detailed account of **the flourishing Buddhist cultures** of southern Asia in the 4th and 5th centuries CE

- In addition to studying the cultures of the places he visits, he also **describes the geography and the flora and fauna**, noting everything that is different from his Chinese homeland

- **Survives a storm on the return voyage** to bring his collection of Buddhist texts back to China

- On his return to China, he spends many years **translating the works he brought back** with the help of the Indian scholar Sramana Buddha-bhadr

MOUNTAIN RETREAT
On his long pilgrimage, Fa Xian found hospitality at Buddhist monasteries. As today, many were isolated retreats high in the mountains, such as this one at Ki Gumpa in northern India, which is 13,500 ft (4,000 m) above sea level.

IN HIS FOOTSTEPS

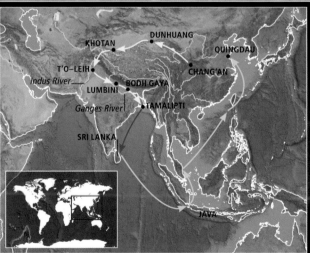

→ **399CE—Pilgrimage begins**
Sets off from Chang'an and crosses into northern India, where he retraces the life of the Buddha

→ **410CE—Sails for Sri Lanka**
After two years in Tamalipti, he sails south to the Buddhist island of Sri Lanka, where he stays for two more years

→ **412CE—Returns to China**
Leaves Sri Lanka and returns to China by sea via Java

THE KINGDOM OF THE LION

From Tamalipti, Fa Xian set out on a merchant's trading vessel to Singhala, "The Kingdom of the Lion" (present-day Sri Lanka). He remained on the island for two years, collecting many Sanskrit manuscripts unknown in China, before beginning the journey home by a sea route.

During his return voyage, Fa Xian's ship was caught in a severe storm and all passengers were ordered to throw their possessions overboard. He held onto his precious manuscripts, recording that, "I have traveled far in search of our Law. Let me by your dread and supernatural power, return from my wanderings, and reach my resting place!" He made it to China by way of Java with his collection of manuscripts intact.

Fa Xian's epic journey had taken him through some 30 countries. He described how his Buddhism had sustained him: "When I look back on what I have gone through, my heart is involuntarily moved, and the perspiration flows forth. That I encountered danger and trod the most perilous places, without thinking of or sparing myself, was because I had a definite aim, and thought of nothing but to do my best in my simplicity … that I might accomplish but a ten-thousandth part of what I hoped."

Xian's companions, Hwuy-Ying, became ill in the severe cold: "a white froth came to his lips" and he urged Fa Xian "do you immediately go away, that we do not all die here." The pilgrimage continued through the Punjab, following the course of the P'oo-na River, where Fa Xian counted 20 monasteries on each bank, housing some 3,000 monks. They crossed the plains to reach the Jetvana Monastery in Awadh. Here, the pilgrims were welcomed as the first men from the kingdom of Han to have reached the site. At Pataliputra (present-day Palibothra), Fa Xian located a copy of the Vinaya containing the rules of the Mahasanghika, setting out how monastic communities should be run, thus completing one of the major goals of his journey. The pilgrims followed the route of the Ganges River to the city of Tamalipti (present-day Tamluk), a sea port and trading center, where he stayed for two years to copy down the sutras.

XUANZANG

BUDDHIST PILGRIM TO INDIA

CHINA   C. 602–C.664

THE BUDDHIST MONK AND SCHOLAR Xuanzang made a 16-year pilgrimage from China to India in the 7th century CE in search of a fuller understanding of his religion. He left behind vivid descriptions of the lands he traveled through on a journey that led him to the mountains and deserts of Central Asia and on to the Buddhist heartlands of northern India. Xuanzang's adventures provided the inspiration for the 16th-century novel *Journey to the West*, better known to Western audiences as *Monkey*.

A LIFE'S WORK

- Follows in **the footsteps of Fa Xian**, who brought back sutras from India 300 years earlier
- **In his autobiography**, provides lively accounts of the lands he has visited
- **Inspires many myths and legends**, which are turned into a novel in the 16th century
- Visits the Great Stupa in Gandhara, thought to be **the tallest building in the world**
- Dedicates the last 20 years of his life to **translating into Chinese** the texts he has collected

Xuanzang was born in the Henan province of China. He joined a Buddhist order of monks at the age of 13, and, by the time of his ordination at the age of 20, had absorbed much of the literature available to him. To gain a deeper insight, he needed to journey to India, the cradle of Buddhism. He began his pilgrimage in 629 after seeing the way forward in a dream.

LEAVING CHINA

In 629, however, Tang China was at war with its Göktürk neighbor and foreign travel was prohibited, so Xuanzang's first test was to find a way out of the country. He traveled across Liangzhou and Qinghai provinces and on into the Gobi Desert, reaching Turpan (in present-day northwestern China) in 630. From there, he skirted the edge of the Takla Makan Desert, following the northern Silk Route to K'iu-Chi. He crossed the Kyzul Kum Desert, observing that, "only by looking in the direction of some great mountain, and following the guidance of the bones which lie scattered about, can we know the way in which we ought to go." Eventually, he reached Samarkand in present-day Uzbekistan, which at the time was one of the great trading cities of Central Asia, and was impressed by the range of goods he found there.

BUDDHIST BACKPACKER
This painting, from the Mogao Caves at Dunhuang, China, depicts Xuanzang carrying Buddhist scriptures in a rack on his back. He holds a lamp to light his way.

CAVE TEMPLES
Xuanzang almost certainly visited the Ajanta Caves in central India, where a spectacular complex of 30 Buddhist temples was carved into the rock in the first century BCE.

Soon, Xuanzang entered Afghanistan, where he saw the Buddhas of Bamiyan. He wrote of one of the immense statues, "Its golden hues sparkle on every side, and its precious ornaments dazzle the eyes." The Buddhas were destroyed by the Taliban in 2001.

INTO INDIA

Xuanzang entered India in 630. He gave a very detailed description of the country and the people. He was particularly impressed with their cleanliness, noting that, "After eating they cleanse their teeth with a willow stick, and wash their hands and mouth." He traveled on to Gandhara, where he saw the Great Stupa, built to

house "a great portion of [the] bodily relics" of the Buddha. He also noted the sacred status of the Ganges River: "This river is called Fo-shwui, the river of religious merit, and can wash away countless sins."

The monk spent the next few years visiting the important Buddhist sites of northern India, including Sankasya, where the Buddha descended from Heaven; Lumbini, the Buddha's birthplace; and Kushinagar, where he died. Xuanzang gave a vivid portrait of the religious devotees gathered at the holy site of Varanasi: "Some cut their hair off, others tie their hair in a knot, and go naked, without clothes; they cover their bodies with ashes, and by the practice of all sorts of austerities they seek to escape from birth and death."

Xuanzang visited Nepal before heading back to China via the southern branch of the Silk Road, which took him through Kashgar and Khotan. By the time Xuanzang had ended his journey in 645, he had collected more than 600 Sanskrit texts. He retired to a monastery, where he spent his remaining years translating the Buddhist texts he had collected into Chinese.

TANG EMPEROR
At the time of Xuanzang's travels, China was ruled by Taizong, who encouraged the monk to translate his collection.

THE JOURNEY WEST

Published anonymously in the 1590s, but thought to have been written by the scholar Wu Cheng'en, *Journey to the West* is based on legends that had grown up around Xuanzang's pilgrimage. The novel's hero, Tripitaka, travels to India in search of Buddhist sutras in the company of three protectors—Monkey, Pigsy, and Sandy—immortals who have agreed to help to atone for past sins. Along the way, the four help locals defeat various monsters.

MAGIC MONKEY THIS 19TH-CENTURY ILLUSTRATION DEPICTS MONKEY BATTLING WITH A MAGICIAN

THE SUTRAS
Xuanzang traveled to India in search of holy texts called sutras, which contain the teachings of the Buddha. Some, like this one, were lavishly illustrated.

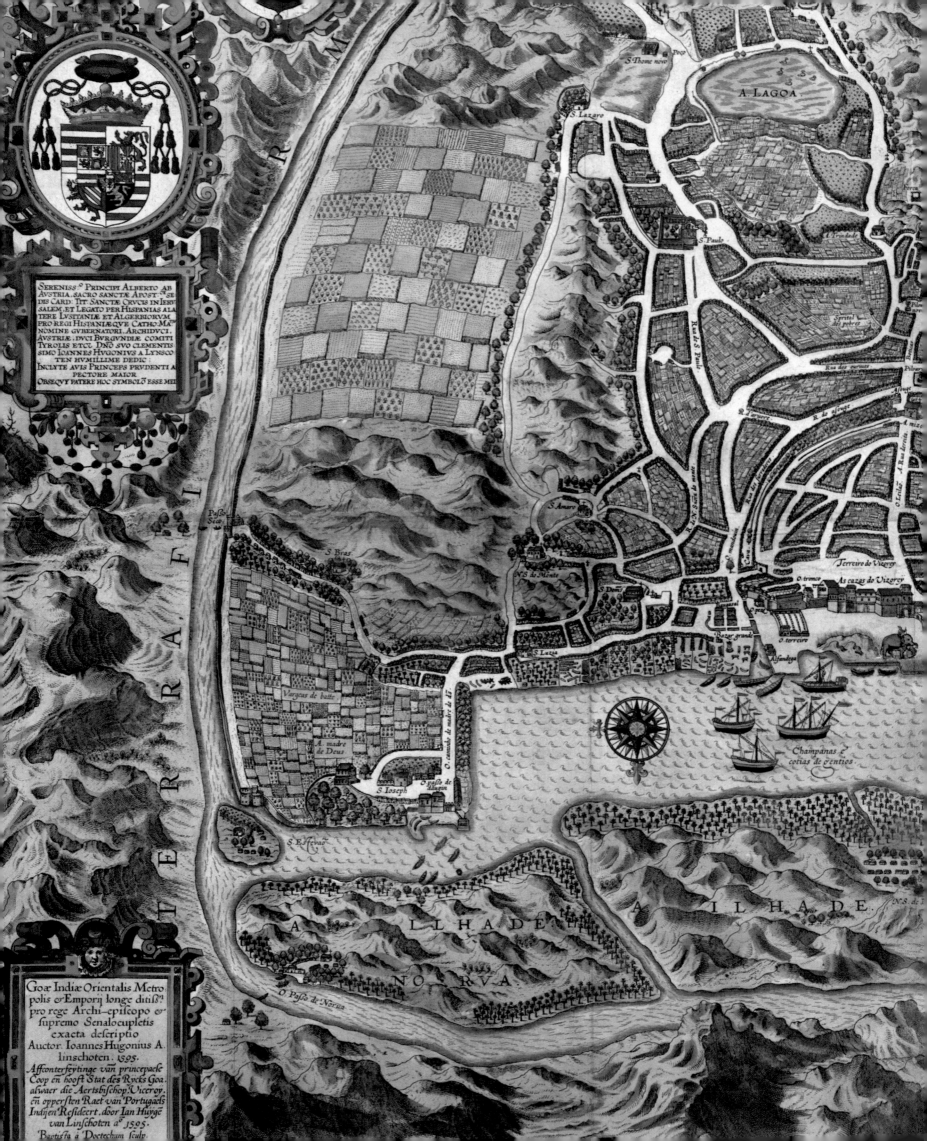

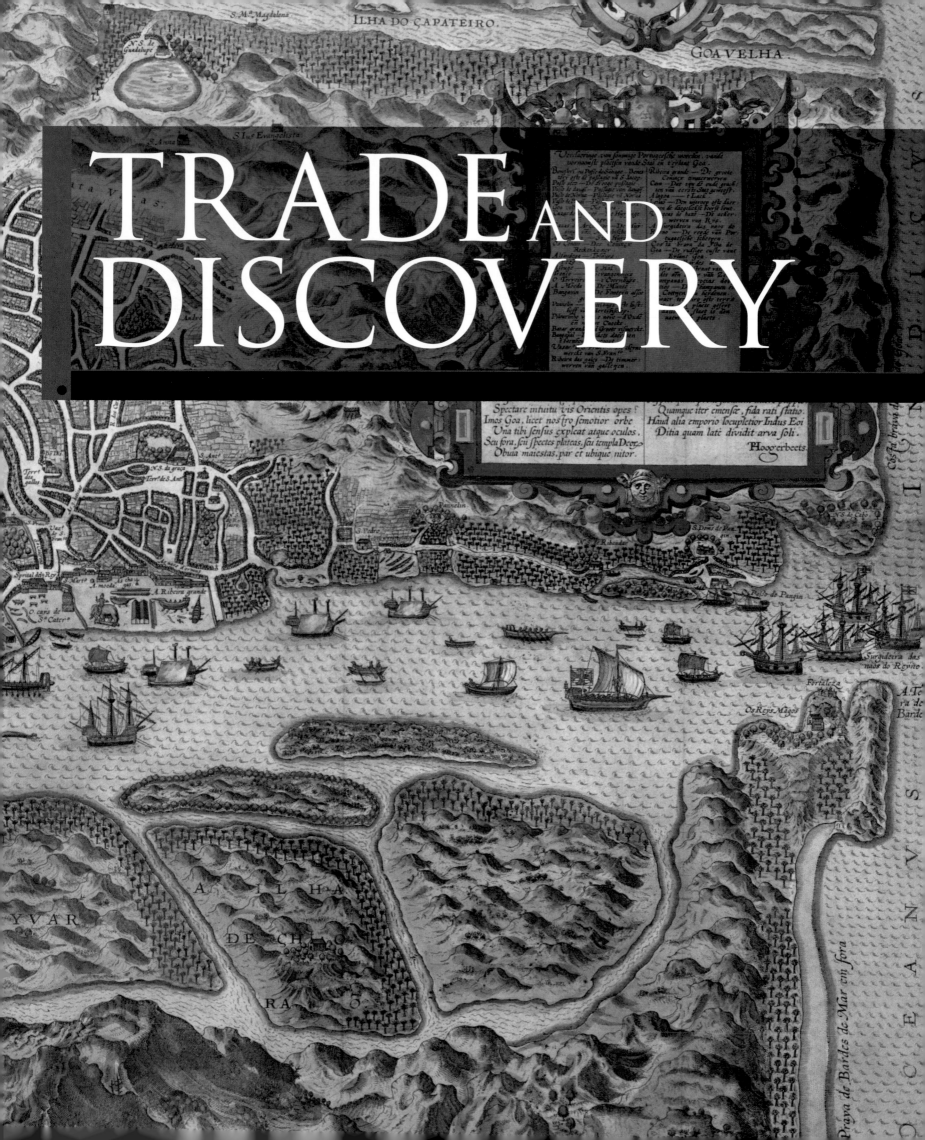

TRADE AND DISCOVERY

TRADE AND DISCOVERY

1000ce	1200	1300

11th CENTURY
The **Tamil Cholas** build an empire in southern India and Sri Lanka, presiding over a 300-year flowering of Hindu culture

▼ 1099
Christian crusaders capture Jerusalem from the Turks and massacre the inhabitants; the city is recaptured by Muslim forces led by Saladin in 1187

► 1206
Genghis Khan unites the nomadic tribes of northeast Asia and founds the Mongol Empire based at Karakoram (in the mountains of present-day Pakistan)

◄ 1324
Mansa Musa, the emperor of Mali, makes a lavish pilgrimage to Mecca, taking with him an entourage of 60,000 men, including a personal retinue of 12,000 slaves

1236
Julian, a Dominican friar, is sent to the court of Batu Khan by Bela IV of Hungary; he is greeted with a demand that the Hungarians submit to Mongol rule

▼ 1246
Umbrian traveler **Giovanni da Pian del Carpini** arrives in Mongolia, where he witnesses the enthronement of Küyük Khan

► 1253
William of Rubruck makes a failed mission to the Mongol court at Karakorum to convert the Mongols to Christianity and win their allegiance against the Muslims (see pp. 54–55)

▲ 1325
Ibn Battuta departs Tangier, Morocco, to start 29 years of traveling, during which he visits most of the Islamic world, including Djenné in West Africa (see pp. 68–71)

► 1342
Franciscan friar **Giovanni dei Marignolli** is sent by Pope Benedict XII to China; during his travels, Giovanni visits Sri Lanka, where he climbs the holy mount, Adam's Peak

▲ c. 1100
The **astrolabe**, an instrument used by navigators and astronomers, is perfected by Andalusian instrument maker al-Zarqali so that it functions at any latitude

► 1271
Venetian **Marco Polo** sets off on a 24-year journey around Asia and is employed as a diplomat by Mongol ruler Kublai Khan (see pp. 56–59)

1280
The **Mali Empire** in West Africa is at its height, spreading its laws and culture along the Niger River; to its south, the **Benin Empire** is growing in power

1368
Zhu Yuanzhang forces the Mongols out of China and founds the Ming dynasty, which goes on to rule the country for the next 300 years

◄ **PP. 48–49** A map of the Portuguese port of Goa on the southwest coast of India, dating from 1595

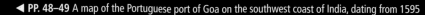

THE ISLAMIC CONQUEST of the Middle East and North Africa in the 7th century opened up a sphere within which Muslim travelers could journey with relative ease. However, the rise of Islam cut off trade routes to the East for Christian Europe. In the 13th century, the search for alternative routes, and for allies against Muslim powers, motivated the despatch of European envoys to the Central Asian lands of the Mongol khans. A century later, Portuguese and Spanish navigators were exploring the coast of West Africa. Then in 1492, Christopher Columbus sailed west in search of a route to Asia and stumbled across the "New World," beginning a series of voyages from Europe that brought the Americas into direct contact with the rest of the world for the first time.

1400

1450

1500

▶ 1483
Diogo Cão reaches southern Africa and plants four *padroes*, stone columns intended to claim the territory in the name of Portuguese king João II
(see pp. 78–79)

◀ 1500
Pedro Álvares Cabral is the first European to land in Brazil, after he was blown off course en route to India
(see pp. 96–97)

▲ 1404
Zheng He embarks on the first of his seven epic voyages from China, crossing the Indian Ocean to reach the Persian Gulf and East Africa
(see pp. 62–65)

▼ 1430s
Prince Henry the Navigator actively supports Portuguese Atlantic exploration, as Portuguese mariners push south along the West African coast

◀ 1488
Bartolomeu Dias rounds the Cape of Good Hope for the first time, naming it the Cape of Storms after the bad weather he encounters there
(see pp. 76–77)

▶ 1492
Christopher Columbus lands on San Salvador, an island in the Caribbean, believing that he has reached East Asia
(see pp. 86–89)

1497
Sebastian Cabot and his father John reach Newfoundland
(see pp. 92–93)

▲ 1502
German cartographer **Martin Waldseemüller** produces a world map on which "America" is named for the first time, shown as a separate landmass from Asia

◀ 1524
Giovanni Verrazano, an Italian explorer in the service of France, is the first European since the Vikings to explore the Atlantic coast of North America around Narragansett Bay

1434
Portuguese navigator **Gil Eanes** rounds Cape Bojador on the western Sahara, which was believed in Europe to be impassable by sea

1444
Portuguese explorer **Dinis Dias** reaches the westernmost point of Africa, which he names Cape Verde ("Green Cape") for the lush vegetation he finds there

◀ 1497
Vasco da Gama rounds Africa to sail to India, the first time Asia has been reached from Europe by sea, bypassing the Muslim-controlled Middle East (see pp. 80–81)

1498
On Columbus's third voyage he becomes the first European to set foot on South America; he continues to believe that he has discovered a route to Asia

▶ 1582
Jesuit priest **Matteo Ricci** arrives in China and establishes a successful mission; he becomes one of the first Western scholars to master the Chinese script

TALES OF ASIA

MONGOL KHAN
Genghis Khan, who completed the conquest of northern China in 1227, was the first of the Mongol Yuan dynasty, which ruled China for nearly 150 years.

R ELATIONS BETWEEN CHINA AND THE WEST DATE BACK AT LEAST TO THE 1ST CENTURY CE, WHEN THE ROMANS BOUGHT SILK FROM A LAND THEY CALLED "SERICA." IN THE MIDDLE AGES, EUROPEAN POWERS SOUGHT CHINESE HELP AS A CHECK TO ISLAMIC EXPANSION, BUT WITH LIMITED SUCCESS.

Although the Romans and Chinese had traded, they did so through intermediaries. Once China became disunited in the 4th century, however, even these contacts with the West ceased until the time of the Tang dynasty (618–907CE). But by then, Islamic caliphates controlled the central portion of the Silk Road, making contact between East and West difficult.

IN SEARCH OF PRESTER JOHN

By the late 11th century, the crusades—religious wars in which the Christian West attempted to wrest control of the Holy Land from the Muslims—were beginning to falter. Seeking aid, the Christian powers began searching for the mythical figure of Prester John, said to be ruler of a Christian kingdom in the Muslim world. The desperation for his military support in the Holy Land led to a series of envoys to the courts of the Mongol khans, any of whom, it was believed, might be the elusive Prester John.

Among the first to travel East was Julian, a Dominican friar sent by King Bela IV of Hungary in 1236, who was greeted with a demand from Batu Khan that the Hungarians submit to Mongol rule. The ensuing Mongol invasion of Europe in 1240–41 did not dispel the belief that the Mongol khans might be useful allies and, in 1246, the Umbrian traveler Giovanni da Pian del Carpini arrived in Mongolia in time to see

A CHINESE VIEW OF EUROPEANS
This is a copy of an effigy of Marco Polo made by Chinese artists during Polo's 24-year stay in Asia, traveling in the service of Kublai Khan.

the enthronement of a new khan, Küyük. Although his attempts to convert the Mongols to Christianity were unsuccessful, he left a priceless account, describing their *gers* (felt-covered tents) and their penchant for *koumiss* (fermented mare's milk). The mission of William of Rubruck (see pp. 54–55) in 1253 was equally unsuccessful, yielding just six converts and no promise of assistance.

TRADING JUNK
The centrepiece of Zheng He's fleets was a series of huge nine-masted "treasure ships," which may have been up to 450 ft (140 m) long.

CHINA IDOL
Until Jesuit scholars such as Matteo Ricci (left) arrived, Christian missionaries made little effort to understand the Confucian and Buddhist religious culture of China.

KUBLAI KHAN

The reign of Kublai Khan (1260–94) saw further European visitors to the Mongol court, most notably the Venetian merchant Marco Polo (see pp. 56–59). But although Polo's account of his travels is an invaluable source on the geography and culture of Mongol Asia, his was a trading rather than a diplomatic venture. Christian envoys did continue to visit the Mongol lands into the 14th century. Among the last of these was Giovanni dei Marignolli, sent by Pope Benedict XII in 1338. He reached

> The Silk Road trade routes through Central Asia were first established during the Chinese Han dynasty in the 3rd century BCE. The routes were retraced in the early 20th century by European explorers such as Marc Aurel Stein and Sven Hedin.

China in 1342 and stayed for three years. In China, the Mongol Yuan dynasty was overthrown by the Ming in 1368. The Ming were less receptive to foreign envoys and decidedly hostile towards Christianity. The renewed self-confidence of China, however, is exemplified by the voyages of Zheng He (see pp. 62–65), whose travels between 1405 and 1433 reached as far as the east coast of Africa. After this, China closed up again. It was only in 1582 that the Jesuit Matteo Ricci arrived there. By the time of his death in 1610, he had founded a successful mission.

SETTING THE SCENE

- The First Crusade **captures Jerusalem in 1099**, and the crusaders establish a series of Christian principalities, but after the Muslims regroup in 1144, the crusaders badly need assistance. They seek allies, among them the Mongol khans.

- A **Mongol invasion of the Middle East** under Hulegu in 1256 seems to aid the crusaders' campaigns. Hulegu sacks the key Muslim stronghold of Baghdad in 1258, but his army is **defeated by the Egyptian Mamluks at Ain Jalut in 1260**.

- Christian envoys and traders continue to visit the Mongol court, but **the Mongols also send emissaries**. In 1287, the Nestorian monk Rabban Bar Sauma goes west to seek European assistance against the Mamluks. He visits Naples, Rome, and Paris, and is even received by the English king Edward II.

- Among **the gifts Giovanni dei Marignolli brings** with him to Beijing in 1342 is a horse. It so pleases the Mongol ruler Toghun Temür that he orders **a portrait and a poem to be made in its honor**.

- After Zheng He's final voyage in 1433, **the Ming rulers turn against such oceanic ventures**. The building of seagoing vessels is forbidden in 1436, and by 1500 the navy has virtually disappeared.

- Matteo Ricci is succeeded at **the Beijing mission** by **Nicolo Lombardi,** and Jesuits continue to operate until 1724, when Emperor K'ang-hsi closes China to missionaries.

HORSE BOWMEN
The Mongol cavalry, riding small, sturdy horses, attacked from a distance using devastatingly effective compound bows. The cavalry was the main component of the Mongols' conquering armies.

WILLIAM OF RUBRUCK

MEDIEVAL CHRONICLER OF THE MONGOLS

FLANDERS   C. 1220–C. 1293

FRIAR AND ENVOY William of Rubruck wrote of the marvels of the Orient decades before the explorations of Marco Polo. Sent by King Louis IX of France as a missionary and alliance-seeker to the Great Khan of Mongolia, the Franciscan recorded his three-year journey in great detail. Although his mission failed in its goal of making the khan a Christian and an ally, his account, *The Journey of William of Rubruck to the Eastern Parts of the World*, is one of the most reliable medieval accounts of the Mongol Empire and its customs.

CAPTURED CRUSADER
While William was on his mission, his patron, Louis IX (later St. Louis), had a less edifying experience—being captured and ransomed by the Muslims during the Seventh Crusade (above).

William was born in the Flandrian village of Rubrouck, now in France, some time in the first quarter of the 13th century. Little is known of this Franciscan monk—even the years of his birth and death are not recorded—other than what is told in the autobiographical account of his travels.

MISSION TO MONGOLIA
William gained the confidence of King Louis IX in Paris, and in 1248 was invited to join the French king on the Seventh Crusade. Following an unsuccessful six-year campaign, Louis changed tack. He wished to win the friendship of the Mongol Empire of the Great Khan—the Tartar people—in the hope of an alliance against the Saracens of the Holy Land. In May 1253, William was sent to take the Christian faith to the Mongol Empire, together with gifts from Louis, and set out from Acre in Palestine with fellow Franciscan Bartholomew of Cremona. He traveled by ox-drawn cart, reasoning that a cart would not require unpacking at every stop, but later admitted that traveling on horseback would have halved the journey time.

The envoys traveled via Constantinople to the court of Batu Khan, ruler of the Volga River region, who refused to convert, but sent them on to Mangu—the Great Khan—at his capital, Karakorum. The overland journey was arduous: east of Lake Balkhash on the Kirghiz steppes, William met "such a wind through that valley that persons cross it with great danger, lest the wind carry them into the sea."

By December, conditions were so severe that his guides begged him to pray against the "devils of the gorges" for safe passage. William obliged, writing out texts for the men to carry, although "it was dangerous, not to say impossible, to speak on questions of the faith." He arrived at Karakorum four months later,

MIGHTY MONGOL EMPIRE

The various nomadic tribes dwelling on the Mongolian steppes were united into a nation by Genghis Khan in 1206. He invaded China in 1211 then expanded across Asia in 1219, forging an empire that continued to grow under his successors. By the time William reached Karakorum, Mongol rule stretched from the Pacific Ocean to the Black Sea, forming the most powerful and dominant empire in the medieval world.

A STATUE OF GENGHIS KHAN STANDS IN ULAN BATOR, CAPITAL OF MONGOLIA

A LIFE'S WORK

- In order to ease his passage through Central Asia, he carries "**fruits, muscadel wine, and dainty cookies** to present to the captains … for among them no one is looked upon in a proper way who comes with empty hands"

- Observes of Mongol fashions: "The women there are **wonderfully fat**, and she who has the least nose is held the most beautiful"

- Learns of Chinese customs from a Tibetan lama, making an early description of **paper money and Chinese script**: "they make in one figure the several letters containing a whole word"

- Proves that the Caspian Sea is an inland sea **that does not flow north into the Arctic** as previously supposed

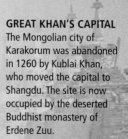

GREAT KHAN'S CAPITAL
The Mongolian city of Karakorum was abandoned in 1260 by Kublai Khan, who moved the capital to Shangdu. The site is now occupied by the deserted Buddhist monastery of Erdene Zuu.

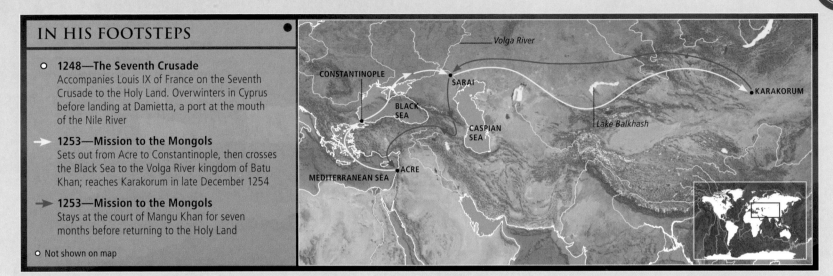

IN HIS FOOTSTEPS

- ○ **1248—The Seventh Crusade**
  Accompanies Louis IX of France on the Seventh Crusade to the Holy Land. Overwinters in Cyprus before landing at Damietta, a port at the mouth of the Nile River

- → **1253—Mission to the Mongols**
  Sets out from Acre to Constantinople, then crosses the Black Sea to the Volga River kingdom of Batu Khan; reaches Karakorum in late December 1254

- → **1253—Mission to the Mongols**
  Stays at the court of Mangu Khan for seven months before returning to the Holy Land

○ Not shown on map

finding it "not as large as the village of St. Denis [a Paris suburb]." He was astounded to find a French woman named Paquette, who had been taken prisoner in Hungary, as well as a master goldsmith from Paris and other foreign captives.

AWAITING AN AUDIENCE

William wrote extensive accounts of Mongolian traditions, such as felt-making, the erection and layout of yurts, and cuisine. He also observed feasting: "when they want to challenge anyone to drink, they take hold of him by the ears, and pull so as to distend his throat, and they clap and dance before him."

The cold became so intense in January 1254 that William was given fur gowns to ward off the subzero temperatures. He complained that he had no house in which to pray for the Great Khan, just a dwelling that was "so small that we could not stand up in it, nor open our books as soon as we lit the fire."

He was granted an audience with Mangu himself, during which the Great Khan looked at copies of the Bible. Despite William's efforts, Mangu was unreceptive to Christianity. Instead, the friar was invited to debate with Buddhists and Muslims before the Great Khan, and to prepare documents for his perusal.

In May 1254, William had a final audience with Mangu, who gently rebuffed the friar's faith with the words: "As God gives us the different fingers of the hand, so he gives to men diverse ways." William departed in July with a letter for Louis IX, arriving at the crusader state of Tripoli in August 1255. He presented the king with a 40-chapter account of his travels, which is held to be a masterpiece of medieval geographical literature. He advised that more missions be sent to the Mongols, with the proviso that they have good translators and "abundant traveling funds."

ETERNAL MONUMENT
Symbolizing eternity and protection, this granite tortoise is one of the last remaining relics of Karakorum.

MARCO POLO

A EUROPEAN AT THE CHINESE COURT

VENETIAN REPUBLIC   1254–1324

MARCO POLO WAS BORN into the prosperous merchant community of Venice, a port city that played a key role in trade between the Mediterranean Sea and the East. Relatively little is known of his early life, but the record of his travels, *The Description of the World*, dictated in later life to a fellow inmate as Polo languished in prison in Genoa, provides the first detailed European accounts of China and Southeast Asia, a first mention of Japan, and many new insights into Persia, India, and remote parts of Central Asia.

The trail Polo would follow was blazed by his father Niccolo and uncle Maffeo, both jewel merchants. In 1260, when Marco was six, they left on a trading expedition to Constantinople (present-day Istanbul) and on to Soldaia, a Crimean port. From there, they ventured north, following the caravan route across the steppes to trade with Barca, the khan of the western Mongol Empire, also known as the "Golden Horde." They remained for more than a year before civil war broke out in the region. Unable to retrace their steps south, the Polo brothers went east to Bukhara in Central Asia, where they stayed for three years. At Bukhara, they met the Mongol ambassador from the court of Kublai Khan, the "Great Khan" of China, who made them an extraordinary offer: to join him

on his return journey to the Chinese court. They accepted, and followed the Silk Road east, reaching Cambulac (present-day Beijing) in 1266.

The Venetians were welcomed at court, where the Great Khan requested that they return to Europe as his envoys to the pope in Rome. They returned to Europe in 1269 as ambassadors of Kublai Khan, hoping that they would one day see China again.

BACK EAST WITH MARCO

Two years later, the brothers set off again for China, this time taking 17-year-old Marco with them. Their route is not clearly defined in *The Description of the World*, and it is often unclear whether they actually visited all the places named in the work. However, we know that their journey took them through Central Asia by way of Turkey, and then southeast to Ormuz in the Persian Gulf, where they had planned to sail to China to avoid the danger of an overland route. The vessels at Ormuz were poor, however, so the men chose an overland route after all, probably traveling northeast into the Oxus Valley, before crossing the Pamir Mountains. They arrived in China in summer, when Kublai Khan's court had moved to the palace of Shandu, or Xanadu, north of Cambulac.

POLO ON THE SILK ROAD
This illustration appears on *The Catalan Atlas*, a six-page map of the known world made in the 14th century. It shows Polo traveling with a camel caravan along the Silk Road, the network of trade routes connecting China with the Middle East and India. The road gets its name from the lucrative Chinese silk trade during the Han dynasty 2,000 years ago, which was the driving force behind the development of such trade routes.

NO OTHER MAN, CHRISTIAN OR SARACEN, MONGOL OR PAGAN, HAS EXPLORED SO MUCH OF THE WORLD AS MESSER MARCO, SON OF MESSER NICCOLO POLO

RUSTICHELLO DA PISA

The educated, 20-year-old Marco made a significant impression on the Great Khan, who selected him to act as a combination of intelligence spy and reporter, sending him first on a year-long solo mission to Yunnan (in southern China) and to Burma. As the text records, "He [Khan] would better like to hear the news and the customs and usages of those countries than he did to hear those matters for which he had sent them; so Marco, when he went on that mission, would fix his attention on all the novelties and strange things he heard and saw in order that he might recount them on his return to the Great Khan."

The Polos remained in China for 17 years. The details of the journeys undertaken by Marco, his father, and uncle are not known in full,

and historians continue to debate the veracity of some of the accounts, but Marco's descriptions of the Pamirs, Kashgar, and Lop Nor—closed, impossibly remote lands to Europeans—were to become one of the few text-based sources of information about Central Asia until northern European explorers traveled the region in the 19th and early 20th centuries. In fact, figures such as Marc Aurel Stein (see pp. 234–37), the Hungarian explorer-archeologist, were still using Polo's geographical descriptions to plan their routes.

SILK SECRET
As a favorite of the Khan's court, Polo would have worn a fine silk tunic similar to this one. At the time, the secret of silk-making was known only in China.

HOME TO VENICE
The Polos returned to the West in 1292, accompanying the Khan's great-nephew as he traveled to Persia with a new bride. Marco Polo's descriptions of coastal China, Southeast Asia, and the Spice Islands, as they sailed from Hangzhou by way of the South China Sea to Ormuz, were to be of great value to later mariner explorers.
The Description of the World

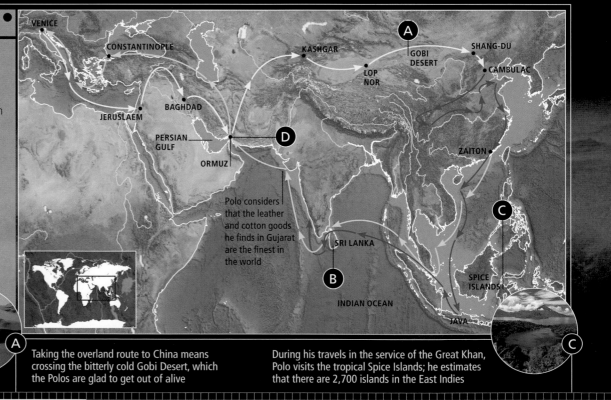

IN HIS FOOTSTEPS

➤ **1271–75—Journey to Cambulac**
The Polo brothers return to Cambulac, which they first visited at the invitation of the Mongol ambassador, following an overland route, and taking the young Marco with them

➤ **1275–91—Working for Kublai Khan**
For 17 years, Marco Polo travels extensively around East Asia in the service of the Great Khan, collecting information on the people living in the various regions of the great Mongol Empire

➤ **1292–95—Return to Europe**
Polo returns to Venice with his father and uncle, this time taking the safer ocean route from China to Europe

VENICE
CONSTANTINOPLE
KASHGAR
SHANG-DU
GOBI DESERT
CAMBULAC
LOP NOR
BAGHDAD
JERUSLAEM
PERSIAN GULF
ORMUZ
ZAITON

Polo considers that the leather and cotton goods he finds in Gujarat are the finest in the world

SRI LANKA

SPICE ISLANDS

INDIAN OCEAN

JAVA

A Taking the overland route to China means crossing the bitterly cold Gobi Desert, which the Polos are glad to get out of alive

C During his travels in the service of the Great Khan, Polo visits the tropical Spice Islands; he estimates that there are 2,700 islands in the East Indies

When Marco is six years old, his father and uncle make their first journey to China

Ten years after leaving Venice, the Polo brothers return to Europe as ambassadors of Kublai Khan

The Khan sends Polo to Java, an island that he has not been able to conquer, where Polo is impressed by the variety of spices

B Polo visits the island of Sri Lanka, which was famed at the time for its jewels, particularly its huge rubies

includes one of the earliest recorded accounts of Japan (whether from personal evidence or report): "Cipangu [the Chinese name for Japan] is an island to the sunrising which is on the high sea 1,500 miles [2,400 km] distant from the land of Mangi [southern China]. It is an exceedingly great island … The Lord that is the chief ruler of that island has a palace which is all covered with sheets of fine gold." Whether or not Polo visited Japan, this was new information to his European readers about a potentially rich source of trade.

"IL MILIONE"

By the time he returned to Venice in 1295, Marco Polo had traveled nearly 15,000 miles (24,000 km) over a 24-year period, an odyssey unprecedented in the medieval world. The Polos disembarked to find that their city was at war with Genoa, and Marco was taken prisoner during the conflict, spending several months in a Genoese prison. This proved fortunate for posterity, however, because it was there that he recounted his tales to fellow prisoner

THE POLOS DEPART VENICE
This illustration of Marco Polo's departure from Venice appears in a 14th-century edition of *The Description of the World,* known as the Bodleni manuscript.

Rustichello da Pisa, who was to write the account of Polo's adventures. Polo's nickname, *Il Milione* ("the Million"), is thought to refer to the extraordinary statistics he recited when describing the size of Kublai Khan's court and the scale of Chinese activities, which his detractors were convinced had to be exaggerations. On his deathbed in 1324, his enemies attempted to have him confess to his "pack of lies." Polo responded simply by saying, "I have only told you half of what I saw."

BENJAMIN OF TUDELA
NAVARRA   C. 1100

A century before Marco Polo, Benjamin of Tudela wrote *The Travels of Benjamin*, a detailed account of his journey from his home in northern Spain through Europe and the Middle East to Persia.

Benjamin's purpose was to find a safe passage for his fellow Jews to travel to the Holy Land. To this end, he documented all the places he found on his route where a Jewish traveler might receive hospitality. He describes thriving Jewish communities as far east as Ghazni, in present-day Afghanistan, a city to which "people of all countries and tongues come with their wares" and with a Jewish population of 8,000. Benjamin documented the customs of the people he encountered, both Jewish and non-Jewish, giving particularly detailed accounts of urban life in the 12th century.

In marked contrast to Polo, he always cited his sources, which has led scholars to judge his account highly trustworthy. It is now considered an important work of medieval geography and ethnography.

ITINERARIUM BENIAMINI,
AN EARLY LATIN TRANSLATION
OF THE ORIGINAL HEBREW TEXT

HIGH MOUNTAINS
Polo would have joined a caravan threading between the glacial waters of the high Pamir Plateau (shown left) as he crossed the Pamir mountain area, which borders present-day Pakistan, China, and India.

D
On both their outward and return journeys, the Polos stop off at Ormuz in the Persian Gulf, which was an important trading port at the time

1292–95   1295–1324

On his return to Venice, Polo becomes involved in his city's war with Genoa; he is taken prisoner by the Genoese and recounts his tales to Rustichello during his imprisonment

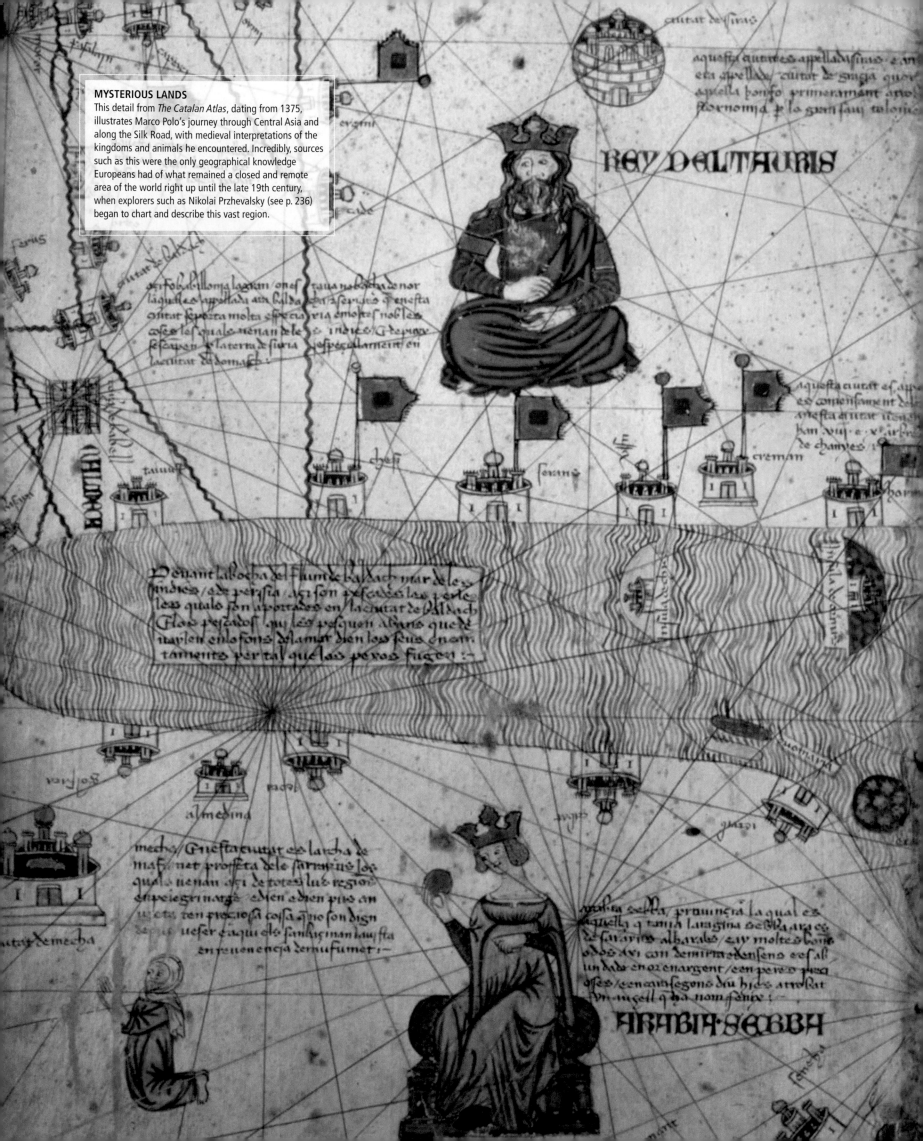

MYSTERIOUS LANDS
This detail from *The Catalan Atlas*, dating from 1375, illustrates Marco Polo's journey through Central Asia and along the Silk Road, with medieval interpretations of the kingdoms and animals he encountered. Incredibly, sources such as this were the only geographical knowledge Europeans had of what remained a closed and remote area of the world right up until the late 19th century, when explorers such as Nikolai Przhevalsky (see p. 236) began to chart and describe this vast region.

REY DELTHAURIS

ARABIA SEBBA

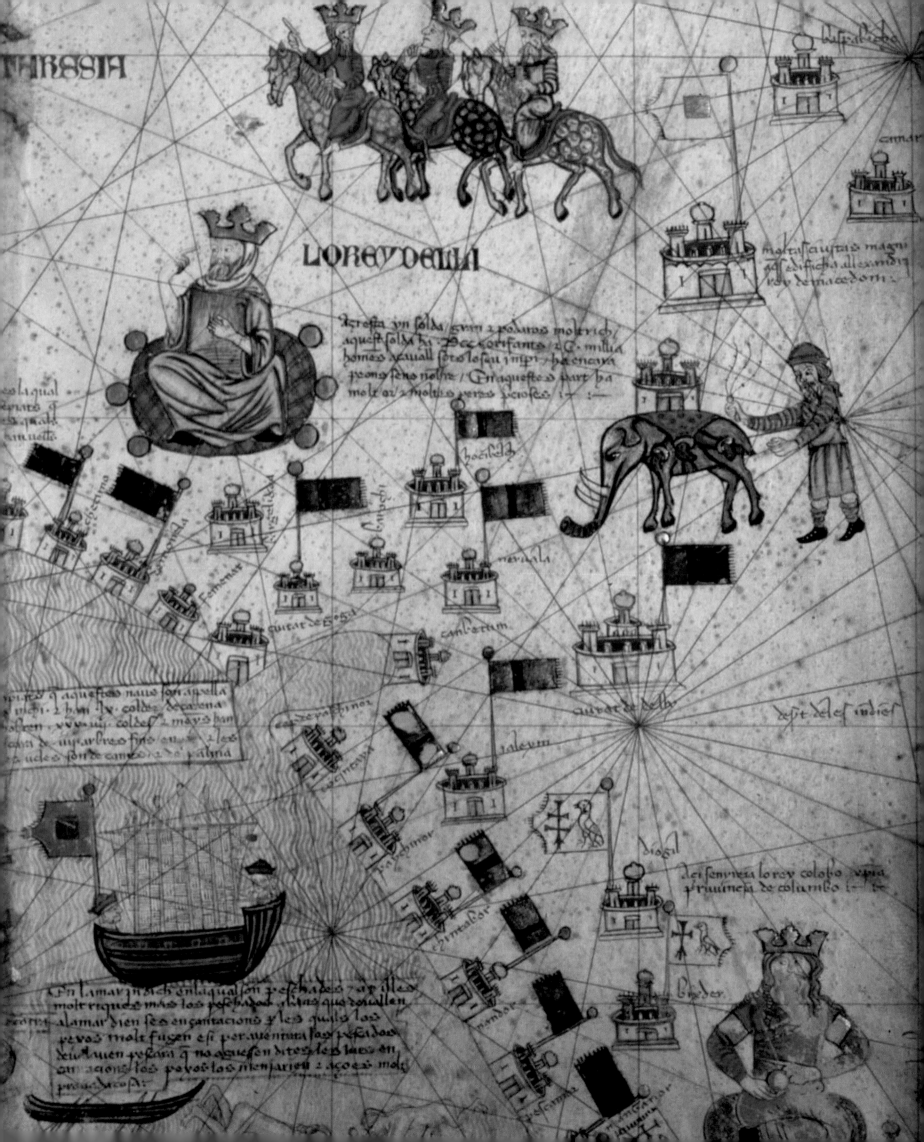

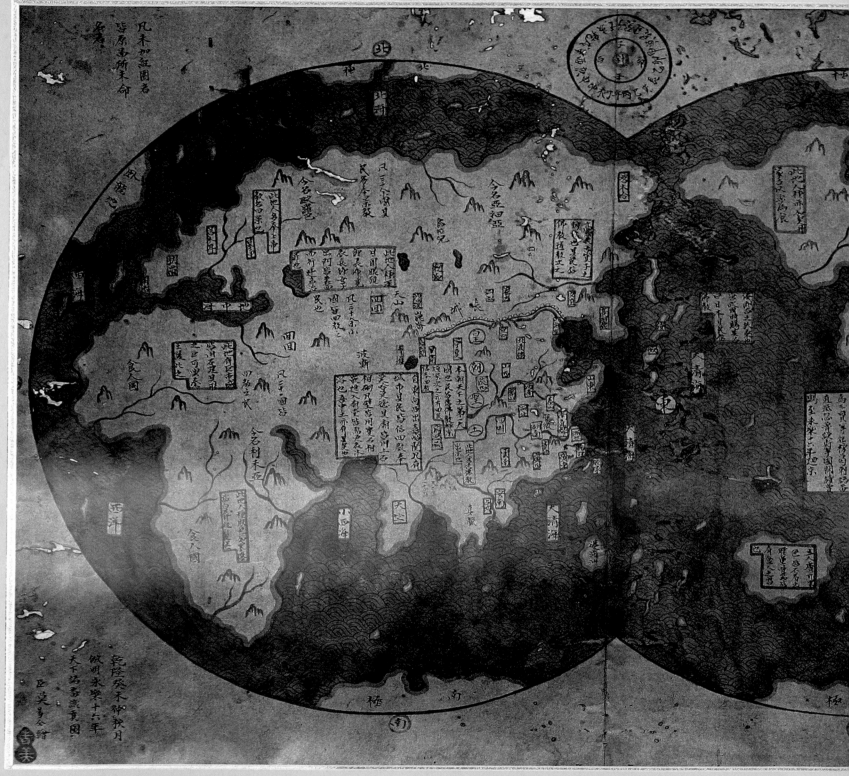

OUR SAILS, LOFTILY UNFURLED LIKE CLOUDS DAY AND NIGHT, CONTINUED THEIR COURSE [AS RAPIDLY] AS A STAR

ZHENG HE

ZHENG HE

MING-DYNASTY CHINA'S MARINER EXPLORER

CHINA   1371–1433

COURT EUNUCH AND ADMIRAL Zheng He made six voyages and directed a seventh around the rim of the Indian Ocean, reaching as far as Malindi on the eastern coast of Africa. Remarkable not only for their attempt to assert Chinese hegemony over the major trading ports of Southeast Asia, Arabia, and East Africa, the voyages were also audacious for their sheer scale. Zheng He's first fleet is said to have comprised more than 300 ships and 28,000 men. A larger fleet would not be seen in the Indian Ocean until the advent of World War II.

Zheng He—whose birth name was Ma He—was born into a Muslim family in Kunyang (present-day Jinning) in the province of Yunnan, southwestern China. At the age of 10, he was captured by the Ming army that had been sent to Yunnan to fight against its Mongol leader. According to common practice at the time, Zheng He was castrated and dispatched to serve at the imperial court in Peking, where he rose to become a trusted adviser of the Ming emperors.

TRADING ACROSS THE WAVES

Timur, the much-feared ruler of the Mongols, died in 1405 after devastating Central Asia and destroying China's overland trade routes. Emperor Yongle of China embarked upon an ambitious program to replace the overland trails with shipping routes across the Indian Ocean, and to draw the overseas ports into tribute to Ming-dynasty China.

Zheng He was chosen to lead this vast enterprise. Historical accounts describe nine-masted "treasure" ships 450 ft (140 m) in length. This is thought by most historians to be an exaggeration, but the vessels were certainly much larger than contemporary European ships. His first fleet contained a host of vessels of different sizes for carrying troops, horses, supplies, and water, as well as patrol boats, warships, and the flagship treasure ships. Zheng He left China in July 1405, calling at Java, Aceh, and Sri Lanka

A LIFE'S WORK

- **Sets out on his maiden** voyage almost 100 years before Christopher Columbus arrives in the Americas

- Like his grandfather and great-grandfather before him, Zheng He is able to **make a pilgrimage to Mecca** to become a hajji

- Zheng He's voyages prove instrumental in the **shift of trade** from the Silk Road to sea routes

before arriving at Calicut (Kozhikode) on the west coast of India in December 1406. Gifts were given to local rulers and Chinese authority was asserted, by force where necessary. On the return journey, Zheng He fought a major battle against the pirate Ch'en Tsu-i, killing 5,000 of his men. The pirate was taken to Nanjing and executed.

Zheng He's subsequent voyages were similarly well-equipped and carried out. His fourth, sixth, and seventh voyages are notable for being documented by Ma Huan, an interpreter who sailed with the fleet. He later drew

NAVIGATING AT SEA
Ming-dynasty mariners used an intricate 24-point compass, featuring a different Chinese character at each point, and sailing charts to navigate at sea.

NOT SUCH A NEW WORLD?
Zheng He's legendary status was given a boost in 2006 when a document purporting to be a 1763 copy of a map he made in 1418 was unearthed. It clearly depicts North and South America and Australia, continents that were not fully mapped by Europeans until the 19th century. Expert opinion has since cast doubt on the map's authenticity. Zheng He has also been suggested as the inspiration for the tales of Sinbad the Sailor in the book *Arabian Nights*.

from his experiences on the three voyages to write *The Overall Survey of the Ocean's Shores*. It is unclear on which of these voyages the specific events described occurred, but his writings paint a vivid picture of Zheng He's achievements.

CROSS-CULTURAL CHRONICLER

Ma Huan recorded the first stop on one of the voyages at Champa, a kingdom located in present-day Vietnam. It was an agreeable destination: "The climate is pleasantly hot, without frost or snow." The fleet next dropped anchor at Java, a major international trading center. Ma Huan observed that, "Foreigners from every place come here in great numbers to trade. Gold, precious stones, and all

IMPERIAL BACKER
Zheng He's voyages were financed by Emperor Yongle. Support for his expensive journeys waned following Yongle's death in 1424.

ISLAMIC SETTLER
As commemorated by this modern, bas-relief bronze, Zheng He encouraged the settlement of Chinese Muslims at Malacca (in present-day Malaysia), which before long had become a thriving port.

varieties of foreign goods are sold in great quantities. The people are very wealthy." They were also fond of entertainment: "They have a class of man who makes drawings on paper of such things as men, birds, beasts, eagles, or insects; he unrolls and exposes a section of the picture, speaking with a loud voice … the crowd listens, sometimes laughing, sometimes crying."

Sailing on, the fleet reached the country of Hsien Lo in present-day Thailand. Although less pleasant than Champa—"the inner land [is] wet and swampy"—the king still managed to impress. "When going about, he mounts an elephant or else rides in a sedan chair, while a man holds [over him] a gold-handled umbrella." Ma Huan also described an unusual local custom: "When a man has attained his twentieth year, they take the skin which surrounds the membrum virile, and with a fine knife shaped like [the leaf of] an onion they open it up and insert a dozen tin beads inside the skin." Hollow gold beads were preferred by the wealthy, into which a grain of sand was placed to make "a tinkling sound" when walking, which was "regarded as beautiful."

IN HIS FOOTSTEPS

→ **1405–09—Voyage to Calicut**
On his first two voyages, he reaches as far as Calicut in southern India, arriving there via Champa, Java, and Malacca

→ **1409–15—To Hormuz and Arabia**
On his third and fourth voyages, he visits the Maldives and crosses the Arabian Sea to Hormuz, before rounding Arabia to Jeddah

→ **1417–19—Reaches Mogadishu**
Sails to Malacca and around the Horn of Africa as far as Mogadishu on his fifth voyage

→ **1421–22—Return to Africa**
On his return to Africa, he pushes farther down the east coast as far as Malindi

● **1430–33—Back to Hormuz?**
Makes final voyage, but route is not known

● Not shown on map

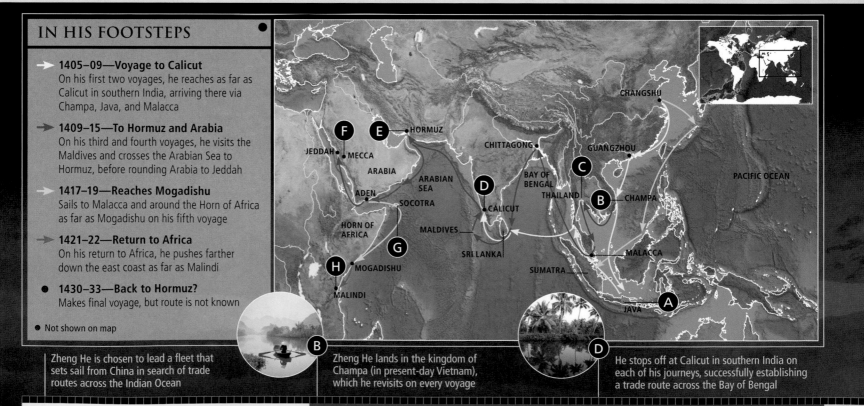

Zheng He is chosen to lead a fleet that sets sail from China in search of trade routes across the Indian Ocean

B Zheng He lands in the kingdom of Champa (in present-day Vietnam), which he revisits on every voyage

D He stops off at Calicut in southern India on each of his journeys, successfully establishing a trade route across the Bay of Bengal

1405–09

1409–15

Feared Mongol leader Timur, who had destroyed China's previous trade routes to India, dies

A On his first voyage, he reaches as far south as Java in present-day Indonesia

C He visits Hsien Lo (present-day Thailand) on his third voyage, which he finds unpleasantly swampy

E He crosses the Arabian Sea from Calicut to the port of Hormuz, an important trading point with the Persian Empire

After calling at Sri Lanka, the fleet reached Cochin (now Kochi) on the west coast of India, where Ma Huan observed the monsoon. The local people "put the roofs of their house in order and prepare their food supplies ... the rain falls in torrents during the day and night, the market streets become rivers ... great personages and little people sit in and wait until the rainy season is over." He described Calicut, farther up the coast, as "the great country of the Western Ocean." Zheng He erected a tablet to mark the friendship between the Chinese and Indian people.

The fleet left India and arrived at the Arabian Peninsula, calling at Dhofar in southern Oman. Ma Huan found the men to have "long, large limbs, and a tall and stout appearance." Aden (now in Yemen) was "rich, and the people numerous." Ma Huan observed the detrimental effect of such wealth: "the people are of an overbearing disposition," but noted that they produced "the most refined and ingenious things, which certainly surpass anything in the world."

MIXED LEGACY

Zheng He is known to have reached farther than the Arabian Peninsula, sailing south along the Indian Ocean coast of Africa on several voyages. He called at Mogadishu and Malindi (in present-day Somalia and Kenya) receiving a giraffe from the Arab Sultan of Malindi as a gift to the emperor. The sighting of a "junk from India" in the Atlantic in 1420, recorded by Venetian cartographer Friar Mauro on his 1459 map, has been used as evidence that Zheng He rounded the Cape of Good Hope. However, most scholars agree that this is unlikely.

Zheng He was appointed Defender of Nanjing by Emperor Hanxi in 1425. He died shortly after completing his next voyage in 1433 and, as was fitting for an admiral, was buried at sea. The Indian Ocean venture was abandoned due to its great cost, but Zheng He's legacy was a vastly expanded trading network that survived despite a lack of imperial assistance. Sadly, most of the reports of his voyages, and even the vessels that he sailed in, were destroyed after his death.

FINE GIFTS AND MERCHANDISE
Zheng He's fleet carried a range of goods for use as gifts and for trading, such as porcelain, gold- and silverware, iron, copper, cotton, and silk.

DETAILED CHARTS
The few documents that have survived from Zheng He's voyages record his journeys in precise detail. This chart, which was reproduced in the 17th-century *Wubei Zhi* ("Treatise on Armament Technology") depicts the west coast of India at the top, Sri Lanka on the right, and Africa along the bottom. The course is charted with a reading from the 24-point compass system, a sailing time and distance, and depth soundings.

TRADING FAIRLY

On his fourth and seventh expeditions, Zheng He docked at the wealthy trading port of Hormuz, now in Iran. Its location at the intersection of a web of overland trade routes from Persia, Central Asia, and the Middle East ensured good trade: "Foreign ships from every place and foreign merchants traveling by land all come to this country to attend the market and trade; hence the people are all rich." But Ma Huan also noted the good spirit of the city's inhabitants: "The king of the country and the people all profess the Muslim religion … There are no poor families; if a family meets with misfortune resulting in poverty, everyone gives them clothes and food and capital and relieves their distress."

G While rounding the Horn of Africa, he stops off at the island of Socotra, part of present-day Yemen

H On his sixth voyage, he sails down the coast of East Africa as far as Malindi

1417–19   1420   **1421–22**   1423–29

F He sails up the Red Sea from Aden to Jeddah and on to the holy city of Mecca, thus completing his hajj, or holy Muslim pilgrimage

He returns to Calicut and Hormuz on his sixth voyage before heading south to Africa

Emperor Yongle, Zheng He's principal backer, dies in 1424, and the finance for further voyages is cut; he makes one more voyage

EXPLORING THE MUSLIM WORLD

THE ISLAMIC WORLD DEVELOPED AN EARLY TRADITION OF SCIENTIFIC INQUIRY THAT LED TO A SERIES OF PIONEERING DEPICTIONS OF THE WORLD. THE DUTY TO VISIT MECCA CONTRIBUTED TO A STREAM OF TRAVELERS THERE, PASSING THROUGHOUT THE VAST MUSLIM REALMS.

NIMBLE VESSEL
The Arab dhow is said to have influenced the later Portuguese caravel, two of which Christopher Columbus took with him on his voyage to the New World.

The establishment of the Abbasid caliphate in Baghdad, in present-day Iraq, in about 750CE initiated a great flowering of culture, the like of which the world had not seen since Athens in the 4th century BCE. The Beit al-Hikma ("house of knowledge") was founded during the reign of Haroun ar-Rashid (786–809), becoming a haven for the Islamic world's leading scholars. There, they had access to Sanskrit works from Persia, as well as the important texts (principally Greek) that had resided in the libraries of the late Roman Empire.

ARAB STARGAZERS

The fruits of this transmission of knowledge to the Arab world were first seen in astronomy, the development of which was critical to safe navigation at sea. In 772, the caliph al-Mansur ordered the translation of a Sanskrit astronomy text *The Perfect Truth*, while in 820 an observatory was founded in Baghdad.

These astronomical ventures soon developed into geography. Sultan

ASTRONOMY TRADITION
The observatory at Galata, near Istanbul, established in 1557 by sultan Suleiman the Magnificent, followed a tradition begun over seven centuries earlier in Baghdad.

Al-Mamoun (813–33) ordered the director of the Baghdad library, Mohammed al-Khwarizmi, to compile a book called *System of the Earth*, which was largely based on the writings of the 1st-century Greek geographer Ptolemy, with a list of place names and their respective latitudes and longitudes. More practical, if on occasions—just like their Western counterparts—a little fanciful, were the works of men such as Amr ibn Bahr al-Jahiz, whose *Book of the Cities and Marvels of Countries* was criticized even at the time for its credulousness.

Later scholars, who engaged in practical travel and observation, such as al-Biruni, a Persian (see p. 33), made more accurate observations. He figured out the latitude of the city of Kath (in present-day Iran) in 990, when he was just 17 years old, and compiled a work on cartography that discussed different map projections. He also calculated the

> From the 16th century, Europeans began to visit the Muslim world, much of which had previously been off-limits. They came initially as ambassadors from powers such as Venice, which depended on trade in the Mediterranean.

circumference of the Earth to within about 60 miles (100 km) of its true value.

A thriving school of cartography had by this time grown up in Baghdad, largely based on the work of Abu Zaid al-Balkhi (850–934), whose *Figures of the Climates* was in essence an atlas of the Islamic world. One of the jewels of this cartographic tradition was the *Al-Rojari* of Ibn Idrisi, an Arab geographer who settled at the court of King Roger II of Sicily in 1125. His ambitious work attempted to describe all the inhabited regions of the world, which he divided into seven climatic zones—a system he adapted from Ptolemy—each in turn subdivided into 10 equal squares.

CURIOUS TRAVELERS

Although for some of the Arab geographers their primary purposes were political or economic there were others who did undertake journeys of enormous extent. In about 840, Caliph al-Mamoun sent Sallam the Interpreter to explore the lands beyond the Caspian Sea, while in about 850, Suleiman al-Tajir provided the earliest Arabic description of China.

At the end of the 9th century, Ahmad al-Ya'qubi's *Kitab al-Buldan* provided detailed descriptions of cities in India, Egypt, and the Maghreb in North Africa, based on firsthand experience. A century later, al-Maqdisi, born in Jerusalem, visited most of the Islamic world to

MAGNIFICENT SULTAN
Ottoman sultan Suleiman the Magnificent (1520–66) was the recipient of one of the masterpieces of Islamic cartography—the Piri Reis map of the world.

FALL OF BAGHDAD
Mongol armies stormed Baghdad in 1258, an event that led to the end of the Abbasid caliphate and the eclipse of the city as a dynamic cultural center.

SETTING THE SCENE

- After the **establishment of the Abbasid caliphate** in the 8th century, the trade routes that lead through Mesopotamia and Baghdad to the Red Sea and the Persian Gulf (and then on to India, Indonesia, and China) and via the Silk Road to Central Asia and China **act as conduits for diplomatic, cultural, and exploratory ventures.**

- Arab astronomy and geography derive much from Greek and Indian models, acquiring the concept of zero from the latter. But they build on both until, by the 10th century, the Islamic world **possesses the most developed expertise** in both fields.

- The **great extent of the Islamic world**, from al-Andalus (Spain) and the Maghreb in North Africa, to India, Central Asia, and Java means that Islamic travelers often cover vast distances **without ever once leaving Muslim-controlled territory.**

  - The most notable late Islamic cartographer is **Piri Reis**, an Ottoman admiral who draws maps showing **unparalleled accuracy** in the distances between continents.

compile his *Knowledge of the Regions* and provided one of the best contemporary descriptions of Jerusalem during the early medieval period.

The best known and most widely traveled of the Arab explorers made his series of journeys at a time when the Muslim world had almost reached its maximum extent. Ibn Battuta (see pp. 68–71) set out from Tangier in 1325 and ended back in Morocco in 1354, having visited or stayed in almost all the regions of the Islamic world. His travels along the Red Sea and down the east coast of Africa were made in one of the great vessels of the Islamic travelers—the dhow. Characterized by a triangular lateen sail mounted at an angle to the mast, dhows were more maneuverable than their square-rigged counterparts and ideally suited to taking advantage of the monsoon winds of the Indian Ocean.

However, the greatest of all Muslim cartographers was working at a time when the West, too, was enjoying a renaissance in the sciences. Piri Reis (*c.* 1465–1554) was an Ottoman admiral who drew maps from his own navigational notes. His first world map, dating from 1513, included a description of Columbus's 1492 voyage (see pp. 86–89), and its surviving portion includes one of the earliest depictions of South America.

BY SUN, MOON, OR STARS
By moving the arms and levers on the astrolabe and correlating them with the movements of the Sun, Moon, and stars, navigators could make an approximate reading of their position.

SCIENTIFIC DEVICES

Among the instruments available to Arab navigators in these waters was the astrolabe, a circular (and in more developed forms, a spherical) device capable of performing mathematical and astronomical calculations to establish the position of the Sun, Moon, and stars. In its very earliest forms a Greek invention, it was introduced in the Muslim world by al-Fazari in the late 8th century and perfected by al-Zarqali in the early 11th century so that it functioned at any latitude. With a marine version of this device, Muslim travelers could voyage with confidence throughout the world.

IBN BATTUTA

SCHOLAR AND TRAVELER WITHOUT EQUAL

MOROCCO   1304–68

IBN BATTUTA WAS A COMPULSIVE TRAVELER, crisscrossing the breadth of the medieval Islamic world and beyond. From Moorish Spain and Timbuktu in the west to Samarkand in Central Asia, and India, Vietnam, and the Philippines in the east, the learned scholar even reached Yuan-dynasty China. Although the full extent of his travels is contested, Battuta was one of the first to travel purely for traveling's sake, making himself indispensible to his many hosts through his guile, charm, and considerable intellect.

A LIFE'S WORK

- Becomes one of the **most-traveled people in the history of the world** when he makes the hajj on **seven separate occasions**

- From his home in Morocco, **travels as far east as China** and **as far south as sub-Saharan Africa**, visiting the whole of the Muslim world of his day

- **Works as an Islamic judge** in many of the places he visits, but his strict judgments are not appreciated in places such as the Maldives, which had only recently converted to Islam

- Suffers several **misfortunes at sea**: a junk due to carry him to China sinks, a second boat taking him from Sri Lanka is wrecked with him on board, while a third ship due to rescue him is attacked by pirates

- Dictates his **life's travels** on the orders of the Sultan of Morocco in 1354 to court poet Ibn Juzayy, later published as the *Rihla*—"Travels"

The name of Ibn Battuta is still relatively unknown in the West, and even in the Muslim world he does not enjoy the fame that his extraordinary travels would merit. He is often compared with Marco Polo (see pp. 56–59), that other great traveler of the medieval period, because both traveled overland to China via many of the same places, but the similarity ends there. Ibn Battuta traveled much further than the Venetian – visiting Arabia, India, Central Asia, China, and trans-Saharan Africa in a journey covering about 75,000 miles (120,000 km). Indeed, he is commonly held to be history's most-traveled individual before the 19th century. While Marco Polo traveled as a merchant and diplomat, Battuta was a pilgrim traveling out of a desire to see and experience new places. He remarked that "it was a habit of mine on my travels never so far as possible to retrace any road that I had once traveled over." He visited every Islamic land then in existence—a remarkable feat that would involve visiting more than 40 countries if it were to be repeated today.

Batutta was born into a Berber family of Islamic legal scholars in Tangier,

STUDENT OF SHARIA
This Moroccan Koran was made in 1344. Ibn Battuta was well versed in koranic law, and occasionally took offense at the lax standards of behavior and dress in the lands he visited.

Morocco, in 1304, and studied Islamic law as a young man. From an early age he was eager to make the hajj, the Muslim pilgrimage to Mecca, and to see the tomb of the Prophet at Medina. He described being "swayed by an overmastering impulse … to visit these illustrious sanctuaries." In 1325, a year after the death of Marco Polo, Battuta decided to make the perilous journey to Arabia, although "it weighed sorely" upon him to leave his parents.

A BORN TRAVELER

Ibn Battuta was 21 when he left on his hajj, and he expected to be away for about 18 months, but in fact it was to be a quarter of a century before he returned, by which time both his parents had died. The pilgrim route to Mecca was well traveled and Battuta soon fell into the company of other pilgrims. He arrived in Cairo—"peerless in beauty and splendor, the meeting place of comer and goer"—after a journey of 2,200 miles (3,500 km), then set about exploring the city. He observed "it is said that in Cairo there are 12,000 water-carriers who transport water on camels, and 30,000 hirers of mules and donkeys, and that on its Nile there are 36,000 vessels belonging to the Sultan and his subjects." After a foray up the Nile, Battuta returned to Cairo and traveled on to Damascus, where he spent Ramadan, then joined a large caravan of pilgrims heading for Medina, a journey

of 930 miles (1,500 km). Moving on to Mecca, Battuta noted that the women were "of rare and surpassing beauty, pious, and chaste," but had such a liking for perfume that they were willing to "spend the night hungry and buy perfume with the price."

BAGHDAD AND BEYOND

After performing the rituals that a hajji—a pilgrim to Mecca—was required to fulfill, Battuta joined another caravan heading to Iraq, making a detour to explore Isfahan and Shiraz in Persia. Once back in Iraq, he visited a hospice for the poor at Umm 'Ubaida, where he witnessed the outlandish custom of the Ahmadi, who, after making a large fire, "went into the midst of it dancing; some of them rolled in the fire, and others ate it in their mouths, until finally they extinguished it entirely".

Arriving in Baghdad in 1327, Battuta found a partially ruined city that had never fully recovered from being sacked by the Mongol army of Hulagu Khan in 1258. There was still much to admire, though, and Battuta was particularly struck by the bath houses, which contained many individual cubicles: "each one of them [is] floored with pitch and having the lower half of its wall [also] coated with it, and the upper half coated with gleaming white gypsum plaster; the two opposites are thus brought together in contrasting beauty."

واشَرْتُ الى الدَّرَاهِمِ فَوَمِنَ بِالسَّرِ المُبْهِمِ وَانَ ابْنَنْ نَرْجِ فَي خَذِي القِطْعَةِ وَاَسَرَ

GREAT AND VARIED WORLD
This 13th-century illustration by al-Wasiti, an Arab
artist, depicts pilgrims embarking on a hajj to Mecca,
accompanied by music and banners. On his first hajj
in 1326, Ibn Battuta was deeply moved by the huge
gathering of Muslims from near and far. It was then
that he realized how great and varied the world was,
and determined to see as much of it as he could.

بِاَنَ فِي اخْلَاصِ البَذْلِ رَاحَةَ النَّمَ وَالاَبْلَجِ الهِمَمِ وَقَالَنَ دَعْ جِدَالَكَ وَبَيْنَا عَمَابَدَكَ الَكَا

After traveling back to Mecca, Battuta branched south to Yemen, Aden, and East Africa in 1328. In Aden he noted that "the merchants among them have enormous wealth, sometimes a single man may possess a great ship with all it contains", but found Zeila in Somalia to be "the dirtiest, most disagreeable, and most stinking in the world" due to the fish landed and camels slaughtered upon its streets.

After visiting the Byzantine empire and the lands of the Seljuk Turks in Anatolia in about 1330, Battuta traveled overland to India via Samarkand in present-day Uzbekistan. His legal knowledge came into good use when he was employed by the Sultan of Delhi as a *qadi*—a judge of Islamic law—a position that served him well on his travels (although he often outstayed his welcome by handing down strict sharia judgments). Battuta described

Delhi as "a vast and magnificent city … surrounded by a wall whose equal is not known in any country in the world," and remained in the city for eight years. Battuta's next adventure came at the invitation of the sultan to go to China as his ambassador in 1342. It was a journey fraught with disaster. The junk Battuta was due to travel in was wrecked before he set off; his entourage was attacked by bandits, and Battuta himself was

CONSTANTINOPLE
Ibn Battuta's first foray outside of the Islamic world came in 1332 in Constantinople, when the magnificent Hagia Sophia was still a Christian church.

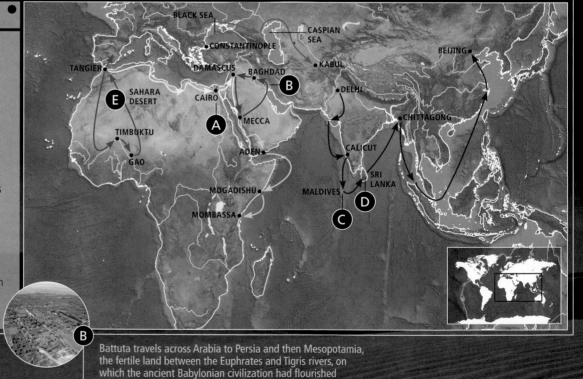

IN HIS FOOTSTEPS

1325–27—First hajj
Ibn Battuta travels overland from Tangier, reaching Mecca via Cairo and the Holy Land

1327–28—Second hajj
Travels from Mecca to Baghdad via Persia, then returns to Mecca via Damascus

1329–30—East Africa and third hajj
Visits the Muslim kingdoms of East Africa

1331–33—East into Asia
Journeys from Constantinople to Delhi across the north of the Black and Caspian seas

1342–44—Sails to China
From the Gujerati coast, he sails to China via the Maldives, Sri Lanka, and Chittagong

1349–54—From Spain to Timbuktu
Travels north from Tangier into Moorish Spain before crossing the Sahara to Timbuktu

(B) Battuta travels across Arabia to Persia and then Mesopotamia, the fertile land between the Euphrates and Tigris rivers, on which the ancient Babylonian civilization had flourished

1325–27	1327–28	1329–30	1331–33

Ibn Battuta leaves Tangier to begin his first hajj; he will not return home for another 25 years

(A) From Cairo, Battuta first attempts to reach Mecca via the Nile; he turns back and reaches his destination via Damascus instead

Reaches as far south as the equatorial Muslim states of East Africa, spending a week in each city he comes across

Battuta disapproves of the cultures of the recently converted Muslims in the lands around the Black Sea

MAKING THE HAJJ

The hajj, the pilgrimage to Mecca, is one of the "Five Pillars of Islam," along with faith, prayer, giving alms, and fasting. Outside trade, it was the main reason medieval Muslims traveled. In Battuta's day, pilgrims assembled in various cities and traveled en masse—sometimes in groups of 10,000—to Mecca. Two of the most famous assembly points were Cairo and Damascus, and Battuta would have joined the hajj in both cities.

nearly executed. He lost all the gifts the sultan had given him to take to China and thereafter dared not return to Delhi. Eventually reaching Zaitun (present-day Quanzhou), he observed that "silk is extremely plentiful … the poor and the destitute dress in it." From Zaitun he traveled to al-Khansa (present-day Hangzhou), which he described as "the biggest city I have ever seen on the face of the earth."

RETURNING HOME

After China, Battuta felt it was time finally to head home, which he did via Mecca for one last pilgrimage. He survived a plague raging through the Middle East and arrived in

Morocco in 1349, the first time he had been there in 24 years. He had set out as an idealistic student, and now reentered the gates of Tangier as a wealthy and famous traveler, with an entourage of servants. In the quarter century of his absence he had met 40 heads of state, acted as an ambassador and a judge, had experienced several brushes with death, married several wives, and made the hajj many times. Within two years he was off again, this time to Moorish Spain and then, on one final adventure, across the Sahara to Timbuktu.

He returned home for good in 1354, and his travels were recorded by order of the Sultan of Morocco in the book the *Rihla* ("Travels"). In it, Battuta comes across as a sympathetic, if occasionally prim, observer—a man as content to rough it with the poor as he was to dine with emperors. His sharia qualifications opened doors wherever he went, and he traveled in relative ease and safety across the Islamic world. But perhaps the most appealing aspect of the *Rihla* was Battuta's willingness to take any opportunity to embark on a journey, to search out new experiences, and to travel for the sheer joy it.

YUAN DYNASTY BUDDHISM
The Mongol emperors of the Yuan dynasty patronized Chinese Buddhist art, such as this seated wooden sculpture. Battuta was familiar with Buddhism before he arrived in China, having served as a judge in the Maldives, which had recently converted from Buddhism to Islam.

SAILING BY DHOW
After his hajj of 1328, Battuta made for Jeddah, taking a series of boats along the Red Sea coast. The boats would have been dhows, similar to these, fishing off the coast of Tanzania.

In Sri Lanka, Battuta climbs Sri Pada (Adam's Peak), a conical mountain in the centre of the island that is held to be sacred in the traditions of Buddhism, Hinduism, and Islam

Battuta crosses the ergs—the great "sand seas" of the northern Sahara—to visit the Muslim lands of West Africa

D   E

1345–48   **1349–54**   1354–68

C   Battuta spends nine mont   he Maldives, finding employment as a judge, his strict decisions are unpopular with the locals

He is impressed by the quality of t   s he finds in China, but the Buddhist and Taoist idols that he finds there trouble him greatly

Ibn Battuta takes up a position as a judge back home in Tangier, where he dies in 1368 or '69

THE MEDIEVAL MUSLIM WORLD
On his travels, Ibn Battuta (see pp. 68–71) would have been familiar with scenes such as those depicted in this 13th-century Arab manuscript. Here, a caravanserai (an inn catering to camel trains) provides respite for pilgrims. In the picture on the opposite page, slaves are inspected and haggled over in a slave market. Ibn Battuta witnessed just such a scene in Timbuktu in 1341.

وكذلك أحسب أنه سبيط رسر زرائى وبغلى السمة على وأحلق الحيث حلق ما اغلف
بل قال أن العبد إذا نزر ثمنة وخفت مونته نرك بمولاه والتحف عليه هؤلاه وألتى

لأوتن نحبت هذ الغلام النك أن أخفت ثمنه عليكم ما بن زهمان شبت
واشكرى ما جبت فنقلنة المبلغ في الكال كما نفد وأرخص الغال وألت

A ROUTE AROUND AFRICA

B Y THE 15TH CENTURY, EXPLORERS HAD LONG BEEN INTRIGUED BY THE POSSIBILITY OF FINDING A SEA ROUTE AROUND AFRICA TO THE MARKETS OF ASIA. ALTHOUGH ATTEMPTS WERE MADE IN ANCIENT TIMES, IT WAS ONLY IN 1488 THAT SUCH A VOYAGE WAS SUCCESSFULLY ACHIEVED.

EXPLORER PRINCE
Prince Henry the Navigator (1394–1460) was the younger son of King João I of Portugal. He gave invaluable support to Portuguese expeditions along the West African coast.

The ancient Egyptians and Phoenicians both sent expeditions that attempted to round Africa. One was sponsored by Pharaoh Necho II in about 670BCE; another was led by the navigator Hanno (see pp. 18–19), whose 60-ship fleet may have reached as far south as Cameroon. The Greeks and Romans were unsure whether Africa was a "great promontory," and could therefore be sailed around, or if it formed a continuous block of land that could not be passed by ship, as those who had read the works of the geographer Ptolemy believed. Their sketchy understanding of conditions beyond the coastal fringes is revealed by the Greek historian Herodotus in the 6th century BCE, who, amid historically verifiable details, writes of a tribe of "dog-faced" men who inhabited Libya.

INCENTIVES TO VOYAGE

The Romans could access the western Indian Ocean from their Red Sea ports in Egypt. Their discovery of how the monsoon winds facilitated trade between Arabia and India, therefore, lessened the motivation for trying to reach the Indian Ocean via an arduous circumnavigation of Africa. The fall of the Byzantine capital of Constantinople to the Turks in 1453, however, provided a fresh reason to seek alternative routes to the East, avoiding lands controlled by Muslim rulers who might block European traders or extract enormous tolls from them.

It was Italian merchants who made the earliest recorded expeditions to the islands off the Atlantic coast of Africa. In 1291, two Genoese brothers, Ugolino and Guido Vivaldi, tried unsuccessfully to reach India by sailing around Africa. Twenty years later, a Genoese navigator named Lanzarote Malocello went searching for the Vivaldis and reached the Canary Islands (where he gave his name to the island of Lanzarote). After this, however, it was the Portuguese who took over the mantle of Atlantic African exploration, sending an

VOYAGE'S END
Vasco da Gama reached Calicut (present-day Kozhikode) in India in May 1498 after a voyage of almost a year, but met with a decidedly frosty reception from the local ruler.

COMOROS LANDFALL
Portuguese vessels first visited the Comoros, situated midway between Madagascar and the East African coast, in about 1505. They became a supply stop for ships heading to India.

COLONIAL WAYS
A 16th-century engraving shows a Portuguese colonist in East Africa being carried in an elaborate litter, possibly influenced by the customs of his Arab predecessors in the region.

expedition to the Canaries in 1341. Portuguese rulers made strenuous efforts to encourage this maritime expansion, in 1377 granting a subsidy to the residents of Lisbon to allow them to cut wood for shipbuilding tax-free. A further stimulus to exploration was provided by the capture of Ceuta (in northern Morocco) in 1415, which provided a Portuguese land-base in Africa from which to make further forays. Between 1418 and 1425, the Portuguese colonized Madeira, and from 1427 began the exploration and settlement of the Azores. The way was now clear for a push southwest along the coastline of Africa itself, with a series of expeditions sponsored by the visionary Portuguese prince, Henry "the Navigator."

PORTUGUESE ASCENDANCY

In 1434, a Portuguese expedition under Gil Eanes rounded Cape Bojador on the western Sahara, previously regarded as an impassable barrier along the West African coast. Two years later, Afonso Baldaia pushed more than 450 miles (650 km) farther, reaching the Rio d'Ouro (in present-day Western Sahara) and returning to Portugal with a large number of sea lion skins.

After a brief hiatus caused by the failure of a Portuguese attack on Tangier in 1437, the African voyages resumed in the 1440s, creeping ever farther south down the West African coast.

In 1444, a Portuguese sailor, Dinis Dias, discovered the Cape Verde Islands. In 1446, another Portuguese sailor, Nuno Tristão, was killed by natives at the mouth of the Gambia River, while by 1448 more than 50 vessels had passed Cape Bojador, less than 15 years after its first rounding.

In 1456, the mariners Alvise da Cadamosto and Antoniotto Usidamare explored the coast of Guinea. Not long afterward, Diogo Gomes sailed along the Guinea coast, though further discoveries were made more difficult beyond Cape Verde, where changeable winds and dense fog rendered sailing conditions treacherous. In the early 1470s, however, the merchant Fernão Gomes pushed on to the Gold Coast, while by 1483 Diogo Cão had advanced even farther, planting a stone pillar on the banks of the Congo River (see pp. 78–79). When Bartolomeu Dias (see pp. 76–77) rounded the Cape of Good Hope in early January 1488 and Vasco da Gama (see pp. 80–81) sighted the coast of India in July 1497, having completed the long sought-for sea-route around Africa, it was the culmination of a maritime venture that had lasted for more than a century.

> The circumnavigation of Africa provided the impetus for the Portuguese (and later Spanish, Dutch, and British) to establish trading colonies around the Indian Ocean and to make overland expeditions into the African interior.

STURDY CARAVEL
The Portuguese caravels that undertook many of the African voyages were said to have been modeled on the traditional Arab dhow, a shallow-drafted vessel with lateen (triangular) sails.

ARAB PRECEDENTS

The coastlines of East Africa that da Gama visited were not unknown to outsiders. As early as the 7th century, the Umayyad caliph Ibn Marwan had sent Syrian settlers to the coast between Somalia and Kenya, while an 8th-century account called the *Kitab al-Zunuj*, lists a string of East African cities whose governors answered to caliph Harun al-Rashid in Baghdad. The Arab settlement in Zanzibar may date to the 9th century, and an inscription from 1107 proves it was ruled by Muslim emirs by that date. By da Gama's time, the whole coastline from Mogadishu to Malindi in Kenya was dotted with Muslim ports that thrived on trade across the Indian Ocean—and did not welcome "interlopers" such as the Portuguese.

BARTOLOMEU DIAS

FIRST EXPLORER TO ROUND AFRICA'S SOUTHERN TIP

PORTUGAL   C. 1450–1500

A PIONEERING FIGURE in Portugal's age of maritime discovery, Dias was the first European to round the Cape of Good Hope, the southwestern tip of Africa. In 1488, his flotilla of three ships sailed farther south and east than any other European expedition, marking their progress along the Atlantic and Indian Ocean coast of Africa with the *padrões* (stone pillars) that staked Portugal's claim to the newly discovered lands. Dias's daring journey prepared the way for Vasco da Gama's voyage to India a decade later.

Little is known of Dias's early life, although he is thought to have joined a voyage to the Gold Coast (present-day Ghana) in 1481. He must have made his mark, because five years later he was chosen by King João II of Portugal to lead an expedition to the southernmost tip of Africa to investigate a possible trade route to India.

ALL POINTS SOUTH

Leaving Lisbon in August 1487 with two caravels—light, maneuverable vessels specially designed for coastal exploration—and a larger store ship, Dias sailed south, stopping at the Gold Coast to pick up provisions. He passed the final *padrão*—a stone pillar erected as a land claim— left by Diogo Cão (see pp. 78–79) some two years earlier at present-day Cape Cross, Namibia. At the end of December the fleet reached Walvis Bay, where the store ship was anchored for the winter. About 300 miles (500 km) farther south Dias ordered the erection of a *padrão* of his own at present-day Dias Point, Namibia. In early January 1488, the weather conditions deteriorated, so Dias ordered his ships farther

A LIFE'S WORK

- Sails farther south than **any other European** before him
- Becomes the first European to **round the southern tip of Africa** and to prove **the existence of a sea route to India**
- Makes observations that allow the **mapping of southern Africa** for the first time
- Falls short of his secondary objective of finding the **fabled kingdom of Prester John**, a legendary Christian priest-king whose domain was thought by the medieval Portuguese to lie somewhere in the region of present-day Ethiopia

ADAPTABLE VESSELS
Dias's caravels, the *São Cristóvão* and *São Pantelon*, were capable of sailing under a square rig of sails, but could also be converted to run a "lateen" triangular sail, making them ideal for exploring coastal waters and estuaries.

IN HIS FOOTSTEPS

→ **August 1487—Departs Lisbon**
Dias heads south, stopping at a Portuguese fort at Elmina on the Gold Coast to pick up provisions; rounds the Cape and reaches present-day Mossel Bay on February 3, 1488; reaches farthest point east when he anchors at Algoa Bay on March 12, and there erects a *padrão*

→ **March—December 1488—Return**
Dias wishes to continue to India, but turns back under pressure from his crew; only on the return does he discover the Cape of Good Hope, which he'd rounded without sight of land on the outward journey

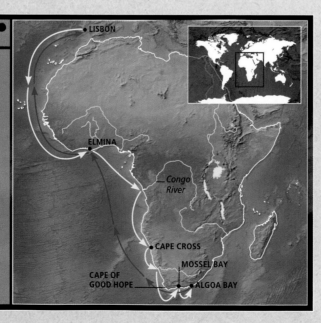

LISBON

ELMINA

Congo River

CAPE CROSS

MOSSEL BAY

CAPE OF GOOD HOPE

ALGOA BAY

A PASSAGE TO INDIA
Dias's observations enabled the mapping of the southern African coast for the first time. A higher temperature and a coastline that bore to the northeast led him to guess, correctly, that he had found a southerly route to the Indian Ocean.

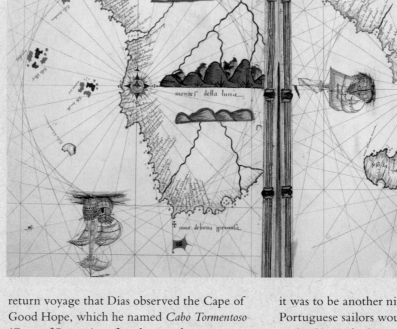

out to sea. The Portuguese chronicler João de Barros wrote some 60 years later: "putting out to sea, the weather forced them to run 13 days with sail at half mast." As Dias discovered to his satisfaction, the storm had blown the ships around the tip of the African continent. He had also discovered the principle of safely rounding the Cape by sailing wide of the dangerous currents.

AROUND THE CAPE

Dias set an easterly course once the storm had passed, reaching present-day Mossel Bay, South Africa, on February 3. Landing to take on supplies of fresh water, it was noted that the African interpreters could not translate the language of the indigenous people, whose appearance was distinctly different from those on the west coast.

Dias continued to follow the coastline eastward and erected another *padrão* at Cape Padrone, east of present-day Port Elizabeth. At this point, Dias seems to have faced a potential mutiny: unsure of their exact position, the crew demanded to return to Portugal. However, Dias held his nerve and the fleet continued east for 60 miles (100 km) along the Indian Ocean coast before turning back at Algoa Bay. It was on the

return voyage that Dias observed the Cape of Good Hope, which he named *Cabo Tormentoso* (Cape of Storms)—after the treacherous conditions in which the ships had first passed. A final *padrão* was erected to mark Portugal's claim and achievement. The two ships retraced their route, collecting the supply ship and visiting the island of Principe off the coast of Equatorial Guinea and Liberia, before reaching Lisbon in December 1488.

SMALL RECOGNITION

No log or first-hand account of Dias's voyage is known to have survived, but it is likely that King João II gave the Cape its current name—"Good Hope"—in expectation of the flow of trade with the East. Despite the importance of the route,

it was to be another nine years before Portuguese sailors would round the Cape again. Vasco da Gama (see pp. 80–81) used the information provided by Dias to extend Portuguese trade across the Indian Ocean.

Dias seems to have received little reward for his efforts. He joined da Gama for the first leg of his pioneering journey to India in 1497, but was never to lead another expedition. His final voyage was to India under Cabral (see pp. 96–97) in 1500, but Dias and his squadron were lost in a storm after leaving newly discovered Brazil.

AN AGE OF DISCOVERIES
Portugal was at the forefront of maritime exploration in the 15th and 16th centuries, as commemorated in the "Age of Discoveries" monument in Lisbon. Dias and Cão are depicted on the right, hauling up a stone *padrão*.

DIOGO CÃO

PORTUGUESE DISCOVERER OF ANGOLA

PORTUGAL   1450–1500

THE DISTINCTION OF EXPLORING the west African coast farther south than any European before him fell to a mariner named Diogo Cão. He recorded his achievements by leaving stone pillars at strategic points along the way. Although written records of the period are scant, the pillars are evidence of two major sea voyages undertaken by Cão. He was the first European to sail up the Congo River and, farther south, he left a pillar in Angola, which became a Portuguese-speaking colony for nearly 500 years.

A LIFE'S WORK

- Makes two journeys down the coast of Africa, becoming the **first recorded European** to sail up the **Congo River**, and the first to set eyes on the **Skeleton Coast**

- Erects four **stone pillars** (*padrões*) at strategic points on his voyages, providing us with knowledge of exactly where he went

- Reinforces Portugal's claims to a trade monopoly **along the Guinea coast**, weakening Spanish influence in the region

- May have commanded **a large fleet** on his **second voyage**, although records are contradictory, and probably dies at some point during this expedition

IN THE NAME OF THE KING
Cão erected the first *padrão* of his second voyage at Cape Cross, in present-day Namibia. The next he planted 160 miles (250 km) farther south. Although crude, the *padrões* proved an effective way of claiming the territories for the Portuguese crown.

Cão lived in a time when Portugal was starting to expand its influence in the world through trade. His first voyage was a mission to enforce existing Portuguese trading rights along the African coast. Cão must have been given orders to explore, too, because he was the first of the Portuguese explorers to carry *padrões* (stone pillars) to mark the progress of his discoveries. Previously, wooden crosses had been used, but the stone markers planted a more durable claim on any new territories. Cão set up four *padrões* during the course of his two voyages, all of which have since been found in their original locations.

THE FIRST VOYAGE
Cão sailed from Lisbon in mid-1482, reaching the mouth of the Congo River by retracing the route of Fernão Gomez, a Portuguese merchant who had made the journey in 1469. The chart of the voyage records that the water was still fresh 15 miles (28 km) out at sea, indicating the strength of the currents at the mouth of the river. Cão sailed briefly up river before his ship was met by canoes and a friendly exchange with the local people was recorded. They explained by hand gestures that a great king lived up river

and Cão sent a party of men to seek an audience. The first of the *padrões* was erected at the mouth of the Congo, and Cão stayed for several months before setting off south along the coast. He reached a point south of Ponta Choca, in present-day Angola, where he set up the second pillar. On

STONE CLAIM
The stone *padrões* Cão carried were inscribed with the arms of King João II of Portugal.

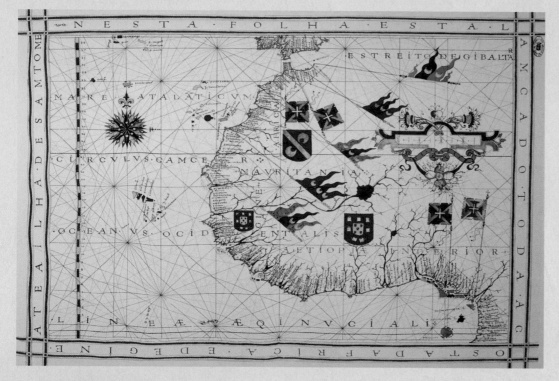

THE SKELETON COAST

On his second voyage, Cão passed the arid coast that borders the Namib desert. The region became notorious among Portuguese sailors as "The Gates of Hell". Dry winds blow from the land, and there is a constant heavy surf, which, in the days of sail, meant it was easier to land than it was to launch from the shore. Its present name, Skeleton Coast, derives from the many wrecks caught by the surf.

THE SKELETON COAST IS KNOWN BY THE BUSHMEN OF NAMIBIA AS "THE LAND GOD MADE IN ANGER"

WEST AFRICA IN THE AGE OF DISCOVERY
Some of the details of Cão's voyages are known only from the legends written on maps like this one from 1571, which uses his observations of the west African coastline.

returning to the Congo, Cão found that his emissaries to the king had not returned. Fearing their abduction (although a later account suggests that they were simply enjoying the king's hospitality), Cão took four men hostage, including Caçuto, a local noble, and returned to Lisbon. There, Caçuto became a favorite of the king and Cão was ennobled, his coat of arms bearing a *padrão*.

Evidence for Cão's second expedition is less well documented. An account from 1493 states, "In 1484 King João sent two vessels to the south, one being commanded by D. Cão … They traded with the Jolof and came to a country where they found cinnamon." Other accounts suggest that Cão returned to the Congo, where he freed his four hostages before sailing south. He erected a third *padrão* at Cape Cross, and a fourth farther along the coast. Some maps record that Cão died at the site of this fourth memorial. Caçuto is known to have been at the Portuguese court in 1490—and renamed João da Silva—suggesting that this second narrative may be the true one.

IN HIS FOOTSTEPS

1482–84—First voyage
Cão is given orders to enforce Portuguese trading contracts along the west African coast, where some Portuguese merchant-mariners have previously explored and established trading links; Cão's expedition presumably comprises soldiers and arms; he also carries royal orders to explore farther to the south and leaves two stone pillars, one at the mouth of the Congo River, the other at Cape Santa Maria (present-day Namibia)

1484–86—Second voyage
Retraces route of first voyage, this time sailing another 870 miles (1,400 km) south, and planting two more *padrões*; one account has Cão dying at sea near Cape Cross

LISBON

AFRICA

MINA SÃO JORGE

Congo River

ATLANTIC OCEAN

CAPE SANTA MARIA

CAPE CROSS

VASCO DA GAMA

DISCOVERER OF A TRADE ROUTE TO INDIA

PORTUGAL   C. 1460–1524

PERHAPS THE MOST RUTHLESS EXPLORER in the European Age of Discovery, Vasco da Gama commanded the first ships to sail directly from Europe to Asia. Da Gama was an ambitious man, eager to exceed the achievements of his Portuguese predecessors in exploring the unknown world. By the late 15th century, Portugal had established maritime dominance along the coastline of Africa. The time was ready for one daring mariner to carry Portuguese expansion beyond Africa to the Indian subcontinent.

A LIFE'S WORK

- Is the first to open a sea route for the **direct import of spices** and other Eastern goods to the West

- Discovers that the east coast of Africa—with its ports offering fresh water, provisions, and lumber—is essential to Portuguese interests, leading to the **colonization of Mozambique** in 1505

- Vigorously and violently **polices Portuguese interests** in India, extracting favorable trading concessions from the *zamorin* (ruler) of Calicut by force after destroying 29 of his ships

- Along with Cabral (see pp. 96–97) opens the way to establishing the Portuguese Empire, the **world's first global empire**

DA GAMA'S ATROCITY
At Cannanore, India, during his second voyage, da Gama encountered a ship returning Muslim pilgrims from Mecca. He gave orders for it to be attacked, burning all on board.

A son of the governor of Alentejo province, da Gama spent his early years in military training and learning the skills of a mariner. When an expedition to find a trade route across the Indian Ocean was planned by King Manuel I, da Gama was chosen to lead it, supported by advice from Bartolomeu Dias (see pp. 76–77), who had rounded the Cape of Good Hope in 1488. Dias had also overseen the construction of two ships, the *São Gabriel* and *São Rafael*, which were to be captained by da Gama and his elder brother Paulo, respectively.

THE FLEET SETS OFF
Setting sail on July 8, 1497, with a fleet of four ships (carrying six stone pillars to erect on newly claimed land), da Gama was accompanied by Dias, who was to become governor of a Portuguese settlement on the coast of Guinea. By December, the ships had reached the Rio do Infante, in the present-day Eastern Cape of South Africa, the point at which Dias had previously turned back. On the *São Gabriel*

TOMB OF A LEGEND
Da Gama's tomb lies in Belém, Portugal. He contracted malaria on his third visit to India in 1524 and died at Cochin.

the crew, frightened by entering unknown waters, threatened to mutiny. Da Gama had both the master and pilot put in chains while his brother Paulo quelled an uprising on the sister ship. Da Gama named the coastline *Natal* (Birth of Christ), since they passed it on Christmas Day 1497.

AFRICAN OASES
On reaching Mozambique in March 1498, the expedition log recorded that many of the crew had become sick with scurvy, "their feet and hands swelling, and their gums growing over their teeth, so that they could not eat." The voyage continued northward, reaching Malindi, north of Mombasa, where the log recorded that: "Mombasa … is very pleasant, being full of orchards, planted with pomegranates, Indian figs, oranges of both kinds, lemons and citrons."

Before departing, da Gama received the consent of the king of Malindi to position one of the stone pillars on a hill above the town. It was there that he also secured the services of Ahmed Mesjid, a skilled pilot of Gujarat, India, whose knowledge of the monsoon winds was instrumental in carrying da Gama's ships across

the Indian Ocean. Continuing from Malindi in April 1498, Mesjid guided the vessels to the Keralan coast of India. With the wind behind them, the journey took just 23 days, sailing by way of the Laccadive Islands (present-day Lakshadweep), off the coast of Kerala.

INDIA AND BACK
Some 10 months after their departure from Lisbon, the ships arrived at the port of Calicut (present-day Kozhikode). An account of da Gama's meeting with Bontaybo, a Portuguese-speaking man in the city, mentions how, "the general and the rest were so surprised to meet with one who could speak their language so far from home, that they wept for joy. After which, da Gama embraced Bontaybo." The local Arabian merchants, however, were less

welcoming. Perceiving da Gama as a threat to their age-old system of trade, they took him hostage. His brother Paulo retaliated by seizing six local nobles. This, coupled with misinformation that da Gama's four vessels were an advance party for a fleet of 50 Portuguese ships, led to a cessation in hostilities and da Gama was freed. After that he departed, sailing along the coast to Cochin (present-day Kochi) before heading home for Lisbon in August.

The return voyage was fraught with difficulties, taking 132 days to reach Malindi due to frequent calms and adverse wind. Scurvy was again recorded in the log: "Those able to navigate our ships were only seven or eight." At Malindi, the *São Rafael* had to be abandoned because of a shortage of crew. On the expedition's return, da Gama's achievements were celebrated and he received the title of "Admiral of the Indian Seas," while King Manuel took the modest moniker of "Lord of the Conquest, Navigation, and Commerce of Ethiopia, Arabia, Persia, and India."

IN HIS FOOTSTEPS

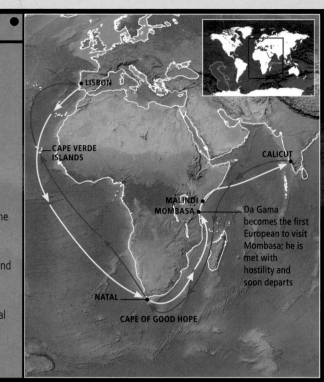

→ **July 1497—Departs Lisbon**
Heads south past the Cape Verde Islands, seeking the South Atlantic westerlies, and in November lands on the South African coast; in six months he covers 6,000 miles (9,600 km) of open ocean, the longest journey out of sight of land made to date

→ **August 1498—Return journey**
Da Gama ignores the monsoon and suffers a long journey with the loss of two-thirds of his crew; he reaches home in August 1499

○ **February 1502—Second voyage**
He returns to India with 20 warships and forces the *zamorin* (ruler) to trade

○ **1524—Third voyage**
Sent by the king to sort out the colonial administration in India, da Gama contracts malaria in Goa and dies

○ Not shown on map

LISBON

CAPE VERDE ISLANDS

CALICUT

MALINDI
MOMBASA

Da Gama becomes the first European to visit Mombasa; he is met with hostility and soon departs

NATAL

CAPE OF GOOD HOPE

CHEAP WESTERN GOODS
A tapestry depicts da Gama greeting the *zamorin* of Calicut. After initial cordial relations, the Portuguese soon encountered problems on account of the poor quality of the goods they had brought to trade, which the *zamorin* considered cheap and undesirable.

CHARTING THE DEVELOPMENT OF...

EXPEDITION NAVIGATION

BEFORE THE DEVELOPMENT OF SCIENTIFIC navigational instruments, sailors relied on their knowledge of the stars, ocean currents, and the migration patterns of birds to estimate their position. In desert regions, even in the 20th century, explorers navigated using dead reckoning, sun compasses, and an estimate of their camel's speed. At the poles, navigation was hugely complicated by drifting ice floes, darkness, and polar magnetic forces, which caused compasses to give false readings.

NAVIGATING AT SEA

From the 13th century onward, the main technique used by mariners to calculate their position at sea was known as dead reckoning. Measurements were recorded at a ship's last known position, which was calculated using portolans (charts, or "pilot books"). Then the direction of travel was worked out using the Sun, Moon, stars, or a compass, and the speed by throwing a log line overboard and counting the number of knots that were pulled off a spool of rope in a given length of time. To make a more accurate measurement of position, the navigator needed two key pieces of information: the ship's latitude (the position on the Earth, north or south of the equator) and longitude (the position east or west of the meridian). Calculating latitude was fairly straightforward, requiring an accurate observation of the Sun, Moon, and stars. The astrolabe, known to the

221 BCE—THE FIRST COMPASS
The earliest compasses date from China in the 3rd century BCE. This later Chinese instrument combines sundial and compass.

800 CE—NORSE WIND
The Vikings navigate using knowledge of prevailing winds.

1268—BLACK STONE
English friar Roger Bacon experiments with magnetic loadstones, the earliest magnetic compasses.

1598—LONGITUDE PRIZE
King Philip II of Spain offers 100,000 crowns for a solution to the longitude problem.

1568—WORLD MAP
Gerardus Mercator publishes his new cylindrical map.

BCE	1100	1000	CE 150	800	1250	1300	1350	1400	1450	1500	1550	1600

1200 BCE— PHOENICIAN SAILORS
The Phoenicians develop a system of navigation by observing the changing positions of certain stars.

1270—COMPASS AND CHART
Alfonso, King of Castile, Spain, orders that all Castilian ships should carry a compass and a chart.

1000 BCE POLYNESIAN SAILORS

Without even the aid of a compass, the **Polynesian islanders were expert navigators**, sailing between islands using **stick charts,** such as this one made from coconut fiber, plant root, and small shells. The charts recorded **wave patterns** around an island, **ocean swells** between islands, and **island-to-island voyages**: known respectively as *mattang, rebbelib,* and *medo* charts.

1492 ASTROLABE

On his first voyage in 1492, Christopher Columbus uses an **astrolabe**, a scientific instrument for measuring with an arm that rotates from its center. The 0° mark is **aligned with the horizon**, and the Sun is sighted using the arm. The height of the Sun can then be measured in degrees. The plate provides a **projection of the celestial sphere** over which a disk shows the positions of stars.

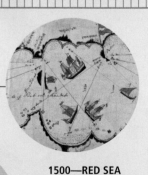

1500—RED SEA NAVIGATION
Arab navigator Ahmad Ibn Majid writes his fullest account of navigation, recording Arab "reef to reef" sailing techniques on the Red Sea.

Greeks and highly developed in the Islamic world by 800CE, gave an accurate measurement of latitude by confirming the height of the Sun at sea. On his voyages across the Atlantic, Christopher Columbus (see pp. 86–89) combined the astrolabe with dead reckoning.

THE LONGITUDE PROBLEM

Precise calculation of longitude, however, was trickier. It depended on the accurate measurement of the angles between objects in view. This accuracy was improved by the octant, invented in the 1730s, which used mirrors to reflect the images of the objects to be measured. By aligning both images into the view on a telescope, the angle between the objects could be determined. Later refinements led to the development of the sextant, which worked on the same principles, but using a 60° scale rather than 45°. Despite these innovations, no truly

accurate method of measuring longitude existed. In London in 1714, the Board of Longitude was formed and offered a large prize to whomever could finally solve the problem. In order to establish a longitudinal position, it was necessary to know the time difference between a ship's position and some fixed point.

The problem lay in establishing the time at a fixed location elsewhere. The solution was the chronometer, invented by English clockmaker John Harrison (1693–1776). He created four watches, or chronometers, that could keep good time at sea. Previously, watches had been too unreliable in the unstable conditions on board a ship (see pp. 142–43) when subjected to large variations in temperature and moisture. Harrison's best chronometer was the H4, made in 1759, a copy of which was taken by James Cook on his second voyage on the *Resolution* (see pp. 156–59).

SHIFTING SANDS

Explorers of the world's great deserts had problems that were in some ways similar to those of the mariners: how to navigate a featureless, ever-shifting vista (see pp. 26–27). British explorer Bertram Thomas, crossing the Arabian Rub' al Khali in 1930 (see pp. 248–49), calculated the distance he had covered by estimating the speed of his camels, making adjustments when the hungry animals encountered scrub. Wilfred Thesiger (see pp. 250–51) acted as his own guide for 150 miles (240 km) in the same desert in 1945, using a compass and protractor to calculate his longitude due to the complete absence of any maps or local knowledge of the region.

THE PROBLEMATIC POLES

Prior to the advent of satellite mapping systems, the terrain of the polar regions posed major navigational problems for

explorers. Arctic explorer Wally Herbert (see p. 309) recorded how, in 1969, the only way to keep track of drifting ice floes was to take regular position measurements with a sextant, using the Sun, Moon, and stars as points of reference. If the weather was overcast, he used a compass mounted on his sled, but the instrument became "sluggish" as he approached the pole.

SATELLITE ACCURACY

The chronometer and other measuring instruments remained essential until the late 1970s, when they were superseded by a satellite network called GPS (Global Positioning System). Despite being able to access accurate positioning information 24-hours a day, however, today's mariners and expedition leaders are still required to have basic navigational skills, and be ready for the moment when the systems go down or the batteries fail.

1714—BOARD OF LONGITUDE
The Board of Longitude is formed in Britain, offering a prize of £20,000, an enormous sum, for a solution to the longitude problem.

1730s—OCTANT INVENTED
The octant, a reflecting instrument is invented almost simultaneously in the US and Britain. It enables the first approximate calculations of longitude.

1841—ORDNANCE SURVEY
French, British, and other European nations create accurate maps for use by their military forces.

1996—SATELLITE ACCURACY
Public access is granted to the US's satellite navigation system, rendering maps and calculations of longitude almost redundant.

1650   1700   1750   1800   1850   1900   1950   2000

1698—MAGNETIC EXPERT
English astronomer Edmond Halley produces a map of the Earth's magnetism as part of his study of the laws governing the variation of compasses.

1772—COOK'S VOYAGES
On his second and third voyages to the Pacific, James Cook takes a copy of Harrison's H4 chronometer with him, and successfully calculates his position throughout.

During the search for a solution to the **longitude problem**, numerous theories are put forward, including one suggestion to create a **chain of ships on ocean-going voyages that would fire cannon or flares** and thereby signal time differences from ship to ship. However, Harrison's elegant and compact chronometer (shown here), a clock that keeps **accurate time at sea**, is the more practical solution.

1759 HARRISON'S CHRONOMETER

Accurate measurements are made on a series of **expeditions to the poles** at the start of the 20th century, including that of Roald Amundsen's South Pole expedition of 1910–11 (see pp. 302–05). Shown here are readings being taken with a **prismatic compass** during Robert Scott's Antarctic expedition of 1910–13 (see pp. 312–15). The measurements are used to create maps of the areas explored, which are of great use to future explorers until the advent of satellite mapping.

1910–13 ANTARCTIC MEASUREMENTS

A NEW WORLD TO SOME

THE "NEW WORLD" OF THE AMERICAS AND THE "OLD WORLDS" OF EUROPE AND ASIA REMAINED IN IGNORANCE OF EACH OTHER UNTIL THE FIRST ENCOUNTER IN 1492. BY THEN THE SO-CALLED "NEW WORLD" HAD GIVEN RISE TO CIVILIZATIONS THAT WERE MORE THAN 2,000 YEARS OLD.

FOREST CITY
The Mayan city of Tikal, deep in the forest of present-day Guatemala, had been abandoned by the time the Spanish arrived. The population may have been driven away by drought.

The Greek astronomer Eratosthenes had made a reasonably accurate calculation of the Earth's circumference in about 240BCE. For centuries, therefore, experts took the view that it was impossible for the ships of the day to sail such a distance westward from Europe and end up in East Asia. Yet in the 1470s and '80s, some began to question this reasoning, including the cosmographer Martin Behaim of Nuremberg, in present-day Germany, who made the world's oldest extant globe in about 1492.

Using the alternative calculations of these revisionists, the Genoese captain Christopher Columbus (see pp. 86–89) came up with a figure some 20 percent lower than the true value of the Earth's circumference. His project to sail due west to China via Cipangu (present-day Japan), said to lie 1,500 miles (2,500 km) to its east, did not seem so fantastical, and so it was on October 12, 1492, that his ship, *Santa Maria* (see pp. 90–91), made landfall in the Caribbean.

FIRST CONACT

The Taino Indians encountered by Columbus on San Salvador Island may originally have come from South America and formed part of a larger group known as the

DREAD WEIGHT
This 26-ton (24-metric-ton) Aztec stone was thought to represent a calendar. It has since been identified as a *temalacatl,* a weight to which sacrificial prisoners were tied.

Arawak. Employing slash and burn farming techniques, largely for the cultivation of cassava, their society, though possessing chiefs and a nobility, was in no position to offer organized resistance to the Spanish. Nor did they have much that the Spanish wanted to acquire.

END OF THE MAYA

Far more sophisticated civilizations awaited in Central America. The Maya, who first encountered Spanish arms in the shape of Francisco Hernández de Córdoba in 1517, had occupied lands in present-day Guatemala, Mexico's Yucatán peninsula, and Honduras since about 2000BCE. Their principal period of cultural flowering, however, occurred in the Classic Period (250–909CE), when the area was ruled over by a competing series of city-states such as Tikal, Yaxchilan, and Palenque. These cities' rulers built huge pyramids and fought debilitating wars with each other in an effort to obtain prisoners and establish themselves as hegemonic powers in the region.

By 1517, however, the Classic Culture had long since collapsed and Mayapan, the last major center of the Post-Classic Period,

> **The Spanish initially established themselves on the islands of the Caribbean. It was not long, however, before they began to send out expeditions to the mainland of Central and South America.**

was itself abandoned in 1441, almost 80 years before the arrival of the Spanish.

AZTEC GOLD

Most enticing to the Spanish was the Mexican empire of the Aztecs. The Mexica, as they termed themselves, had migrated from a mythic homeland called Aztlán far to the north in 1168. Two centuries later, they were well established in central Mexico, where they forged an empire based around the great city of Tenochtitlán. An alliance established in 1429 with the neighboring cities of Texcoco and Tlacopan allowed the Aztecs to dominate the valley of Mexico. With a strong military ethos, the Aztecs controlled most of the trade routes in and around Mexico, allowing the building of enormous temples and the amassing of huge quantities of gold artifacts. However, they subjected nearby tribes to a rule so harsh—it included the regular provision of captives to feed the sacrificial hunger of the Mexica gods—that their subjects were more than willing to cooperate with the Spanish when Hernán Cortés arrived in 1519 (see pp. 106–09).

LAND OF FOUR QUARTERS

Far to the south in the Andes Mountains, the Inca Empire's ruler, the Sapa Inca, exercised absolute power. The Inca had first established themselves in the foothills of the Andes in about 1300, but they began a dramatic expansion

AZTEC CROPS
Corn was a common crop grown by the Aztecs that was unknown to the Spanish. Other crops that were unknown to the Old World were chiles and tomatoes.

SUN WORSHIPERS
Inti, the Sun god was the chief deity of the Inca Empire. The festival of Inti was held during the winter solstice (around June 24) in Peru. It began with three days of fasting.

SETTING THE SCENE

- Christopher Columbus believed he would probably make first landfall in **Cipangu** (Japan), which, **according to Marco Polo,** lay 1,500 miles (2,500km) to the east of China. When he lands in the Caribbean in 1492, this is where Columbus thinks he has arrived.

- At the **height of their power** the Maya construct great buildings such as the palace for **K'inich Janaab' Pakal,** who rules the city of Palenque from 615 to 683CE.

- The Aztecs believed that the god **Quetzalcoatl** ("the feathered serpent") would one day return from the east. When the Spanish arrive, there is **confusion** as to whether they are the deity and his entourage, which **saps the Aztecs' initial resistance** to the invaders.

- The **fragmentation of the Maya** means that the Spanish cannot simply capture their rulers, (as they had captured those of the Aztecs and Inca), but have to **take their cities one by one**. The last, Tayapan, falls only in 1697.

- The Inca state is only just emerging from a **civil war** when the victor, **Atahualpa**, is forced to face the Spanish invaders.

under Emperor Pachacuti from 1438, who swept aside the Chimú (the previously dominant power), whose capital fell in 1470. By 1493, the Inca ruled as far as Ecuador in the north and as far as Peru in the south, a vast territory they called *Tawantinsuyu* ("The Land of the Four Quarters"). Acting as the spine of this great domain was a network of roads along which runners carried orders from a complex bureaucracy. Great temples housed treasures in gold. As Tupac Inca and Huayna Capac, the last Inca rulers before the Spanish arrived in 1532, extended the bounds of the empire to the edge of the Atacama Desert and into the Bolivian highlands, the Incas' dominance of the continent must have seemed unassailable.

OLD AND NEW
This is the first map showing the Old and New Worlds together. It was made by Columbus in Spain after returning from his second voyage. By that time, he had visited South America in addition to the Caribbean.

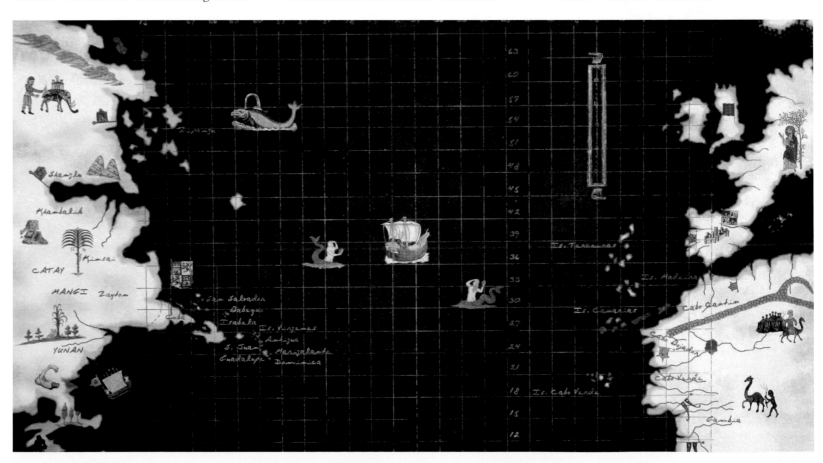

CHRISTOPHER COLUMBUS

EXPLORER OF THE NEW WORLD

GENOESE REPUBLIC

C. 1451–1506

GENOESE NAVIGATOR AND MARINER Christopher Columbus became the most famous explorer in history for discovering the Americas by chance. His goal had been to find a westward sea route to China and India, and it was in the mistaken belief he had reached Asia that he set foot on San Salvador Island in the Bahamas in 1492. Although he was not the first European to reach America, his four voyages across the Atlantic would set in motion the widespread colonization of the "New World" by European settlers.

Little is known of Columbus's early life, but it is likely that he became a merchant-mariner at a young age. At the time, Genoa (in present-day Italy), was a leading center for nautical science, so a career at sea may have been an obvious choice for him. He sailed to the Canary Islands in 1478 to ply the sugar trade, and gained experience of the Atlantic, joining at least one merchant voyage to Ghana in west Africa. By 1485, however, he was living in Lisbon, Portugal, where his brother Bartolomeo was a mapmaker. With combined expertise, the two men hatched an "Enterprise of the Indies"—a daring plan to sail west, not east, in search of a sea route to Asia.

THE "NEW WORLD"

At first, the brothers had no luck in finding a sponsor. Their proposal was rejected by King João II of Portugal, who believed that they had grossly underestimated the circumference of the Earth. (As it turned out, the king was right.) However, the late 15th century was a time when Europe's kingdoms were competing for wealth from new sea routes and colonies and, in 1486, the brothers' risky plan caught the attention of the Spanish monarchs, Ferdinand II of Aragon and Isabella of Castille.

After a long delay over funding, a fleet of three ships, the *Santa Maria*, the *Pinta,* and the *Niña*, departed from Palos, Spain, in August 1492. Columbus's plan was to sail due west, in the belief that China would be the first land he sighted. So confident was he of this that he assured his captains that Asia would be reached in a matter of weeks.

On October 11, 1492, land was first sighted by Rodrigo de Triana, a sailor aboard the *Pinta*. But it was not Asia—Christopher Columbus's fleet had reached an island in the Bahamas off

ROYAL REWARDS
This manuscript from 1492 details the generous rewards promised to Columbus by the Spanish crown for successfully discovering new lands for Spain.

I FIND [THAT] THE WORLD IS NOT ROUND ... IT IS THE SHAPE OF A PEAR

CHRISTOPHER COLUMBUS

88

the coast of North America. Naming the island San Salvador, and believing it to be near the East Indies, he referred to its inhabitants as "*Indios*," or "Indians." Columbus wrote in his journal of the native people, "they were friendly to us … I presented them with some red caps, and strings of beads to wear." By Christmas Day 1492, a full exploration of the local islands and the northeastern coast of nearby Cuba had been completed. Arriving close to the northern coast of another large island (present-day Haiti and Dominican

THE FIRST FLEET
In a reenactment of Columbus's first voyage to the Americas, these specially built replicas of the *Santa Maria*, *Pinta*, and *Niña* set sail from the southern Spanish port of Huelva on October 13, 1991.

Republic), Columbus recorded that "more than a thousand of the inhabitants visited the ships, every one bringing something."

On the evening of Christmas Day, disaster struck. The *Santa Maria* was driven aground near Cap Haïtien. Columbus had to cut away the mast and throw overboard any items that could help to right the rapidly listing ship. A local king, Guacanagari, came to his aid, offering the use of craft to offload cargo. Columbus ordered a fort settlement to be built, making this the first European colony in the Americas. He named the large island La Española (Hispaniola) and the town La Navidad, before making plans to return to Spain. Forty colonists, including craftsmen, were left behind with provisions and other supplies. Columbus returned in triumph to Palos on March 15, 1493, bringing with him gold and

THE KNOWN WORLD
This map is believed to have been drawn by Columbus's brother, Bartolomeo, in 1490. Details of sea routes peter out below West Africa; the map is blank west of the Atlantic Ocean.

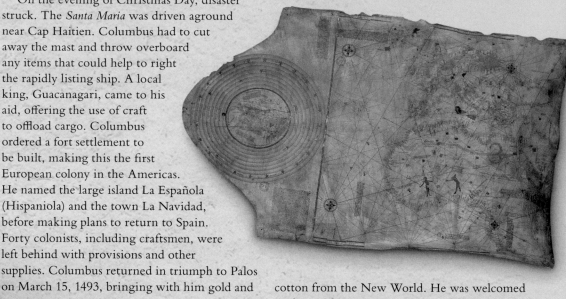

cotton from the New World. He was welcomed to the royal court at Barcelona in May and given a new title—"Admiral of the Oceans"—to reflect his status. With the promise of even greater riches, Columbus made three further voyages of discovery to the Americas. His second expedition, aboard a new *Santa Maria*, consisted of 17 ships carrying some 1,200 colonists. When he arrived at La Navidad in November 1493, by way of more island discoveries in the Caribbean, or "West Indies," he was shocked to discover that the settlers he had left behind had been massacred by the natives after his departure the previous year. A new colony, named Santo Domingo, was set up to the east of La Navidad, with Bartolomeo Columbus as governor, and it was not long before the new arrivals began mining for gold.

SOUTH AMERICA

In May 1498, Columbus made a third voyage, with a smaller fleet. Sailing by way of Hispaniola to the south coast of Trinidad, he explored the Gulf of Paria (which divides the island from the coastline of Venezuela). There he made landfall, and his party became the first Europeans to set foot in South America. Columbus knew he had landed on a new continent, but believed that it hung down from China, bulging out to make the Earth pear-shaped. His belief in the Asian connection was influenced partly by the discovery of pearls, which he knew were a major source of East–West trade from China. He wrote to his Spanish patrons that "the way to pearls and gold is now open—

IN HIS FOOTSTEPS

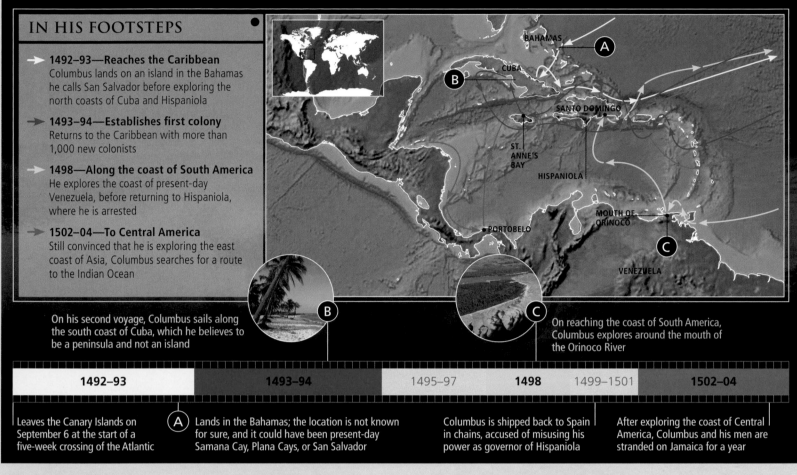

➤ **1492–93—Reaches the Caribbean**
Columbus lands on an island in the Bahamas he calls San Salvador before exploring the north coasts of Cuba and Hispaniola

➤ **1493–94—Establishes first colony**
Returns to the Caribbean with more than 1,000 new colonists

➤ **1498—Along the coast of South America**
He explores the coast of present-day Venezuela, before returning to Hispaniola, where he is arrested

➤ **1502–04—To Central America**
Still convinced that he is exploring the east coast of Asia, Columbus searches for a route to the Indian Ocean

On his second voyage, Columbus sails along the south coast of Cuba, which he believes to be a peninsula and not an island

On reaching the coast of South America, Columbus explores around the mouth of the Orinoco River

1492–93	1493–94	1495–97	1498	1499–1501	1502–04

Leaves the Canary Islands on September 6 at the start of a five-week crossing of the Atlantic

(A) Lands in the Bahamas; the location is not known for sure, and it could have been present-day Samana Cay, Plana Cays, or San Salvador

Columbus is shipped back to Spain in chains, accused of misusing his power as governor of Hispaniola

After exploring the coast of Central America, Columbus and his men are stranded on Jamaica for a year

LUNAR MAGICIAN
Shipwrecked and hungry on Jamaica, Columbus used mathematics to predict a lunar eclipse. The awed natives then produced food for his men.

had been hanged. On hearing the reports of disenchanted settlers, Bobadilla had Columbus and his brother put in chains and shipped back to Spain.

FALL FROM GRACE

Although he was permitted to argue his case and reconcile with the Spanish monarchs, Columbus would never forget the dishonor of his arrest. Believing a fourth voyage to be the only chance of recovering his reputation, he set sail in May 1502 with his 13-year-old son, Fernando.

The fleet consisted of four ships with only 150 men and again Columbus was convinced that he would reach Asia and set up trading routes with Spain. It was not to be—reaching Hispaniola in June 1502 during a terrible storm, Columbus's ships were refused entry to the port at Santo Domingo by the governor. Forced to continue at

sea, Columbus reached Panama, where he and his men became the first Europeans to explore Central America, spending two months investigating the coasts of present-day Honduras, Nicaragua, and Costa Rica. In Panama, the expedition uncovered some gold, before the men were forced back to their ships by the local Indians.

Desperate for food and water, they headed for Hispaniola, but the ships' timbers were riddled with worm and the two surviving ships had to be beached side by side on the Jamaican coast in June 1503. The crew remained shipwrecked until a rescue party reached them a year later.

Columbus returned to Spain in 1504. He was wealthy, but Jamaica had broken him physically. He wrote, "I have not a hair on my body that is not gray, and my body is infirm." He died on May 20, 1506, still convinced that his voyages had been along the east coast of Asia.

"ADMIRAL OF THE OCEANS"
This coat of arms was designed for Columbus in 1492. It was one of the honors that had been promised to him if he ever made it back to Spain—many doubted that he would.

a thousand things can be expected with confidence." However, his promises were beginning to sound hollow. On Hispaniola, food was scarce and the promised gold harder to mine than expected. The colonists rose against Bartolomeo in a mutiny, which was brutally suppressed. A new governor, Francisco de Bobadilla, was despatched to the island, where he found that several of the colonist mutineers

LEGENDARY FIRST VESSEL TO THE NEW WORLD

THE *SANTA MARIA*

ON CHRISTOPHER COLUMBUS'S FIRST VOYAGE to the New World in 1492, his flagship was the *Santa María de la Inmaculada Concepción*. Built at Pontevedra in Galicia, Spain, it was probably a carrack (an ocean-going, three-masted vessel), and larger than the *Niña* and *Pinta,* the caravels (maneuverable sailing ships) that made up the fleet. With one deck and three masts, the conditions on board were relatively spartan. Although the *Santa Maria* was a slow and sturdy ship capable of surviving the rough conditions of the Atlantic Ocean, she ran aground on Christmas Day, 1492, and had to be abandoned at Cap Haitien, Hispaniola.

▼ IN FULL SAIL
The ship had three masts—fore, main, and mizzen—each of which held a sail: the fore and main were both large square sails, while the mizzen was triangular, known as a lateen sail, as shown on this 1994 replica. The ship also carried a small sail on the bowsprit.

▶ HIGH RIGGING
On sighting land, Columbus gave thanks to God as the men scrambled up the rigging to verify the claim. The larger sails would have displayed a red cross, as was the custom in Spain at the time, but Columbus also made sure that each ship carried a flag with a green cross as a standard to be flown in the New World.

▲ PRONE TO ROTTING
Rope was stored where it was least likely to get wet, since it was prone to rotting.

◀ "LOMBARDS"
With a range of 300 yd (275 m), the Lombard cannon was fired to measure distance.

▲ STONE MARKER
The *Santa Maria*, *Niña*, and *Pinta* may have carried stone markers similar to the Portuguese *padrões*, to plant on any new land claimed for Spain.

◀ CRAMPED CONDITIONS
Below deck there was little space. The crew worked on four-hour shifts and slept wherever there was room.

► THE CARRACK
The history of the carrack can be traced back to the merchant lighters, or barges, that plied early trade routes in the Mediterranean. The foremast (left) was originally designed to aid the steering of the vessel.

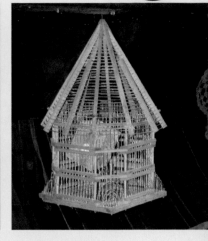

▲ LIGHTING THE WAY
Spanish ships of the period carried wax candles. Their use would have been limited, with nighttime compass readings taken by candlelight.

▲ CAGED BIRDS
On his return to Spain, Columbus displayed "gorgeously colored parrots" from the New World. The ships were equipped with basket-work, such as this cage, to hold such finds.

▲ SHIP'S BELL
The ship's bell would have been rung to mark the hour and quarter-hour and to summon assistance in times of need.

▲ ON DECK
The main deck would have served as mess for the men, with food prepared in a fire box. Space was also given over to livestock, supplies, and fresh water, stored in casks similar to those shown here.

▲ FOOD FROM THE SEA
Turtles, clams, mullet, crabs, and other seafood were caught by the sailors to vary their spartan diet of crackers, pickles, and salted meat.

◄ STEERING A COURSE
Only the pilot was permitted to steer the ship and negotiate harbors and reefs.

SEBASTIAN CABOT

MASTER MERCHANT MARINER

ENGLAND   C. 1474–1557

SEBASTIAN CABOT MAY HAVE sailed over more of the world than anyone else in his day, but very little is known of his life. He was the son of John Cabot, a Genoese merchant adventurer who had settled in the English port of Bristol by 1489. Records show that the Cabots were instrumental in the departure of many voyages of discovery from the city, before Sebastian eventually transferred his allegiance to Spain in 1512. His chief legacy is the introduction of the log as the standard form of ship's record-keeping.

IMPASSABLE SEA
In his search for a northeast passage, Cabot was forced back by the icy White Sea. With typical élan he turned a failed mission into a success by forming trade links with the Russian mainland, founding the Muscovy Company.

Cabot was probably born in Bristol in 1474. When he was about 22 his father, aware of Christopher Columbus's success in discovering the New World (see pp. 86–89), petitioned King Henry VII for a charter "to sail to all places, lands and seas, of the East, West, or North." The conditions of the charter were clear: Cabot and his sons were to sail to and from Bristol and to pay over one-fifth of any spoils to the crown.

On May 2, 1497, Cabot set sail with his father on board the *Matthew*, navigating a direct course to the west and reaching the coast of Newfoundland on June 24. The ship sailed up the coast of Labrador, where he recorded the sighting of "monstrous great lumps of ice swimming in the sea, and continual daylight," an ordeal that almost drove the men to mutiny. The expedition had to be abandoned, with the ship returning to Bristol in July. Their return brought accounts of a sea so full of fish that "the kingdom will have no more business with Islande [Iceland]".

Although greatly celebrated in Bristol, the royal response to this achievement was somewhat muted. Having almost certainly hoped for a rich supply of gold and treasure, Henry VII offered a payment of just £10 for the discovery of the new land.

THE SEARCH FOR NEW ROUTES
In 1498, the Cabots undertook a second voyage, this time crossing the Atlantic with more than 300 immigrants and a plan to colonize the coastline of Newfoundland. Little is known of the fate of these people and there are scant details about the voyage, but it is likely that John Cabot died at sea, with command effectively passing to his son, Sebastian.

WEST TO A NEW WORLD
A painting of 1906 romanticizes the moment of Cabot's departure for Newfoundland in 1497. Although he failed to return with gold, he found lucrative fishing grounds.

A LIFE'S WORK

- Finds **Newfoundland** and leads an expedition to colonize it

- Is the first to use a **ship's log** for daily ship-keeping records

- Establishes **Spain's first military presence** in what are now Argentina and Uruguay

- Abandons attempt at finding northeast passage and travels **overland to Moscow** to set up a trading company

By 1512, Cabot had transferred his allegiance to Spain, attracted by the Spanish crown's active support for exploration. He undertook several expeditions to the Gulf of Mexico before being appointed as pilot master for Spain. In 1526, Cabot set off on his most ambitious expedition from Sanlúcar, Spain. Sailing with 200 men in four ships, the plan was to carry settlers to the Moluccas (the Spice Islands, Indonesia) and continue westward in a circumnavigation of the world.

On reaching the coast of Brazil in June, however, Cabot heard rumors of Inca treasure and abandoned his mission in order to explore the Río de la Plata, farther down the coast. The expedition was not a success. Unimpressed with his helmsmanship, three of the crew revolted and were set ashore. Cabot then spent five months exploring the river, establishing Spain's first forts in what are now Argentina and Uruguay. But after battling rapids and losing 18 men in an Indian ambush, he had found no treasure and returned to Spain in 1530. A trial awaited him. He was fined for disobedience and for his treatment of his men and exiled to North Africa. However, he may have received a royal pardon, because he remained a pilot master for Spain until 1547.

In about 1528, Cabot returned to England, and he led an expedition to search for a northeast passage to Asia. He got as far as the northwest coast of Russia, and forged strong Anglo-Russian trading ties. It was his final voyage. He retired and was made life governor of the "Company of Merchant Adventurers."

IN HIS FOOTSTEPS

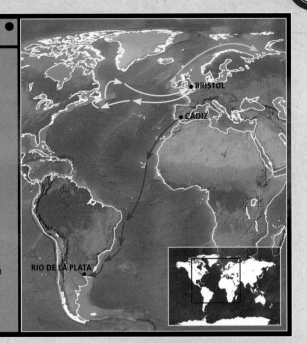

1497—Sails for Newfoundland
Cabot accompanies his father on board the *Matthew*. He finds plentiful sources of fish but no treasure; almost nothing is known of a second voyage in 1498 to Newfoundland with 300 settlers

1527—Sails on a Spanish expedition to the Spice islands
He is waylaid by rumors of gold in South America and explores the Río de la Plata, founding two Spanish forts; he never reaches the Spice Islands.

1528—Attempts to find a northeast passage to Asia
Cabot's final voyage reaches northwest Russia before weather conditions force him to abandon the attempt

BRISTOL

CÁDIZ

RIO DE LA PLATA

CABOT'S WORLD
Although Cabot kept records of all his voyages, these have been lost. All that remains of his work is a copy made from a map he drew in 1544, shown here. The map is interesting for the extent of the New World known in the 52 years since Columbus's discovery, and for the light it sheds on Cabot's American voyages.

AMERIGO VESPUCCI

CONFIRMER OF THE FOURTH CONTINENT

REPUBLIC OF FLORENCE   C. 1454–1512

A MAN OF LEARNING AND COMMERCE who took to exploration late in life, Amerigo Vespucci's exact journeys are the subject of some debate. What is certain is that he crossed the Atlantic on at least two occasions, sailing along the coast of what he realized was not the eastern seaboard of Asia—as maintained by Columbus— but an entirely new continent. That he has been immortalized in the names of two continents—and the largest nation in the western hemisphere—is largely due to the whim of a mapmaker.

Vespucci was born in a village outside Florence, in present-day Italy, and was educated by his uncle. He later went on to study the sciences before working for the powerful Medici family in 1483. He became a trusted figure in the Medicis' various commercial enterprises, but there was little to indicate that he would one day become a celebrated navigator, let alone give his name to a vast and newly discovered landmass.

EXPLORATION FEVER
Vespucci's work for the Medicis took him to Seville, Spain, in 1496, where he was involved in shipping. The voyages of Christopher Columbus (see pp. 86–89) were the talk of the town, and Vespucci became determined to join

the rush for new discoveries. Although in his forties and with no previous nautical experience, he managed to secure a position as astronomer and cartographer to the Spanish expedition of the explorer Alonso de Ojeda.

Leaving Spain in May 1499, Vespucci parted company with Ojeda somewhere in the Caribbean, and joined another ship sailing southeast. Soon, he encountered a coast "so full of trees it was a great marvel." However, the dense vegetation prevented the crew from landing, so the ship continued along the coast until they found "something marvelous in that sea; fifteen leagues [about 50 miles or 80 km] from land, we found the water as fresh as a river, and drank from it, filling all our empty casks."

Vespucci had probably reached the point at which the enormous freshwater outflow of the Amazon River enters the Atlantic. Whether he had set foot in Brazil just before or just after Cabral's celebrated landing of April 1500 (see pp. 96–97) is not known for certain.

RED LIKE A LION'S MANE
The Soderini letter described the natives as having "flesh of a color that verges into red like a lion's mane ... if they went clothed, they would be as white as we."

NEW WORLD PROPAGANDA
Letters bearing Vespucci's name were copied, translated, printed, and sold throughout Europe. This image was printed on the cover page of a printed copy of the letter that was allegedly sent to Florentine magistrate Soderini, and published in 1505.

AN EARTHLY PARADISE
Upon reaching the twin mouths of the Amazon, Vespucci ventured into the great river with 20 men in two boats. They observed "an infinite number of birds of various forms and colors … and trees so beautiful and fragrant that we thought we had entered the Earthly Paradise." They also came upon "a snake or serpent some eight braccia long [a braccia is equal to a man's arm], and the width of my waist: it frightened us very much, and at the sight of it we returned to the sea."

Vespucci turned back after reaching as far as Recife, in present-day Brazil, sailing north to the island of Trinidad, where he found the inhabitants to be friendly but fearful. He reassured them "with great effort, by means of signs," discovering that they were cannibals, although "they do not eat one another, but navigate in certain vessels … called canoes … to neighboring islands or lands in search of prey."

After sailing past the mouth of the Orinoco River (in present-day Venezuela) and on to the Caribbean island of Hispaniola, Vespucci

HIGHLY REGARDED
In this letter to his son, Christopher Columbus praises Vespucci and speaks of the "rewards he in justice should have." Columbus admired the Florentine, who had advised him prior to his 1498 voyage.

MAPMAKER'S MISNOMER

Vespucci was propelled to the top of the pile of New World explorers when "America," the feminine form of his first name, was chosen by Martin Waldseemüller as the name of the new continent. The German cartographer seems to be familiar with the letters, allegedly written by Vespucci, that describe his journeys to the new continent.

WALDSEEMÜLLER'S MAP WAS WIDELY CIRCULATED FROM 1507

returned to Spain, arriving in 1500. He joined a second expedition in 1501, this time sailing for Portugal under the command of Gonçalo Coelho. Vespucci claimed that the voyage charted "nearly 2,000 leagues of continental coast and more than 5,000 islands." This would have taken him as far south as Patagonia, which seems unlikely, since he makes no mention of the mouth of the Plate River.

Whatever the truth of these extravagant claims, the people, flora, and fauna he observed on his second voyage convinced Vespucci that he was not sailing along the coast of Asia, but had reached a new continent. After returning to Spain he was appointed Pilot Major, making him the chief instructor for the Spanish admiralty. He died in Seville in 1512.

CONFUSING CORRESPONDENCE

Vespucci's achievements have been somewhat clouded by letters that he was purported to have written. *Mundus Novus* (New World) describes a voyage of 1501–02 and was sent to the Medicis, while *Lettera di Amerigo Vespucci delle Isole Nuovamente Trovate in Quattro Suoi Viaggi* (Letter of Amerigo Vespucci Concerning the Isles Newly Discovered on his Four Voyages) is an account of four journeys between 1497 and 1504 that was sent to an associate of the Medicis, Piero Soderini. Both letters are now thought to have been written by supporters of Vespucci rather than the man himself, and were widely circulated—partly thanks to the fascinating descriptions they contained. These lavish accounts further muddied the waters.

Vespucci did not claim to have discovered the New World, leaving that honor to Columbus. His contribution to the story of the Americas has been not the use of his name, which derives from a chance appearance on a map made by the German cartographer Waldseemüller (see box, above), but the realization that the new land was a continent in its own right.

SURVEYING THE STARS
Navigating by the stars was critical to marine exploration in the Middle Ages, so Vespucci's astronomical skills—as depicted in this print of 1491—were in demand.

PEDRO ÁLVARES CABRAL

NAVIGATOR OF ROUTES TO THE EAST AND WEST

PORTUGAL   C. 1467–1520

ONE OF THE GREATEST PORTUGUESE NAVIGATORS, Pedro Álvares Cabral was the first European to discover Brazil, which he sighted by chance en route to India. Following Vasco da Gama's discovery of a viable sea route to India in 1499, King Manuel I of Portugal was determined to establish a Portuguese hegemony over the lucrative spice trade with the subcontinent. Cabral was chosen as a successor to da Gama, tasked with spreading Christianity and fighting the Arab merchants who controlled the sea routes.

FLEET ON PAPER
An early 16th-century manuscript records the fate of the 13 new vessels in Cabral's fleet. All appear to be carracks, one of the key vessels of the Age of Discovery.

Little is known of Cabral's early life, except that his father was the governor of the Portuguese districts of Beira and Belmonte. With such a connection, Cabral and his two brothers spent some time as royal courtiers. Presumably, he also gained experience as a mariner because, in 1499, King Manuel I selected him to command a fleet of 13 new ships carrying 1,500 men. Among them were priests and at least one other notable explorer: Bartolomeu Días (see pp. 76–77).

TRADE MISSION

Cabral's mission was to continue the work of da Gama (see pp. 80–81), establishing permanent trading relations in India and spreading Catholicism, by force of arms if necessary. Sailing from Lisbon on March 9, 1500, and intending to follow da Gama's route to India,

Cabral's fleet veered too far to the west. They made landfall on April 23 on a coastline Cabral believed to be an island, naming it Ilha de Vera Cruz ("Island of the True Cross"). This was in fact the coastline of present-day Brazil on the South American continent. The native people, speakers of the Tupi, Macro-Ge, and Arawak languages, communicated with the new arrivals by sign language. Cabral left two convicts behind to learn the native tongues. (Why he was carrying convicts in his fleet is not clear.)

Setting sail once more, the fleet headed southeast to the Cape of Good Hope, where it ran into a storm so bad that several ships, including that of Días, were lost.

On September 13, 1500, Cabral finally reached his destination: Calicut (present-day Kozhikode) on the Keralan coast of India. The Portuguese brought with them four Keralan men who da Gama had taken back with him to Portugal after his visit to Calicut in 1498. Their safe return—dressed in Portuguese finery—impressed the *zamorin* (ruler) of Calicut. Relations with the *zamorin* began well, with

A LIFE'S WORK

- Is **the first European** to set foot in Brazil, claiming it for Portugal; he gets there due to strong winds and navigational errors

- His voyage carries some of the first **Christian missionaries** to India

- Establishes **trade treaties** with Cochin and Cannanore (present-day Kochi and Kannur)

IN HIS FOOTSTEPS

→ **First leg**
Cabral stops at Cape Verde, after which he is blown westward to Bahia, Brazil; one ship immediately returns to Portugal with news of the momentous discovery

→ **Second leg**
The fleet is depleted by a storm off the Cape of Good Hope; rounding the Cape they become the first Europeans to find Madagascar, naming it São Lourenço; they then cross the Indian Ocean to Calicut, India

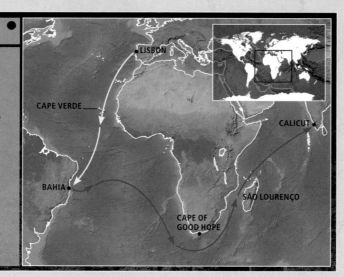

CLAIMING BRAZIL

After making landfall on the coast of Bahia, Brazil, in 1500, Cabral took possession of the region for Portugal by erecting a cross and holding a Christian service. Brazil was a Portuguese colony from 1500 onward, although settlement did not begin in earnest until 1534. The Portuguese assimilated some indigenous peoples, while countless others were enslaved or killed. During the Napoleonic Wars of the early 19th century, the Portuguese empire relocated to Brazil, before the colony became independent from Portugal in 1822.

the Portuguese capturing a ship from Ceylon (present-day Sri Lanka) carrying elephants, which were presented as gifts to the delighted ruler. In return, Cabral demanded trading privileges over the local Arab merchants.

Eventually, the *zamorin* agreed to the foundation of a spice factory and the loading of Cabral's ships with fine spices and pepper. The Arab traders were furious in their complaints to the *zamorin*, and when Cabral seized an Arab ship while it was being loaded, believing it to be in breach of his deal with the *zamorin*, Cabral's factory was besieged by the local Muslim population, who killed the workers. Cabral was soon forced to

flee, sailing north on to Cannanore (present-day Kannur). There he received a friendlier welcome, and found a land rich in "ginger, cardamoms … and tamarinds."

Fully loaded, and having achieved the goal of making a trade treaty without competition from Arab traders, Cabral's ships retraced their route, arriving in Lisbon by July 1501. The cost of the expedition had been high, however, with only four of the 13 ships making it back to Portugal.

KERALAN SPICES
Cabral's expedition was among the earliest European attempts to control the sea routes for the highly lucrative spice trade. Since ancient times, the main route had been overland from Asia.

TAKING ILHA DE VERA CRUZ FOR PORTUGAL, CABRAL HELD A SERVICE WITH FRANCISCAN FATHER HENRIQUE DE COIMBRA

BRAZILIAN TREASURE
The earliest Portuguese settlers soon began extracting Brazilwood from the rainforest. It was valuable as lumber and as the source of a distinctive red dye.

CHARTING THE DEVELOPMENT OF...

EXPEDITION MAPPING

THE EARLIEST KNOWN MAP is a town plan discovered at Catalhöyük in Turkey, which dates from about 6000BCE. Maps improved with the mathematical innovations of the ancient Greeks, Romans, and Arabs, so that the charts produced to incorporate the discoveries of European explorers of the 15th century were increasingly accurate. Today, online users can view customized maps produced to their own specifications by websites whose databases are constantly updated with the latest information.

THE ANCIENT WORLD

Greek philosopher Anaximander of Miletus was credited with the creation of the first map of the world in the 6th century BCE. His treatise on geography also included a map depicting the Earth as a disk. Few in the ancient Greek world produced maps based on physical data; much was based on the interpretation of myth and religious belief. However, in the 2nd century BCE, the Greek mathematician Eratosthenes calculated the circumference of the Earth with relative accuracy based on the notion that the planet was spherical. By the second century CE, Claudius Ptolemy had published his *Geographia*, which may have included a series of maps showing lands beyond the boundaries of the Roman Empire. The few Roman maps that survive include the *Tabula Peutingeriana*, a road map showing routes throughout the empire. As Roman

2500BCE—CLAY BORDER
Babylonian tablets record settlement boundaries.

490BCE—ROUND WORLD
Greek mathematician Pythagoras develops a theory of a spherical world.

1134—TOPSY-TURVY
Andalusian scholar al-Idrisi produces a world map for Roger II, King of Sicily, in which he places South at the top of the map and North at the bottom.

1290—MAPPA MUNDI
Medieval maps such as this one from Hereford, England, showed Jerusalem at the center of the world.

1477—FIRST PRINTED MAP
A world map based on Ptolemy's information is published in Bologna, Italy.

| BCE | 2000 | 1000 | CE | 100 | 300 | 500 | 1150 | 1200 | 1250 | 1300 | 1350 | 1400 | 1450 |

350BCE— ANAXIMANDER
Greek philosopher Aristotle collects the maps of Anaximander, drawn three centuries previously.

600—ROUND, OR DISK?
In his *Etymologiae*, Isidorus of Seville describes the Earth as round, or even disk-shaped.

1350—PORTOLANS
Maps known as portolans are based on realistic descriptions of ports and distances surrounding the Mediterranean Sea.

1492—FIRST GLOBE
Martin Behaim (above) of Nuremburg, Germany, produces the first terrestrial globe made in modern times.

100CE — PTOLEMY'S GEOGRAPHIA

In creating his *Geographia*, **Ptolemy relies on accurate figures of latitude and longitude from a variety of sources**. It is not known if he himself compiles maps from this information, but he certainly leaves instructions on how to do so. From the 15th century onward, copies of his work circulate in western Europe in manuscript form, and after the first printed edition of 1477 many others follow, and maps such as this are made from it.

1375 CATALAN ATLAS

Produced by the leading cartographers of Majorca, the Catalan Atlas, left, is **one of the most important maps of the medieval period**. In addition to the latest astronomical, cosmological, and astrological data, the original six vellum leaves of the map also include **religious and literary references,** including Marco Polo's *Book of Marvels*.

rule diminished, the information that had been gathered to create such maps was dispersed from libraries and lost or neglected.

ARAB GOLDEN AGE

Although Ptolemy's maps have not survived, the calculations he made to draw them informed geographical thinking for 14 centuries. His work was widely known in the Islamic world from about 800CE and was preserved by Arab scholars, who made huge progress in mathematics and science during the 9th century—their Golden Age. The most accurate map of the world for 300 years was the *Tabula Rogeriana*, made by Andalusian geographer al-Idrisi in 1134, which shows the whole of Eurasia and North Africa.

Johannes Gutenberg's invention of the printing press in 1439 enabled maps to be made more widely available.

Meanwhile, the Turkish conquest of Constantinople (Istanbul) in 1453 led to the closure of European land routes to the East, encouraging Spain and Portugal to seek alternative routes to sustain the supply of spices and other luxuries from Asia. Under the patronage of Prince Henry the Navigator (1394–1460), the Portuguese moved quickly to produce maps and charts in support of Portuguese exploration of the coastline of Africa and into the Indian Ocean, led by Bartolomeu Dias (see pp. 76–77).

SHOWING THE NEW WORLD

In 1507, a landmark map by German cartographer Martin Waldseemüller was published, the first printed map to include a depiction of the newly found continent with the name "America." In 1569, the Flemish mapmaker Gerardus Mercator published his famous cylindrical map projection and a year later, Mercator's

contemporary, Abraham Ortelius, published the first printed modern Atlas, *Theatrum Orbis Terrarum*. The Dutch were preeminent in mapmaking throughout the 17th century, with names such as Hondius, Blaue, Janssonius, and de Wit producing finely illustrated works.

NATIONAL SURVEYS

France was the first country to establish a national survey made under the auspices of Sanson and Cassini, which led to the publication in 1789 of the *Atlas Nationale*. As the director of the Paris Conservatory, César-François Cassini collaborated with his British counterpart General William Roy at Greenwich to carry out joint survey work. In Britain, this led in 1791 to the formation of the Ordnance Survey, which would go on to provide the most detailed mapping yet known in Europe. Colonial expansion was the motivation behind much of the

cartographic work of the rival powers, France and Britain. Napoleon's failed invasion of Egypt in 1798 led to the first detailed survey of the country, while the British consolidated power in India in the 19th century by mapping new territories.

In 1884, maps were internationally standardized at a conference in Washington, D.C., at which Greenwich in London was adopted as the Prime Meridian. The French continued to show Paris at the center of their world maps, finally conceding defeat to Greenwich in 1914, although the Paris Meridian is marked on some French maps even today.

In the modern era, computers have revolutionized the way we think about maps. Geographic information systems store raw data that can be displayed in a variety of different ways. Cartographers no longer decide how to project the information, but rather provide users with the means to project it themselves.

1569—MERCATOR MAP
Adopted throughout Europe, Gerardus Mercator's projection includes parallel lines of latitude.

1635—ORTELIUS
The *Theatrum Orbis Terrarum* of Flemish cartographer Abraham Ortelius (shown right) contains 70 new maps.

1755—MITCHELL MAP
A map of North America under British colonial rule is produced.

1791—ORDNANCE SURVEY
Founded to prepare accurate mapping for southeast England in the event of a possible French invasion.

1959—SATELLITE IMAGES
The first satellite images from NASA's *Explorer 6* provide new insights. By the 1990s, thermal images of the Earth's oceans (right) are produced.

1500 1550 1600 1650 1700 1750 1800 1850 1900 1950 2000

1513—PIRI REIS
Ottoman cartographer Piri Reis (see p. 67) produces a map showing the coast of Brazil, discovered by Europeans 13 years previously.

1890—PARIS STREET MAP
Mapping of European urban areas is detailed and accurate.

German cartographer Martin Waldseemüller produces the first map to depict the lands across the Atlantic as a new continent separate from Asia. **He calls this continent "America,"** it is thought in honor of Amerigo Vespucci (see pp. 94–95), who may have suggested as early as 1504 that the lands he had seen are **not part of Asia, as Columbus and others have assumed**. The map is made six years before the first recorded European sighting of the Pacific.

1507 WALDSEEMÜLLER MAP

1658—JANSSONIUS
The Dutch cartographic master produces a series of fine maps of the Netherlands.

From about 1914 onward, new types of map are developed for the particular requirements of **aviation**. They take into account a **third dimension**, showing not only the lie of the land, but the likely state of the atmosphere above it: **where icing may be likely, or where turbulence is predicted**. The earliest maps for airplanes, such as this one from the beginning of World War I in 1914, show the location of the newly dug trenches at the Somme, northern France. Some were based on photographic reconnaissance.

1914 AVIATION MAP

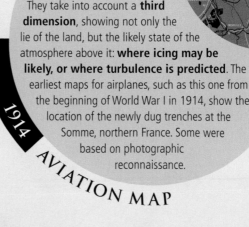

CONQUEST AND COLONIZATION

CONQUEST AND COLONIZATION

1500ᴄᴇ   1525   1550

1502
Dominican friar **Bartolomé de las Casas** arrives in Hispaniola (now Haiti and Dominican Republic), where he deplores the enslavement of the Taíno people

▲ 1513
Conquistador **Vasco Núñez de Balboa** becomes the first European to see the Pacific Ocean; he duly claims it for the Spanish crown
(see pp. 120–21)

◄ 1513
Conquistador **Juan Ponce de León** is the first European to set foot on Florida, which he believes to be an island
(see pp. 116–17)

▼ 1513
Ferdinand Magellan leads a voyage to circumnavigate the world; Juan Sebastian Elcano completes the voyage after Magellan is killed at Cebu in the Philippines
(see pp. 138–41)

1521
Hernán Cortés overthrows the Aztec Empire, taking the city of Tenochtitlán, which he renames Mexico City, and capturing the Aztec emperor, Cuauhtémoc
(see pp. 106–109)

► 1532
Spanish conquistador **Francisco Pizarro** overthrows the Incas at the Battle of Cajamarca in northern Peru, capturing the Inca emperor, Atahualpa
(see pp. 112–15)

◄ 1534
French explorer **Jacques Cartier** reaches the Gulf of St. Lawrence, naming the land that he finds there the "Country of Canadas"
(see pp. 130–31)

1542
Spanish conquistador **Francisco de Orellana** reaches the mouth of the Amazon River after a voyage down the entire length of the river

► 1542
Conquistador **Hernando de Soto** reaches the banks of the Mississippi River, where he is greeted by local chief Aquixo and a fleet of 200 canoes
(see pp. 118–19)

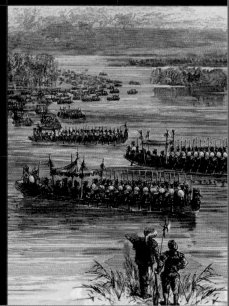

1540
Starting from Mexico, conquistador **Francisco Vásquez de Coronado** explores the southwest of North America, and some of his party reach as far inland as the Grand Canyon

1576
Sponsored by the Muscovy Company, English navigator **Martin Frobisher** makes the first of three voyages in search of the Northwest Passage

▲1580
English privateer **Francis Drake** completes the second circumnavigation of the world
(see pp. 144–45)

1585
John Davis explores the west coast of Greenland and Baffin Island, sailing along the strait that now bears his name in search of a route to China

1595
Spanish navigator **Álvaro de Mendaña** dies on his second voyage into the Pacific in search of the "Terra Australis," a continent believed to lie to the south of the ocean

1597
Simon Ferdinando, a Portuguese navigator working for English queen Elizabeth I, lands on the coast of Maine in North America

◄ PP. 100–01 The Aztec capital Tenochtitlán is captured by Hernán Cortés in 1521 (see pp. 106–109)

JUST A FEW DECADES AFTER the Spanish first landed in the Bahamas, the conquest and colonization of much of South and Central America had largely taken place. In North America, however, explorers (and European colonies) were largely confined to the coastal fringes of the continent. Voyages of exploration now became more adventurous, as the first complete circumnavigations of the globe opened up possibilities for trade that would enrich the European nations that controlled it. A new sphere for exploration was also opened with the first ventures into the South Pacific. European explorers found island groups such as the Solomons and New Guinea, and then a series of Dutch voyages at the beginning of the 17th century resulted in the discovery of an entirely new continent—Australia.

1600 **1650** **1700**

1656
Portugal loses its stronghold at Colombo, Sri Lanka, to the Dutch, who become the dominant trading power in the Indian Ocean

◄ 1704
Alexander Selkirk, the inspiration for the novel *Robinson Crusoe*, is stranded on Juan Férnandez Island in the Pacific where, in his isolation, he hallucinates about talking animals

▼ 1708
William Dampier sets sail on his third circumnavigation of the world, working as sailing master for the English privateer Woodes Rogers (see pp. 146–47)

▲ 1603
Frenchman **Samuel de Champlain** arrives in "Nouvelle France" in North America, founds a settlement on the site of present-day Quebec City (see pp. 126–27)

1605
Portuguese navigator **Pedro de Quirós** makes landfall on Espiritu Santo in the New Hebrides and returns to Mexico by way of California

1740
George Anson sets sail to fight the Spanish in South America and achieves a circumnavigation of the world, losing more than 1,000 of his men to scurvy on the way (see pp. 148–49)

1766
Louis Antoine de Bougainville sets off on a three-year circumnavigation of the world for France (see pp. 150–51)

1621
French explorer **Étienne Brûlé** is the first European to see Lake Superior

▲ 1673
Christian missionaries **Marquette and Jolliet** set out in bark canoes from Michigan to meet and convert indigenous tribes along the Mississippi River (see pp. 132–33)

▲ 1642
Dutch mariner **Abel Tasman** finds New Zealand, which the Maori discovered in about 1300 (see pp. 160–61)

◄ 1682
Robert de la Salle sails the length of the Mississippi River from the north to the south, claiming the area around it for France (see pp. 134–35)

▲ 1768
Captain James Cook sets sail on the first of three epic voyages to the Pacific during which he travels over more of the Earth's surface than anyone before him (see pp. 156–59)

► 1785
La Pérouse sets sail on a scientific mission to the Pacific at the behest of French king Louis XVI; he visits the remote Easter Island a year later (see pp. 162–63)

CRUEL CONQUISTADORS

CHRISTOPHER COLUMBUS'S DISCOVERIES WHILE SEARCHING FOR A PASSAGE TO THE EAST IN 1492, AND FERDINAND MAGELLAN'S CIRCUMNAVIGATION OF THE WORLD IN 1519, LED TO THE RAPID EXPANSION OF SPAIN'S TERRITORIES IN THE NEW WORLD AT THE START OF THE "AGE OF DISCOVERY."

ADVOCATE OF THE AMERINDIANS
In 1550, Fray Bartolomé de las Casas won a debate in the Spanish court at which he advocated the equal treatment under the law of the native peoples in the Americas.

In the light of Columbus's discovery, Queen Isabella and King Ferdinand of Spain requested clarification of their rights to the new territories against those of their archrival, Portugal. To this end, Pope Alexander VI ordered a line to be drawn on a world map, 370 leagues (1,100 miles/1,800 km) west of the Cape Verde Islands in the Atlantic Ocean. All lands to the west of the line could be claimed by Spain, and to the east by Portugal. The treaty was signed at Tordesillas in Spain on June 7, 1494, and Spain's conquest of the Americas was set to begin.

THE CONQUERORS

The men who would carry out Spain's exploration, the conquistadors ("conquerors"), included a cross-section of society from noble to commoner. Many had seen action during the *Reconquista*, the century-long war against the Moors in southern Spain, which had ended in 1492, the year Columbus reached the Caribbean (see pp. 86–89). The top tier of conquistadors included figures from the aristocracy. The second tier consisted of Hidalgos ("men of high standing") and included Hernán Cortés, conqueror of Mexico (see pp. 106–09). A third category called Hidalgos de Gotera ("lesser nobility") completed the framework.

For most conquistadors, the main motivation for traveling to the New World was the potential to amass great personal

BEFORE THE AZTECS
Several civilizations flourished in Mexico before the Aztecs. Huge pyramids were built at Teotihuacán 2,000 years ago. This mosaic-covered wooden mask was found there.

wealth. The Spanish state took a large cut of the returns from all expeditions, but reports from the Americas of vast reserves of gold, silver, and pearls were nonetheless enticing, since routes to fortune in war-weary Spain were limited. Many of the conquistadors were also driven by a desire to establish hereditary claims as landowners and colonial rulers in the new dominions; others invested their own money to fund their journeys, but not all would achieve their goals.

GOLD FEVER

Following the overthrow of the Aztecs by Cortés in 1521 and the Incas by Pizarro in 1532 (see pp. 112–15), the notion of El Dorado, the Kingdom of Gold, infected the psyche of Spain. By the 1570s, many had followed in these men's footsteps. Estimates of the value of gold and silver from the Spanish colonies in the 16th century are placed in the region of $1.5 trillion at today's rates. Each conquistador negotiated a percentage share of his spoils

> **Spain and Portugal divided South and Central America between them in the 16th century; North America was explored by the French and English in the 17th century, and it would be their colonies that would go on to dominate the New World.**

with the Spanish crown, and in the process many became very wealthy. This lust for gold, however, had a deadly impact on the indigenous populations.

SUPERIOR ARMS

To the civilizations of Central and South America, the foreign invaders were truly an alien force. The horse was unknown before the arrival of the Spanish, and mounted soldiers posed a deadly new challenge to their warriors. In addition to cavalry, the conquistadors were equipped with a wide range of high-tech weaponry: swords of fine Toledo steel were light and swift; and the arquebus (a forerunner of the musket) had been developed to deliver a deadly blow against European plate armor, and would have had a far more bloody impact against Aztec shields, which were designed to protect against darts or wooden swords in which obsidian (volcanic glass) was embedded.

The sheer power of Spanish cannon was often used to devastating effect. When the Aztec emperor Moctezuma sent messengers to Veracruz in 1519, Cortés fired his cannon as a show of power. According to an account, written 50 years later, the Aztec messengers fainted on the spot.

The military devastation of the people of the Americas was accompanied by equally deadly new diseases. The Europeans brought with them a range of infections and viruses to which the native peoples had little or no

PRE-COLUMBIAN CIVILIZATIONS
At Chichen Itza on the Yucatán peninsula in Mexico, the Spanish found evidence of a sophisticated Mayan civilization that had been abandoned to the forest centuries earlier.

SACRIFICIAL OFFERINGS
The Aztecs practiced ritual human sacrifice, cutting out the victim's heart to offer it to the gods. Cortés described it as "a most horrid and abominable custom which truly ought to be punished."

SETTING THE SCENE

- The papal treaties granting rights in the New World to Spain and Portugal are issued on the basis that **the conversion of the indigenous population to Catholicism** is at the heart of all exploration. The two countries assume that their mutual dominance of the seas is so great that no other countries will participate in the European division of newfound spoils.

- **The legend of El Dorado** exists in pre-Columbian South America. It may have grown out of **a ceremonial tradition of the Muisca people of the high Andes**. A new king is anointed with oils and gold before being sent out into Lake Guatavita aboard a raft heavy with perfumes and incense. Once he reaches the middle of the lake, nobles are said to cast gold into the water to complete the coronation.

- Spanish voices of **dissent against the brutality of the conquistadors** begin to emerge in the early 16th century. **Bartolomé de las Casas, a Dominican priest** who emigrated to Hispaniola in 1502, writes of his shock at the brutality of the *encomienda* system of native slavery and the subsequent mass slaughter of Cuban tribes by Spanish soldiers. His eyewitness accounts would contribute to some of the earliest forms of human rights law.

immunity. Cholera, smallpox, measles, and diptheria spread across the continent in epidemics. Within just 20 years of the arrival of the Spanish, the indigenous population had been decimated by a combination of disease and military might.

RECORD OF AZTEC LIFE
This illustration of high-ranking Aztec warriors is from the Codex Mendoza, created about 20 years after the Spanish conquest. Codices were books illustrated with Aztec pictograms. This one, made for the Spanish king, records details of Aztec daily life.

HERNÁN CORTÉS

THE CONQUEROR OF MEXICO

SPAIN   1485–1547

IF A MAN'S LIFE is judged by the consequences of his actions, then Hernán Cortés must surely rank as one of the most significant men in history. With his small band of hardy adventurers, he overthrew a well-organized and sophisticated empire ruling over as many as 15 million people. In doing so, he prized open the gates through which a flood of conquering Europeans would jostle to carve up the New World. Cortés found fame for his exploits, but did not receive the power and riches he thought he deserved.

Cortés was born in 1485 in the Spanish province of Extremadura to impoverished parents of the minor nobility. Extremadura, meaning "hard extreme," was an unforgiving land that bred hardy, determined people. These two factors—place and parentage—were the key to Cortés's character. He was aware that to make something of himself he would have to leave Spain for the New World, where land and wealth were available to those with determination and talent.

He sailed for the Caribbean island of Hispaniola in 1504, and set himself up as a planter in Santo Domingo. Within a few years he was successfully established, but his ambition led him to join an expedition to conquer the neighboring island of Cuba. The expedition was led by Diego Velásquez, who had already played a major part in conquering Hispaniola. Following the conquest of Cuba, Cortés rose to become one of the colony's leading men. In 1517 and 1518, Velásquez sent

AZTEC GOLD
Lust for gold was the driving factor for Cortés's men. They prized small, portable ornaments, such as this.

two expeditions from Cuba to reconnoître the coasts of Yucatán and Campeche in Mexico, which brought back intelligence that the mainland supported an advanced civilization with a military structure capable of resisting Spanish incursions. This civilization ruled large parts of the mainland and had subjugated other peoples, who paid them tribute. Toward the end of 1518, a third expedition comprising 500 men was sent to Mexico, led by Cortés.

TO THE MAINLAND

In March 1519, Cortés landed on mainland Mexico at Tabasco, planning to negotiate with the local people. His small force was attacked by a militia from the town of Potonchán, and despite driving them off, Cortés was impressed by the fighting ability of his opponents. He realized that he would need to use diplomacy to split the enemy and gain allies. To this end, he put on a show of force for the locals, firing his cannons to demonstrate their power, and telling the people that if they became subjects of the

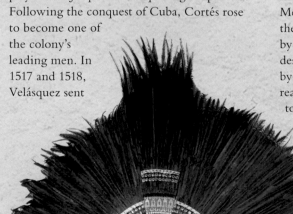

MOCTEZUMA'S HEADDRESS
Aztec nobles wore fine, highly decorated clothes. The emperor himself wore this splendid feathered headdress.

DEATH OF MOCTEZUMA
With Cortés away at the coast, the Aztec emperor Moctezuma, a weak figure, asked Cortés's deputy, Pedro de Alvarado, for permission to celebrate the spring festival of Toxcatl. During the celebration, however, Alvarado and his men broke into the Main Temple and massacred the celebrants. This provoked a rebellion (shown here) in which Moctezuma was stoned to death by his own people for allowing the massacre.

Spanish crown he would protect them. The local leaders at Tabasco told Cortés of the wealth of the Aztecs, or Mexica as they preferred to be called, a great civilization far inland. Cortés determined to confront them. He sailed farther up the coast and landed in the region of the Totonacs. These once-dominant people were now subjects of the Aztecs and appealed to Cortés to protect them. This was the breakthrough Cortés needed. He now had an ally who knew the way to the Aztec capital, Tenochtitlán. The Totonacs advised Cortés to seek an alliance inland with the Tlaxcalans, who were bitter enemies of the Aztecs.

No alliance was to be made with the Tlaxcalans, however, until after some fighting with an estimated 100,000-strong Tlaxcalan army. The Tlaxcalans resisted the intruders fiercely at first, but eventually sued for peace, inviting the Spanish to visit their capital, Tlaxcala. Cortés wrote of the city,

JOIN WITH CORTÉS?
This contemporary codex (written record) shows Mixtec chiefs discussing whether to join Cortés in his attack on the Aztecs. Such meetings took place as the Spanish progressed inland.

"I feel assured that the little I say will scarcely be credited, since it is larger than Granada and much stronger, and contains as many fine houses and a much larger population." With the Tlaxcalans now allies, Cortés had the military might to challenge the Aztec ruler, Moctezuma. As he progressed inland, it became clear to him that many of the cities of the interior regarded Moctezuma as a tyrant.

VAST CITY

When the Spanish finally entered the city of Tenochtitlán in November 1519, they were overawed by its size and grandeur, with Cortés noting that at the main market alone, 60,000 people were assembled. Tenochtitlán was one of the largest cities in the world at the time, with a population of at least 200,000.

At first, relations between the Spanish and the Aztecs were cordial, if strained. Trouble was brewing for Cortés, however. Fearful of Cortés's growing power, Velásquez had despatched another expedition

SERPENT GIFT
This double-serpent pectoral ornament, representing the Aztec god Tlaloc, was given to Cortés by Moctezuma.

to oppose him. Cortés left for the coast to deal with his rivals, leaving a garrison of 200 men behind. He returned to Tenochtitlán to discover a shocking situation: that Moctezuma had been killed by his own people (see p. 107) and that his garrison was under siege after it had carried out a massacre. Cortés fought his way into the city, then all the Spanish fought their way out.

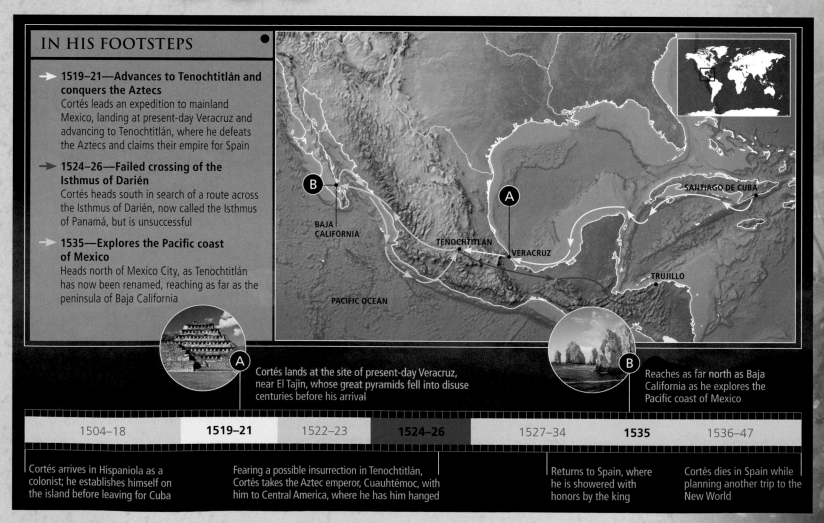

IN HIS FOOTSTEPS

➤ **1519–21—Advances to Tenochtitlán and conquers the Aztecs**
Cortés leads an expedition to mainland Mexico, landing at present-day Veracruz and advancing to Tenochtitlán, where he defeats the Aztecs and claims their empire for Spain

➤ **1524–26—Failed crossing of the Isthmus of Darién**
Cortés heads south in search of a route across the Isthmus of Darién, now called the Isthmus of Panamá, but is unsuccessful

➤ **1535—Explores the Pacific coast of Mexico**
Heads north of Mexico City, as Tenochtitlán has now been renamed, reaching as far as the peninsula of Baja California

B BAJA CALIFORNIA
A TENOCHTITLÁN VERACRUZ
SANTIAGO DE CUBA
TRUJILLO
PACIFIC OCEAN

A Cortés lands at the site of present-day Veracruz, near El Tajin, whose great pyramids fell into disuse centuries before his arrival

B Reaches as far north as Baja California as he explores the Pacific coast of Mexico

1504–18	**1519–21**	1522–23	**1524–26**	1527–34	**1535**	1536–47

Cortés arrives in Hispaniola as a colonist; he establishes himself on the island before leaving for Cuba

Fearing a possible insurrection in Tenochtitlán, Cortés takes the Aztec emperor, Cuauhtémoc, with him to Central America, where he has him hanged

Returns to Spain, where he is showered with honors by the king

Cortés dies in Spain while planning another trip to the New World

THE AZTEC EMPIRE

"Aztec" is a Nahuatl word meaning "people from Aztlán," a mythical city north of Mexico from which all Nahuatl people were said to have come. By the start of the 16th century, the empire of the Nahuatl had extended its power across large parts of present-day Mexico. Its power base was in the Valley of Mexico, a high plateau that was home to the city states of the Aztec Triple Alliance: Tenochtitlán, Texcoco, and Tlacopan. The alliance's dominance was brief: its biggest city, Tenochtitlán, fell to Cortés less than 200 years after it was founded.

THE CITY OF TENOCHTITLÁN WAS SITED ON LAKE TEXCOCO IN THE VALLEY OF MEXICO

In 1521, Cortés returned to lay siege to Tenochtitlán, and slowly but surely the Spanish gained control. The fighting was fierce and Cortés and his local allies lost many men. For those captured by the Aztecs the outlook was grim. Cortés wrote, "the enemy ... sacrificed them naked, opening their breasts and taking out their hearts to offer them to their idols." Cortés captured the city, which he then officially renamed Mexico City, and killed the new emperor, Cuauhtémoc. He went on to lay waste to the entire Aztec Empire, securing vast treasure for the Spanish crown. The native population, who had no immunity to Old World diseases such as smallpox and measles, was decimated. In 1524, after three years as governor of the new territory, Cortés was replaced by a civilian administrator. He went on to make an unsuccessful attempt to find a channel across the Isthmus of Darién before returning to Spain a bitter—if wealthy—man.

Cortés returned to Mexico in 1530 with the new title of Marquis of Oaxaca, but little power, and mounted several expeditions to the Pacific coast of Mexico. Never far from controversy, he fell from royal favor at the end of his life. In 1547, Cortés died as he had started out: in Spain, in debt, and planning a trip to the New World.

I HAVE GIVEN YOU MORE PROVINCES THAN YOUR ANCESTORS LEFT YOU CITIES

HERNÁN CORTÉS, IN A LETTER TO CARLOS V OF SPAIN

THE TAKING OF TENOCHTITLÁN
A dramatic painting shows Cortés returning to lay siege to the city of Tenochtitlán. The Spaniards' horses and metal armor gave them a key advantage over the defenders.

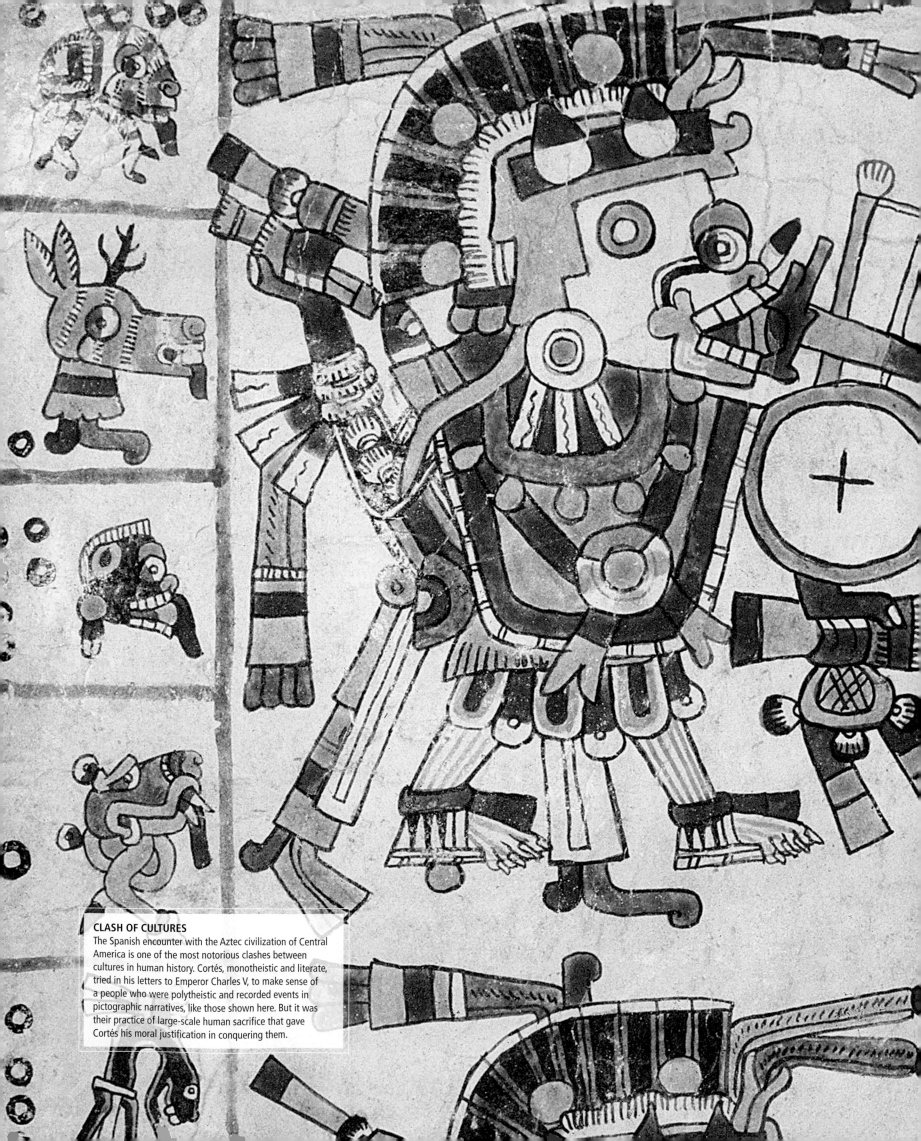

CLASH OF CULTURES

The Spanish encounter with the Aztec civilization of Central America is one of the most notorious clashes between cultures in human history. Cortés, monotheistic and literate, tried in his letters to Emperor Charles V, to make sense of a people who were polytheistic and recorded events in pictographic narratives, like those shown here. But it was their practice of large-scale human sacrifice that gave Cortés his moral justification in conquering them.

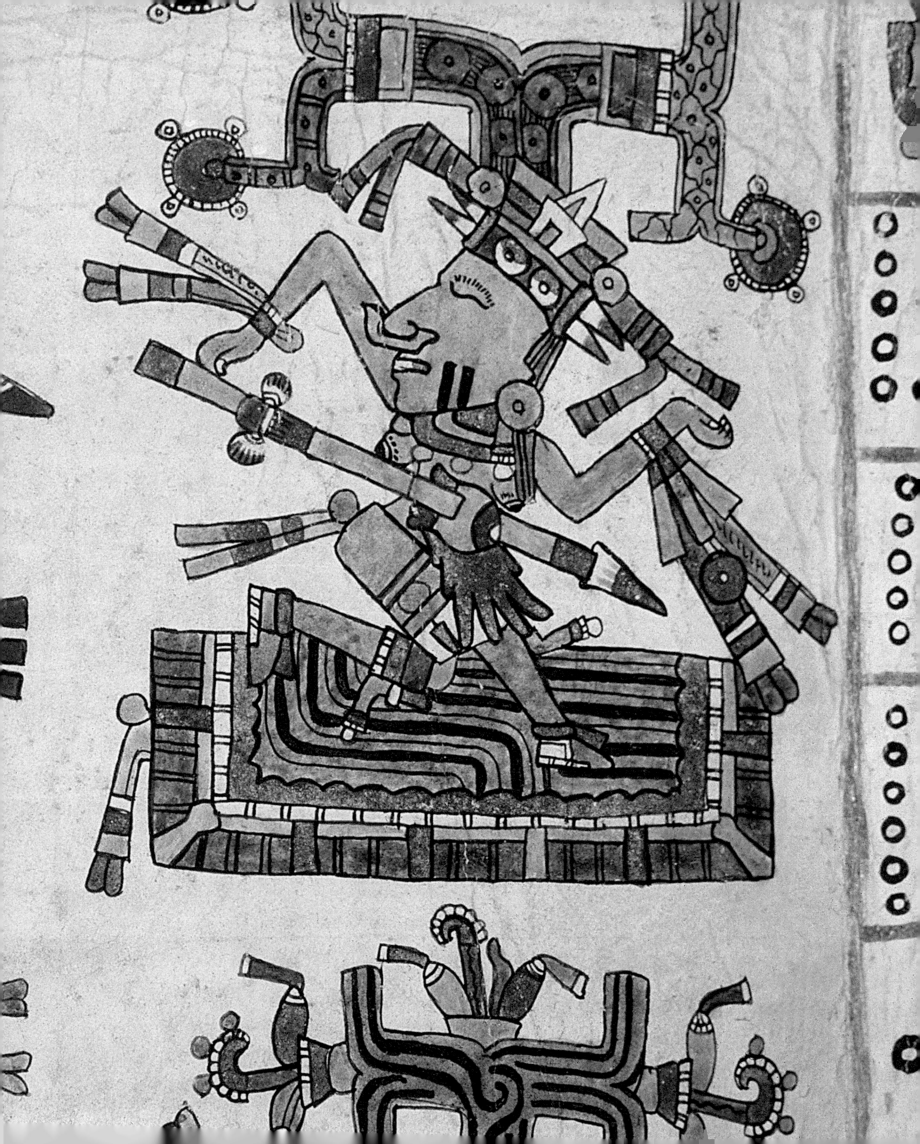

FRANCISCO PIZARRO

CONQUISTADOR WHO CLAIMED PERU

SPAIN   1471–1541

THE MAN WHO BROUGHT DOWN the mighty Inca Empire and subjugated a vast region of South America was an unlikely conquistador. Illegitimate and illiterate, Francisco Pizarro was just one of thousands of colonists arriving in Panama from Spain, hoping to find a new life. He spent 20 years working his way up through colonial society before putting together his first expedition. Spurred on by tales of a fabulously wealthy civilization to the south, Pizarro began his campaign of conquest at the advanced age of 60.

Although a second cousin of the illustrious conquistador Hernán Cortés (see pp. 106–09), Pizarro was from a lowly background. He arrived in the New World in 1502 as part of a large fleet of 30 ships carrying 2,500 Spanish colonists. Most of them were from humble stock; all of them were eager to find fortune. By 1524, Pizarro had transformed himself into a leading figure in Panama society. But, like his cousin before him, he was also driven by a desire to find lands to conquer and a fortune to plunder. He had already taken part in the expeditions of other explorers, including Nuñez de Balboa (see pp. 120–21), whom he accompanied to the Pacific coast in 1513. Now he was ready to set out on his own expedition, joining forces with a soldier, Diego de Almagro (see box, p. 115), and a priest, Hernando de Luque, to sail south and explore the west coast of South America.

A BAD START

This first expedition did not go well. Pizarro and his party reached no farther than the coast of present-day Colombia before bad weather, fierce resistance from the local people, and a severe shortage of food forced them to beat a retreat back to Panama. During the expedition, de Almagro lost an eye when they were attacked by local warriors. At one point they were forced to land while they waited for supplies. The crew named the place "Port Famine" after they were reduced to boiling up and eating a cowhide.

After such a disastrous first voyage, it was not easy to find men willing to make another journey south. The governor of Panama was also reluctant to sanction a second expedition. However, with the arrival of a new governor, Pedro de los Ríos, in 1526, Pizarro's luck began to change. A second expedition was approved and Pizarro set out once again down the west coast.

FINDING GOLD

While he explored the swampy shores of Colombia, he sent his chief pilot, Bartolomé Ruiz, down the coast of present-day Ecuador, where he found Tumbes, an Inca settlement abounding with gold, textiles, and emeralds. This was exactly what avaricious conquistadors were after, and it was a tantalizing sign of the wealth of the lands farther south.

INCA TREASURE
The Spaniards placed no value on the art of the Inca goldsmiths. Gold ornaments such as this exquisite figurine were melted down.

THERE LIES PERU WITH ITS RICHES; HERE, PANAMA AND ITS POVERTY. CHOOSE, EACH MAN, WHAT BEST BECOMES A BRAVE CASTILIAN

FRANCISCO PIZARRO

GOLD LUST
This engraving from 1602 appeared in an early history of the conquest of the Americas. It shows the Incas bringing gold as payment of a ransom for the release of the Inca emperor Atahualpa, whom Pizarro had captured at Cajamarca (in present-day Peru). Despite having received the ransom in full, Pizarro had Atahualpa executed.

LINE IN THE SAND
As his men wavered in the harsh conditions of the Peruvian Andes, Pizarro is said to have drawn a line in the sand and dared them to follow him to glory.

When the governor refused to sanction a third expedition, Pizarro returned to Spain to make a direct appeal to Emperor Charles V. The king was impressed by his tales of rich new lands, and Pizarro returned to the New World with a Royal Commission to establish a new Spanish colony with himself as its governor. Back in Panama, Pizarro and de Almagro organized the next expedition, and in 1532 they sailed down the coast.

They landed at Tumbes, where they immediately drew the hostility of the local Punian people. Finding that Tumbes was not a safe place to stay, Pizarro headed inland and established the first Spanish settlement in Peru at San Miguel de Piura. From there, he despatched one of his men, Hernando de Soto (see pp. 118–19) to explore farther inland. De Soto returned with an envoy from the Inca emperor, Atahualpa himself.

HEARTLANDS OF THE INCA
The Spaniards' timing could not have been better. They had entered Peru at a time of civil war—as Atahualpa fought his brother Huáscar for the succession to the Inca throne. Having just defeated Huáscar, Atahualpa was resting in the northern Inca city of Cajamarca. Pizarro embarked on a two-month march to Cajamarca with a tiny force of 106 foot-soldiers and 62 horsemen. Ironically, the Incas' strongly

THE CAPTURE OF ATAHUALPA
This 19th-century painting illustrates the moment that Atahualpa was taken prisoner during the Battle of Cajamarca. Inca society was very hierarchical, and once the Inca warriors saw that their leader had fallen, their resistance soon crumbled.

centralized and organized empire, with its excellent system of roads, made it easier for an invader to gain access to their heartland. For soldiers in armor, unused to the high altitudes of the Andes, the Inca roads must have been an unexpected bonus. When Pizarro reached Cajamarca, the emperor, backed by an army numbering more than 50,000 men, did not consider Pizarro's tiny force a threat, and dismissed his demand to enter the city. However, Atahualpa's complacency was to prove his downfall. Pizarro gathered his men together. They appeared to be stuck—unable to retreat without being pursued, yet faced with overwhelming odds against them. Pizarro reminded them how Cortés had taken Mexico with a similarly tiny force. The only option was to attack. On November 16, 1532, Pizarro's men sprang a surprise attack on Atahualpa's

PIZARRO'S GOBLET
This wooden goblet was made for Pizarro by Inca artisans. It is decorated with scenes from his conquest of Peru.

unprepared, and mostly unarmed, force. They targeted Atahualpa himself in order to decapitate the Inca chain of command.

CAPTURE OF THE EMPEROR
The Battle of Cajamarca, as it became known, was in reality little more than the slaughter of thousands of unarmed men by the heavily armed Spanish. Atahualpa was captured and Pizarro, with the iron confidence that his Christian god was on his side, said to him, "When you have seen the errors in which you live, you will understand the good we have done you by coming to your land." Fearing the Spaniards would kill him, Atahualpa offered a ransom saying, "I will give gold enough to fill a room twenty-two feet long and seventeen wide." Over the next few weeks, Atahualpa's supporters diligently brought load after load of precious metal objects until the room

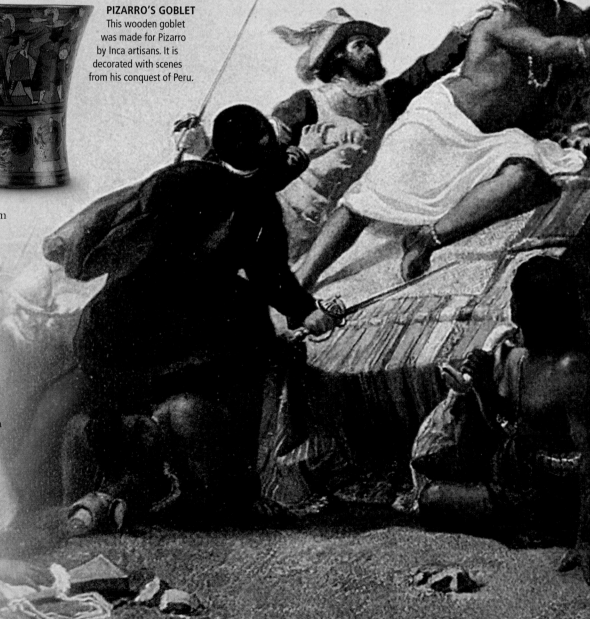

was full. Pizarro knew, however, that as long as Atahualpa lived he would be a threat to his ambitions, and so, with the connivance of his officers, he sentenced the Inca emperor to death on a trumped-up charge of treason. Atahualpa was to be burned at the stake. Horrified, he converted to Christianity in a bid to escape this barbarous fate (he believed burning would prevent his soul from passing to the afterlife), and instead, at his own request, was fastened to a pole in an open space and garotted.

ONWARD TO CUZCO

A year after executing the Inca emperor, Pizarro entered the Inca capital, Cuzco, now with a force of indigenous troops to help him. Pizarro had made Atahualpa's younger brother, Túpac Huallpa, the new puppet emperor, and he took Cuzco amid little resistance. The illiterate Pizarro ordered one of his officers to write to Emperor Charles V, "This city is the greatest and the finest ever seen in this country or anywhere in the Indies … We can assure your Majesty that it is so beautiful that it would be remarkable even in Spain." Situated up in the mountains, Cuzco was at too high an altitude and too far from the sea to serve as the capital of Pizarro's

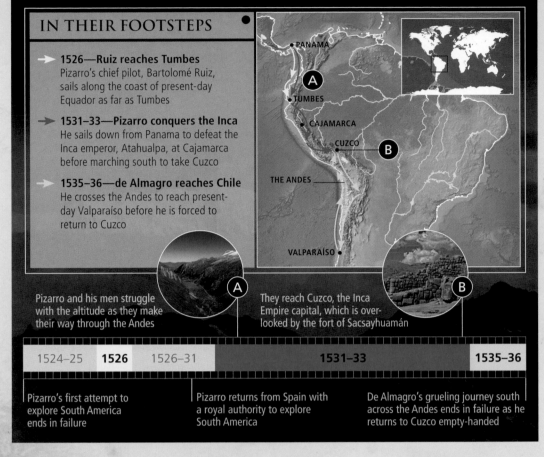

IN THEIR FOOTSTEPS

1526—Ruiz reaches Tumbes
Pizarro's chief pilot, Bartolomé Ruiz, sails along the coast of present-day Equador as far as Tumbes

1531–33—Pizarro conquers the Inca
He sails down from Panama to defeat the Inca emperor, Atahualpa, at Cajamarca before marching south to take Cuzco

1535–36—de Almagro reaches Chile
He crosses the Andes to reach present-day Valparaíso before he is forced to return to Cuzco

Pizarro and his men struggle with the altitude as they make their way through the Andes

They reach Cuzco, the Inca Empire capital, which is overlooked by the fort of Sacsayhuamán

1524–25	**1526**	1526–31		1531–33	**1535–36**

Pizarro's first attempt to explore South America ends in failure

Pizarro returns from Spain with a royal authority to explore South America

De Almagro's grueling journey south across the Andes ends in failure as he returns to Cuzco empty-handed

new colony, so he established the city of Lima on the coast in 1535 and settled down to enjoy his new governorship.

A CONQUISTADOR'S FATE

Pizarro had used the authority granted him by the Royal Commission to take the lion's share of Atahualpa's treasure for himself. Unsurprisingly, this high-handed attitude alienated some of his former comrades, including de Almagro. Rather than confront the newly powerful Pizarro, however, de Almagro decided to travel south to explore present-day Chile, hoping to find his own civilization to conquer. Finding only hostile tribes and no sign of gold, he returned reluctantly to Peru, where he persuaded the new puppet Inca ruler, Manco, to join him in an attack on Cuzco. There, in 1538, de Almagro was defeated by Pizarro's brother, Hernando, who proved to be just as ruthless as his sibling. Hernando had no sympathy for de Almagro as he begged for his life, telling him, "You are a gentleman with an illustrious name; do not display compassion." De Almagro was executed, and his body displayed in the main square. Pizarro was not to enjoy his victory for long, however, as he was assassinated three years later by supporters of de Almagro's son.

Remarkably, Pizarro had conquered Peru with even fewer men than Cortés had used in his conquest of Mexico. He ruthlessly imposed

Christianity and placed almost no value on the indigenous culture, a mistake that has had long-term effects for the region. The Spanish did not understand the value of the Incas' tiered mountainside farming system, and to this day, Peruvian agriculture has not fully recovered from its demise.

DIEGO DE ALMAGRO

SPAIN   1475–1538

Pizarro fell out with his long-serving second-in-command, de Almagro, after the conquest of Peru.

Unhappy at what he saw as the unfair distribution of the spoils, de Almagro set out in 1535 with his own expedition, following the Inca trail south to present-day Chile. His force of 500 men was ill-equipped for the rigors of the Andes, however, and stiff resistance from the local Mapuche people, combined with a bitterly cold winter, persuaded them to return to Peru. There, a still resentful de Almagro plotted to overthrow Pizarro, but he was captured and executed by Hernando, Pizarro's brother.

PONCE DE LEÓN

THE SPANISH DISCOVERER OF FLORIDA

SPAIN
1474–1521

A SPANISH NOBLE who, like many of his class, saw his future in the New World, Juan Ponce de León conquered the island of Puerto Rico for Spain and became its governor. When he was deposed during unrest on the island, he turned his attention northward, taking a fleet of ships to become the first European to set foot on Florida. Enthused by the fertile land he found there on this first voyage, Ponce de León returned to Florida to take possession of it for Spain, but was killed in a skirmish with the local people.

SAILING ALONG THE FLORIDA COAST
This engraving shows Ponce de León's ship, the *Santiago*, in the Florida swamps. He took two other ships, the *San Cristobal* and the *Santa Maria*, on the first voyage.

A LIFE'S WORK

- **Sails for the New World** with Christopher Columbus's second expedition

- Is made **governor of Puerto Rico** after subduing the island's Taíno population, but **is soon deposed** from his position

- On a voyage of discovery north from Puerto Rico, is the first European to **make landfall on the east coast of Florida**, which he believes to be a large island

- Returns to Spain to receive **royal consent to conquer Florida**

- Is **killed in a skirmish** with the locals on his return to Florida

Little is known of Ponce de León's early years. His name first comes to prominence during the *Reconquista*, the Spanish taking of Andalucia from the Moors, which was completed in 1492. With the Moors driven out of Spain, Ponce de León found employment in short supply, so in 1493 he joined the second expedition of Christopher Columbus (see pp. 86–89). Their destination was Hispaniola (present-day Haiti and Dominican Republic), but on the way they stopped off briefly at a large island called Boriquén by the locals (present-day Puerto Rico).

For the next few years, Ponce de León disappears from history, resurfacing in 1504 when the

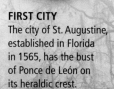

FIRST CITY
The city of St. Augustine, established in Florida in 1565, has the bust of Ponce de León on its heraldic crest.

governor of Hispaniola, Nicolás de Ovando, gave him a lead role in crushing a rebellion by the local Taíno people. Ponce de León was rewarded for his efforts with a substantial land grant, and made governor of a new frontier province called Higüey.

RICHES ON BORIQUÉN

At about the time that he was establishing his new estate, Ponce de León began to hear tales of the riches to be found on Boriquén. The locals told him that the island was very fertile and that its rivers carried much gold. It was an enticing prospect to a Spanish noble in search of his fortune. He gained permission to lead an expedition to the island in 1508. It is likely that he had carried out an earlier, clandestine visit in order to satisfy himself that it was worthy of a major expedition. At this time, the Spanish called the island San Juan Bautista. Landing at San Juan Bay, they moved inland and built a fortified house and storeroom. According to the chronicler Antonio de Herrera, who compiled a history of the conquistadors from reports sent back to Spain, the local chief "conducted [Ponce de León] all over the Island, showing him the Rivers, among them two that were very rich, the one called Manatuabon, and the other Cebuco, whence much Treasure was afterwards drawn." The island itself was found to be very attractive with "high Mountains, some of them covered in fine Grass, like that in Hispaniola … few Plains, but many Vales, with agreeable Rivers running through them, and all is very fruitful."

REVOLT AND DISMISSAL
In 1509, the Spanish had collected sufficient gold to return to Hispaniola. Ponce de León was promptly made governor of the new colony with the right to put the Taíno people to work

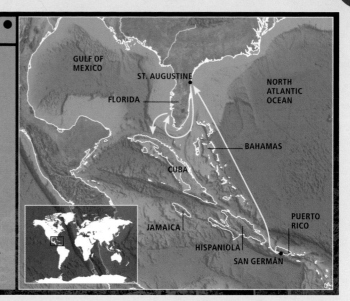

IN HIS FOOTSTEPS

○ **1508—Explores Puerto Rico**
He finds gold on the island and returns the following year to conquer it

→ **1513—Discovers Florida**
Hearing of rich islands to the north, he reaches the east coast of Florida and sails around to the west coast, believing it to be an island

○ **1521—Returns to Florida**
He returns to Florida intending to become its new governor, but is struck in the shoulder with a poisoned arrow and dies soon after

○ Not shown on map

GULF OF MEXICO
ST. AUGUSTINE
FLORIDA
NORTH ATLANTIC OCEAN
BAHAMAS
CUBA
PUERTO RICO
JAMAICA
HISPANIOLA
SAN GERMÁN

THE FOUNTAIN OF YOUTH
Following his death, a legend grew that Ponce de León had gone to Florida in search of the mythical Fountain of Youth, whose water restored the youth of all who drank it.

for him. But hard labor in the gold mine and European diseases soon decimated them, and once again Ponce de León had to put down a revolt. As unrest grew, Spanish political machinations led to him being relieved of the governorship.

This was undoubtedly a blow to such an ambitious man, but he was ever resourceful and "having gathered much Wealth, he resolved to do something that might gain him Honor, and increase his Estate; and being informed that there were lands to the Northward, thought fit to go make Discoveries that Way."

THE LAND TO THE NORTH
Ponce de León sailed north from Puerto Rico in late March 1513. In early April, his fleet of three ships and 200 men arrived off the coast of what they believed to be another island. According to de Herrera, "They named it Florida, because it appeared very delightful, having many pleasant Groves, and it was all level; as also because they discovered it at Easter, which the Spaniards call Pasqua de Flores, or Florida."

Soon after landing, they made contact with the local inhabitants, who at first seemed friendly. However, the situation soon turned ugly, with one of the local people "stunning a Sailor with a stroke of a Cudgel he gave him on the Head, [and] the Spaniards were obliged to fight, and had two of their men wounded with Darts and Arrows pointed with sharp Bones." After several skirmishes, Ponce de León withdrew his men, satisfied that Florida was worthy of settling.

He soon retuned to Spain to have himself confirmed as the rightful discoverer of the new "island" and to prepare a second expedition that would take possession of his new colony. This time, however, Ponce de León's luck had run out. In a skirmish with the local Calusa people, he was struck in the shoulder with a poisoned arrow and, after withdrawing to Cuba, he died. Some said that Ponce de León had been searching for the fabled Fountain of Youth in Florida but, as with the later conquistadors, it was probably land and gold that motivated him. It was left to others to settle and exploit his "discovery."

LUSH EVERGLADES
Ponce de León was impressed by Florida's lush tropical vegetation. He saw it as the perfect place to colonize after he had been ousted as governor of the equally lush Caribbean island of Puerto Rico.

HERNANDO DE SOTO

FIRST EUROPEAN TO REACH THE MISSISSIPPI

SPAIN   1496–1542

A FAMED EXPLORER AND CONQUISTADOR, Hernando de Soto journeyed from Spain to the New World in 1514, drawn by the promise of military glory and unbounded wealth. He gained renown as a leader, tactician, and fighter during the conquest of Central and South America, but became notorious for his brutal methods. De Soto was the first known European to lead an expedition deep into the present-day United States, where he suppressed hostile natives and discovered the Mississippi River.

FLORIDA EXPEDITION
De Soto and his men spent their first few months on North American soil in Florida. Their winter camp was at Anhaica, an Apalachee Indian town.

In 1514, an ambitious 18-year-old Hernando de Soto sailed from Spain to Central America with Panama's new governor, Pedrarias Dávila. He was to serve in Dávila's administration for 15 years, reaching the rank of regidor (governing officer) of León in Nicaragua. There, de Soto reaped substantial rewards from his interests in the slave trade, but had his sights set on even greater riches. Hearing of the Inca wealth described by Francisco Pizarro (see pp. 112–15), de Soto resolved to join him on an expedition to Peru, his lust for gold kindled. Dávila, however, refused permission for de Soto to leave his position, and it was not until the governor's death in 1531 that the budding conquistador was free to go.

Reaching Pizarro's base on the island of Puná (in present-day Ecuador), de Soto found the small army of Spaniards sick with infections and under attack from natives. Pizarro, grateful for de Soto's help, made him a captain. Proceeding south into the heart of the Inca Empire, the Spaniards met the emperor, Atahualpa himself, at the town of Cajamarca. Skilled as a diplomat, de Soto attempted to parley with him but was rebuffed, so Pizarro attacked, taking Atahualpa hostage. De Soto then led a vanguard force to Cuzco, the capital, where plunder, and his share from Atahualpa's ransom, made him extremely rich.

TO NORTH AMERICA
De Soto returned to Spain a hero in 1533. As a reward for his success, he was made governor of Cuba, where he served for six years before departing on his next expedition in search of a route through North America to the East. On May 12, 1539, he set sail with nine ships, 350 horses, and more than 1,000 soldiers and settlers. On landing in what is now Florida, he named the spot Espiritu Santo (present-day Tampa Bay). Despite the hostility of the American Indians, de Soto negotiated safe passage

west with Chief Hirrihigua of the Uzita tribe, whose land bordered the coast. He also secured the services of Juan Ortiz, a young Spaniard who had learned the local dialects and routes as a guide on an earlier, failed expedition. Ortiz chose to dress like the natives, appearing "naked like them, with a bow and some arrows, his body decorated like an Indian." Despite Ortiz's assistance, de Soto's expedition west was dogged

DE SOTO AT WORK
An engraving of 1540 depicts de Soto's brutal methods. Here, he is torturing Florida Indians in his search for treasure.

A LIFE'S WORK

- His observations of the landscape and peoples of North America pave the way for **Spanish colonization**

- **Claims large parts of North America** for the Spanish crown

- His expedition introduces **measles, smallpox, and chicken pox** to the American Indian population; with no resistance to the diseases, many Native American peoples are devastated by epidemics

DISCOVERING THE MISSISSIPPI
This romanticized painting depicts de Soto's discovery of the Mississippi. The broad river, patrolled by hostile natives, was a major obstacle; de Soto's party crossed it using rafts.

by skirmishes with hostile locals. Finally, in May 1541, his party reached the banks of the Mississippi in what is now Tennessee—the first Europeans to do so. With no trace of the hoped-for gold, the loss of many men and horses, and under attack, the dispirited party made its way west toward present-day Texas. Changing tack again, they headed back toward the Mississippi, reaching the settlement of Guachoya on the western banks of the river. There, de Soto contracted a fever and died on May 21, 1542. His body was placed in a hollowed-out tree trunk and submerged in the Mississippi. The remaining expedition members, malnourished and clothed in animal skins, reached the Spanish frontier town of Pánuco in Mexico. Only half of the original party survived.

IN HIS FOOTSTEPS

- **1531–33—Conquering the Incas**
  Fights the Incas under the command of Pizarro, leading a force into the Inca capital, Cuzco (see pp. 112–15)

- **1539–42—Explores the northern mainland**
  Lands in Florida and heads north, then west to the Mississippi River; his men make their own way back to Mexico after de Soto dies

○ Not shown on map

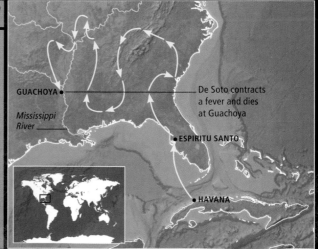

GUACHOYA

De Soto contracts a fever and dies at Guachoya

Mississippi River

ESPIRITU SANTO

HAVANA

NÚÑEZ DE BALBOA

CONQUISTADOR DISCOVERER OF THE PACIFIC

SPAIN   1474–1519

LIKE MANY OF THE CONQUISTADORES, the ambitious Vasco Núñez de Balboa was born into a noble but impoverished family, in his case from the Jerez region of Spain. He scented opportunity when news of Columbus's discoveries reached Europe, and joined a mission to South America, setting sail in 1501. After establishing the earliest permanent European settlement on the mainland of the Americas, Balboa crossed the Isthmus of Panama to become the first European to reach the Pacific Ocean from the New World.

A LIFE'S WORK

- Witnesses the **burial practice** among the Comagre, in which the cremated remains are threaded with precious stones and suspended in a burial hall

- Balboa's **name for the Pacific Ocean**, "Mar del Sur," remains in use until the explorations of Ferdinand Magellan six years later

- He names the **Archipiélago de las Perlas** (Pearl Islands) off the Panama coast, a title they still bear today

At the age of 27, Balboa set sail from Cádiz under the command of Rodrigo de Bastidas. This expedition explored the coast of Colombia and northeastern South America while collecting gold, pearls, and other precious cargo through trade with the indigenous people. On their return journey to Spain, the ships were caught in a storm in the Caribbean and forced to make for the island of Hispaniola.

Balboa remained on Hispaniola and managed a farm at Salvatierra on the coast. His experience as a farmer was not a happy one, however. In 1509, deeply in debt, he smuggled himself onto a boat bound for the settlement at San Sebastián de Urabá (in present-day Colombia), hiding in a cask being shipped from his farm. Once the ship was at sea, Balboa made himself known to the commander, Martín Fernández de Enciso, who threatened to cast him adrift. Enciso was on a relief mission to provide support against a hostile indigenous population that was

attacking San Sebastián de Urabá and Balboa pleaded successfully to remain on board, citing his previous experience of the region.

SEIZING THE MOMENT

San Sebastián was under fierce attack when the relief force arrived, and it was clear that the settlement would have to be relocated. Balboa suggested moving north to the region of Darién, between present-day Panama and Colombia, where the land was more fertile. Following this advice, the Spanish took control of an existing coastal settlement and renamed it Santa María la Antigua del Darién. Balboa's stock was rising rapidly as he skillfully represented the settlers' complaints against Enciso's rule as mayor, and he successfully overthrew his protector. A shrewd strategist, Balboa ensured his own

FOREST RELOCATION
The forested area of Darién, on the Isthmus of Panama, was chosen by Balboa as the site for the permanent settlement of Santa María la Antigua del Darién in 1510.

SIGHTING THE PACIFIC
On finally reaching the coastline, Balboa walked into the sea. Waist deep in the water, he proclaimed Spain's dominance of the "seas, lands and coasts, and islands of the south."

IN HIS FOOTSTEPS

→ **1501—Explores the coast of Colombia**
Balboa sails with Rodrigo de Bastidas, exploring the northern coast of South America; they are forced to land at Hispaniola instead of returning to Spain

→ **1509—Into Central America**
After smuggling himself onboard a ship to the mainland, Balboa rises to power as governor of Darién

→ **1513—Sights the Pacific**
Crosses the isthmus and becomes the first European to set eyes on the Pacific, "taking possession" of it in the name of Spain

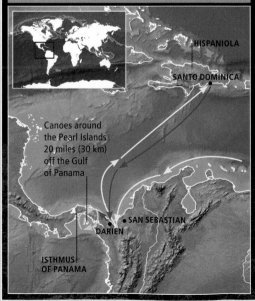

protection by sending gold to the royal treasurer at Hispaniola, asking for royal approval to act as governor of the Darién region. While still only in unofficial control of the region, Balboa heard of the friendly chief of the Careta people, based at Coyba to the north. Balboa set out for Coyba, where the chief told him of a territory to the west ruled by the Comagre, where a "mighty sea" lay and gold aplenty. Balboa made it his immediate mission to reach this bounteous sea.

A MONSTER'S DOGS
Balboa, known for using ruthless force against the indigenous peoples, set his dogs on the Quarequas people for their tolerant attitude toward homosexuality.

REACHING THE NEW OCEAN
Balboa set out from Santa María in September 1513 with a party of 190 Spaniards plus several Darién Indians to act as interpreters. They struggled across the rocky landscape, navigating rapids in hastily constructed rafts. Disease had reduced the party to 67 when, on September 25,

they spied the Pacific Ocean. Balboa gave thanks to God and took possession of the ocean in the name of Spain. The party canoed around an archipelago of tiny islands, which Balboa named the Pearl Islands after he had been assured that this treasure was plentiful there, but they were forced back by bad weather.

Balboa returned to the Pacific in 1519 with a force of 300 men, and once again explored the islands. Back on the Caribbean coast, however, his luck had run out. The new governor, Arias de Ávila, accused Balboa of treason, and on his return, he was convicted and beheaded.

CHARTING THE DEVELOPMENT OF...

EXPLORATION AND MEDICINE

EXTREME CONDITIONS can result in severe medical problems, even for the best planned expeditions. Scientific advances and medical training have done a great deal to mitigate the worst effects of the illnesses and injuries that most commonly affect explorers, although frostbite can still strike within minutes of exposure to the coldest temperatures. Earlier travelers and explorers encountered new diseases and brought old ones with them, while scurvy was the scourge of sailors for centuries.

DEADLY MALARIA
The disease malaria has affected humankind for thousands of years. Theories relating to its diagnosis and treatment were recorded as early as the 6th century BCE. Today, malaria kills more than a million people each year, the majority in sub-Saharan Africa. Scientists believe that the malaria parasite reached Central and South America in the 16th century with slaves shipped from West Africa by Spanish colonizers. By the 17th century, it had been found that a tincture made from the root of the cinchona tree in South America was an effective treatment. In the 19th century, Alexander von Humboldt (see pp. 266–69) published the first scientific paper on the tree, and in 1820, the effective alkaloid was separated from the powdered bark. The new drug was named quinine, and it soon became an essential item for explorers visiting malarial regions.

5TH CENTURY BCE— MEDICAL SCHOOL
The Greek physician Hippocrates of Cos founds a school of medicine, establishing the subject as a distinct discipline.

1253—RUBRUCK'S RHUBARB
Flemish monk William of Rubruck (see pp. 54–55) records the skills of Mongolian doctors in their use of medicinal plants, including rhubarb.

1348—BLACK DEATH
Bubonic plague reaches its peak in Europe, spread by rats carrying infected fleas; the disease was brought from Asia along the Silk Road.

1497—TRADE IN CURES
Vasco da Gama (see pp. 80–81) buys bezoars—stones from the stomachs of cattle (shown being administered, left)—believed to be antitoxins.

1530—NO IMMUNITY
Smallpox, carried by Spanish settlers, decimates native populations in Mexico.

BCE 400	CE 70	1250	1300	1350	1400	1450	1500	1550

1350—IBN BATTUTA
The Arab traveler is cured of heart palpitations by the emperor of Hindustan.

Greek pharmacologist Pedanius Dioscorides publishes his *Materia Medica*, one of the **first pharmacopeias to include descriptions of Indian and Arabic herbs**. The knowledge had reached the West from Asia Minor via military and trade connections. Dioscorides's works were still current in medieval times. This medieval illustration is from his *Tractatus de Herbis*.

70CE MATERIA MEDICA

1493 MASTIC LEAVES

While on a visit to the Greek island of Chios in 1493, Christopher Columbus (see pp. 86–89) describes the efficacious effects of a **gum made from the bark of the mastic tree**, the leaves of which are shown here. At the time, it is used to treat a variety of ailments and to make toothpaste. Columbus believes it can **cure cholera**, and the gum has indeed since been found to have some **antibacterial qualities**.

1520—DEADLY SCURVY
On Magellan's circumnavigation (see pp. 138–41), the crew is devastated by scurvy, with a fatality rate of more than 80 percent.

In addition to malaria, European explorers in Africa faced the dangers of blackwater fever (an aggravated form of malaria), dysentery, and innumerable infections and parasitic conditions then unknown in Europe. The death toll to disease of the first European explorers was high, and even by the end of the 19th century, many succumbed to illness, including Mary Kingsley, who died of dysentery in South Africa in 1900 (see pp. 212–13). By Kingsley's time, the well-equipped explorer, with or without the added benefit of a medical expert on the expedition, would travel with a medicine chest containing a comprehensive range of curatives.

THE SCOURGE OF SAILORS

While exchanges of pharmacological information helped travelers in new lands, many cures were forgotten or lost over time. The cause and cures for scurvy, one of the single largest causes of death during the 15th-century European voyages of exploration, had been forgotten, despite accounts of the condition dating back to antiquity. In the late 15th century, the Italian anatomist Hieronymous Fabricius recorded a "new and unheard of disease, spreading as supposed by contagion." Little was known about the disease or its true cause—a deficiency in vitamin C. It was described in the accounts of Vasco da Gama's voyage in 1497 (see pp. 80–81) as *Amalati de la Boccha* ("Curse of the Mouth").

A lack of vitamin C in the diet could be equally serious on land. In 1535, trapped by ice during his exploration of the St. Lawrence River, French explorer Jacques Cartier (see pp. 130–31) carried out one of the earliest autopsies on a member of his scurvy-ridden crew to establish an internal cause for the swollen and blackened limbs of the corpse. A local tribesman proffered needles from the *arborvitae* tree, and an infusion made from them led to a swift recovery among the remaining men.

Following the publication of British naval surgeon James Lind's *Treatise on Scurvy* in 1753, preventative treatments began to be put in place. James Cook followed Lind's advice to the letter on his voyages between 1768–79 (see pp. 156–59), insisting that his men eat sauerkraut, a source of vitamin C. With improved knowledge, scurvy became less of a threat to life on board ship.

IN THE FROZEN WASTES

On land, Lind's cure was slower to catch on. Polar explorers continued to suffer from scurvy, believing it was caused by tainted canned food. Scurvy was not the only disease. During Scott's *Discovery* expedition of 1901 (see pp. 312–15), Dr. Edward Wilson recorded how members of the party suffered from snow blindness, colic, rheumatic pain, and frequent diarrhea, in addition to minor and more major cases of frostbite. In comparison, on the Norwegian Antarctic Expedition of 1910–12 (see pp. 302–05), Roald Amundsen dispensed with the services of a doctor, preferring to rely on a medical kit "carefully chosen and beautifully arranged." Polar explorers often had to endure the effects of frostbite alone (see p. 294). In his diary on the return journey from the South Pole, Scott wrote bleakly that "amputation is the least I can hope for." In 1908, Robert Peary (see pp. 308–09) set off for the North Pole undeterred by having lost seven toes to frostbite on an earlier expedition. Even today, the missing digits of many explorers bear testament to the danger of frostbite, despite advances in clothing and protection.

1795—AFRICAN MEDICINE
Trained surgeon Mungo Park (see pp. 194–97) observes the writing of saphias—words written on a board, washed off, and the liquid drunk as a cure—during his expedition in search of the Niger River.

1804—INDIAN CURES
Lewis and Clark's Corps of Discovery (see pp. 174–77) carries simple medical supplies in Indian medicine bags for its exploration of the Louisiana Purchase.

1873—ANTIMALARIAL
David Livingstone (see pp. 220–23) and other explorers take quinine to combat malaria.

1910—*TERRA NOVA*
Antarctic explorer Cherry-Garrard suffers frostbite after two minutes without gloves.

1969—ASTRONAUT HEALTH
Apollo astronauts take eye drops, bandages, antibiotics, and painkillers into space.

1600 1650 1700 1750 1800 1850 1900 1950 2000

1740—PLAGUE OF THE SEA
More than 1,200 men die from scurvy on George Anson's voyage around the world (see pp. 148–49).

1820—QUININE
The drug is first extracted from the cinchona tree.

1953 OXYGEN TANKS
Hilllary and Tenzing use oxygen tanks on Mt Everest to combat the effects of altitude.

1753
JAMES LIND

British naval surgeon **James Lind** makes a study of **scurvy**. In an experiment (shown here), one group of sailors is given **two oranges and one lemon per day**, while others are given **normal rations**. The results are dramatic, as the citrus-eaters develop the disease more slowly. British sailors are the first to benefit from Lind's discovery, earning the nickname **"limeys"** from their policy of sailing with supplies of limes and other citrus fruit.

1871
CHARLES HALL

Following the death of Arctic expedition leader Charles Hall, his body is found to contain **high doses of arsenic, a notoriously poisonous metalloid**. Many medical preparations of the day, such as those shown here, **contain the poison in small doses**, and it is possible that a misjudgment in self-medication led to his death. Medicines containing arsenic have been **superseded by modern antibiotics** and other drugs.

NORTHERN ALLIANCES

THE EARLY EXPLORATION OF CANADA SAW INTENSE COMPETITION BETWEEN THE ENGLISH AND FRENCH TO SECURE CONTROL OF NORTHERN AMERICA. SOLDIERS, MISSIONARIES, AND FUR TRADERS ALL PLAYED THEIR PART IN THE EXPLORATION OF THE CANADIAN INTERIOR.

TRADING PLACES
The Hudson's Bay Company maintained an extensive network of trading posts, many of them in very isolated positions, such as this one in the Yukon Territory.

The first European landings in North America, by Norsemen sailing from Greenland in about 1000CE, did not lead to any permanent settlement. The continent was instead left to its indigenous peoples: in Canada, principally the Inuit, who occupied an arc of land from the northern St. Lawrence River through to the Arctic at the mouth of the Mackenzie River, and the Algonquians and Iroquois who lived to the south. While the Algonquians tended to be migratory fishermen and hunters, the Iroquois lived in large palisaded villages, which represented possibly the highest pre-Columbian population density in North America.

> Although the west coast of Canada was reached in 1793, much of its interior and that of the United States to the south was still unexplored, a process that was carried forward by Lewis and Clark in the following decade.

RETURN OF THE EUROPEANS

It was the Genoese John Cabot who made the next European landfall in Canada (see p. 92), reaching a point on the Labrador coast on June 24, 1497. He had been sponsored by King Henry VII of England, who feared that the English might be excluded from the spoils of the New World discovered by Christopher Columbus five years earlier (see pp. 86–89). The French began their long-standing rivalry with the English over North America with the arrival in 1524 of Giovanni da Verrazano, a Florentine in the service of Francis I of France, who surveyed the coast from New York and the Hudson River as far north as Newfoundland.

The Spanish-sponsored voyage of Esteban Gómez in 1524–25 attempted to enter the Gulf of St. Lawrence and skirted the Nova Scotia coastline, threatening to bring the area into the Spanish sphere. However, the Spanish did not follow up Gómez's voyage. Instead, it was the French who made the first real penetration of Canada, in the shape of Jacques Cartier (see pp. 130–31), who visited the Iroquois settlement of Stadacona on the future site of Quebec City in 1534.

The English, meanwhile, were preoccupied with the search for the hoped-for Northwest Passage around the tip of North America as an alternative means of reaching Asia. In 1576, Martin Frobisher discovered the strait that came to bear his name, while in 1585–86, John Davis found the Davis Strait and explored along the coast of Baffin Island and Labrador. English knowledge of the Canadian north was further extended by Henry Hudson (see pp. 286–87), who encountered Hudson Bay in 1610, and William Baffin, who in 1615-16, in the service of the Anglo-Russian Muscovy Company, entered Baffin Bay and sailed along the whole east coast of Baffin Island.

The French concentrated their explorations on the St. Lawrence Valley, where Samuel de Champlain (see pp. 126–27) founded Quebec, the oldest permanent settlement in Canada, in 1608. De Champlain's lieutenant, Étienne Brûlé, pushed even farther, becoming the first European to enter Lake Superior in 1621. Another of de Champlain's subordinates, Jean Nicolet, traveled up the Ottawa and Fox rivers in 1634 to reach the lands of the Winnebago Indians. Nicolet's curious habit of dressing in a Chinese silk robe—since he expected to encounter Asian peoples at any moment—led some local Indians to believe him to be a god.

MISSIONARY EXPLORERS

Increasingly, French exploration came to be led by Jesuit missionaries. In 1673, Father Jacques Marquette (see pp. 132–33) reached the Mississippi River and overwintered near Chicago. René de la Salle (see pp. 134–35) traveled down the Mississippi all the way to the Gulf of Mexico. By now, the territories of "New France"

BEAR NECESSITIES
Among the many hazards faced by fur traders was attack by bears, a danger that made necessary the use of bear traps such as this one.

BUYING SECURITY
Good relations with local Indian tribes were crucial for fur traders, who depended on their goodwill to cross the vast expanses of the Canadian interior in safety.

FUR POST
These hanging furs are at Lower Fort Garry, established by the Hudson's Bay Company as a trading station in 1830, and now the oldest surviving stone trading fort in North America.

SETTING THE SCENE

- There are indications that ships from Bristol, England, may have **fished the Newfoundland banks** even before John Cabot. In 1480, a ship under Captain Thylde sails in search of the island of "Brasylle" to the west of Ireland, but is forced back after nine months at sea.

- **The Iroquois** live in villages with **up to 100 longhouses**. In the 16th century, the villages group together in a **tribal confederacy** that resisted European encroachment. Known as the Iroquois League, it comprises five nations: the Mohawk, Oneida, Onondaga, Cayuga, and Seneca. The Tuscarora join in the 18th century.

- In 1501, the **Portuguese navigators Miguel and Gaspar Corte-Real** visit the Labrador and Newfoundland coasts, but the authorities in Lisbon fail to follow this up.

- **Quebec City**, the capital of New France, finally **falls to the English in 1759**. During the assault on the city, both the English and French commanders, James Wolfe and the Marquis de Montcalm, are mortally wounded.

- In 1821, the **Hudson's Bay Company** and **Northwest Company** merge. The combined company retains its monopoly on the fur trade until this is abolished in 1870.

were well-established, based around the colonial capital of Quebec, and reinforced by the establishment of new settlements such as Montreal, which was founded in 1642.

The fur trade was one of the principal economic motives for the exploration of Canada, both for the English and French. In 1670, the Hudson's Bay Company was established. It was to dominate the fur trade for two centuries and

provide a bulwark for English—and later British—interests in Canada. Henry Kelsey, an English trader for the Hudson's Bay Company, made the earliest penetration into the Canadian prairies in 1690–91, becoming the first European to encounter buffalo. (The account of his journey was lost until 1926.) His discoveries were not followed up until 1755, when the English trader, Anthony Henday, reached the Red Deer River in Alberta.

CROSSING THE CONTINENT

The rivalry between Britain and France ended with the British acquisition of almost all of "New France" by the Treaty of Paris, which ended the Seven Years' War in 1763. There was much left of Canada still to explore, however, and in 1770–72, the English fur trader Samuel Hearne reached the Coppermine River on the Arctic coast. By now the Hudson's Bay Company had a serious commercial rival in the shape of the Northwest Company, founded in 1779 in Montreal. It was a "Nor'wester," the Scottish fur trader Alexander Mackenzie, who set off to find a route across Canada to the Pacific. He was thwarted in his first effort, naming the waterway he thought would lead him to the coast the "River of Disappointment," but he succeeded in 1792–93 to become the first European to cross America north of the Spanish possessions in Mexico.

SEA TRAVEL
In the far north, the local Inuit (or in Alaska, the Aleut) traveled in sea kayaks constructed of seal skin stretched over a bone and driftwood frame.

SAMUEL DE CHAMPLAIN

FATHER OF "NEW FRANCE"

FRANCE   1580–1635

SOLDIER, NAVIGATOR, AND GEOGRAPHER, Samuel de Champlain established the first permanent French settlements in North America. He made many voyages to the continent, exploring the rivers and lakes around the St. Lawrence River, and considerably expanded the geographical knowledge of the area. He forged alliances with American Indian tribes, making a point of learning everything he could from them about this new land. He also fought several battles with the Iroquois, the sworn enemies of his new allies.

FOUNDING A MISSION
Samuel de Champlain (right) accompanied Father Joseph le Caron (center) to found a mission at Caragouba, now La Fontaine, Ontario, Canada on August 12, 1615.

De Champlain was born at Brouage on the Atlantic coast of France. His father and uncle were mariners and, as de Champlain grew up, it was natural for him to learn how to navigate and make charts. Following a period of service in the army of King Henri IV, de Champlain followed his father to sea. He learned his skills on board his uncle's ship, which was chartered to carry Spanish troops to the Caribbean in 1598. This voyage was to last two years.

At Portobelo in Panama, he observed that, "if the four leagues of land which there are from Panama to this river were cut through, one might pass from the South Sea to the ocean on the other side, and so shorten the route by more than 1,500 leagues …" This is one of the earliest written suggestions for a canal across Panama.

A LIFE'S WORK

- Explores the area around the eastern **Great Lakes**, making detailed maps

- Searches for an elusive path to the east and a **river route to the Arctic Ocean**

- Founds the first permanent settlement of New France on the site of **Quebec City**

- **Forges allegiances** with American Indian peoples, but begins a **long period of enmity** between French settlers and the Iroquois

On his return to France, de Champlain was made Royal Hydrographer in charge of producing coastal charts, and heard with fascination the fishermen's accounts of North America's Atlantic coast. In 1602, he received royal assent to join an expedition to "Nouvelle France" (New France) in North America.

EXPLORING NEW FRANCE

Arriving in the New World, de Champlain explored the area around Tadoussac, where the Saguenay River flows into the St. Lawrence River. He did not find a suitable site for a settlement or a trading post, but gathered much information about the Great Lakes and the possibility of a river route to the Arctic Ocean. His second voyage to New France began in 1604. He took with him 100 tradesmen, who it was hoped would form the nucleus of a new settlement. He explored the coast from the Bay of Fundy to Cape Cod, looking for possible sites. Two attempts to found a settlement failed due to the severity of the winter and scurvy. He described the symptoms of the latter: "their teeth became loose, and could be pulled out without causing them pain." On his third voyage in 1608, he established a settlement

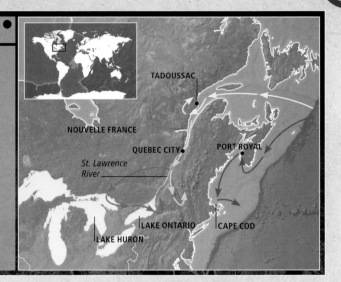

IN HIS FOOTSTEPS

→ **1603—To Nouvelle France**
De Champlain explores the Tadoussac for a suitable settlement site

→ **1604–06—Along the coast**
He sails as far south as the coast of present-day Massachusetts but fails to establish any settlements

→ **1608–09—Founds a settlement**
De Champlain founds a settlement on the site of Quebec City

→ **1615–16—Explores Great Lakes**
He explores the shores of Lake Huron and Lake Ontario

on the site of present-day Quebec City, 120 miles (200 km) up the St. Lawrence River from Tadoussac.

The following spring, de Champlain began a concerted effort to forge good relations with the local Indians, and made an alliance with the Huron and Algonquin. The agreement included a commitment to fight his new allies' great enemies, the Iroquois. To reach Iroquois territory, de Champlain and his allies paddled up the Richelieu River to the lake that now bears his name. There, his men were confronted by 200 Iroquois warriors. De Champlain killed two chiefs with one shot from his musket, and the warriors were put to flight. He returned to France in September 1609, but was back in New France in the spring of 1610, when he joined his Algonquin allies in another successful attack on the Iroquois. His aggression toward the tribe set the tone for Franco-Iroquois relations for the rest of the century.

DEFEAT OF THE IROQUOIS
Accompanied by his Indian allies, de Champlain is seen here attacking the Iroquois with musket fire, an unmatched battle that opened the way for French settlement of New France.

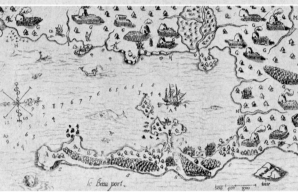

EXPLORER AND MAPMAKER
De Champlain made many maps, including this one of Gloucester Harbor in present-day Massachusetts, which he visited in 1606 and named "Beauport."

De Champlain made several more voyages to New France between 1611 and 1632, pushing farther up the St. Lawrence River to the present-day site of Montreal. But he failed to find a river route to the Pacific Ocean. Quebec was captured by the English in 1629, and de Champlain was taken back to England. The region was returned to the French in 1632, and de Champlain ended his days there in 1635.

THIS WINTER ALL OUR LIQUOR FROZE; CIDER WAS DISPENSED BY THE POUND

SAMUEL DE CHAMPLAIN

HAVEN IN CANADA
This manuscript map from 1542 shows French explorer Jacques Cartier and his crew disembarking in Canada with the coastline newly mapped. He made three voyages of exploration in dangerous, uncharted waters without once losing a ship, and entered and departed some 50 undiscovered harbors without serious mishap. Of all the great explorers, Cartier may be considered one of the most skilled seamen.

Rio de canada

JACQUES CARTIER

FRENCH PIONEER OF "NOUVELLE FRANCE"

FRANCE   1491–1557

JACQUES CARTIER WAS A COOL-HEADED sea captain with a genius for navigating dangerous coasts, charting new lands, and surviving hostile natives—without once losing a ship or facing a revolt from his men. He was the first European to map the great Gulf of St. Lawrence. While his original mission was to find a northwest passage to the East, his three expeditions were instrumental in staking the territory of present-day Canada for France.

A LIFE'S WORK

- Proves himself a **capable explorer and leader** by forging alliances with indigenous peoples whose loyalty is far from guaranteed, and not once faces an uprising from his men despite great hardships

- Invents the **name for Canada** by transcribing the Iroquois word for a settlement, *kannata*, which he mistakenly takes to be the indigenous name for the country itself

- Upon tasting the food of the Iroquois people, Cartier decries the **poor fare** of the New World, exclaiming, "they eate nothing that hath any taste of salt."

THE *GRANDE HERMINE*
The ship that Cartier piloted on his second voyage was a carrack, an ocean-going vessel of sufficient size to carry ample provisions and stable enough to withstand high seas.

Jacques Cartier was born in the port of Saint Malo on the northern coast of France in 1491. Little is known of his early career, but in 1533 he wrote to the high admiral of France, Philippe de Chabot, setting out his ambition: to sail along the American coast in search of new discoveries.

JOURNEY OF DISCOVERY

Cartier set sail on April 20, 1534 with three ships and 61 men. After crossing the Atlantic in just 20 days, he reached Newfoundland on May 10 but was obliged to harbor at a bay to the south, which he named St. Katherin's Haven, due to

"the great store of ice that was alongst the sayd land." Cartier continued north, passing through the narrow Strait of Belle Isle. He explored several "islettes," taking on plentiful supplies of duck eggs, and took "a good store of salmon" from the waters of the newly named St. James River. There, Cartier showed his navigational skill, steering his ships through the myriad shallow inlets, while carefully noting ocean depths and features for future mariners. He described the sighting of walruses, "beastes as great as oxen, which have two great teeth in

their mouths like unto Elephants." By mid-July 1534, bad weather had forced the ships to shelter at the Bay of Gaspé, where Cartier met a large fishing party of Iroquois. Their chief, Donnacona, objected to the construction of a "great Crosse" and Cartier's subsequent land claim for France. However, the chief permitted his sons Domagaya and Taignoagny to return to France with Cartier. Domagaya would later serve as an interpreter.

IN HIS FOOTSTEPS

➤ **1534—the Gulf of St. Lawrence**
Spends three months exploring the Gulf of St. Lawrence and its surrounding coastline and islands

➤ **1535–36—St. Lawrence River**
Returns to further explore the St. Lawrence River in search of a trade route to the East

○ **1541–42—Attempts to found a colony**
Now certain that no route to the East exists, Cartier returns as part of an expedition to colonize the area

○ Not shown on map

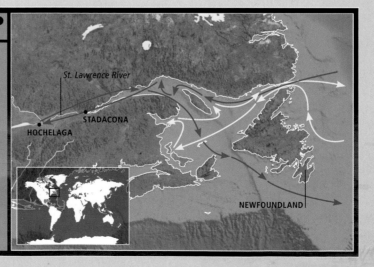

St. Lawrence River

STADACONA

HOCHELAGA

NEWFOUNDLAND

FOLLOWING THE RIVER
Believing that a channel he had sighted might hold a northwest passage to the East, Cartier set out on a second voyage in May 1535. During a 50-day crossing, the three vessels—the *Grande Hermine*, *Petite Hermine*, and *Emerillion*— were separated during severe Atlantic storms, but regrouped at Blanc Sablon on the Labrador

coast. Cartier sailed west into the channel and into the mouth of a great river, which he named the St. Lawrence, reaching Donnacona's settlement of Stadacona (in present-day Quebec) in September 1535. After continuing to the larger settlement of Hochelaga (present-day Montreal), Cartier observed from a nearby high point, which he named Mount Royal, that the St. Lawrence soon turned to rapids, precluding farther advance to the west.

NEW FRANCE

The party returned to Stadacona for the winter, building a small fort, since Cartier was uncertain of the Iroquois' true intentions. But in December a different enemy struck—"a strange and cruell disease"—scurvy. Eight French and 50 Iroquois died before a remedy was discovered by the interpreter Domagaya in March 1536. Tea made from the branches of the white cedar proved so

successful that a "tree as big as any Oake in France was spoiled and lopped bare." Once the ice had thawed in May, Cartier set sail for home, this time with Donnacona himself. In 1540, King François I sent Cartier on a third expedition to start the first colony in "Nouvelle France" (New France). He departed in May 1541, but was dogged by "contrary winds and continuall torrents" across the Atlantic. On arriving at Stadacona, he built the fort of Charlesbourg nearby, and was forced to rely on its protection when the Iroquois attacked later that year. Surviving the winter, Cartier sailed for France the following June with a cargo of precious stones and gold. But the true worth of his expeditions proved to be the strategic advantage that "New France" offered to the French state.

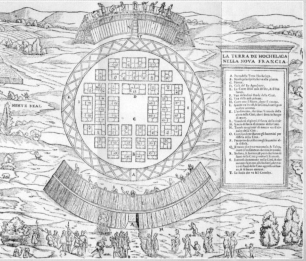

WOODEN CITY
Cartier was impressed by the city of Hochelaga (shown here), later writing: "There are in the town about 50 houses … built all of wood … very finely and cunningly joined."

DISCOVER ISLANDS … WHERE THERE ARE SAID TO BE GREAT QUANTITIES OF GOLD AND OTHER RICHES

KING FRANÇOIS I TO JACQUES CARTIER

PEACEFUL PIONEER
Cartier is shown here greeting tribes along the St. Lawrence River. The cordial relations he enjoyed with the indigenous people were a key factor in the success of his first and second expeditions. He deplored the cruel attitude shown by the Spanish elsewhere in the New World.

JOLLIET AND MARQUETTE

EXPLORERS OF THE UPPER MISSISSIPPI FOR FRANCE

FRENCH CANADA   1645–1700
FRANCE   1637–75

LOUIS JOLLIET

JACQUES MARQUETTE

FAITH AND EMPIRE were the factors driving the French navigation of the Mississippi during the 17th century. The great North American river had long been described to trappers and missionaries by the indigenous tribes of the area. Jolliet was the Quebec-born hardened explorer chosen by New France to follow the river to its southern end, while Marquette was the missionary selected by the Jesuits to take Christianity to the new lands.

Jacques Marquette was born at Laon, a city northeast of Paris, and entered the Jesuit order at the age of 17. He was sent as a missionary to the French colonies in present-day Canada in 1666, initially working in Quebec. Proving himself adept at the Huron language, he was sent west to a Jesuit mission at La Pointe, Lake Superior, in 1669. Louis Jolliet received a Jesuit education and chose the life of a fur trader. Born close to Quebec City, he had grown up well accustomed to the ways of the indigenous peoples.

IN SEARCH OF THE MISSISSIPPI

The two men were brought together for their missionary, linguistic, and expeditionary skills by the Comte de Frontenac, the governor of New France. Seeking to enhance his career,

NEVER IS THE SUN SO BRIGHT, O FRENCHMAN, AS WHEN THOU COMST TO VISIT US

ELDER OF THE PEORIAS TRIBE

A LIFE'S WORK

- Marquette masters six Indian tongues, despite being variously described by his teachers in France as **"mediocre," "bilious,"** and **"melancholic"**

- In addition to being a rugged explorer accustomed to the ways of indigenous peoples, Jolliet was an **accomplished musician**, adept at playing the harpsichord, flute, and trumpet

he sent them to see whether the river named by the Indians as the "Mississipy" flowed into the Gulf of Mexico or the Sea of Cortez.

In May 1673, they set out from St. Ignace, Michigan, in two bark canoes with a crew of five, carrying a small supply of corn and jerk meat. Paddling into Green Bay on Lake Michigan, Marquette described the water as "full of mischievous vapors, which cause the most grand and perpetual thunders." The men traveled on up the Fox River, pulling their canoes against the force of the rapids, and reached a village inhabited by the Miamis, Mascouten, and Kickapoo tribes.

At its center stood a large wooden cross, marking the farthest point yet reached by Europeans. The party left the village on June 10 with two Miamis guides, who led them—on foot and carrying their canoes—to the Wisconsin River. They followed this river with occasional difficulty due to sand banks, but the lushness of the vines and surrounding meadows impressed them. On June 17, Jolliet and Marquette reached the Mississippi River, the latter describing it as "a joy that I cannot express."

MISSIONARY ZEAL

Marquette was successful in helping to found several missions. It was at the mission of Sault Ste. Marie (now in Michigan) that he made contact with the Illinois people who described the Mississippi River.

WERE ILLINOIS AND IN TOKEN OF PEACE PRESENTED THE PIPE TO SMOKE

SMOKING THE PEACE PIPE
Jolliet and Marquette won the friendship of the indigenous populations of the Illinois River region, such as the Potawatomi tribe, who welcomed the French explorers with the offer of a peace pipe.

The two men found the Mississippi to be a place of welcome. Deer and buffalo were plentiful, and their first human contact came near the mouth of the Iowa River. Following footprints left on the bank to a small town, they were greeted by four elders, who described themselves—over a peace pipe—as the Peorias tribe of Illinois. A four-course feast was held in their honor, although the Frenchmen declined the third course of dog.

They left the village the next day with an escort of 600 men, but from this time were constantly on their guard, damping down fires and anchoring midstream during the night. Passing two great tributaries, the Missouri and Ohio rivers, they traveled downstream to the Akamscas (now Arkansas), where Marquette proffered his peace pipe to win the trust of the

FINAL JOURNEY
Marquette kept a promise to return to the Kaskaskia tribe on the Illinois River, despite being weakened by dysentery. He preached to 500 elders and 1,500 braves but died on May 18, 1675.

elders. They were invited to dine at a feast in return, and on this occasion, readily ate the dog and corn that was offered. Marquette also noted that the people used only stone tools.

Realizing that hostility from indigenous peoples was more likely the farther south they traveled, and also fearful of Spanish colonists into whose territories they were now venturing, they began to retrace their steps on July 17. One of the last indigenous groups they encountered

told them they were just 10 days from the Gulf of Mexico, thus confirming their observations that the Mississippi flowed south into the gulf.

Returning to the Illinois tribes, Marquette wrote "nowhere … did we see such grounds, meadows, woods, buffaloes, stags, deer, wildcats, bustards, swans, ducks, parroquets [sic], and even beavers." The party rejoiced on their return to Green Bay in September 1673. Although Jolliet's report to his superiors dashed any hope that the Mississippi might be a highway to the east, the mighty river proved to be the artery of future French colonial expansion into the district of Louisiana.

LOST RECORDS

Jolliet's logbook and maps were lost when his canoe overturned in the St. Louis rapids upstream of Montreal in May 1674, while a duplicate set that he had left with the Jesuit missionaries at St. Marie, Lake Superior was burned in a fire. Marquette's diary was also lost. The only record of the expedition comes from firsthand accounts given to Claude Dablon, the Superior General of Jesuit missions in Canada.

NEW FRANCE JOLLIET'S MAP OF 1673–74 INCLUDES THE UPPER MISSISSIPPI RIVER

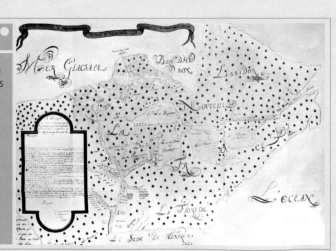

RENÉ-ROBERT DE LA SALLE

EXPLORER OF THE GREAT LAKES

FRANCE 1643–87

ALTHOUGH HE TOOK VOWS to become a priest, the young René-Robert de la Salle left the church lured by the prospect of a new life in America. He began his career as a pioneer farmer, but was eager to establish trade routes through the Great Lakes, and also to explore the "Father of the Rivers," the Mississippi, which he had heard about from Indian traders. This ambition would eventually lead him to explore the Mississippi basin, reaching the Gulf of Mexico and claiming the vast Louisiana Territory for France.

La Salle arrived in "Nouvelle France" in 1667 and joined his first expedition two years later, canoeing up the St. Lawrence River. The journey inspired in him ambitious ideas for a network of forts and river trading routes, which he took back to France with him in 1674. Impressed, King Louis XIV ennobled him, and gave him a grant of rights to the fort of Catarouci (which he renamed Fort Frontenac) on Lake Ontario, together with a fur-trading concession and permission to build frontier forts. La Salle set out from Quebec City in 1678 with

30 skilled craftsmen brought from France plus a number of local shipbuilders and carpenters. The party traveled upriver, reaching Fort Frontenac in December 1678, which was rebuilt in stone.

The following year, La Salle sent two of his party, Lucière and Hennepin, to explore the Niagara River. A boatyard was established at the site of present-day Buffalo, where a new, light ship, the *Griffon*, was constructed to enable trade between the Great Lakes—a prototype for future trade along the course of the Mississippi.

A NEW START
A 19th-century painting depicts La Salle's colonists sailing for Louisiana in 1684. La Salle mistakenly landed west of the Mississippi delta, a navigational error that cost him his life when the colonists mutinied.

IN HIS FOOTSTEPS

→ **1678–80—Around the Lakes**
In an attempt to set up trading routes around the Great Lakes, La Salle paddles through the lakes and down the Illinois River to build Fort Crèvecoeur

→ **1681–82—Down the Mississippi**
From Fort Crèvecoeur, La Salle reaches the Mississippi River and paddles down to the Gulf of Mexico

→ **1684–87—Ill-fated return**
La Salle arrives in the Gulf of Mexico with hundreds of colonists from France, but he cannot find the Mississippi and is killed in a mutiny

MONTREAL
FT FRONTENAC
St. Lawrence River
BUFFALO
Illinois River
FT CRÈVECOEUR
The *Griffon* is lost in Lake Ontario, presumed to have been attacked by the Ottawa Indians
Mississippi River
MISSISSIPPI DELTA
MATAGORDA BAY
GULF OF MEXICO

The ship was despatched for Fort Frontenac loaded with a cargo of fur, but was lost, presumed to have been attacked by Indians.

TRIPLE MISADVENTURE

La Salle paddled along the St. Joseph and Illinois rivers, establishing a fort he named Fort Crèvecoeur before returning overland to Frontenac. The overland journey lasted an arduous 65 days through uncharted land. On reaching Niagara, however, La Salle found that the *Griffon* was lost. He continued on to Frontenac and to further bad news: he had been reported dead and his creditors had seized the fort. Even worse, La Salle then returned to Fort Crèvecoeur to find it had been destroyed in a mutiny. His first attempt to establish a trading network had failed. He returned to the Illinois River in June 1681. From the rebuilt Fort Crèvecoeur, he pushed on west, reaching the Mississippi on February 6, 1682. Traveling with a French and Indian crew, he canoed downstream and reached the delta of the Mississippi on April 6. Sighting the Gulf of Mexico, he claimed the Mississippi and the surrounding lands for the French crown, naming it "Louisiana" in honor of Louis XIV. Sorties were made around the gulf before La Salle retraced the journey upstream to the Illinois River. There, he constructed a new fort, Saint-Louise, which became a highly successful fur trading post.

FATAL RETURN

La Salle returned to France in triumph, having found a new territory ideal for colonization. Colonists rallied to him and in July 1684, he set a course for the Mississippi delta with four ships full of settlers for the new Louisiana. The voyage was to end in disaster. After surviving attacks from Spanish pirates in the Gulf of Mexico, La Salle mistook Matagorda Bay on the coast of Texas for the Mississippi. The colonists

OPENING UP THE LAKES
This stained-glass mural depicts La Salle landing at the site of present-day Detroit in Michigan.

landed, but shortly afterward the store ship was wrecked on a reef, with great loss of supplies. Realizing his mistake, La Salle made three failed attempts to reach the Mississippi overland. Finally, in 1687, he was shot dead by mutineers, whose dream of a new life had turned sour. La Salle's life had ended in failure, but in the decades to come, the French would consolidate the routes he had opened, building new forts and colonizing the vast territory of Louisiana.

BUILDING ALLIANCES
La Salle established good relations with the tribes he met and even learned the Iroquois language. Here, he is pictured enjoying a feast with the Illinois, a confederation of tribes who lived around the upper Mississippi.

SAILING AROUND THE WORLD

THE FIRST CIRCUMNAVIGATION OF THE EARTH WAS ACHIEVED IN THE 16TH CENTURY, BUT IT WAS NOT UNTIL THE MID-18TH CENTURY THAT THE DETERMINATION OF LONGITUDE AT SEA BECAME POSSIBLE, ALLOWING CARTOGRAPHERS TO CREATE ACCURATE WORLD MAPS FOR THE FIRST TIME.

GLOBE TROTTER
In 1577–80, Francis Drake's galleon, the *Golden Hind*, sailed around the world. On his return to England, he was richly rewarded for his exploits against the Spanish along the way.

Early Greek maps, such as that of Anaximander of Miletus (610–546BCE), had portrayed the world as a flattened disk, surrounded by an Ocean of unspecified (or limitless) size. The philosopher Aristotle (384–322BCE), by contrast, was firmly convinced of the Earth's spherical nature, using simple observations such as the shape of the Earth's shadow on the Moon during an eclipse to bolster his case. In about 325BCE, the Greek explorer Pytheas of Marseilles (see pp. 20–21) took accurate readings of latitude, determining that of his hometown. Eratosthenes (c. 274-19BCE) devised a map with divisions called *sphragides* ("seals"), prefiguring the grid system of modern maps. The greatest cartographer of the ancient world, Ptolemy of Alexandria (c. 90–168CE), experimented with different projections to make the portrayal on a flat map approximate to a sphere. Ptolemy's great treatise, *Guide to Geography*, would remain the authoritative reference on world geography for the next 1,500 years.

EXPANDING HORIZONS

Although eventually it became widely accepted that the Earth was spherical, the idea of actually sailing around it did not take hold until Columbus's discovery of the Americas (see pp. 86–89). Up till then, the concept had been considered too far-fetched. When the Spanish and Portuguese occupation of the New World got underway, however, the voyages of Vasco da Gama (see pp. 80–81) and his successors led to similar European empires around the Indian Ocean. Now, linking these two new spheres of European activity became a prime objective.

FIRST CIRCUMNAVIGATOR
Ferdinand Magellan died in a skirmish on the island of Mactan in the Philippines in April 1521, some 19 months after he had set sail from Spain. Although he failed to make it home, he is credited with the first major attempt to circle the Earth.

THE TIME AT SEA
The English watchmaker John Harrison finally solved the problem of measuring longitude at sea when he invented a chronometer that could keep good time on rough oceans.

VOLCANIC DISCOVERY
This volcano is located on Bougainville Island, which was named after the French explorer Louis Antoine de Bougainville (see pp. 150–51), who completed a circumnavigation in 1769.

see pp. 150–51

SETTING THE SCENE

- Parmenides of Elea (*c.* 480BCE), a disciple of the great Greek mathematician Pythagoras, **teaches that the Earth should be regarded as a sphere** (although on no better grounds than that this form is a symbol of perfection).

- **Magellan's circumnavigation is completed by his subordinate Juan Elcano**, who brings Magellan's remaining ship, the *Vittoria*, back to Spain in September 1522.

- **Louis Antoine de Bougainville** leads the first French expedition to circumnavigate the Earth, in 1766–69, **losing only seven of his 200 crewmen to scurvy**, a far lower death toll than on previous, similar voyages.

- Larcum Kendall's improved model **pocket watch, the K2** is taken by **Captain William Bligh** on the ill-fated voyage that ended in the mutiny on the *Bounty* in 1789.

- In 1898, American Joshua Slocum completes **the first single-handed circumnavigation** aboard a small yacht called the *Spray*.

- The **first nonstop circumnavigation** is achieved in 1968–69 by English yachtsman Robin Knox-Johnson in the ketch *Suhali*.

FINAL SUCCESS

The first sighting of the Pacific Ocean by a European, Vasco Núñez de Balboa (see pp. 120–21), took place in April 1514. By this time, the Spanish were already challenged by the problem of reaching the Moluccas, or the Spice Islands, without having to sail around Africa and pass through the Indian Ocean—territory contested by their Portuguese rivals. So it was that Ferdinand Magellan (see pp. 138–41) set sail from Sanlúcar de Barrameda in September 1519, entering the Pacific by the storm-lashed strait at the tip of South America that came to bear his name. Although Magellan died in the Philippines, the survivors of the expedition reached Tidore in the Spice Islands in November 1521. It was, however, almost as an afterthought that they continued westward to reach home, thereby achieving the first circumnavigation of the world.

As the 16th century wore on, the number of nations that could claim their own circumnavigation multiplied, with Francis Drake (see pp. 144–45) becoming the first Englishman to achieve it in 1577–80 and Olivier van Noort doing so for the Dutch in 1598–1601. In 1711, the English privateer and explorer William Dampier (see pp. 146–47) became the first man to circle the globe three times.

By Dampier's time, the problem was not so much that of circumnavigation, but of accurately determining one's location. Although

> In the 18th century, navigators turned from the pursuit of circumnavigations to maritime exploration of specific regions, such as the South Pacific, or the search for a navigable seaway to the north of the Americas.

it was possible to calculate latitude at sea with some ease using the length of the day, the height of the Sun at noon, or the relative position of certain stars, the accurate determination of longitude was far more difficult. In order to do so, navigators had to compare the time at their location to that in their home port. Changing the clock on the ship at noon each time and taking the difference between this and the home port would in theory allow seamen to calculate the distance between these two points (at 15 degrees of longitude, or 1,000 miles [1,600 km] per hour). Unfortunately, the most accurate clocks of the time, driven by pendulums, were very unreliable at sea.

LONGITUDINAL PROBLEM

In 1714, the British parliament offered a handsome reward to anyone who was able to solve the longitude problem. In 1731, John Hadley invented the octant, a combination of a mobile arm and mirror to observe the Moon and celestial horizon. In combination with tables of the Moon's positions, it ought to have allowed the calculation of the time on a ship at sea, but it turned out not to be accurate enough.

In 1736, the Yorkshire clockmaker John Harrison tested a newly devised clock, H1, which had a host of features to counteract the normal malfunctioning of chronometers at sea, including a pendulum made of two metals, brass and steel, allowing Harrison to compensate for their expansion and cooling as temperatures varied. Harrison was never awarded the full prize money, but was granted a lesser amount for his most advanced version, the H4, in 1773.

A copy of H4, made by another clockmaker, Larcum Kendall, and named the K1, was taken by James Cook (see pp. 156–59) on his second voyage to the South Pacific in 1772–75. Cook highly praised its accuracy compared to the use of lunar tables. By 1815, there were an estimated 5,000 chronometers in use on ships worldwide, so that mariners could now crisscross or even circumnavigate the globe, confident in the knowledge that they would always be able to determine their location with reasonable accuracy.

EVOLUTION TIMEPIECE
Chronometers had become so common in the early 19th century that when HMS *Beagle*, with Charles Darwin aboard, set out in 1831, the ship had 22 of them.

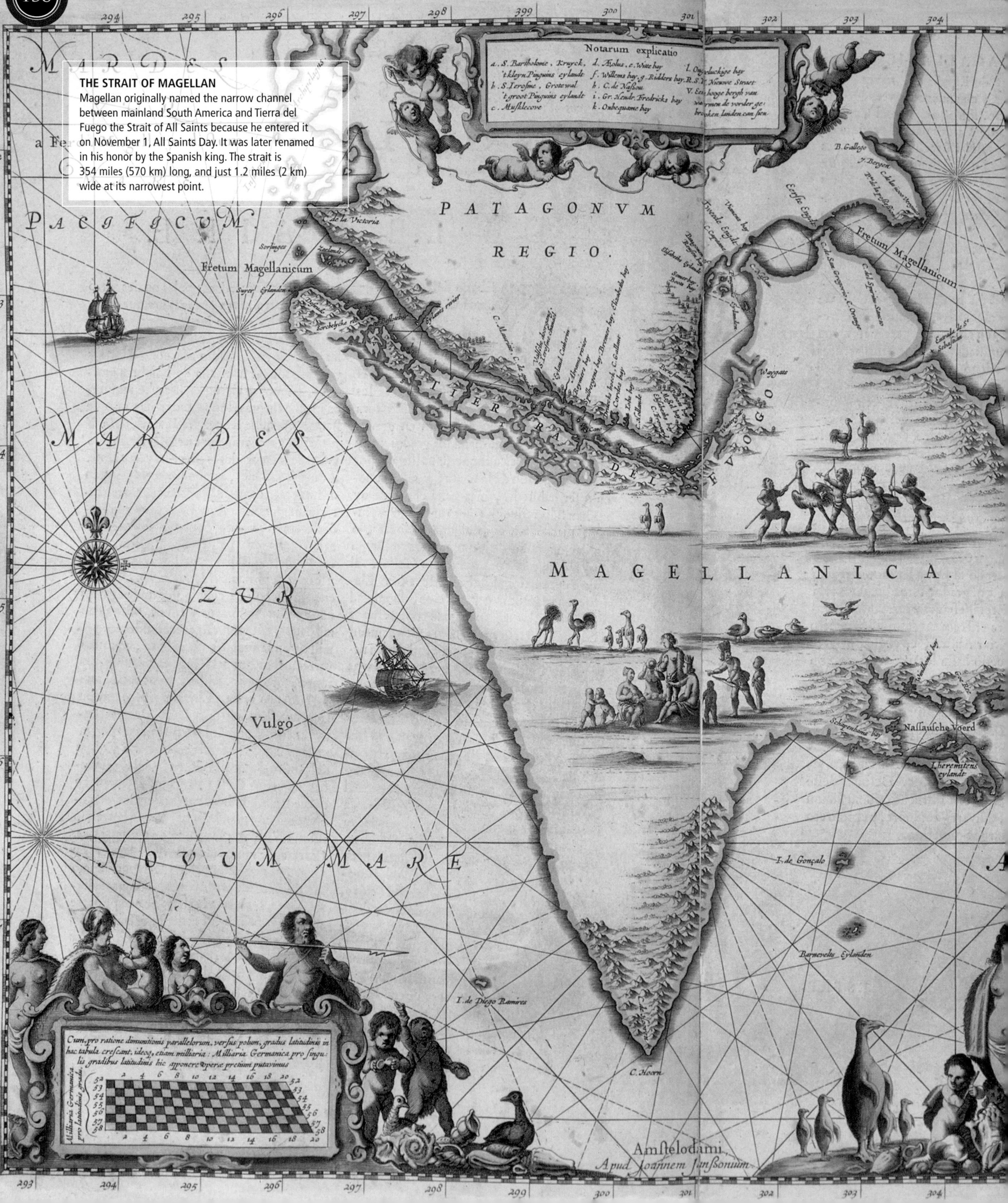

294 295 296 297 298 399 300 301 302 303 304

M A R D E S

PACIFICVM

52

a Fe

O

THE STRAIT OF MAGELLAN
Magellan originally named the narrow channel
between mainland South America and Tierra del
Fuego the Strait of All Saints because he entered it
on November 1, All Saints Day. It was later renamed
in his honor by the Spanish king. The strait is
354 miles (570 km) long, and just 1.2 miles (2 km)
wide at its narrowest point.

Notarum explicatio

a . S. Bartholome . Kruyck .   d . Aolus .   e . Witte bay .   l . Ongeluckige bay
'tkleyn Pinguins eylandt   f . Willems bay .   g . Ridders bay . R.S.T. Nieuwe Struet
b . S. Ierosme . Grotewal .   h . C. de Nassou .   V. Eers hooge bergh van
't groot Pinguins eylandt .   i . Gr. Hendr. Fredricks bay   waer men de voorder ge-
c . Musflecove .   k . Onbequame bay .   breuken luiden can sien .

B. Gallego

de la Victoria

Soringes

Fretum Magellanicum

PATAGONVM

REGIO.

Fretum Magellanicum

53

M A R D E S

54

Z V R

MAGELLANICA.

55

Vulgo

56

N O V V M   M A R E

I. de Gonçalo

57

Barnevelts Eylanden

I. de Diego Ramires

Cum, pro ratione dimuutionis parallelorum, verfus polum, gradus latitudinis in
hac tabula crefcant, ideoq; etiam milliaria : Milliaria Germanica pro fingu-
lis gradibus latitudinis hic apponere operæ pretium putavimus

C. Hoorn

58

293 294 295 296 297 298 299 300 301 302 303 304

FERDINAND MAGELLAN

MARINER OF NAVIGATIONAL GENIUS

PORTUGAL   1480–1521

IN ONE OF THE GREATEST FEATS of courage in maritime history, Ferdinand Magellan led a major expedition in search of a western route to Asia. Despite mutinous crews, foul weather, and starvation, Magellan showed a navigational genius in rounding South America and crossing the Pacific Ocean, only to be killed while aiding a local chief in a war in the Philippines. Eventually, his expedition was continued by Juan Sebastián Elcano, whose small band of survivors completed the first circumnavigation of the globe.

Magellan's first experience at sea came in March 1505, when he joined the fleet of warships sent to enforce the Portuguese monopoly on trade around the Cape of Good Hope. He was injured in battles at Cannanore, India, and on the island of Diu in the Indian Ocean, as the Portuguese consolidated their control of shipping routes. Magellan was in the city of Malacca (in present-day Malaysia) in the summer of 1511 when it was successfully taken for the Portuguese crown. There, he received letters

LAST SHIP HOME
Of the five ships that left Seville, only the *Vittoria* returned, carrying just 18 of the original 237 crew.

from the Portuguese explorer, Fransisco Serrão, who had made the earliest recorded European visit to the Moluccas Islands farther east of Malacca. The letters told of the great riches of the islands, including pepper, cinnamon, ginger, and cloves: all highly prized in Europe. In his accounts, Serrão exaggerated the distance of the islands from Malacca, a fact that would have a profound impact on the course of Magellan's career.

SWITCHING ALLEGIANCE

In July 1512, Magellan volunteered to join an expedition to Morocco, where he served in the Battle of Azamor against the Moors. Despite a Portuguese victory, Magellan was accused of the unauthorized sale of cattle to the enemy. This badly affected his status at court. Although the charge was eventually dismissed, his request to return to the Moluccas Islands was refused by King Manuel I. His career blighted, Magellan looked to Spain for new opportunities. He arrived in Seville in southern Spain in October 1517, and soon set about studying Serrão's

A LIFE'S WORK

- **Leaves Portugal** in disgrace after he is falsely accused of **trading with the enemy**

- Puts down **a mutiny** by two of his **Spanish captains**, who resent being led by a Portuguese commander

- Is the first to successfully navigate **the Magellan Strait** from the Atlantic to the Pacific

- Takes up arms on behalf of **a local chief** in the Philippines to fight the chief's rival, and is killed in the battle by a **poison arrow**

- Magellan's expedition is taken on by **Elcano**, who completes **the first circumnavigation**

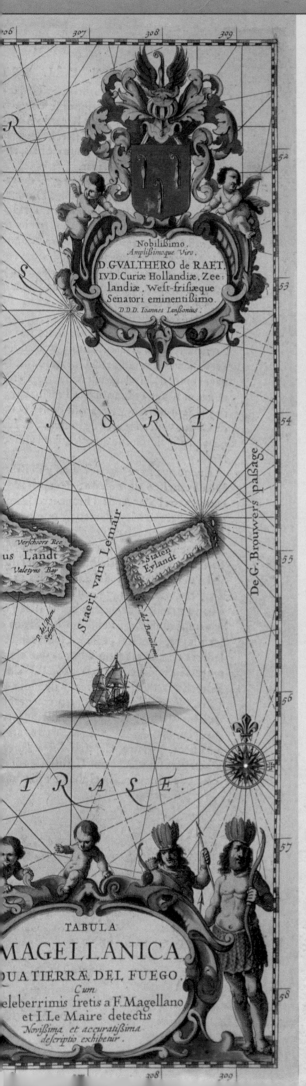

Nobilißimo, Amplißimoque Viro
D. GVALTHERO de RAET,
IVD. Curiæ Hollandiæ, Zee-
landiæ, West-frisiæque
Senatori eminentißimo.
D.D.D. Ioannes Lanßonius.

TABULA

MAGELLANICA,
QUA TIERRÆ DEL FUEGO,
Cum
celeberrimis fretis a F. Magellano
et I. Le Maire detectis
Novißima et accuratißima
descriptio exhibetur.

account to work out the location of the Moluccas Islands. Under the 1494 Treaty of Tordesillas, Spain and Portugal had agreed to an east–west division of the New World, with all unclaimed territories to the east of an imaginary line falling to Portugal, and those to the west falling to Spain. Magellan's calculations placed the Moluccas so far to the east of Malacca that they fell into Spain's western half of the world. King Charles I granted him an audience at the court of Valladolid, excited by the prospect of neutralizing Portugal's control of the route east by finding an alternative western route to the riches of Asia. Magellan promptly renounced his Portuguese nationality and was granted leadership of the expedition.

TROUBLE IN THE RANKS

A fleet of five vessels set sail from Seville in August 1519, with Magellan in command of the flagship, *Trinidad*. They sailed south along the west coast of Africa, crossing the equator in October 1519, then headed southwest. They touched the coast of Brazil in December and reached the Bay of Guanabara (Rio de Janeiro) by Christmas Day. The ships maintained contact through an elaborate system of daytime sail signals. At night, each ship sailed sufficiently close to the *Trinidad* for watchmen to hail the flagship. As the voyage progressed, however, resentment grew toward Magellan's dictatorial methods. Two of the captains led a mutiny against him, but it failed to win enough support from the crew to succeed. Magellan had one of the rebellious captains beheaded, while the other was left marooned on the coast.

INTO THE STRAIT

As the voyage continued south, Magellan's assistant, Antonio Pigafetta, charged with keeping a journal of the voyage, recorded the marvels of the new landscape, including the discovery of the pineapple, which he described as "like huge round cones, but very

PATAGONIAN PENGUINS
Magellan recorded seeing small birds that swam in the sea as he passed the coast of Patagonia. These little penguins are now called Magellanic penguins.

sweet and more tasteful than any other fruit." He also noted the large-footed local Indians, who came to be known as "Patagones."

On October 21, 1520, Magellan came to the strait that now bears his name, where he observed fires on the shores of the inhospitable coast, naming it *Tierra del Fuego* (Land of Fire). The fleet endured a grueling 38-day voyage through the strait. Short of rations, Magellan knew he had to continue forward. One ship was wrecked, while another deserted and returned to Spain, taking with it vital food supplies. In November, the three remaining ships—the *Vittoria*, *Trinidad*, and *Concepción*—emerged into a still ocean lit by a golden sunset. Magellan broke down and wept, and named the ocean the Pacific, for its calm waters.

PACIFIC ORDEAL

Like Columbus before him, Magellan had grossly underestimated the circumference of the globe. He calculated it would take three days, perhaps four, to cross the Pacific and reach the Moluccas. As errors go, it was a major one. The journey across the immense ocean went on for month after month, and the men began to starve. Pigafetta described the condition of the men: "We [had] passed three months and

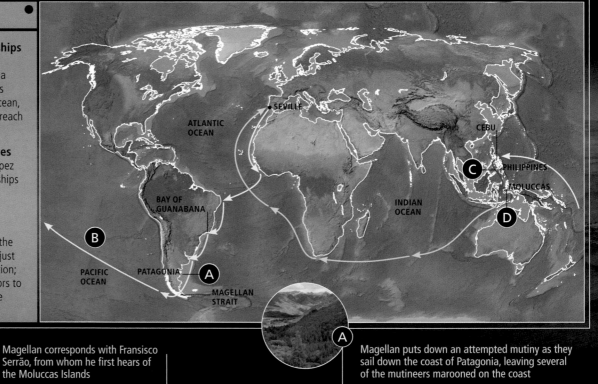

IN THEIR FOOTSTEPS

→ **1519–21—Magellan's fleet of five ships sets sail from Seville**
Magellan has been charged with finding a western route to the Moluccas; he rounds South America and crosses the Pacific Ocean, but dies in the Philippines before he can reach the Moluccas

→ **1521—Confusion after Magellan dies**
Command is eventually taken by João Lopez Carvalho, who leads the two remaining ships on a slow six-month voyage through the Philippines to the Moluccas

→ **1521–22—Journey home**
Elcano takes charge of the last ship left, the *Vittoria*, and sails it back to Europe with just 17 other original members of the expedition; they reach Spain to become the first sailors to complete a circumnavigation of the globe

SEVILLE

ATLANTIC OCEAN

CEBU

C

PHILIPPINES

BAY OF GUANABANA

INDIAN OCEAN

MOLUCCAS

D

PACIFIC OCEAN

PATAGONIA

A

MAGELLAN STRAIT

B

A

Magellan corresponds with Fransisco Serrão, from whom he first hears of the Moluccas Islands

Magellan puts down an attempted mutiny as they sail down the coast of Patagonia, leaving several of the mutineers marooned on the coast

Magellan sails to India in a fleet of

On emerging from the turbulent B

twenty days without obtaining any provisions, eating powdered biscuit, riddled with worms … rats were sold for half a ducat each, and even then they could not be got." Magellan had thrown his remaining charts overboard in despair when, after three and a half months, the three ships sailed into the Ladrones Islands (the present-day Marianas) to take on much needed supplies. They had missed several islands that were near their route.

MAGELLAN DIES

Magellan continued through the Philippines to the island of Cebu, where he agreed to take up arms on behalf of the local chief. It was a grave mistake. He was killed on the neighboring island of Mactan by a chief named Lapu-Lapu in a skirmish on April 27, 1521.

Following further skirmishes, too few crew were left to sail all three ships, so one was abandoned. Just one ship, the *Vittoria*, under the command of Elcano (see right), made it back to

AGILE FLEET
Magellan's ship, the *Trinidad*, (depicted here in the strait) was a caravel—an agile design with lanteen sails. The rest of the fleet were carracks—small ships with square rigging.

Spain, arriving on September 8, 1522, to complete the first circumnavigation of the world. Just 18 of the original crew of 237 had made it all the way around. Four survivors from the *Trinidad* eventually returned home via India.

JUAN SEBASTIÁN ELCANO
PORTUGAL   1486–1526

Elcano was a ship's master aboard the *Concepción* on Magellan's expedition. He took part in the failed mutiny and spent five months in forced onboard labor, but went on to bring the last ship back home.

When Magellan was killed in the Philippines, command was initially taken jointly by Duarte Barbosa and João Serrão. Both were killed just days later in a massacre at a feast held by this same chief. Under the weak leadership of João Lopez Carvalho, with Elcano now second-in-command, the remaining two ships spent the next six months sailing slowly through the Philippines. On November 6, 1521, they finally reached the Moluccas Islands, Magellan's original destination, where they loaded up with spices. The day they were due to leave, the *Trinidad* sprung a leak, so it was agreed upon that Elcano would forge ahead in the *Vittoria*, taking 17 European survivors and four Timorese men with him. They reached Spain eight months later. Elcano was awarded a coat of arms by King Charles I featuring a globe and the motto *Primus circumdedisti* ("You went around me first" in Latin). In 1525, Elcano embarked on a second circumnavigation of the globe, but he died of malnutrition while crossing the Pacific.

BATTLE OF MACTAN
A fanciful depiction shows the moment of Magellan's death on Mactan beach, surrounded by hordes of hostile islanders. A monument subsequently built on the site records the foolhardiness of Magellan and the heroism of his killer.

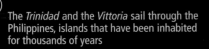

C   The *Trinidad* and the *Vittoria* sail through the Philippines, islands that have been inhabited for thousands of years

D   Upon reaching the Moluccas, the remaining ships take on cargoes of spices; the *Trinidad* springs a leak, so the *Vittoria* sets sail on its own

Elcano dies while crossing the Pacific in an attempt at a second circumnavigation of the globe

1521   **1521–22**   1522–26

Elcano reaches Spain, where he is ennobled by King Charles I for his achievement; Antonio Pigafetta is among the survivors and brings back his detailed journal of the voyage

EXPERIENCING LIFE...

ON BOARD SHIP

THE FUNDAMENTALS OF SAILING the ocean waves have always remained constant. From the Mediterranean voyages of the Phoenicians and the emigrations of the Vikings, to the Portuguese navigators who charted far-flung coasts, mariners have always needed to read the winds and the tides. Technology has added to seafaring expertise, increasing maritime safety and precision, and the risk of mutiny or disease has all but vanished. However, the sea remains dangerous and unpredictable, so that even today crossing the world's oceans by ship is not always plain sailing.

LASHINGS OF BEER

Beer was given to sailors on British Navy ships in the 18th century, and was even brewed by William Parry on his 1821 Arctic expedition. As a brewed drink, it was less likely to harbor dangerous bacteria than casked water or supplies from local sources. Parry issued canned meat, vinegar, lime juice, and sugar to his men rather than ship's biscuits. He even used mold on a warm pipe in his cabin to grow mustard and cress.

SEA BISCUIT
Washed down with beer from the keg, the ship's biscuit, made with flour, water, and salt was a long-life ship's staple.

SEAFARERS' SCOURGE

From the expansion of maritime exploration in the 15th century, scurvy was one of the biggest killers of sailors. One of the most significant losses of life occurred during George Anson's global circumnavigation (see pp. 148–49), when two-thirds of the crew died. Scottish naval surgeon James Lind conducted an experimental trial among scurvy sufferers in 1747, proving the effectiveness of citrus fruit as a cure. He varied the diets of separate groups, and those who ate oranges and lemons recovered fully. In 1753, Lind published *A Treatise on Scurvy*, which also explained that sailors should wash and shave regularly, and the ship should be fumigated below decks. Nevertheless, scurvy remained a killer of sailors and polar explorers well into the 20th century, and it was not until the discovery of the cause—a lack of vitamin C—by US scientists Albert Szent-Györgyi and Charles King in 1932 that the disease was eradicated.

DEALING WITH COASTAL HAZARDS

Coral reefs and sand banks posed a major challenge to pilots in the 16th century. Smaller boats could be deployed to reach the shore, while the lead-line system was used to calculate depths. This involved a "leadsman" attaching a lead weight or "plummet" to a line to establish the depth of water. For the major scientific expeditions of the late 18th and early 19th centuries, smaller, more maneuverable ships were commissioned that were more suitable for sailing in shallow waters. While sailing on board the *Beagle*, Charles Darwin (see pp. 278–81) formulated his theory of how coral atolls are formed, enabling mariners to be better prepared for sudden changes in depth around coral formations.

RUN AGROUND
After sustaining storm damage near Cuba, Columbus's *Santa Maria* was wrecked off the coast of Jamaica in June 1503.

NAVIGATING AT SEA

A range of instruments evolved over the centuries to assist navigation on the high seas (see pp. 82–83). The astrolabe, compass, and sextant were followed in 1764 by the chronometer. Invented by British horologist John Harrison, it enabled mariners to fix their longitude and establish a position at sea. The use of nautical almanacs further enhanced the knowledge of the maritime navigator. A further advance was made for Antarctic exploration in the early 20th century, in the form of the gyroscopic compass.

ANTARCTIC NAVIGATION
This gyroscopic compass, which can find true north despite magnetic disturbance, was used on the 1910–13 *Terra Nova* expedition.

THE MISERY I ENDURED FROM SEASICKNESS IS FAR BEYOND WHAT I EVER GUESSED AT

CHARLES DARWIN

LIFE ON THE OCEAN WAVES

A strict onboard routine while at sea was long held to be the key to maintaining a healthy crew. In addition to his dietary innovations, William Parry introduced several precautions to ensure the well-being of his sailors during the long Arctic winter. The decks were cleared so that the men could exercise, by running while singing to organ music. The men's minds were kept active with the foundation of an expedition newspaper, *The North Georgia Gazette and Winter Chronicle*, while theatrical performances were staged by the Royal Arctic Theater. On Sundays, church services were held.

Daily inspections were made of the men, their clothes, and bedding in order that any infestations might be caught at an early stage. Hygiene below decks was improved by replacing bunks with hammocks, which enabled air to circulate. The men were also divided into four watches, with each watch responsible for wiping the interior of the ship with cloths in order to avoid the build up of humidity and ice.

MUTINOUS MARINERS

MUTINY ON THE HIGH SEAS
After spending a harsh winter stuck fast in the ice of Hudson Bay (now Canada), Henry Hudson was cast adrift by his tired, rebellious crew in June 1611. Nothing was heard of him again.

During the expansion of seafaring in the 15th and 16th centuries, crews were often poorly clothed, ill-equipped, untrained, and press-ganged. Sailing into the unknown, superstition combined with a fear of danger often resulted in mutinous feelings toward the ship's officers. The Spanish and Portuguese captains attempted to instill discipline through regular daily prayers, while promises of future reward were often made to motivate crewmen and masters alike. Perceived weakness in command— or the fact that the commander was a foreigner, as in the case of Ferdinand Magellan (see pp. 138–41) in 1519— could lead to outright mutiny. The penalty for mutiny might be death, the lash, or marooning on a foreign shore, as experienced by Magellan's second-in-command Juan de Cartagena. Mutiny became less common with the establishment of set routes, regular trading patterns, and formalized crew conditions, which removed some of the motivations for disobedience on board ship.

MAN THE PUMPS!
As first experienced by Captain Cook, sea conditions in the Southern Ocean are among the most severe in the world. Here, the *Terra Nova* bucks and rolls in a gale off Antarctica in 1912 as water is pumped from the ship.

FRANCIS DRAKE

PRIVATEER, BUCCANEER, EXPLORER

ENGLAND   C. 1540–96

ARISE, SIR FRANCIS
So as not to antagonize the Spanish, Drake's booty-laden return was not celebrated publicly. He was knighted by Queen Elizabeth in a low-key ceremony on board the *Golden Hinde*.

BEST KNOWN IN BRITAIN for his defeat of the Spanish Armada in 1588, Francis Drake is remembered in the Spanish-speaking world as a pirate of the high seas. His raids on Spanish vessels accumulated an enormous fortune for his secret sponsor—the English monarch, Queen Elizabeth I. As an explorer, Drake completed the second circumnavigation of the globe, and was the first captain to make it all the way around. During the voyage, he became the first European to land at present-day California.

Drake's flamboyant career as a ship's captain began on voyages running slaves between West Africa and America. He made several journeys to the Caribbean, where he crossed the Isthmus of Darién. When he first set eyes on the Pacific Ocean he felt a burning ambition to sail over it.

The journey that would fulfill this ambition began in 1577. Drake set sail in December with a fleet of five ships, including his flagship, the *Pelican*. Only one ship would make it all the way. The fleet reached the Bay of Montevideo (in present-day Uruguay) in April of the following year. As the fleet negotiated a

LUCKY DRUM
Drake carried this snare drum on his travels. According to legend, whenever England is in danger, the drum beats of its own accord.

passage south, a Spanish pilot, Nuno da Silva, was captured and, under duress, aided Drake's navigation down the coast of Patagonia. In August 1578, three of the five vessels sailed into Port St. Julian, where they would spend the winter before tackling the treacherous Strait of Magellan. Two boats had already been abandoned due to the loss of so many crew members. At Port St. Julian, they found the gibbet that Magellan had used 50 years earlier to execute mutineers (see pp. 138–41). Bad weather and heavy losses had been fomenting similar discontent among member of Drake's crew. One of the conspirators was Drake's close friend, Thomas Doughty. Found to be working for the Spanish, Doughty was summarily executed.

RAIDS ON THE SPANISH
As winter abated, the three vessels sailed on for the Pacific. One boat sank in heavy seas, and the remaining two ships became separated. Nonetheless, Drake pressed on in the *Pelican*, now renamed the *Golden Hinde*, and carried out a series of dramatic raids on Spanish vessels and land stores, taking valuable booty. Drake then made sail for home. En route, he landed at what would become Port San

Francisco, where, according to contemporary accounts, the native Californians "supposed the Englishmen to be gods, and would not be persuaded to the contrary."

The *Golden Hinde* left the Americas in July 1579, and Drake kept detailed records of the route he took back home, passing the Philippines and the East Indies before rounding the Cape of Good Hope. He arrived back in Portsmouth in September 1580 to become the first captain to circumnavigate the globe (Magellan before him having died halfway around). The *Golden Hinde* was laden with Spanish treasure of such value that investors in Drake's voyage, including Queen Elizabeth I, received £47 for every £1 invested. Drake was duly knighted by a grateful monarch, whose share of the spoils enabled the crown to pay off England's national debt.

Drake's circumnavigation was to be overshadowed by his later achievements, notably his leading role in the defeat of the Spanish Armada in 1588. However, with this important voyage, he had set the course for England's development as a sea-faring nation.

DRAKE'S FLAGSHIP
This replica of the *Golden Hinde*, built in 1973, has itself sailed round the world. The vessel is now permanently moored in London.

A LIFE'S WORK

- Completes a **circumnavigation** of the globe, the first ship's captain to achieve this feat, since Magellan had died before reaching home

- Becomes **notorious in Spain** as a pirate after mounting raids on Spanish ships around the coast of the Americas

- Amasses **an immense fortune** for his secret sponsor, Queen Elizabeth I

- Accumulates important information about the Pacific, laying the foundations for England's emergence as a **naval power**

- Defeats the **Spanish Armada** in 1588, as one of the three commanders of the English fleet

IN HIS FOOTSTEPS

→ **1577–1578—Reaches Patagonia**
Three of the five ships make it to Port St. Julian, where Drake puts down a mutinous plot against him

→ **1578–79—Around Cape Horn**
Only Drake's ship, the *Golden Hinde*, survives the treacherous waters of Cape Horn; he sails up the coast to land in California

→ **1579–80—Return leg**
After a swift crossing of the Pacific Ocean, Drake makes his way home via the Philippines and the East Indies

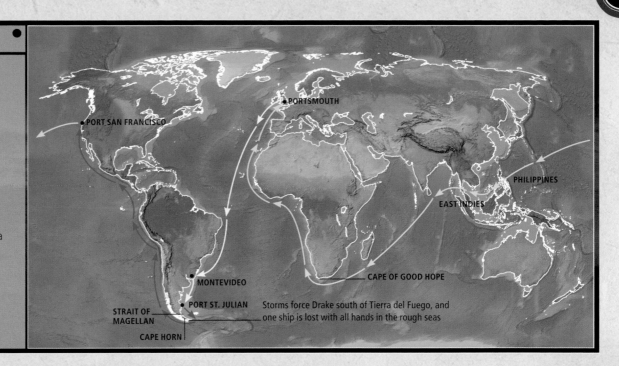

PORTSMOUTH

PORT SAN FRANCISCO

PHILIPPINES

EAST INDIES

MONTEVIDEO

STRAIT OF MAGELLAN

PORT ST. JULIAN

CAPE HORN

CAPE OF GOOD HOPE

Storms force Drake south of Tierra del Fuego, and one ship is lost with all hands in the rough seas

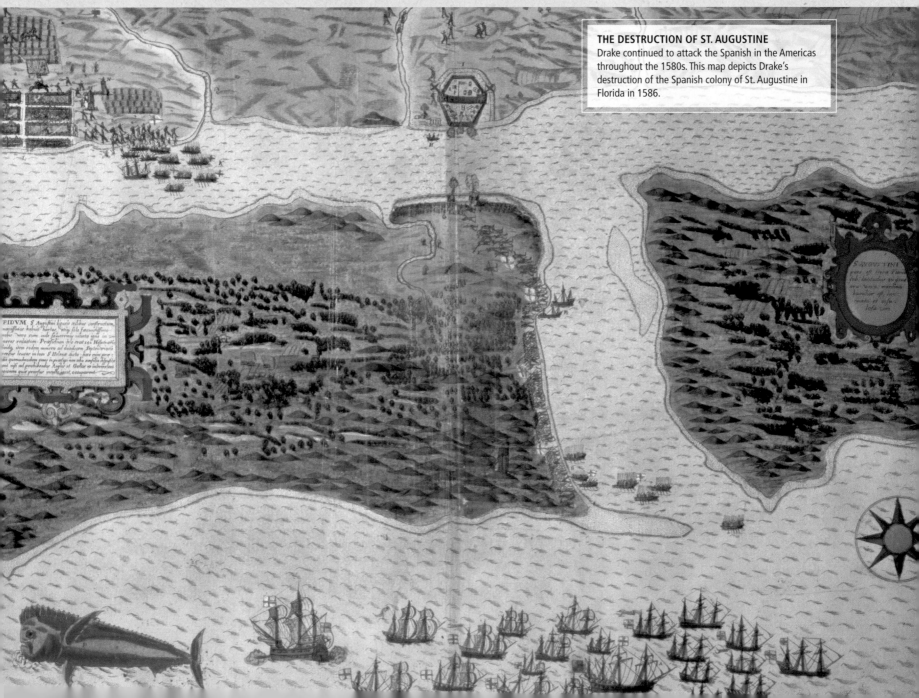

THE DESTRUCTION OF ST. AUGUSTINE
Drake continued to attack the Spanish in the Americas throughout the 1580s. This map depicts Drake's destruction of the Spanish colony of St. Augustine in Florida in 1586.

WILLIAM DAMPIER

BUCCANEER TURNED CIRCUMNAVIGATOR

ENGLAND   1651–1715

ADVENTURER, PIRATE, AUTHOR, and naturalist, William Dampier was one of the most remarkable figures of the 17th century. From a modest background, he became the first person to circumnavigate the world three times and was renowned in England both as a celebrity author and for his scientific observations. Dampier has been credited as the inspiration for the scientific expeditions of Charles Darwin and Alexander von Humboldt, while his innovations in navigation were studied by James Cook.

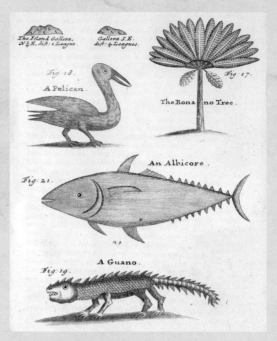

FLORA AND FAUNA
Dampier recorded valuable details of the flora and fauna he met with on his voyages, including (above) a "Bonano tree," a pelican, an albacore, and an iguana.

A LIFE'S WORK

- Works on a **sugar plantation** as a **logger** and a **gunner** in between voyages with various buccaneers

- His book, *A New Voyage Round the World*, earns him **fame** and a **commission** to command a ship to New Holland (present-day Australia)

- On his final circumnavigation, he rescues **castaway Alexander Selkirk** from Juan Fernández island in the Pacific

- Dies before he can collect his share of the **enormous booty** collected on his last voyage

There he joined a hardy group of Englishmen who made their living cutting logwood, which was used to make dye. He remained with them until 1676, when a great storm blew down the trees they depended on. Ever resourceful, Dampier soon found a new occupation that set him on a career of high adventure: sailing with the buccaneers attacking Spanish settlements and ships in the New World.

CELEBRITY PIRATE

In 1683, Dampier sailed to the Galápagos Islands with buccaneer captain John Cook. Following Cook's death, he joined another buccaneer captain, Charles Swan, and sailed across the Pacific, eventually reaching New Holland (present-day Australia) in 1688. Dampier left the buccaneers in the Nicobar Islands in the Indian Ocean, and his remarkable career twisted and turned once more. He survived a five-day voyage to the island of Sumatra in an open canoe, and briefly served as a gunner at the English fort at Benkulen on the island. From there, he returned to England, taking with him Jeoly, a heavily tattooed man from Miangis Island (Indonesia). He displayed Jeoly at freak shows around England under the moniker "the painted Prince."

In 1697, the publication of his book, *A New Voyage Round the World*, brought Dampier to the attention of the British Admiralty. He was given command of the

SPANISH BOOTY
During his time as a pirate, Dampier's brief was to capture as much gold as possible, as well as wine, gunpowder, and even valuable maps.

Dampier's first experience of life at sea came at the age of 18, when he sailed aboard a trading ship to Newfoundland. This voyage gave him both a taste for ocean travel and an aversion to the cold. In 1671, his preference for warmer climes led him to board a ship bound for the Dutch Spice Islands in Indonesia. A year later, the Third Anglo-Dutch War broke out and Dampier saw service aboard the *Prince Royal*, before he was wounded and sent home.

After his convalescence, he took up a chance to manage a sugar plantation in Jamaica. However, the lure of the sea was too strong and after nine months Dampier was on a trading ship bound for the Yucatán Peninsula, Mexico.

WHOEVER HAS ILL FORTUNE WILL HARDLY BE ALLOWED A GOOD NAME "

WILLIAM DAMPIER

IN HIS FOOTSTEPS

- **1678–91—First circumnavigation**
  Dampier sails around the world as a crew member of various privateers.

- **1699—Surveys New Guinea**
  As captain of the *Roebuck*, he surveys New Guinea and New Britain

- **1700–01—Return voyage**
  Retraces his route along New Guinea, intending to head south to New Holland, but is forced to turn back due to the poor condition of his ship

- **1703—Second circumnavigation**
  As captain of the gunship *St. George*, Dampier sails round the world again, attacking French and Spanish ships

- **1708–11—Third circumnavigation**
  Sails as pilot of the *Duke*, under the privateer Woodes Rogers

- Not shown on map

CERAM

NEW GUINEA

NEW BRITAIN

TIMOR

NEW HOLLAND (AUSTRALIA)

leaky vessel *Roebuck* in 1699, and charged with exploring New Holland. Dampier's lack of experience soon told, and his second-in-command, Fisher, held him in contempt. Dampier was forced to put Fisher ashore in Brazil to maintain control.

He surveyed the coasts of New Guinea and New Britain before reaching New Holland in July 1699. The poor repair of his ship forced him to return to England. The *Roebuck* finally sank near Ascension Island, and the crew had to be rescued by passing ships.

He was to make two further circumnavigations as a privateer. On his final voyage, he rescued castaway Alexander Selkirk (the inspiration for Daniel Defoe's *Robinson Crusoe*) from his Pacific island. This last voyage amassed a huge booty worth $30 million in today's money, but Dampier died before receiving his share.

OBSERVATIONS OF INDIANS
On meeting the Miskito Indians living on the coast of present-day Honduras and Nicaragua, Dampier described them as "tall, well-made, raw-bon'd, lusty, strong, and nimble of Foot."

CELEBRITY AUTHOR

Dampier's fame, if not fortune, was secured with the publication in 1697 of *A New Voyage Round the World*. He had carefully documented his voyages, preserving the charts, observations, and accounts in "a large Joint of Bambo, which I stopt at both Ends, closing it with Wax, so as to keep out any Water." This data made his circumnavigation not only an exciting tale of adventure and a literary sensation, but also a valuable scientific treatise.

GEORGE ANSON

NAVAL OFFICER WHO SAILED AROUND THE WORLD

ENGLAND   1697–1762

GEORGE ANSON was a British naval captain who rose through the ranks to become a vice admiral. He commanded the British fleet in several battles, including a victory over the French at the Battle of Finisterre in 1747. As an explorer, he is famous for one of the most heroic and dangerous circumnavigations of the globe ever achieved. He lost nearly the whole of his fleet, but returned home in a ship laden with Spanish booty. Anson had left with orders to fight the Spanish, but returned to find that the French were the enemy.

SPANISH AMERICA
This contemporary map shows the scale of the enemy territory. The stricken ships had to return from Cape Horn to Portuguese-held Brazil to avoid parts of the coastline in Spanish hands.

A LIFE'S WORK

- Takes charge of his first ship **at the age of 19**
- Achieves his first success commanding a ship patrolling the coast of **South Carolina**, battling pirates and Spanish ships
- Despite poor provisions and bad weather, completes a **circumnavigation of the globe**
- Crosses the Pacific Ocean with just **a pocket compass and a homemade quadrant** to guide him
- Returns to Britain to **great public acclaim**
- Commands a victorious British fleet against the French at the **Battle of Finisterre**
- Rises to the rank of **vice admiral** and is made a lord for his achievements

When war broke out between Britain and Spain in 1740, Anson was made a commodore in charge of eight ships, including his flagship, HMS *Centurion*. His mission was to attack Spain's South American dominions. On paper, his fleet was formidable, with a crew of 1,696 men. However, more than 250 of the men were sick, and the food supplies were poor.

A HAZARDOUS VOYAGE

Despite these handicaps, the ships sailed from England on September 18, 1740. They reached the Brazilian coast on December 18, mooring at the island of St. Catherine. After a month's rest and recuperation, the ships continued south. A series of terrible storms dogged the fleet as they negotiated the Strait of Magellan. Two of the ships, the *Severn* and the *Pearl*, were forced to turn north to Rio de Janeiro, while the *Wager*

was wrecked on the coast of Chile. As he entered the Pacific Ocean, Anson recorded his depleted fleet: 292 of the *Centurion*'s crew were dead from scurvy; the *Tryal* had been reduced to its captain and four other men, from an initial crew of 80. In desperation, Anson made for Juan Fernández, the uninhabited island on which Alexander Selkirk—the inspiration for Daniel Defoe's novel *Robinson Crusoe*—had been cast adrift 30 years earlier. Anson and his men rested there for more than three months, surviving on a diet of fish and seal meat. Using Juan Fernández as a base, the reduced fleet continued on its way north up the Pacific coast, seizing

IN HIS FOOTSTEPS

- **1740—Crossing to Brazil**
  Anson leads a fleet of eight ships across the Atlantic to St. Catherine, where they rest up for a month

- **1741–42—Brazil to China**
  Rough seas reduce the fleet to one ship by the time Anson attempts a crossing of the Pacific

- **1742–44—Return leg**
  Anson returns to Britain with a ship laden with Spanish booty

- **1747—Battle of Finisterre**
  Commands a fleet to victory over the French; Anson goes on to oversee a massive expansion of the Royal Navy as Britain becomes the dominant naval power in Europe

○ Not shown on map

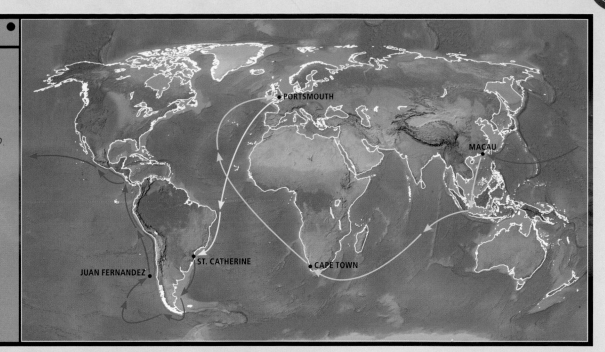

Spanish merchant ships as they went. By the time Anson sailed across the Pacific to China, only the *Centurion* was left.

Anson assumed, optimistically, that this voyage would take seven weeks. In fact, it was five months before the *Centurion* reached Macau. Anson had crossed the Pacific with little more than a pocket compass and a homemade quadrant. He was puzzled by the lack of interest from the Chinese upon their arrival: "Though many of their vessels came close to the ship, yet they did not appear to be at all interested about us … which insensibility, especially of maritime persons about a matter in their own profession, is scarcely to be credited."

Anson returned to Britain in June 1744, by way of Table Bay, Cape Town. He was stunned by the news that his country

SEEING THE WAY
The navigational instruments of Anson's day did not allow for exact calculation, so optical observation was essential. Anson would have had his telescope continually on hand.

was now at war with the French, not the Spanish, although this did not make his haul of Spanish treasure any less welcome. It took 32 wagons to transport the treasure from the south coast to London. As Anson remarked modestly in a letter, "Though the expedition has not had all the success the nation expected of it, which is of great misfortune to me, I am persuaded no misconduct can justly be laid to my charge as Commander-in-Chief."

BATTLE OF FINISTERRE
On his return to Britain, Anson was quickly pressed into service in battle against France. He commanded his fleet to a famous victory over the French in 1747 at the Battle of Finisterre.

JOHN BYRON
ENGLAND   1723–86

John Byron was the grandfather of the poet Lord George Byron. He served in Anson's fleet as a midshipman on board HMS *Wager*, which was lost in fog off the coast of Patagonia and ran aground on the southern coast of Chile in 1741.

Byron joined a party of survivors in a longboat sailing along the coast of Chile. He was captured by the Spanish and returned to Britain five years later. By 1766, Byron had completed his own record-breaking circumnavigation, achieved in a little over 22 months, with only six deaths on board ship and none from scurvy—a rare achievement for the time. During his voyage Byron located the Falkland Islands. He had first sighted the islands in January 1765.

"BYRON MEETS THE PATAGONIANS," AN ILLUSTRATION FROM A CONTEMPORARY ACCOUNT OF BYRON'S VOYAGE

LOUIS ANTOINE DE BOUGAINVILLE

FRENCH SETTLER OF THE FALKLAND ISLANDS

FRANCE   1729–1811

A GIFTED MATHEMATICIAN, Louis Antoine de Bougainville was also an accomplished military commander. His academic prowess and leadership skills came to the fore in his completion of the first French circumnavigation of the globe between 1766 and 1789. These voyages helped to extend French influence around the world, and his experiences in the South Seas in particular provided new scientific knowledge about the people and islands in a vast, uncharted region of the world.

PICTURES FROM THE VOYAGE
This illustration from the book *Bougainville's Voyage* (1772) shows a sailor from de Bougainville's crew presenting a Patagonian woman with a cookie for her baby.

Born in Paris in 1729, Louis de Bougainville lived at the time of the Enlightenment—a movement among European nations for a rational, scientific understanding of the world. Well-connected at the court of King Louis XV, the young aristocrat established an early reputation as a gifted mathematician. In 1754, de Bougainville was elected to the Royal Society of London in recognition of his published work on calculus. Destined for a military career,

MEDAL OF HONOUR
Minted in France in 1931, this commemorative medal celebrates Louis de Bougainville's achievements for his country.

he served as a captain during the Seven Years' War (1756–63), the conflict in North America involving most of the European powers.

In 1763, at the end of the war—and at his own expense—he distinguished himself further by founding a French outpost on the Îles Malouines, now the Falkland Islands.

De Bougainville carried out two separate excursions to the islands, describing his impressions of them in his log: "The horizon terminated by bald mountains, the land lacerated by the sea ... the fields bearing a dead aspect, for want of inhabitants; no woods to comfort those who intended to be the first settlers."

Despite this rather forbidding account, he had recognized the strategic value of the islands as a halfway point for French shipping heading to the Pacific. In recognition of his contribution, de Bougainville was given charge of the first

official French expedition to the Pacific. He received permission from Louis XV to circumnavigate the globe, sailing to China by way of the Strait of Magellan, with the option of taking possession for France of any new land he came across. Setting sail in November 1766, he hoped to make new discoveries and find an outlet for French expansion.

EXPLORING THE SOUTH SEAS
During the three-year expedition, de Bougainville commanded the French navy frigate *Boudeuse* and the former merchant ship *Étoile*. The expedition visited and surveyed Tahiti, Samoa, and the New Hebrides. He also named Bougainville Island, located off Australia's north coast, after himself.

A LIFE'S WORK

- Elected to the **Royal Society, London,** for his work on calculus

- Founds a French outpost on the **Îles Malouines** (the present-day Falkland Islands) but has to surrender them to Spain, which has a prior claim

- **Circumnavigates the globe** on a three-year expedition; names **Bougainville Island**

- Surveys the **South Seas** and claims the island of Tahiti for France

CANOE CROSSING
On the way to Montevideo, in present-day Uruguay, de Bougainville's men crossed the St. Lucia River in a canoe. Horses were brought across alongside them.

ISLAND PARADISE
In his reports of Tahiti, de Bougainville described the island as an innocent paradise, removed from the corrupting influence of civilization.

While berthed at Tahiti, a young Tahitian named Aotourou joined the French expedition. De Bougainville and his crew benefited greatly from Aotourou's presence, learning much about South Seas customs and life. Nearing the Great Barrier Reef, de Bougainville came close to claiming the discovery of Australia for France but was turned away by heavy seas. The expedition returned to France in March 1769, having lost only seven men out of a complement of 200, despite food shortages. As de Bougainville described it, "hunger ... was always on board." Although de Bougainville made few important discoveries or land acquisitions for France, the expedition mapped many of the Pacific island groups for the first time. In addition, his reports of Tahitian people living in happy innocence strongly appealed to the Enlightenment concepts of human nature and the revolutionary ideas fomenting in France.

IN HIS FOOTSTEPS

1766–67—Into the Pacific
On the first leg of his circumnavigation, de Bougainville reaches Tahiti; his description of the island as an egalitarian paradise has a strong influence on French revolutionary thinkers in Paris

1767–69—Return voyage
Crosses the Pacific and surveys the Solomon Islands before returning to France via Batavia; he almost claims Australia for France, but heavy seas prevent his landing

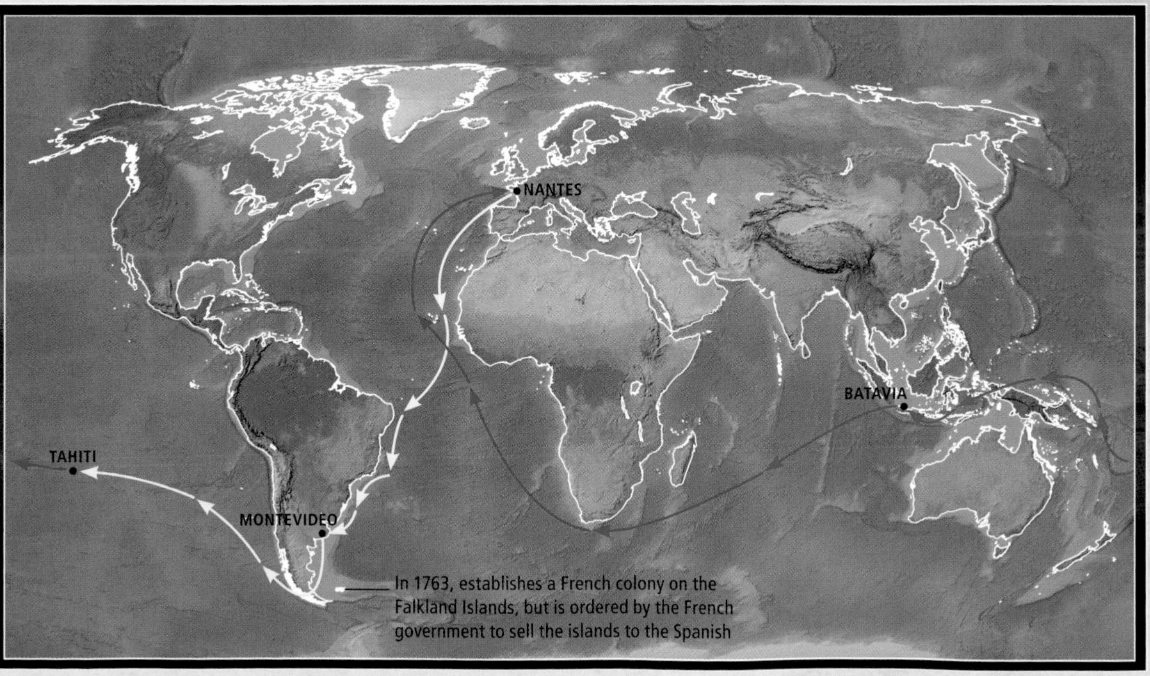

NANTES

BATAVIA

TAHITI

MONTEVIDEO

In 1763, establishes a French colony on the Falkland Islands, but is ordered by the French government to sell the islands to the Spanish

CHARTING THE DEVELOPMENT OF...

EXPEDITION COMMUNICATION

THE SUCCESS OR FAILURE of an expedition can depend on the quality of communications between members of a party, and with home. Up until the 19th century, communication over long distances traveled no faster than horse or sailing ship, and explorers would often be away for years with no news from or to home. The development of the telegraph and now satellites has made communication almost instant, and explorers can remain in contact with civilization from anywhere in the world.

ANCIENT ROADS

In 600BCE, Darius the Great established a network of post roads through Persia, enabling messages to be sent quickly through his kingdom using a relay of men and horses stationed at fixed points on routes. Riders crisscrossed the kingdom, covering up to 200 miles (300 km) per day, with texts transcribed onto lightweight papyrus.

Later, in medieval China, Marco Polo (see pp. 56–59) was to witness the system of post roads, which were not without danger. He described how, when stopping on the Silk Road, travelers would sleep close to each other and hang bells from their animals to raise the alarm should they be attacked by bandits.

SEA SIGNALS

At sea, early communication between vessels was limited to fire or flare. During the first crossings of the Atlantic, early

---

334BCE—GREEK INTELLIGENCE
Alexander the Great (see pp. 22–25) employs a network of scouts who travel in advance of his troops, gathering information.

200BCE—THE SILK ROAD
The 5,000-mile (8,000-km) trade route acts as a communication highway linking Asia with Europe and Africa.

1000CE—VIKING EXPLORATION
The Icelandic Sagas record the achievements of the families migrating to Greenland and North America.

1584—TRAVEL WRITER
Through his books, English geographer Richard Hakluyt communicates general knowledge of distant lands.

THE PRINCIPALL NAVIGATIONS, VOIAGES AND DISCOVERIES OF THE English nation

---

BCE 500	CE 100	500	1000	1550	1600	1650	1700	1750

399CE—MONK NETWORK
Pilgrim Fa Xian (see pp. 44–45) is supported en route to India by a network of Buddhist monasteries.

1520—SMOKE SIGNALS
Ferdinand Magellan (see pp. 138–41) sees fires along the coast of Tierra del Fuego, thought to be the smoke signals of the Patagonian Yámana people.

1740—LATE NEWS
At war with Spain, Britain sends George Anson (see pp. 148–49) on a mission to attack Spain's Pacific ships. He returns in 1743 to find that the enemy is now France.

500BCE GREAT WALL OF CHINA

The Great Wall acts as a **barrier to invaders from the north**, but also facilitates communication. Beacon towers located along the Wall, such as this one on the Jinsanling section, signal potential attacks **using a combination of smoke** (day time) and **flares** (at night) alongside **drum-beat patterns**. Communication signals are first used in this way during the period 475–221BCE.

1534 JACQUES CARTIER

During Jacques Cartier's first encounters with the indigenous people in Canada (see pp. 130–31), he **kidnaps the two sons of an Iroquoian chief**. The chief, shown here greeting Cartier, allows the explorer to take his sons to France **on condition that they come back laden with European goods**. Cartier returns the sons home on his second journey in 1535 **full of information about the life** they have seen in France.

marine navigators, such as Christopher Columbus (see pp. 86–89) would establish a night system of verbal call-outs between the ships of the fleet in order to establish position and to warn of hazards. By day, simple signals could be provided by raising and lowering sail. From the 18th century, a formal system of lantern night signals was established in the UK, which could be accompanied by rockets or flares. Semaphore, a handheld flag-signaling system, was first used during the Napoleonic wars in the early 19th century, and later adapted as a flag-hoist system for ships by English author Frederick Marryat (1792–1848).

LANGUAGE BARRIERS

The lack of a common language with the people of other lands was a major issue for early Spanish and Portuguese explorers. In 1488, for example, Bartolomeu Dias (see pp. 76–77)

resorted to kidnap to solve the problem, carrying West African translators on his journey east. Unfortunately for Dias, his captives were unable to understand the languages of the continent's east coast.

The need for translators and intermediaries continued to be of crucial importance if local knowledge and expertise were to be understood. During their exploration of the American West, Lewis and Clark (see pp. 174–75) hired the services of a Shoshone Indian woman named Sacagawea as a translator of the Shoshone and Hidatsa languages. They also used a Shawnee sign language that had been developed by the trapper George Drouillard. Although there was a misconception that the Indian nations shared common signage, in 1805, Lewis recorded that "the strong parts of the ideas are seldom mistaken." In Africa, British Victorian figures such as John Hanning Speke (see pp. 204–07),

Augustus Grant, and others were dependent on the support of their translators when crossing tribal boundaries from Zanzibar to the interior.

CABLE AND WIRELESS

The electric telegraph system was first successfully demonstrated in 1844 by American inventor Samuel Morse, and soon the telegraph offered instant communication across land as thousands of miles of cables were laid around the world. In 1867, a British Naval officer, Vice Admiral Philip Colomb, invented a system of flash signaling based on the Morse system, enabling dramatic improvements in seaboard communication. Although such systems were often disrupted by poor weather, their speed and reliability meant that messengers were soon replaced. In 1876, the telephone was invented by Scottish engineer Alexander

Graham Bell and it became possible to telegraph human speech. By 1892, the first trials of wireless telegraphy were being undertaken by Italian radio pioneer Guglielmo Marconi, allowing Morse code to be transmitted from land to sea. In addition to providing a method of verbal communication, wireless technology also improved the accuracy of longitude measurements in the field by using wireless time signals.

MESSAGES FROM SPACE

Today's explorers remain in constant touch with home, even from the world's remotest places, by speaking or emailing from satellite radio. Laptop computers, now more compact than ever, can be transported virtually anywhere. Even from space, astronauts on board the International Space Station share their experiences with thousands of people on Earth via regular blogs.

1839—MORSE CODE
Samuel Morse first outlines his theory of the electromagnetic telegraph.

1804—INDIAN SIGNALS
Lewis and Clark (see pp. 174–77) communicate with various American Indian nations using sign language.

1990 SATELLITE RADIO
Satellite technology enables remote connections to the internet.

1953—EVEREST CODE
Sleeping bags are laid in a "T" shape on Mt Everest, a coded signal that the summit had been reached.

2010—SPACE BLOG
Subscribers all over the world follow the blogs of the International Space Station, as astronauts describe their experiences.

1800 | 1850 | 1900 | 1950 | 2000

1800—SEMAPHORE CATCHES ON
The basic handheld flag signaling system is adopted in the maritime world.

1840s—ARCTIC SEARCH
Message balloons are used in the search for the "Lost Expedition" of John Franklin (see pp. 292–93).

1934—NEAR-DEATH BY RADIO
US Polar explorer Richard E. Byrd is almost killed by carbon monoxide from his radio generator.

1897—POLE PIGEONS
Swedish balloonist August Andrée takes homing pigeons on his ill-fated flight to the North Pole.

Captain Frederick Marryat of the British Royal Navy publishes his *Code of Signals for the Merchant Service*. **Based on a system of hoisted signal flags**, it is eventually adopted as an **international code**, and by 1854, Marryat's system is known as the **Universal Code of Signals**. Today, all signaling by non-naval vessels, whether semaphore or lamp signals, is organized under the International Code of Signaling.

1817 MARINE SIGNALING

By the early 20th century, wireless technology is freely available to explorers, but **many consider it too heavy and cumbersome to carry**. Robert Peary (see pp. 308–09) is offered a wireless set for his 1909 attempt on the North Pole but **declines to take it**. His colleague Matthew Henson (see pp. 310–11) later writes that radio "has helped to blaze new trails." Shown here is a suitcase-sized wireless receiver being operated in Niger in 1927.

1909 WIRELESS RADIO

INTO THE PACIFIC

FROM THE 16TH CENTURY, THE LURE OF A FABLED SOUTHERN CONTINENT DREW EUROPEAN EXPLORERS INTO THE PACIFIC. THEIR SEARCH LED TO THE EXPLORATION OF THE PACIFIC ISLANDS, AUSTRALIA, AND NEW ZEALAND, AND ENDED WITH THE DISCOVERY OF ANTARCTICA.

ROGUE TRADERS
In 1615, Dutchmen Willem Schouten and Jacob Le Maire sailed west around South America to reach the Moluccas. Their goal was to break the Dutch East India Company's trade monopoly.

The first true Pacific explorers were not Europeans but Polynesians. They were descended from people from southern China who first colonized western Polynesia, reaching Tonga and Samoa in about 1000BCE. Some 1,300 years later, they began another series of migrations, traversing the seas between island groups in large canoes, carrying the typical Polynesian larder of breadfruit, taro, yam, and sweet potatoes to sustain the colonies they established. By 700CE, they had reached Hawaii and as far east as Easter Island, guided by an accurate knowledge of the winds and currents, and the construction of maritime charts from sticks. Between 700 and 1100, they moved even farther afield, ultimately reaching New Zealand, where their descendants became the Maori.

A GLOBAL PICTURE

In Europe, the rediscovery of the works of Ptolemy in the early 15th century gave rise to the notion that there might exist a large southern landmass that joined Africa to Asia. The circumnavigation of Africa by Vasco da Gama in 1499 (see pp. 80–81) made it clear that Ptolemy was wrong, but notable cartographers such as Abraham Ortelius and Gerard Mercator then began to depict a southern continent, which they

MAORI ART
When Cook landed in New Zealand in 1769 he found an advanced Maori culture, capable of producing sophisticated totems in wood.

named *Terra Australis nondum cognita* ("southern continent not yet known"). Although there are some suggestions that Portuguese navigators reached the coastline of Australia in the 1520s, which a few French cartographers labeled Java la Grande ("Great Java"), nothing is proven.

SPANISH SUCCESS

More tangible discoveries in the western Pacific were made by the Spanish, beginning in 1521 with Ferdinand Magellan's landing on Cebu in the Philippines (see pp. 138–41). In 1527, the conquistador Hernán Cortés (see pp. 106–09) sent an expedition under Alvaro de Saavedra to find a secure route from Mexico to the Philippines. On the return journey, he skirted the coast of New Guinea for the first time and reported on the customs of the local Papuan people. In 1567, the Spanish sent out another expedition, this time from Peru, intent on finding the land of Ophir, where King Solomon's Mines—the potential source of a fabulous treasure in gold—were said to lie. The mines proved to be a pipe dream, but Alvaro de Mendana discovered Guadalcanal, naming the archipelago in which it lay the Solomon Islands, as a nod toward the objective of his voyage.

> Once the coastlines of Australia and New Zealand had been surveyed, explorers turned their efforts to finding the Southern Continent even farther south, ultimately leading to the discovery of Antarctica.

In 1605, Pedro de Quirós, a Portuguese explorer in the service of Spain, made landfall on Espiritu Santo in the New Hebrides before returning to Mexico by way of California. De Quirós had abandoned one of his ships in the New Hebrides, and it was the captain of this vessel, Luis Váez de Torres, who came tantalizingly close to discovering a new continent as he sailed past southern New Guinea through the Torres Strait, sighting Long Reef at the northwestern tip of Australia.

DUTCH EXPANSION

It was left to the Dutch to begin the real exploration of *Terra Australis*. Their expeditions were sponsored by the Dutch East India Company, established in 1602 to further Dutch commercial exploitation of the countries around the Indian Ocean. The company founded a string of colonies, most notably in Sri Lanka, Java, and the Moluccas, and soon eclipsed Spanish and Portuguese interests in the area.

In 1605, Willem Janszoon sailed south along the New Guinea coastline and then followed the coastline of Cape York south for 200 miles (300 km), making the first known landfall by a European in Australia. In 1623, Jan Carstenz explored Arnhem

SEAT OF POWER
The city of Batavia (present-day Jakarta) was captured by the Dutch in 1619, becoming the seat of the Dutch governor-general and the de facto capital of their empire in the East Indies.

AROUND THE HORN
By the 19th century, ships were regularly sailing around South America into the Pacific. The need to make this dangerous journey ended in 1914 with the opening of the Panama Canal.

SETTING THE SCENE

- Some time in about 1600, **the Polynesians who have colonized Easter Island** cut down the last trees on the island. Their expenditure of resources on the construction of **hundreds of enormous stone heads**, called *moai*, results in an ecological disaster. Recent pollen analysis of the island shows that it was almost totally covered in forest as recently as 1200.

- **The Portuguese lead the way** in exploring the Indian Ocean, reaching Sri Lanka by 1506 and capturing Malacca in 1511. By the mid-17th century, they have been **eclipsed by the Dutch**, losing their stronghold at Colombo to Dutch East India Company forces in 1656.

- In 1621, John Brooke's ship, the *Tryall*, breaks up near the North West Cape of Australia. The 46 survivors, who reach Java five weeks later, are **the first Englishmen to have sighted the coastline of Australia**.

- Captain James Cook's first voyage in 1768–71 is officially despatched **to observe the Transit of Venus across the Sun**, but its secondary mission is to thwart the French by discovering and asserting British ownership of new lands in the South Seas.

Land, and by the 1640s the Dutch had a good understanding of the northern and western coastlines of Australia, which they called Nova Hollandia ("New Holland").

In 1642, Abel Tasman (see pp. 160–61) made the last major Dutch discoveries on the continent as he sailed northwest from the southern Indian Ocean to sight Tasmania (which he called, more modestly, Van Diemen's Land, after the governor-general of the Dutch East Indies). Farther still, he reached New Zealand, where his crew became the first recorded Europeans to land there.

THE ENGLISH ARRIVE

The English established their own East India Company in 1600, and began to take a greater interest in

FRENCH PACIFIC VOYAGER
This is a replica of de Bougainville's frigate, *Boudeuse*, which led the first French circumnavigation in 1766 via the Tuamotus, Tahiti, and Samoa. A valet on board was unmasked as Jeanne Baré, mistress of the ship's botanist. She became the first woman to circle the world.

the South Pacific. As early as 1621, an East India Company ship attempting to reach Java was wrecked off northwest Australia, but the first deliberate exploration was undertaken by William Dampier (see pp. 146–47), who landed at Cygnet Bay on King Sound early in 1688, returning again in 1699, when he landed near Sharks Bay in Western Australia.

A LAND WORTH EXPLORING

Dampier's reports on his landings in New Holland portrayed a dry, cheerless land with little worth exploiting. It was only when French and British commercial rivalry turned to war in the 1750s that a race to explore and occupy the remaining blanks on the Pacific map broke out. In 1768, Louis-Antoine de Bougainville (see pp. 150–51) came to within less than 120 miles (200 km) of the Queensland coast. The following year, James Cook (see pp. 156–59), mapped almost the entire coastline of New Zealand before sighting the mainland of eastern Australia for the first time on April 19, 1770.

In the decades that followed Cook's voyages, European trade with the Maori increased, and Christian missionaries began to settle in New Zealand in the early 19th century. The British secured European rights over the islands in the 1840 Treaty of Waitangi with the Maori, and established their first penal colony in eastern Australia in 1788. In 1828, they formally laid claim to the whole continent.

JAMES COOK

EXPLORER OF THE SOUTH SEAS

ENGLAND   1728–79

A HIGHLY SKILLED NAVIGATOR, cartographer, and explorer, James Cook commanded three voyages of discovery for Britain. He circumnavigated the globe twice, and mapped the northwest coast of the American continent. Cook's encounters with the inhabitants of the South Sea Islands also brought several Polynesian cultures into contact with Europeans for the first time. His exploration of Australia led to its future colonization by European settlers, but his greatest goal, the discovery of a vast southern continent, eluded him.

In three voyages to the Pacific, James Cook discovered more of the Earth's surface than any other explorer in history, but his early life gave little indication of the heroic career that awaited him. As a young man, he worked in the merchant navy, shipping coal along the English coast, but a desire for adventure led him to volunteer for the Royal Navy in 1755. Distinguished service during the Seven Years' War saw him promoted to the rank of master— qualifying him to navigate a ship. As master of the warship HMS *Pembroke*, Cook crossed to North America, where he displayed further talents as a cartographer, making an accurate chart of the St. Lawrence River. This helped earn him his first command, HMS *Grenville*, in which he charted the coast of Newfoundland.

VOYAGE TO TAHITI

By 1768, Cook's outstanding navigational skills had brought him to the attention of Britain's Royal Society, which appointed him to lead a scientific expedition to Tahiti in the South Pacific. Accompanied by two astronomers, Cook's mission was to measure the key astronomical event of

COOK'S SEXTANT
Made by the English instrument-maker John Bird (1709–76), this sextant was the most advanced scientific measuring instrument of its day.

1769: the transit of the planet Venus across the Sun. Cook was given command of a newly refitted Royal Navy vessel, HMS *Endeavour*, which set sail from Plymouth on August 25, 1768. His crew included the young English botanist Joseph Banks (see p. 197) and Banks's Swedish and Finnish counterparts Daniel Solander and Herman Spöring. Cook made good progress, arriving at the recently discovered island of Tahiti on April 13, 1769. The measurement of the transit of Venus was carried out efficiently, and the data collected would eventually help scientists accurately determine the size of the solar system.

Cook then carried out a second, secret instruction, following orders from the British Admiralty to sail due south from Tahiti. His new mission was to establish whether a great, undiscovered continent lay waiting there—and to claim it for Britain if it did. At the time, it was widely believed that a huge continent existed in the southern hemisphere—known as the *Terra Australis Incognita* (Latin for "unknown land of the south")—which balanced the large land masses of the north. If no continent was found, Cook was to sail for New Zealand to annex the land and chart the coastline.

In October 1769, Cook arrived in New Zealand, having failed to find the southern continent. He surveyed New Zealand's North Island and South Island, confirming the theory of Abel Tasman (see pp. 160–61) that these were indeed islands, and not connected to a larger landmass. From New Zealand, Cook sailed west. On April 19, 1770, he landed

(see p. 197)
(see pp. 160–61)

A LIFE'S WORK

- Observes and records the **transit of Venus** across the Sun from the island of Tahiti

- Confirms the theory that **New Zealand** is made up of two islands

- Leads the first recorded **European expedition** to make landfall on the southeastern coast of **Australia**

- Circumnavigates the **Antarctic Circle**

- Travels to the **Bering Strait** in search of the **northwest passage**

- Opens up the northwest coast of America to **trade and colonization**

- Discovers the **Hawaiian Islands,** which he names the **Sandwich Islands**

- Ensures that none of his crew dies of **scurvy,** as he insists that they have a **proper diet,** including **orange extract**

(3,000-km) eastern coastline, successfully navigating the treacherous Great Barrier Reef.

On his return to Britain, Cook was celebrated as the country's most accomplished sailor, but his achievements were overshadowed in the public eye by the scientific discoveries of Joseph Banks. The voyage was to establish a long tradition of scientists traveling with naval expeditions.

circumnavigation of the Antarctic before he was forced north to Tahiti to take on fresh supplies. He returned home with conclusive proof that any southern continent that might exist was not the great *Terra Australis* that had been hoped for.

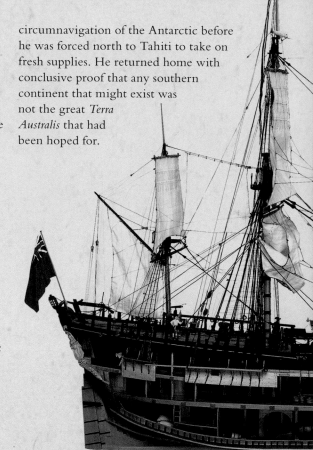

MAORI RESISTANCE
Cook encountered resistance from the Maori as he sailed around New Zealand. At one point, the Maori rowed out to meet him in war canoes, and he was forced to fight them off.

on the coast of the land that Tasman had sighted and named "New Holland" nearly 200 years earlier—Australia.

Banks and his fellow botanists named the spot where they landed "Botany Bay," after the huge number of specimens of new plants they collected there. Cook claimed the lands for the British crown, naming them "New South Wales." He also spotted people on the shore, but did not make contact with them. Cook then surveyed the whole of the 2,000-mile

THE SECOND VOYAGE

Despite the huge achievements of Cook's first voyage, the question of the great southern continent remained unanswered. In June 1772, Cook received his second set of secret orders from the Admiralty. Commanding HMS *Resolution*, accompanied by its sister ship, HMS *Adventure*, his mission was to sail farther south than any of his rivals. Cook crossed the Antarctic Circle in January 1773, discovering and mapping the island of South Georgia in the southern Atlantic. He sailed along the edge of the ice shelf, suspecting that a smaller polar continent lay beyond this barrier, but was unable to break through the ice to find it. He completed a

IN HIS FOOTSTEPS

→ **1768–71—First voyage**
Cook sails to Tahiti, where he observes the transit of Venus across the Sun, before sailing in search of a new southern continent; in the process, he surveys New Zealand and the eastern coast of Australia

→ **1772–75—Second voyage**
Completes a circumnavigation of the Antarctic but cannot break through the ice to find the continent that lies beyond

→ **1776–79—Final voyage**
Returns to the Pacific, this time to search for a northwest passage; after failing to find a way through the Bering Strait, Cook is killed on his return to Hawaii

→ **1779–80—Cook's crew sails for home**
Following the death of Cook, Captain Charles Clerke takes charge of the expedition, and the crew makes one more attempt to pass through the Bering Strait before returning to Britain

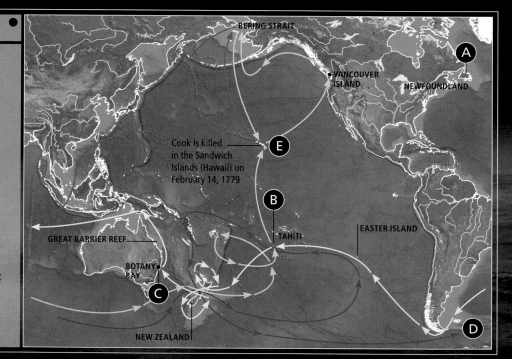

Observes the transit of Venus from Tahiti, an island that Cook will return to on each of his three voyages into the Pacific Ocean

Cook joins the Royal Navy at the age of 27 after several years in the merchant navy

(A) Makes his reputation as a superb navigator and cartographer by charting the coast of Newfoundland

(C) Makes landfall on the Australian continent, naming the spot Botany Bay

Safely negotiates the Great Barrier Reef, although he is forced to put ashore for repairs at one point

THE EXPLORER'S END

In July 1776, Cook set sail on his third voyage, again on the *Resolution*, this time eyeing the Arctic Ocean. His goal was to find a northwest passage from the Pacific to the Atlantic oceans across the top of America. As they sailed north through the Pacific, Cook's crew became the first Europeans to land at the Hawaiian Islands (which Cook named the Sandwich Islands after his sponsor, the Earl of Sandwich).

THE *ENDEAVOUR*
This model of Cook's most famous ship shows its three decks, which provided crew cabins, mess facilities, and a large storage hold.

AMBITION LEADS ME ... AS FAR AS I THINK IT POSSIBLE FOR MAN TO GO

JAMES COOK

He continued his survey work when he reached the coast of California, stopping for a month in Vancouver Island, where he traded uneasily with the local Yuquot people. He then sailed north as far as the Bering Strait, where he found that there was no navigable passage.

In 1779, Cook returned to Hawaii, where his even-handed dealings with the local people were to prove his downfall. While investigating the alleged theft of a boat by an islander, he was stabbed to death by angry locals. His expedition arrived back in Britain a year later. Cook left behind a considerable legacy: the standards of behavior he set both on board and on shore; the precision of his measurements; and a new spirit of peaceable, scientific exploration.

GEORGE VANCOUVER
ENGLAND   1757–98

A surveyor of the northwest coast of North America, George Vancouver was a British naval officer who gained his early nautical experience on Cook's voyages.

Serving as a midshipman, he was aboard HMS *Resolution* for Cook's second voyage (1772–75) and HMS *Discovery* on the third expedition. He went on to serve in the West Indies, and was later given command of an expeditionary task force. Setting sail with two vessels in April 1791, he visited Cape Town in South Africa, Australia, New Zealand, Tahiti, and the Sandwich Islands (present-day Hawaii), surveying coastlines and selecting botanical samples. Next, Vancouver headed for North America, where he surveyed the western coastline from California to Alaska (Vancouver Island in British Columbia, and the cities of Vancouver in Washington state and in Canada, were all named in his honor). Revisiting the Sandwich Islands in 1794, Vancouver accepted their submission to Great Britain, although this was never formally ratified. He was renowned for his sympathetic treatment of the people of the places he visited, holding unscrupulous Western traders in contempt.

EASTER ISLAND
On Cook's second voyage, he visited Easter Island in 1774. One of the world's most isolated islands, it has a subtropical climate and is made up of three extinct volcanoes. Seen here is the volcanic crater of Ranu Kao at Rapa Nui. Easter Island is famed for the mysterious statues that face seaward along the shoreline. When Cook visited, he reported that many of the statues were in a state of disrepair or had fallen down.

D Charts the island of South Georgia during a complete circumnavigation of Antarctica, but fails to find the polar continent

E On his final voyage, Cook discovers Hawaii, naming them the Sandwich Islands

1775–76   1776–79   1779–80

Cook is forced by the ice to turn back at the Bering Strait, meaning that he cannot find a northern passage from the Pacific to the Atlantic oceans

ABEL TASMAN

DUTCH EXPLORER OF THE "GREAT SOUTH LAND"

THE NETHERLANDS   1603–59

SEA CAPTAIN ABEL TASMAN led the first European expedition to the southern reaches of the "Great South Land," with the goal of expanding the Dutch East India Company's trading empire. His first voyage yielded the new lands of Tasmania, New Zealand, Fiji, and Tonga, but not the rich trading grounds that his employers had hoped for. Tasman's achievements were little appreciated during his lifetime, and it would be 200 years before the island of his first discovery bore his name.

A LIFE'S WORK

- Proves his **company loyalty and patriotism** with the names he gives to new discoveries, such as Van Diemen's Land (Tasmania) and Cape Marie Van Diemen (the northern tip of New Zealand's North Island), after his superior and superior's wife

- Navigates the southern reaches of a new continent and **discovers several unknown Pacific island groups**, but his exploratory efforts are unappreciated by his employers

- Achieves some recognition for his **exploratory journeys** in 1648 due to the publication of fellow-Dutchman Joan Blaeu's world map

Tasman was born in Lutjegast in the northeastern Netherlands, and was listed as an ordinary sailor on his 1632 marriage certificate. He joined the Dutch East India Company a year later and climbed the company's ranks, sailing to Batavia (present-day Jakarta), its base in the East Indies, as commander of the *Engel* in 1638.

SEARCHING THE SOUTH

Eager to extend the company's trading interests, Anthonie Van Diemen, governor-general of Batavia, sent Tasman to explore the lands known as the "Great South Land" in 1642, and to investigate a route to South America. Tasman set sail on August 14 with the *Heemskirk* and *Zee-Han*, sailing west to Mauritius to make the most of prevailing winds. Heading back across the Indian Ocean, by November 24 Tasman had "discovered land … which I called Van Diemen's Land." Nothing was seen of the inhabitants other than smoke rising inland. Tasman wrote, "I perceived also in the sand the marks of wild beasts' feet, resembling those of a tiger … we did nothing more than set up a post,

KEEPING GOOD COMPANY
The Dutch set up a company to gain a slice of the lucrative spice trade in 1602. The initials VOC stood for *Vereenigde Oost-Indische Compagnie* (United East India Company).

on which everyone cut his name, or his mark, and upon which I hoisted a flag."

AN UPLIFTED LAND
Departing Van Diemen's Land, Tasman sailed east, aiming for the "Islands of Solomon." Instead, he spied the shore of "a large land, uplifted high"—New Zealand—on December 13. The ships anchored at Cape Farewell, South Island, where Tasman reported an "abundance of inhabitants." A few days later, a Maori canoe approached the ships, attacking

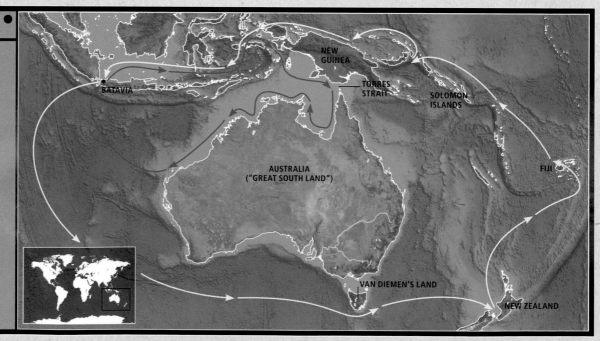

IN HIS FOOTSTEPS

→ **1642–43—Van Diemen's Land**
Departs Batavia, catching the prevailing winds via Mauritius, and sails southeast; makes one landing on present-day Tasmania in rough weather before being blown out to sea; becomes the first European to set foot on New Zealand; returns to Indonesia via Tonga, Fiji, and New Guinea after a 10-month voyage

→ **1644—New Guinea and Australia**
Sent to establish whether a land bridge exists between Indonesia and Australia; follows the south coast of New Guinea westward but misses the Torres Strait; maps the coast of northern Australia and makes observations of its geography and inhabitants

NEW GUINEA

BATAVIA

TORRES STRAIT

SOLOMON ISLANDS

AUSTRALIA ("GREAT SOUTH LAND")

FIJI

VAN DIEMEN'S LAND

NEW ZEALAND

FIRST CONTACT
Tasman sketched the Maori and described their "black hair tied together right on top of their heads, in the way and fashion the Japanese have it … On the tuft … a large, thick, white feather. They were naked from shoulder to waist."

a support boat from the *Zee-Han*. Four of the crew were killed and the rest swam for their lives. Tasman set sail immediately for North Island. Although in need of fresh water and provisions, he decided not to land on the nearby Three Kings Islands due to "thirty or five-and-thirty persons … men of very large size, and each of them had a large club in his hand." Sailing northeast in bad weather, the islands of Tonga were sighted in

January 1643. Tasman met "[an] abundance of rain, a strong wind … with dark cold" at Fiji in February, then sailed west via the Solomon Islands and New Guinea, reaching Batavia on June 15, 1643.

Although Tasman's voyage added significantly to Dutch knowledge of the Pacific, he failed to deliver the hoped-for lucrative shipping route to South America. He was despatched again in January 1644 to ascertain whether New Guinea and Australia were part of the same landmass, but turned back before reaching the Torres Strait, which separates the two. It was to be the last voyage to Australia until James Cook's expedition 126 years later (see pp. 156–59), and ended the Dutch East India Company's interest in the "Great South Land."

CEREMONIAL MAORI CLUB
The Maori that Tasman encountered were armed with stone and hardwood weapons, such as this elaborately engraved club. The haliotis shell represents a bird's eye.

TRADING NEAR AND FAR
Batavia became the East Indies headquarters of the VOC in 1619. It grew into a thriving city thanks to the burgeoning spice trade. By the mid-17th century, the Dutch company had become the wealthiest private organization the world had ever seen.

LA PÉROUSE

CARTOGRAPHER WHO VANISHED OFF THE MAP

FRANCE   1741–c. 1788

A DECORATED NAVAL COMMANDER, the Comte de la Pérouse led a major French expedition to circumnavigate the world. His goal was to build on the scientific endeavors of Captain James Cook, whom he admired. He took with him leading French scientists on what was intended to be a model scientific expedition, equipped to compete with the British, Spanish, and Dutch in the Pacific. It was not to be. La Pérouse's ships vanished en route to New Caledonia and decades were to pass before his fate was discovered.

ILLUSTRATED MAP
This illustration of one of La Pérouse's ships, *La Boussole*, appeared on a map of the Pacific Ocean drawn using surveying data La Pérouse sent back to France.

Jean-François de la Galaup was born near Albi, southern France. "La Pérouse" was the title of a family estate that he added to his name. At the age of 15 he went to naval college and saw action in North America against the British during the Seven Years' War (1756–63), rising to the rank of commodore.

In 1785, King Louis XVI appointed La Pérouse to lead an expedition that would continue the mapping work of James Cook (see pp. 156–59), open new trade routes, and enrich French scientific knowledge.

VOYAGE TO THE PACIFIC
The expedition set sail from Brest harbor in August 1785 with two ships, *L'Astrolabe*, captained by a Paul-Antoine de Langle and *La Boussole*, captained by La Pérouse. They

ANGLE MEASUREMENTS
La Pérouse used this graphometer to survey the northwest Pacific coast. It was used to measure angles as part of the process of trigonometry.

rounded South America to reach Easter Island, where La Pérouse acknowledged Cook's visit of 1772: "it is to the kindness with which those navigators conducted themselves toward this people that we owe the confidence they seemed to place in us." He then sailed to the northwest Pacific via the Hawaiian Islands.

La Pérouse surveyed the coastline of the Canadian northwest up into present-day Alaska, but after failing to find the Northwest Passage, returned south to the Monterey coastline of Alta California, the first European to visit the area since Francis Drake in 1579 (see pp. 144–45).

ONWARD TO ASIA
In September 1786, La Pérouse left Monterey Bay and sailed southwest across the Pacific, arriving at Macao off the coast of China the following January. From Macao, collections and journals from the expedition were despatched to Paris. The ships proceeded to the Philippines and by April 1787, were sailing along the coastlines of Japan and Korea and into the Sea of Okhtosk. La Pérouse made harbor in the Bay of Terney on June 23. This, finally, was a land that Cook had not visited, and La Pérouse enthusiastically collected specimens. Records of Tartar

settlements and culture were also made and the men ate fish flavored with local herbs, which La Pérouse identified as a protection against scurvy. After sailing part of the way along the coast of the Russian island of Sakhalin, he was unable to establish whether the landmass was a peninsula or an island, and continued on to Kamchatka, from where more collections were despatched across Siberia to Paris. While in Kamchatka, La Pérouse received orders from France to cross for a third time into the southern hemisphere to investigate British activities in Australia.

A LIFE'S WORK

- Leads naval frigate *Astrée* to **victory against the British** in the Battle of Louisbourg, 1781

- Wins fame when he **captures two British forts** in Hudson Bay, North America, in 1782

- Builds on the **surveying work** of James Cook, proving the rigor and safety of Cook's methods

- His survey of flora and fauna along the California coast stands for centuries as **the most exact record** of the species in the region

FUR WARS

In addition to his scientific endeavors, King Louis XVI also required La Pérouse to keep an eye on British naval activities and to establish a French foothold in the lucrative fur trade of the Pacific northwest. This pitted him against the Russians, who controlled the fur trade across the Pacific, selling American pelts to Asia.

LA PÉROUSE (CENTER) IS DEPICTED HERE BUYING FURS FROM A CANADIAN INDIAN CHIEFTAIN

IN HIS FOOTSTEPS

1785–86—Surveys North America
La Pérouse enters the Pacific and sails north to Alaska; from there, he sails down the Pacific coast of North America as far as present-day California, surveying as he goes

1786–88—Across the Pacific
From California, he crosses the Pacific to Macao, where he sends the surveying data he has gathered back to France, before heading north to explore the coast of Siberia

1788—Lost in the Pacific
He receives fresh orders to sail for Australia and, after a difficult journey, reaches Botany Bay on the same day that the British are changing the site of their original settlement; from there, he heads for New Caledonia

1825—Wreckage found
The wrecks of La Pérouse's two ships are found on the Santa Cruz Islands; some of the crew survive the wreck, but their fate is unknown

○ Not shown on map

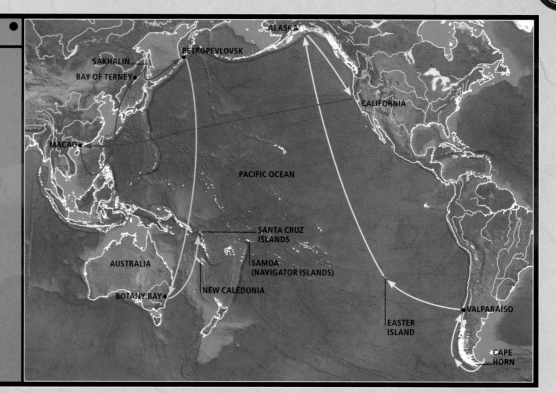

DISAPPEARANCE

La Pérouse set sail for the Navigator Islands (present-day Samoa), where 12 of his men, including Captain de Langle, were killed in a skirmish with the islanders. He forbade reprisals, and the two ships continued on to South Australia. They reached Botany Bay during a gale on January 26, 1788, at the exact moment that a British frigate was in the process of transferring the colony to the safety of Sydney Cove. The British received La Pérouse cordially, despite some British convicts attempting to volunteer for service on the French ships, and several French crew stowing away on the English ships for an early return to Europe.

On March 10, La Pérouse sailed for New Caledonia, after which nothing was ever heard of him again. A relief expedition was sent in 1791, but it was not until 1825 that a British captain reported seeing a cross of the Order of St. Louis on the Santa Cruz Islands. Further investigation in 1828 confirmed that La Pérouse's ships had been wrecked near Vanikoro Island, where the surviving crew had built a small boat from the wreckage and vanished into the unknown.

EASTER VACATION
This engraving shows La Pérouse and his crew relaxing with the locals on Easter Island, where they received a warm welcome. The engraving appears in an illustrated atlas of his voyages that was published in France in 1797.

FILLING IN THE GAPS

FILLING IN THE GAPS

1800	1825	1850	1860

1825
English explorer **Hugh Clapperton** and his manservant **Richard Lander** explore the lands around the Niger River in West Africa (see pp. 200–01)

1827
Frenchman **René Caillié** becomes the first European to visit the city of Timbuktu and leave it alive, before crossing the Sahara to Tangier (see p. 201)

▶ **1860–61**
Burke and Wills cross Australia from south to north, but die on the return journey (see pp. 188–91)

▲ **1804**
Lewis and Clark set out to explore the lands of the newly acquired Louisiana Purchase; they travel from St. Louis across North America to the Pacific coast (see pp. 174–77)

▲ **1850**
German **Heinrich Barth** travels across the Sahara north to south; in 1852, he makes his way alone along the Niger River to Timbuktu (see pp. 202–03)

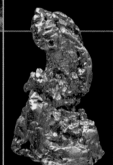

◀ **1868**
After two years of conflict, a peace treaty is signed between the **gold miners** of Dakota and the **Oglala Sioux Indians**

◀ **1805**
Scot **Mungo Park** returns to West Africa to explore the Niger; he is attacked by locals and drowns near the Bussa Falls while attempting to escape (see pp. 194–97)

▶ **1854–56**
David Livingstone crosses Africa from west to east, starting in Luanda in Angola, and finishing in Quelimane near the mouth of the Zambezi River (see pp. 220–23)

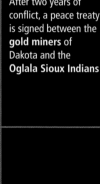

1868
English artist and explorer **Thomas Baines** explores southwest Africa, keeping a record of his travels with paintings and photography (see pp. 208–09)

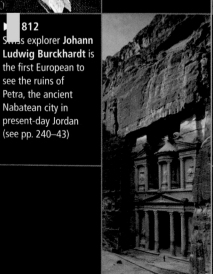

◀ **1812**
Swiss explorer **Johann Ludwig Burckhardt** is the first European to see the ruins of Petra, the ancient Nabatean city in present-day Jordan (see pp. 240–43)

▲ **1840**
English farmer **Edward Eyre** begins his epic journey west across Australia, setting out from the recently founded city of Adelaide (see pp. 186–87)

◀ **1857**
Richard Burton joins John Hanning Speke to search for the source of the Nile River (see pp. 204–07)

▶ **1871**
German geographer **Ferdinand von Richthofen** travels extensively around China, identifying the ancient Silk Road trails through the Qilian Mountains (see pp. 258–59)

▶ **1843**
John Frémont searches for routes for settlers to pass westward through the Rocky Mountains of the United States (see pp. 180–81)

▶ **1858**
John McDouall Stuart makes the first of six journeys into the Australian interior, which will culminate in a successful crossing from south to north (see pp. 184–85)

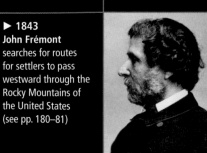

1872
HMS *Challenger* sets sail from Portsmouth, UK, to begin its four-year voyage of scientific discovery, during which more than 4,000 new marine species are discovered

◀ **PP. 164–65** A Tang Dynasty Buddhist painting from the Mogao Caves, near Dunhuang in Central Asia, which Marc Aurel Stein visited in 1907 (see pp. 234–37)

By 1800, most of the world's landmasses, aside from Antarctica, had at least in part been explored. Within them, however, lay regions where political turmoil or remote conditions meant that knowledge was limited. In Australia, the United States, and Canada, a series of concerted pushes during the first half of the 19th century opened up the interior. In sub-Saharan Africa, European explorers began to use the great waterways of the Congo, Nile, and Zambezi to move inland, and to solve the mysteries of the source of these rivers, which had long vexed outsiders. In areas where European control was less certain, such as East Asia, North Africa, and Arabia, explorers still penetrated, continuing to fill in areas that had seemed for centuries—at least in Europe—to be mere "blanks" on the map.

1875

▲ 1874–77
Henry Morton Stanley becomes the first European to travel all around the great lakes Victoria and Tanganyika in Central Africa (see pp. 214–15)

► 1876
Charles Montagu Doughty begins his two-year journey around Arabia (see pp. 246–47)

◄ 1893
Mary Kingsley makes her first journey to West Africa, spending time with the Fjort people of the Congo and traveling along the Gabon River (see pp. 212–13)

1900

► 1900
Hungarian **Marc Aurel Stein** makes his first expedition to Central Asia, exploring routes along the southern edge of the Takla Makan Desert (see pp. 234–37)

◄ 1904
Francis Younghusband heads the British Tibet mission to Lhasa, which is intended to strengthen British interests in the "Great Game" with Russia (see p. 231)

► 1906
Swede **Sven Hedin** travels around southern Tibet, an area previously unknown to Europeans, where he conducts extensive land surveys (see pp. 228–31)

► 1909
Getrude Bell travels around Mesopotamia, conducting archeological work at Ukhaidir and Carchemish, where she collaborates with T. E. Lawrence (see pp. 252–53)

► 1917
Harry St. John Philby is the first European to complete an east–west crossing of Arabia, his safe passage proving that the future king, Ibn Saud, has the loyalty of the tribes in the region (see pp. 238–39)

1922
The **tomb of Tutankhamun** is discovered by English archeologist Howard Carter in Egypt's Valley of the Kings

1925

► 1930
Freya Stark makes her first visit to the remote region of Uristan in western Persia; she draws detailed maps of the area (see pp. 254–55)

◄ 1930
Bertram Thomas embarks on his crossing of the forbidding Rub' al Khali, or Empty Quarter, in southern Arabia (see pp. 248–49)

1931–36
Pole **Kazimierz Nowak** travels 25,000 miles (40,000 km) across Africa on foot and by bicycle

► 1945
Wilfred Thesiger makes his first long journey through the Rub' al Khali, during which he studies the culture and survival techniques of the Bedouin people (see pp. 250–51)

MAPPING THE LAND

THE SURVEYING AND MAPPING OF UNKNOWN LANDS WAS THE MAIN DRIVING FORCE FOR MANY EXPLORERS. THIS WAS PARTICULARLY THE CASE IN AUSTRALIA, RUSSIA, AND THE UNITED STATES, WHOSE INTERIORS WERE LARGE, UNEXPLORED CONTINENTAL LANDMASSES.

SIBERIAN SCENE
A Cossack map of Siberia from 1571 shows the paucity of geographical information about the Russian East. It formed the basis of a more detailed map by Semyon Remezov in 1687.

The tradition of cartography in Europe dates at least as far back as the 6th century BCE and the maps of Greek philosophers Anaximander and Hecataeus. The idea of surveying the land using scientific instruments to establish a precise measurement of distances also has classical precedents. In Roman times, surveyors called *agrimensores* measured the territory around new colonies, dividing the area into squares in a process known as centuriation, which can still often be detected in the organization of landholdings nearly 2,000 years later. In the Middle Ages, *Practica Geometriae* by Leonardo of Pisa outlines the use of a quadrant in surveying, while the Renaissance humanist Leon Battista Alberti described a number of different surveying techniques, including the use of triangulation to fix positions.

MAPPING THE NEW WORLD

Following Columbus's first landfall in the Americas in 1492 (see pp. 86–89), the new data available to European mapmakers increased enormously. Within a century, much of the coastline of the Americas, Africa, and the East Indies was charted. This, combined with the popularization of the new printing process, led to an explosion in the number of maps in circulation—from a few thousand before 1450, to millions by the end

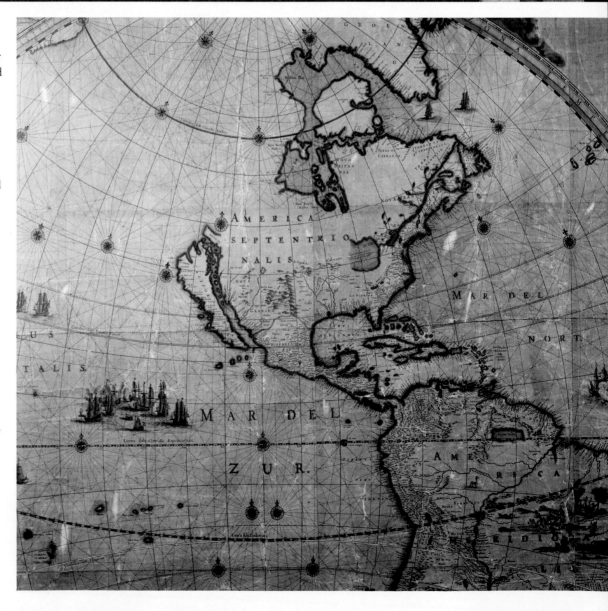

ERRONEOUS ISLANDS, BLANKS, AND VOIDS
This mid-17th-century map of the world is remarkable for showing California as an island, and the northwestern United States still as a complete void yet to mapped.

MOUNTAIN SURVEY
The American explorer, mountaineer, and cartographer Henry Bradford Washburn made the first ascents of more than a dozen Alaskan peaks.

RAIL FREEDOM
The construction of railroads across the continental United States and, later, across Russia into Siberia helped to cement the political cohesion of those two countries.

SETTING THE SCENE

- **Roman surveyors** use a *groma*, a stafflike instrument with cross arms to lay out plots, setting sights against a second *groma* positioned a predetermined distance away.

- Although **Vitus Bering sails through the Bering Strait** dividing Asia from the Americas (see pp. 170–71), he fails to travel far enough to the northeast to prove definitively that the two continents are not joined.

- Many maps in the early 1840s show the **"Buenaventura River"** flowing from the Great Salt Lake in Utah. Frémont's 1844 expedition spends a great deal of time searching for **this fictitious waterway**.

- The Russian military explorer Nikolai Przhevalsky (see p. 236) makes **four journeys into Central Asia** from 1870–85 as Russia and the UK compete for influence in the region in **"the Great Game."** An avid naturalist, Przhevalsky studies the fauna and flora, but is contemptuous of the people he meets, comparing the Chinese to "mean Moscow pilferers."

- The first successful **east–west crossing of Australia** is achieved by Edward Eyre (see pp. 186–87) in 1840–41, traversing the Nullarbor Plain to Albany, Western Australia.

- The completion in May 1869 of **the first transcontinental railroad in the United States** means that passengers can now cross the continent in relative ease.

ARTIFICIAL HORIZON
Surveyors used artificial horizons to take measurements when the actual horizon was not visible, using the reflection of the Sun or stars against its mirror.

of the 16th century. The increased accessibility of this knowledge itself fueled further investigation, as explorers sought to fill in the "blanks" on the map, sometimes propelled by erroneous notions portrayed on them, such as the existence of the southern continent of *Terra Australis* or a "great inland sea" in Australia. At other times, they searched for features such as the sea passage between Asia and the Americas or the Northwest Passage across the top of Canada, which were initially elusive but eventually proved to be real.

SURVEYING SIBERIA

The need to establish the topography and resources of lands immediately beyond areas that were already settled impelled some of the greatest 19th-century expeditions. Throughout the late 16th century, Russian expeditions moved progressively east across Siberia, establishing settlements such as Tobolsk (in 1587) and exploring the great waterways of the Ob, Enisei, Amur, and Anadyr. The first general map of Siberia was produced in 1667 under the auspices of Peter Godunov, the military governor of the province. The tradition of central sponsorship of mapping and exploration continued into the

reign of Peter the Great (1682–1725). The Russian czar conceived the Great Northern Expedition, led by Vitus Bering (see pp. 170–71), which surveyed a great stretch of the northern coast of Siberia from 1733–43 and traversed the Bering Strait between Russia and America.

OPENING UP THE WEST

The fledgling United States faced the problem of expanding westward into unknown territories, while at the same time fending off the competing claims of France to Louisiana, Spain to Florida, Texas, and California, Great Britain to Oregon, and Russia to Alaska. The acquisition in 1803 of more than 1 million sq miles (2 million sq km) of formerly French territory by the Louisiana Purchase opened up an area in need of exploration. The Lewis and Clark expedition of 1804–06 (see pp. 174–77) surveyed the new lands and established a route to the Pacific.

Further expeditions followed in their wake, including those of John Frémont (see pp. 180–81), who from 1842–46 traveled far along the Oregon Trail and into the Sierra Nevada, pioneering routes along which many thousands of settlers would travel. As expeditions, adventurers, and settlers surged across the continent, the "blanks" in the map between the East and West coasts closed up.

> Satnav systems mean that maps are now available instantly to travelers almost anywhere in the world, but remote parts of Amazonia, Africa, and Central Asia have still not been completely surveyed.

THE AUSTRALIAN INTERIOR

Exploration of the Australian coastline proceeded rapidly in the late 18th and early 19th centuries, and English navigator and cartographer Matthew Flinders circumnavigated the continent in 1801–03. The arid interior presented enormous challenges, but the challenge of traversing the continent from south to north—a feat first achieved by John McDouall Stuart in 1862 (see pp. 184–85)—led to the exploration of much of central Australia. The belief that there was a large sea at the heart of the continent provided the motive for a number of explorers, notably those of English officer Charles Sturt, who led several expeditions into the interior. Sturt's last attempt in 1844 resulted in 18 months of extreme privation, enduring temperatures of more than 127°F (53°C) and finding only the most meager watercourses in the Great Stony Desert.

VITUS BERING

FIRST SCIENTIFIC EXPLORER OF SIBERIA

DENMARK   1681–1741

THE DANISH-BORN NAVIGATOR Vitus Bering explored the northwest Pacific under the patronage of Russian czar Peter the Great. At the beginning of the 18th century, this vast region was still a blank on the map. The czar sent Bering to find out whether Asia and America were linked by land. During his second expedition to search for a land bridge, Bering discovered Alaska and the Aleutian Islands. He died during the return voyage, when he and his crew were forced to spend the winter on an Arctic island.

A LIFE'S WORK

- Is criticized for **his first voyage**, when he fails to find the coast of Alaska
- Returns to the northwest Pacific 10 years after his first voyage and **successfully crosses from Russia to Alaska**
- The expedition's large group of scientists **collects extensive data** about the geography, and flora and fauna of the region
- **Dies during the return voyage** when he and his crew are forced to spend the winter on the island now called Bering Island
- Paves the way for **Russian expansion** eastward

Bering was selected to lead an expedition to the northwest Pacific in 1725, as part of Russia's territorial expansion under Peter the Great. A land bridge, linking Cape Chukchi on the Kamchatka peninsula to the North American continent, was an intriguing possibility. The expedition party, complete with provisions, was transported at great expense from Moscow across Siberia to Russia's far east, from where the exploration was to begin.

HUGGING THE COAST

By 1728, Bering was ready to set sail on the *Gabriel*, a vessel specially built for the expedition on the coast of Kamchatka. He headed north, following the Russian coast so closely that he sailed between the two continents without sighting America, although he was only some 70 miles (110 km) away. Bering returned to Moscow in 1730 and provided detailed reports on the flora and fauna of the region, but could not offer solid evidence of a land bridge.

Three years later, he was commissioned to return to the northwest Pacific by Czarina Catherine I, Peter's successor. The Great Northern Expedition, as it was known, was a huge undertaking, involving more than 3,000 men, including eminent scientists from all over Europe, one of whom was the German naturalist Georg Wilhelm Steller, who later wrote a detailed account. Bering was not only to map the coast of North America, but also to establish Russia's interests in the wider Pacific region.

After 10 years of preparation, two new ships were built at the Okhotsk shipyard: the *St. Paul*,

STELLER'S SEA COW
This large, slow-moving mammal was first described during Bering's 1740–41 expedition. An easy source of meat for hungry sailors, it was hunted into extinction just 27 years after it was discovered off the coast of Kamchatka.

commanded by Bering, and the *St. Peter*, captained by Alexei Chirikov, his lieutenant on the first voyage. Bering sailed in September 1740, overwintering in Awatchka Bay before sailing for the American coast in June 1741. America was sighted on July 18. Bering spoke to the assembled officers and gentlemen in his cabin: "Now we think we have found everything, and many are full of expectations like pregnant windbags! But they do not consider where we have reached land, how far we are from home, and what accidents may yet happen." The naturalist, Steller, joined a small landing party, which went ashore in the vicinity of Kayak Island, and became the first European to set foot on Alaskan soil.

DISASTROUS RETURN

On the return voyage, the crew of the *St. Paul*, which had become separated from the *St. Peter*, fell victim to an outbreak of scurvy, and the ship was forced to

TAMING SIBERIA

Peter the Great saw the untapped resources of Siberia as key to Russian development. Siberia was first conquered by Russia in 1582, when Yermak Timofeyevich defeated the Mongols at the Battle of Cuvash Cape. Yermak later drowned under the weight of his chain mail as he fled a surprise Mongol attack, and the Russians withdrew. Yermak had explored the river routes through central Siberia and the Russians retook the region using this knowledge in the decades that followed, pushing east to the Pacific coast. The Kamchatka peninsula, which Bering used as a base, was first explored and settled by Vladimir Atlasov in 1700.

SIBERIAN SHAMAN
This engraving, from Georg Wilhelm Steller's work, *Description of the land of Kamchatka* (1774), shows a shaman from the Kamchatka peninsula dressed in leather robes and carrying a ceremonial drum and drumstick.

WE HAVE ONLY COME TO AMERICA TO TAKE WATER TO ASIA

GEORG WILHELM STELLER, ON BEING TOLD THAT THEY WILL ONLY BE STAYING AT KAYAK ISLAND LONG ENOUGH TO TAKE ON WATER

land on the Komandorskiye Ostrova island group, which they mistook for the coastline of Kamchatka. The decision was taken to overwinter in grim conditions with the men constructing sub-surface shelters dug below the permafrost. Many of the party perished, including Bering, who died on December 19, 1741. Only 46 of the remaining party survived.

Although he had not survived his expedition, the reports, mapping, and samples from Bering's exploration set the course for Russian expansion into the east for the next century. The American territories that would eventually become the state of Alaska were held by Russia until they were sold to the United States in 1867.

IN HIS FOOTSTEPS

→ **1728—First voyage**
Bering sails along the Siberian coast from the Kamchatka peninsula in search of a land bridge to America; he reaches as far north as the strait that now bears his name, but does not sight the coast of Alaska

→ **1740–41—Reaches Alaska**
He returns to Siberia with a major scientific expedition, and discovers Alaska and the Aleutian Islands; Bering dies during a fraught return journey

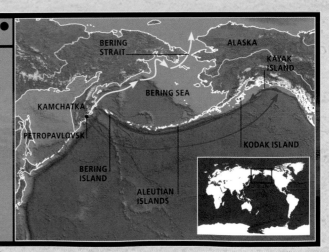

EXPERIENCING LIFE IN THE...

STEPPE AND TUNDRA

STEPPE AND TUNDRA ARE TWO DISTINCT CLIMATE ZONES. Both environments have provided explorers with challenges that could only be met by adopting the skills of local nomadic peoples. Steppe is characterized by grassland plain, while tundra, found in the far northern hemisphere, is characterized by subsoil permafrost. The Eurasian steppe, mostly within Central Asia, is crisscrossed by the ancient paths of the Silk Road.

PEOPLE OF THE COLD

Initial contact between Europeans and the Inuit people of the Arctic occurred with the arrival of the Vikings in Greenland in about 985CE. The Vikings never fully adapted to the harsh environment, however, and it wasn't until the 19th century that European explorers learned valuable lessons from the Inuit. The Inuit's relationship with the landscape, captured in their phrase "Our Land is our Life" provided explorers such as Matthew Henson (see pp. 310–11) with an awareness of the value of Inuit dress, food, and transportation to survive extreme cold. Farther south, the nomadic peoples of the Eurasian steppe experienced an interplay with cultures from East and West along the Silk Road.

DRESSING TO SURVIVE

When traversing the frozen wastes of the Canadian Arctic or Alaska, European explorers found that adoption of Inuit clothing was essential to limit exposure to frostbite, wind-chill, and hypothermia. In the Arctic, the Inuit made use of sealskin for summer clothing and caribou in winter. In the Inuit tradition, all parts of an animal were used, with shoes made from seal and caribou hide, toughened by chewing. The "anorak" (an Inuit word) was a heavy jacket with a hood to protect the face. It was invented by the Caribou Inuit for protection against wind-chill while hunting and kayaking. The garment was regularly coated in fish oil, which made it waterproof, if pungent. On the Eurasian steppe, thick padded felt clothing made from yak and sheep's wool and camel hair provided protection against subzero winds. The "parka," another type of hooded jacket, is a Nenets word from Russia (pictured below).

NOMADS OF THE TUNDRA
Here, a Nenets tribesman of western Siberia herds caribou, his main livelihood. The Nenets also breed Samoyed dogs to help herd and pull sleds.

TRANSPORT CHALLENGES

In the Arctic Circle, caribou- and dog-drawn sleighs have provided transportation (and at times, food) for centuries. As Marie Herbert, wife of British explorer Wally Herbert remarked, "dogs don't break down … and when you run short of food, you can't eat a Skidoo." On the Kirghiz Steppe in the late 19th century, Swedish explorer Sven Hedin (see pp. 228–31) rode Kirghiz horses. Central Asian nomads are skilled horsemen and their horses, much prized, are capable of digging for grass under the snow, unlike European breeds. Motorized transportation arrived in the steppe of Mongolia after World War I. Although the grassy terrain was suited to motor transportation, information on early routes was difficult to obtain and all parts and towing equipment had to be carried. Gasoline too, had to be transported and carried.

LONG-HAUL CAMEL
A Bactrian camel being loaded in Mongolia. With their ability to drink brackish water and survive long periods without sustenance, camels are invaluable on long trips.

SHELTER KNOW-HOW

Inuit expertise in building temporary winter hunting lodges, or igloos, in the Arctic Circle was a skill picked up by some explorers. On his crossing of Baffin Island in 1924, J. Dewey Soper found shelter in a large snow hut at Kognung. Lit by blubber lamps, the hut included a raised sleeping platform and, despite frosts, was warm and offered facilities for drying wet clothing, "an inestimable advantage in all phases of winter work in the Arctic."

NOMAD HOSPITALITY

In 1891, on the Mongolian steppe, Sven Hedin enjoyed the protection of "blanket tents" or yurts, while sampling a *dastarkhan* (a "spread") of mutton, rice, sour milk, and tea with his Kirghiz nomad hosts.

MONGOLIAN MOBILE HOME
The traditional Mongolian home, the yurt, is a felt-covered, lattice-framed structure, with thicker walls than a tent.

A MAN WHO HAS CARIBOU HAS FOOD, TRANSPORTATION, GODS, AND FRIENDS

NENETS SAYING

FINDING FOOD

The Arctic has a seasonal supply of seals, fish, and game in the spring and summer months, with the Arctic fox available year-round as prey. Despite this, scurvy has historically been the killer disease of Europeans exploring the steppe and tundra, with even well-stocked expeditions succumbing to the tell-tale symptoms of fatigue, weakness, and aching joints.

UNDERSTANDING NUTRITION

By the late 19th century, a reliance on canned food, fresh meat, and an understanding of antiscorbutics (cures for scurvy) was vital. For example, in 1893 on Franz Josef Land, US explorer Frederick J. Jackson described preferring the meat of bears and walruses to his canned fare. Later explorers on Baffin Island in the 1930s were cautious about reliance on game: "large 'blanks' exist in the Arctic where no game at all exists … in any of these a party might easily meet death by actual starvation." They made sure they had adequate canned stock.

PREPARING FOOD FOR WINTER
Here, Inuit women preserve fish as food for the winter by smoking them in a tent.

COPING WITH EXTREMES

In the Central Asian steppe, temperatures can range from -40°F (-40°C) to 104°F (40°C), depending on the season. The spring thaw made progress difficult through the "sea of mud" recorded by European travelers, while in winter, pack horses sank in snow drifts. Sven Hedin's Kirghiz guides advised him to lay sheets of yurt blanket for the horses to walk on. In the Arctic, temperatures may fall to -90°F (-68°C). In such conditions, the Inuit return to the shelter of a regular hunting bay and relocate ice holes to where they know seals can be killed for food and blubber burned for warmth and light.

INUIT MITTENS
These 19th-century Inuit mittens are made from sealskin, with fur linings. No synthetic materials have yet improved on fur's ability to trap warmth.

LEWIS AND CLARK

HEROES OF THE AMERICAN WEST

UNITED STATES 1774–1809; 1770–1838

MERIWETHER LEWIS　　**WILLIAM CLARK**

MERIWETHER LEWIS AND WILLIAM Clark led an expedition across the United States in 1804–06, charting the territories that had been purchased from the French in 1803. They made maps of the vast new regions, and notes on the people and wildlife, relying on their American Indian guide Sacagawea to communicate with the tribes they met. Lewis and Clark's expedition greatly increased understanding of the lands they crossed.

In 1803, France's Emperor Napoleon Bonaparte sold the entire Louisiana territory to the United States for $15 million. The Louisiana Purchase, as it became known, effectively doubled the size of the United States overnight. Given the enormous breadth of the new lands, US President Thomas Jefferson immediately commissioned a survey party to explore the landscapes, assess the potential for settlement, and identify a route west to the Pacific. To this end, he appointed Captain Meriwether Lewis to lead the expedition. Lewis, a Virginian with experience of the frontier lands, selected William Clark, a fellow Virginian, to help him. The two men assembled a team for a "Corps of Discovery" comprising 33 men, later to be joined by a Shoshone woman, Sacagawea, as a translator of the American Indian languages, Shoshone and Hidatsa.

SETTING OUT

The Corps set off along the Missouri River in April 1804, entering Indian tribal lands hardly known to the US government. Indeed, the Corps soon came to depend on the knowledge and goodwill of the local tribes. Not all would be so well disposed toward the explorers, however.

Lewis knew that once they reached the headwaters of the Missouri, they would have to ask the Shoshone people for horses to carry them safely through the Rocky Mountains. As Patrick Gass, a sergeant with the Corps, stated in his journal, "We were to pass through a country possessed by numerous, powerful, and warlike nations of savages, of gigantic stature, fierce, treacherous, and cruel; and particularly hostile to white men." Fortunately, Sacagawea's presence removed the threat of attack from many of the tribes, and even more so following the birth of her baby son during the expedition.

Sailing by keelboat (a shallow riverboat) up the Missouri, the party encountered many Sioux and French traders who were taking their pelts and animal fat downriver by canoe. Despite good morale and a plentiful supply of deer and other game shot for food, Clark and others complained of illness as the expedition proceeded. As Clark noted in his idiosyncratic prose style: "The party is much afflicted with Boils, and Several have the Deassentary, which I contribute to the water (which is muddy) … The Ticks and Musquiters are verry troublesome [sic]."

GIFT FOR A PRESIDENT
Lewis and Clark described more than 100 new species of animal. They sent a Black-Tailed Prairie Dog (left) in a cage as a gift to President Jefferson.

I DO NOT BELIEVE THAT THERE IS IN THE UNIVERSE A SIMILAR EXTENT OF COUNTRY EQUALLY FERTILE AND WELL WATERED

MERIWETHER LEWIS, ON THE MISSOURI VALLEY

LEWIS AND CLARK COUNTY, MONTANA
The party reached the area of the present-day state of Montana on April 27, 1805. Just east of Wolf Point, Clark and George Drouillard, who was an excellent hunter and translator, killed the largest grizzly bear they had yet come across. On the same day, Clark peered into a den of wolf pups.

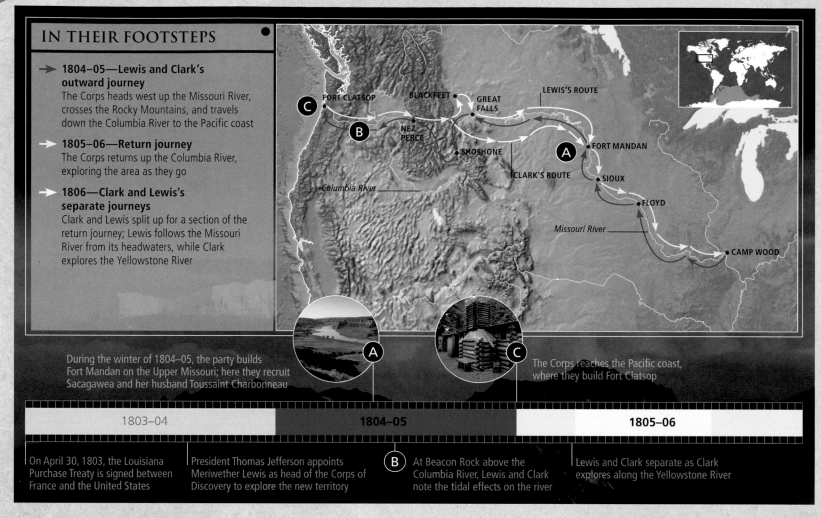

IN THEIR FOOTSTEPS

→ **1804–05—Lewis and Clark's outward journey**
The Corps heads west up the Missouri River, crosses the Rocky Mountains, and travels down the Columbia River to the Pacific coast

→ **1805–06—Return journey**
The Corps returns up the Columbia River, exploring the area as they go

→ **1806—Clark and Lewis's separate journeys**
Clark and Lewis split up for a section of the return journey; Lewis follows the Missouri River from its headwaters, while Clark explores the Yellowstone River

FORT CLATSOP   BLACKFEET   GREAT FALLS   LEWIS'S ROUTE

NEZ PERCE

SHOSHONE   FORT MANDAN

CLARK'S ROUTE   SIOUX

Columbia River   FLOYD

Missouri River   CAMP WOOD

During the winter of 1804–05, the party builds Fort Mandan on the Upper Missouri; here they recruit Sacagawea and her husband Toussaint Charbonneau   Ⓐ

Ⓒ   The Corps reaches the Pacific coast, where they build Fort Clatsop

1803–04	**1804–05**	**1805–06**

On April 30, 1803, the Louisiana Purchase Treaty is signed between France and the United States

President Thomas Jefferson appoints Meriwether Lewis as head of the Corps of Discovery to explore the new territory

Ⓑ At Beacon Rock above the Columbia River, Lewis and Clark note the tidal effects on the river

Lewis and Clark separate as Clark explores along the Yellowstone River

INDIAN NATIONS

In August 1803, Lewis led a council with members from the Oto and Missouri Indians. This first meeting set a template for future encounters, and as the expedition progressed, Lewis recorded his impressions of the tribal groups. These accounts point to a growing understanding of the indigenous civilizations as contact increased. In October 1804, Lewis recorded the earth dwellings of the Mandan and Hidatsas people in North Dakota, noting that the settlement held more than 4,500 people.

LEWIS AND CLARK ATTEMPT TO WIN FAVOR WITH A LOCAL TRIBE IN THE LOUISIANA TERRITORY

On June 13, 1805, the expedition reached what Lewis described as "the grandest sight I ever beheld"—the Great Falls of the Missouri River, above which lay the headwaters of the river. As the Corps edged closer to Sacagawea's homeland, Lewis recorded that, "The Indian woman recognizes the country and assures us that this is the river on which her relations live … This piece of information has cheered the sperits [sic] of the party who now begin to console themselves with the anticipation of shortly seeing the head of the Missouri." Despite this positive note, many members of the expedition were suffering badly from fatigue. Lewis's concern on reaching the continental divide was clear: without the aid of horses, crossing the Rocky Mountains would be all but impossible: "If we do not find them or some other nation who have horses I fear the successfull issue of our voyage will be very doubtfull [sic]."

TO THE PACIFIC

Progress upriver became more difficult as the rapids increased in strength, but on August 12, 1805, Lewis finally reached the source of the

HISTORY BOOK
The Louisiana Purchase, signed with France, is preserved inside this elaborately embroidered single volume.

Missouri, which brought a great deal of satisfaction. Lewis wrote, "Thus far I had accomplished one of those great objects on which my mind has been unalterably fixed for many years … after refreshing ourselves we proceeded on to the top of the dividing ridge from which I discovered immense ranges of high mountains still to the West of us … here I first tasted the water of the great Columbia River." Shortly afterward, the Corps finally encountered a Shoshone village where, with the help of Sacagawea, Lewis procured much-needed horses and mules. The party proceeded along the Columbia toward Oregon until Clark spotted the snowy peak of Mount Hood in October 1805. The Corps descended into the forests of the Pacific Northwest, and reached Gray's Bay on the Columbia River's estuary, some 20 miles (30 km) from the Pacific coast. As Patrick

TRIBAL CONFERENCE
In 1825, Clark met with many of the tribes at Prairie du Chien, Wisconsin (shown here). The goal was to limit the tribes' land claims and to end their feuding.

Gass recorded, "We are now at the end of our voyage, which has been completely accomplished according to the intention of the expedition, the object of which was to discover a passage by the way of the Missouri and Columbia rivers to the Pacific ocean; notwithstanding the difficulties, privations and dangers, which we had to encounter."

For the remainder of the expedition, Lewis and Clark frequently broke off into smaller parties to explore the Louisiana Territory in greater detail before the return journey east. In September 1806, the Corps returned to St. Louis, prompting a great celebration of their achievement. Lewis was appointed governor of the Louisiana Territory, with Clark serving as liaison officer with the American Indian peoples. But tragedy was to ensue as Lewis, unsuited to his desk-bound role, suffered from financial problems, administrative failures, and charges that he planned to split the Louisiana Territory from the United States. Accused of treason, Lewis may have committed suicide during a journey to Washington to clear his name, although some believed that he was assassinated as part of a wider political conspiracy.

Today, Lewis and Clark are widely celebrated in the United States for carrying out one of the first major explorations of North America, which was achieved with minimal force and a greater understanding of the role and contribution of native peoples than had previously been shown.

CABEZA DE VACA

SPAIN   C. 1490–1559

Long before Lewis and Clark, another expedition was not so fortunate in its encounters with the American Indians.

Álvar Núñez Cabeza de Vaca was one of only five survivors of an ill-fated, 300-man expedition led by conquistador Pánfilo de Narváez through the lands around the Gulf of Mexico in 1537–28. They were attacked by local tribes and suffered disease. Cabeza de Vaca's account of the experience included some of the earliest descriptions of the area's indigenous tribes.

LANGUAGE PUZZLE
Here, Sacagawea interprets the party's intentions to Chinook Indians. Although she spoke no English, her French-Canadian husband, Toussaint Charbonneau, could translate her words into French, which in turn was translated into English by the Corps.

IN THEIR OWN WORDS

LEWIS AND CLARK

DURING THEIR EPIC JOURNEY of 1804–06, Meriwether Lewis and William Clark led the Corps of Discovery in making some of the most significant species discoveries in the history of the United States. By the time of their return, they had identified more than 300 new species of flora and fauna. They recorded their other scientific discoveries in a series of elkskin-bound field books, accompanied by journals, which documented their achievement for the newly created nation.

E   SNOW ON THE MOUNTAIN
Euphorbia Marginata is an annual flower native to North America. William Clark collected native specimens from the area of Fort Atkinson, Nebraska, and the Yellowstone River, Montana in 1804 and 1806 respectively.

A   CLARK'S DIARY
This is the diary kept by William Clark from 1804–06. The outer canvas wrapper provided protection from the elements as they traveled.

B   ILLUSTRATION OF A TROUT
Clark's drawing of the "cutthroat trout" (with a distinctive red color to the jaw). It was given the species name *Oncorhynchus clarki* in his honor.

C   "COCK OF THE PLAINS"
A sketch by Clark of the Sage Grouse, or Cock of the Plains, was drawn in his diary. Clark described how he "Sent out Hunter to shute the Prairie Cock, a large fowl which I have only seen on this river."

D   FLATHEAD NATION
Along the Columbia River, Clark encountered the Indian Flathead Nation. He illustrates the bizarre method the Indians used to flatten their heads.

Clarksville 17th July 1803

Dear Lewis

[handwritten letter, partially legible]

F LETTER OF ACCEPTANCE
This is William Clark's letter accepting Lewis's invitation to join the Corps of Discovery, written from Clarksville and dated 1803. Lewis had been commissioned earlier that year to explore the newly purchased territory of Louisiana by President Thomas Jefferson, who had described the goals of the expedition: **To explore the Missouri River and such principal stream of it as by its course and communication with the waters of the Pacific ... the most direct and practicable water communication across this continent.**

G FRONTISPIECE
The frontispiece "A Canoe Striking on a Tree" from the *Journal of the Voyages and Travels of a Corps of Discovery*, written by Patrick Gass, sergeant on the expedition and published in this edition of 1811. Gass was the expedition's head carpenter and organized the construction of the Corps' winter quarters.

H GASS'S JOURNAL
Patrick Gass had kept a journal of the expedition, which was first published to popular acclaim in 1807, and sold for a dollar a copy in Pittsburgh, Pennsylvania. He was responsible for coining the phrase "Corps of Discovery."

JOURNAL
OF THE
VOYAGES AND TRAVELS
OF
A CORPS OF DISCOVERY,

Under the command of Capt. Lewis and Capt. Clarke
of the army of the United States,

FROM THE MOUTH OF THE RIVER MISSOURI THROUGH
THE INTERIOR PARTS OF NORTH AMERICA
TO THE PACIFIC OCEAN,

During the Years 1804, 1805, and 1806.

CONTAINING

An authentic relation of the most interesting transactions

JOHN FRÉMONT

FOUNDER OF FREE STATE CALIFORNIA

UNITED STATES   1813–90

SOLDIER AND POLITICIAN John Charles Frémont was born in Savannah, Georgia, to a French immigrant and the runaway wife of a Virginia planter. Despite the social ignominy of his birth, Frémont won fame leading several expeditions to map vast regions of the United States. His pioneering became political when he incited an uprising against Mexican rule in California in 1846, after which he became the first Republican Party candidate to run for president, on an antislavery ticket.

Frémont studied at Charleston College, South Carolina, where he exhibited a considerable talent for mathematics. In July 1838, this was to win him the position of second lieutenant in the Corps of Topographical Engineers, in which role he joined two expeditions tasked with mapping the vast region between the Missouri and Upper Mississippi rivers.

FIRST EXPLORATION

In 1842, Frémont led an expedition of his own. His goal was to return to the Mississippi and the lands to the west of it to find the most practical crossing point for settlers traveling west through the Rocky Mountains. During the journey, he carried out a land survey, combining botanical and geological data with detailed drawings. His report was published by Congress, setting off a wave of immigration to the West. This success

led to a second expedition, in 1843, to the Columbia River in the Pacific northwest, and southward into the mountains of the Sierra Nevada (in present-day California and Nevada). The southward leg of the journey became increasingly hazardous as Frémont and his men trekked through deep snow. At one point, a mule, loaded with botanical samples, hurtled to its death from a clifftop, and the Indian guides refused to accompany him farther into the wilderness. Yet he succeeded in his goal of being the first to map the mountains, to which Gold Rush settlers soon came to mine their fortunes.

CALIFORNIA ADVENTURE

In May 1845, Frémont's third expedition was to the most remote areas of the West, through the Mexican Republic into the desert parts of Alta California. At the borders of Mexican-controlled California, Frémont left his men, making his way alone to Monterey, where he received permission from the Mexican governor to explore

PRESIDENTIAL CANDIDATE
Frémont's running mate for the 1856 presidential election was William Dayton (right). They lost to Democratic candidate James Buchanan (President, 1857–61).

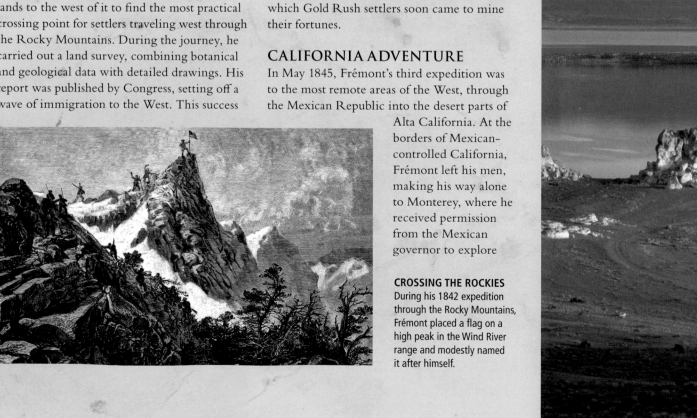

CROSSING THE ROCKIES
During his 1842 expedition through the Rocky Mountains, Frémont placed a flag on a high peak in the Wind River range and modestly named it after himself.

the San Joaquin Valley. It seems that exploration was not on Frémont's mind, because once there, he set about inciting rebellion against the Mexican authorities among the American settlers, which had perhaps been his brief from the start. Mexican troops attacked, and Frémont hurriedly left for Oregon. En route, he encountered US soldiers carrying orders to the US consul in Monterey, and to Frémont, to claim rights in the region of California. Returning to Sacramento, Frémont took command of the American settlers, and, within 60 days, the northern part of California was taken from Mexican control. On July 4, 1846, Frémont proposed to the settlers that they should declare themselves free of Mexican rule, and that California should become a free state.

ARREST AND DISHONOR

On January 16, 1847, Frémont was appointed military governor of California. Then, despite his achievement, he was arrested and charged with mutiny. The complaint was made by US General Kearney, who claimed he had orders from the president and secretary of war to serve as governor instead. Frémont was convicted of the offense and discharged from the army. In order to restore his good name, Frémont undertook a fourth, private expedition in 1848,

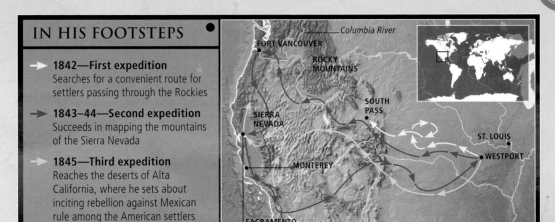

IN HIS FOOTSTEPS

→ **1842—First expedition**
Searches for a convenient route for settlers passing through the Rockies

→ **1843–44—Second expedition**
Succeeds in mapping the mountains of the Sierra Nevada

→ **1845—Third expedition**
Reaches the deserts of Alta California, where he sets about inciting rebellion against Mexican rule among the American settlers

to the head of the Rio Grande, on the US–Mexico border. The expedition ended in disaster when the party was caught in a severe snowstorm. Frémont sent men back to the nearest settlement for help. After 16 days with no sign of relief, Frémont set out with three men and soon came upon the despatched party in a state of terror and starvation, close to the body of their leader, who they had partially eaten. He succeeded in reaching help, however, and returned to his original camp, where many had perished. Undeterred by the experience, Frémont carried out his planned expedition, successfully finding a route to Sacramento.

After a bid for the presidency as a Republican candidate, Frémont served in the Civil War. His work in mapping huge areas of the United States opened up the West for settlement, but he died in New York at aged 77, a largely forgotten figure.

RIDING TO THE WEST
Here, Frémont, in his "prairie" uniform, leads the men of his third expedition westward to California.

VAST NEW LAND
On his 1843–44 expedition into the Sierra Nevada, Frémont became the first person to map the mountains, as well as the first non-American Indian to lay eyes on Pyramid Lake (shown here) and Lake Tahoe.

WAGON TRAIN

FOLLOWING IN THE FOOTSTEPS of the explorers Lewis and Clark came the waves of pioneers who would tame the "Wild West." They traveled in trains of heavy freight wagons, such as the Conestoga, which were basic but stoutly built. Later pioneers would benefit from the "Chuck wagon." Thought to have been invented in 1876 by Charles "Chuck" Goodnight, the Chuck carried the food that sustained the hungry settlers during their arduous journeys. It would blaze a trail ahead of the main train, setting up camp in advance of the settlers' arrival. The Chuck wagon could carry provisions for 30 days, and from it a cook prepared basic but hearty fare.

► **CHUCK BOX**
Located at the rear of the Chuck wagon, the Chuck box was the nerve center of the wagon. The box was protected by a hinged wooden lid, which converted into a table for the cook's exclusive use. It contained drawers and compartments for equipment and provision stores.

▼ **CLEANING UP**
The "wreck" or "round up" pan was stored on top of the Chuck box. During a meal, it was put beneath the cook's table and dirty dishes were placed inside it.

► **SAFE STORAGE**
The gaps in the floorboards of the Conestoga wagon were filled with tar to make them waterproof. This ensured that goods were kept dry when the wagons had to cross rivers.

▼ **CUTTING DOWN TREES**
Double saws and axes were carried on the side of the wagon to chop firewood and clear camp areas.

► **ROUGH RIDER**
Wooden wagon wheels rotated around tough iron axles, which could endure rough routes.

◄ **COWHIDE BAGS**
Durable and waterproof, hide bags were ideal for protecting valuables from getting soaked.

▲ **RIDING HIGH**
The cook sat under the semi-shelter of the front canvas on the Chuck wagon. His seat was often crudely sprung to remove some of the jolt on the wagon, which had no suspension.

► CLEAVING THE MEAT
Salt pork was a common staple, to which a resourceful cook would add game, shot en route by settlers.

▲ THE "JEWELRY CHEST"
The chest contained strips of torn raw hide for repairs, horse-shoeing equipment, and other items that required quick access.

◄ LIGHTING THE WAY
Lamp oil was an expensive resource and its use was rationed between "outfitting" stations on the trail.

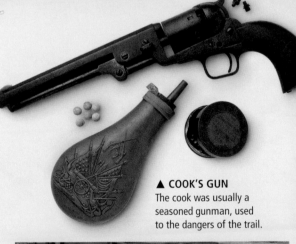

▲ COOK'S GUN
The cook was usually a seasoned gunman, used to the dangers of the trail.

◄ EXTRA STORAGE
Bedding and clothing were stored under the protection of canvas, but a wagon would carry additional store boxes (shown here) on sideboards between the wheels.

▲ STURDY TRANSPORTER
The hard-wearing Conestoga, the classic wagon of the pioneers, could carry up to 11,000 lb (5,000 kg) of cargo. Many poorer settlers traveled in more rudimentary converted farm wagons.

▲ WATER SOURCE
A water barrel was positioned on the side of the wagons. It contained enough water for about two days.

IN NO TIME OR COUNTRY HAS ANY PIONEER MORE DIRECTLY ADVANCED THE INTERESTS OF A COLONY THAN MR STUART

SIR RODERICK MURCHISON, THEN PRESIDENT OF THE ROYAL GEOGRAPHICAL SOCIETY

CHAMBER'S PILLAR
Stuart was the first European to set eyes on this rocky outcrop just south of Alice Springs when he reached it in April 1860. The 160 ft (50 m) sandstone pillar was an important landmark to aid the navigation of later explorers. Its Aboriginal name is Idracowra.

JOHN McDOUALL STUART

PIONEER OF AUSTRALIAN EXPLORATION

SCOTLAND   1813–66

A CIVIL ENGINEER FROM SCOTLAND, John McDouall Stuart immigrated to Australia in 1838 to become one of the key surveyors of the continent's vast interior. He became an accomplished bushman, learning the craft on the 1844 expedition of English explorer Charles Sturt, which discovered the Simpson Desert, before leading six expeditions of his own. Stuart's final expedition saw him cross the continent from south to north, but the rigors of the journey ruined his health and he died soon afterward.

UNDER ATTACK
This wood engraving from 1879 depicts Aboriginal Australians attacking Stuart's camp during his 1862 crossing of the continent.

On his first expedition, in 1858, Stuart explored the northwest area of South Australia, looking for new pasture land and minerals. In the process, he discovered a permanent waterway he named Chamber's Creek. After a journey of 1,500 miles (2,400 km), he returned to Adelaide to apply for a lease on the land extending from Chamber's Creek before returning to the area to survey it. In March 1860, Stuart crossed the northern boundary of South Australia and progressed steadily to the center of the continent. On April 22, he became the first European to reach the heart of the continent, planting the British flag "on a hill which I named Central Mount Sturt, after the father of Australian exploration."

TELEGRAPH ROUTE
Stuart's success led the state authority to support a further expedition to establish a route plan for the new overland telegraph. Stuart set out from Chamber's Creek

STUART'S SEXTANT
Stuart carried this sextant with him on his expeditions. He used it both to measure the angles between landmarks for his charts and to measure the angle of the Sun to calculate his position.

in January 1861 with 11 men and 49 horses. The journey was difficult, and lack of water and supplies forced him to turn back.

He tried again in January 1862, but by now the traveling was taking its toll, and he felt that his health was failing, while the horses on the expedition suffered badly from heat exhaustion. The group pushed northward to the coast, where Stuart was "gratified and delighted to behold the water of the Indian Ocean."

Stuart's premonition about his own condition proved correct: during the return journey, he suffered two strokes and had to be carried on an improvised stretcher between two horses. The party struggled back to Adelaide, arriving on December 17, the first Europeans to make a return crossing of the continent. Half-blind and partially crippled, Stuart returned to London, where he died at the age of 50. He would not be forgotten, however, as his route formed the backbone for the Australian telegraph system, the railroad line from Adelaide to Darwin, and the eponymous Stuart highway.

IN HIS FOOTSTEPS

- **1858—First expedition**
  Makes his first exploration of South Australia in search of new pastures
- **1859–60—Pushes north**
  Explores farther into northern South Australia during his second and third expeditions
- **1860–61—Into the interior**
  On his fourth and fifth expeditions, he reaches the center of Australia, the first European to do so
- **1861–62—Coast to coast**
  On his final expedition, he makes it right across the continent

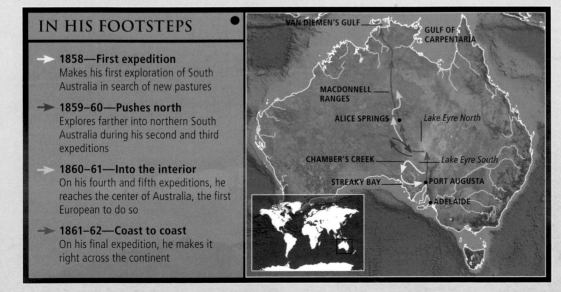

EDWARD EYRE

DROVER TURNED EXPLORER OF AUSTRALIA

ENGLAND   1815–1901

A SHEEP FARMER who went exploring for new grazing pastures, Edward Eyre greatly increased knowledge about the land surrounding the new city of Adelaide in South Australia before embarking on a daring journey west. In the company of his Aboriginal guide, Wylie, Eyre trekked 1,200 miles (2,000 km) from Adelaide to Albany in Western Australia, covering territory that was completely new to Europeans. He later went on to govern Jamaica, where his reputation was ruined by allegations of brutality.

EYRE AND WYLIE ARE RESCUED
When they reached the coast near the end of their epic trek west, Eyre and Wylie were picked up by a French whaling ship, whose captain, Rossiter, took them on board to recuperate.

A LIFE'S WORK

- Explores the **land surrounding Adelaide**, concluding that it was not suitable for settlement

- Journeys along the **south coast of Australia**, making it to Albany with his guide, Wylie, after his two other guides had murdered his European companion

- His **career ends in disgrace** when, in 1865, as governor of Jamaica, he is accused of using excess force to put down a rebellion

northwestern Victoria, which would significantly shorten the journey. Other drovers had avoided that scorched, waterless waste with good reason, and as his cattle began to die and men threatened to quit, Eyre was forced to retrace his steps and take the conventional route. The profit he made from the sale of his stock in Adelaide was to fund his future exploration.

IN SEARCH OF NEW PASTURES

In May 1839, Eyre and his overseer, John Baxter, set out in search of a viable, well-watered route from Adelaide west across the Spencer Gulf to Port Lincoln. Hugging the coast the distance would be about 400 miles (640 km), but Eyre wanted to explore inland in the hope of finding undiscovered grazing land. Traveling north from Adelaide, they reached the head of the gulf, from where they explored north, west, and east, finally finding decent grazing land around the Murray River to the east. Eyre then attempted the journey in reverse. They traveled northeast from Port Lincoln, but soon ran short of water and had to detour across what is now called the Eyre Peninsula to Streaky Bay. From there he traveled east to Mount Arden, discovering a vast dry salt lake just to the north which "I distinguished with the name of Colonel Torrens," before turning back to Adelaide.

Eyre grew up in Yorkshire, England, the son of a parson. At the age of 16 he intended to join the army, but was dissuaded by his father, who suggested he try his luck in Australia, an idea that appealed to Eyre's adventurous spirit. He arrived in Sydney in 1832 and soon established himself as a sheep farmer with a station at Molonglo Plains near Canberra. In 1837, he met the English explorer Charles Sturt, whose tales of exploration fueled his own urge to explore.

Eyre decided to drive his sheep overland to Port Phillip, near Melbourne, a four-month journey through difficult terrain. He sold the flock at Port Phillip, and thereafter resolved to combine business with exploration. His next venture was to drive cattle to Adelaide by crossing the desert of

EYRE'S WATCH
Eyre carried this watch on his expeditions. A watch was crucial to help him work out his position, and he kept it safe in a wooden case.

- The first European to locate the **Niger River**, establishing the direction of its flow and charting its partial course

- Inspired by the work and dedication of his champion, **Sir Joseph Banks**

- Through his careful observations, creates an important **geographical record** of the West African landscape

- Provides detailed information on the economics of the **slavery systems**, which informs the abolitionist debate in Britain

MUNGO PARK

A YOUNG MAN OF NO MEAN TALENTS

SCOTLAND   1771–1806

IN 1795, A YOUNG SCOT with a yearning for adventure set off on one of the greatest journeys of exploration in West Africa. Mungo Park was born to tenant farmers in the Scottish borders. A studious boy, he had been expected to make his career in the church, but a youthful self-belief and a fascination for the natural world led him to study medicine at Edinburgh. Soon, he had the globe in his sights and a desire to "acquire a greater name than any other ever did" by voyaging to Africa in search of the Niger River.

After Edinburgh, Park's medical studies had taken him to the College of Surgeons in London, where he was introduced to the influential naturalist Sir Joseph Banks (see p. 197). It proved a fateful meeting. On Banks's recommendation, the 21-year-old Park was given the position of surgeon's mate on board the *Worcester,* an East India Company ship bound for Sumatra in Southeast Asia in February 1793. The three-month journey was uneventful, but Park's passion for adventure had been ignited. Although nominally only a surgeon's mate, on his return he presented a paper on the discovery of eight new species of fish.

In the late 18th century, the interior of Africa was a mystery to Europeans. To promote research, the African Association had been founded in 1788, and Banks lost no time in presenting Park. Soon it was agreed to that the young adventurer would depart on an expedition to seek out the mysterious Niger, a mission Park embraced gladly, despite the fact that the previous man given the job had been apparently murdered en route to Timbuktu.

Park was given a £200 letter of credit for presentation to Dr. John Laidley, whose trading station was at Pisania on the banks of the Gambia, and a party of 50 men.

GOING IT ALONE

Whether through impatience or a desire to go it alone, Park took a passage on the brig *Endeavour* before the party could be formed, sailing in May 1795. He arrived at the trading station on July 5 and soon came down with malaria. With typical determination, he spent his convalescence mastering the Mandé language used in Gambia and other areas of West Africa, knowing how vital communication would be to his mission.

In December 1795, Park left on his journey to find the Niger River supported by Johnson, a Mandingo guide, and Demba, a slave boy. He took with him a horse, two asses, a sextant, a

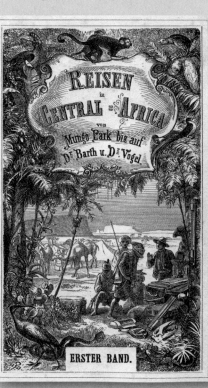

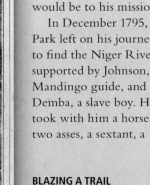

BLAZING A TRAIL
Park's explorations of Central Africa inspired many in Europe to follow him. This German book, written decades after his death, honors Park as a trailblazer in the region.

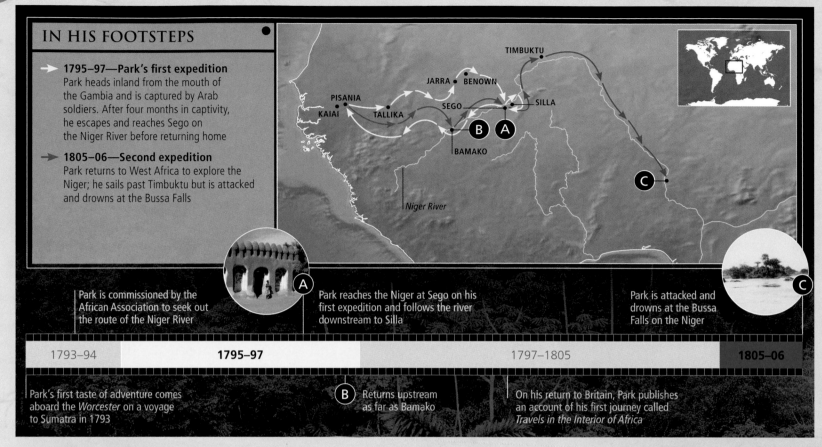

IN HIS FOOTSTEPS

→ **1795–97—Park's first expedition**
Park heads inland from the mouth of the Gambia and is captured by Arab soldiers. After four months in captivity, he escapes and reaches Sego on the Niger River before returning home

→ **1805–06—Second expedition**
Park returns to West Africa to explore the Niger; he sails past Timbuktu but is attacked and drowns at the Bussa Falls

---

A Park is commissioned by the African Association to seek out the route of the Niger River

A Park reaches the Niger at Sego on his first expedition and follows the river downstream to Silla

C Park is attacked and drowns at the Bussa Falls on the Niger

1793–94	**1795–97**	1797–1805	**1805–06**

Park's first taste of adventure comes aboard the *Worcester* on a voyage to Sumatra in 1793

B Returns upstream as far as Bamako

On his return to Britain, Park publishes an account of his first journey called *Travels in the Interior of Africa*

---

compass, two fowling pieces, two pairs of pistols, and an umbrella. As goods for exchange or barter he carried a small quantity of beads, amber, and tobacco. Park followed a route east to Medina, then onward to Simbing, and farther into the interior and the semidesert area of Kaarta. There he was a vulnerable figure. Without an obvious intention to trade, why would a white man travel, apparently aimlessly, in such a way?

As he made his way through the upper Senegal basin, he was arrested and held for four months by the local Moorish king, Ali. By his own account, Park's behavior, clothing, and language fascinated the king. Although threatened with violence, Park survived his imprisonment. His possessions were removed, except for the compass, which he was allowed to keep because it was seen as having magical properties. Throughout his incarceration, Park made detailed descriptions of his Arab captors, their sensibilities and trading systems.

In May 1796, King Ali agreed that Park could accompany him on a journey to Jarra, and the young man took the opportunity to escape on horseback with nothing but his compass and diary. He reached Sego on July 21, 1796, and there he saw "with infinite pleasure the great object of my mission—the long sought-for majestic Niger, glittering to the morning sun, as broad as the Thames at Westminster." Park was the first European to see the river and to establish the direction of its flow—eastward. He followed it downstream as far as Silla before turning back. His return journey began on July 30, 1796, following the river's course for some 300 miles (500 km), during which time he became ill again, and survived only thanks to the care of Karfa Taura, a trader who gave him food and shelter for seven months. Still riddled with disease, Park joined a line of slaves heading west and staggered back to the Gambia coast. He finally reached Pisania on June 10, 1797, and sailed for England on December 22.

RETURN TO AFRICA

Park arrived home to a hero's welcome but soon grew bored of the attention. He returned to Scotland to finish his diaries, which were published to great acclaim in 1799. The lure of Africa remained strong, however, and five years later he accepted a second mission to the Niger. This expedition of 1805 was to be on different terms. Park proposed that it was for "the extension of British commerce and the enlargement of our geographical knowledge." In response, the Colonial Office asked him to assess the potential for European settlement. The scale of the expedition was ambitious. It included a force of 30 soldiers and the

MUMBO-JUMBO AND OTHER CULTURAL MATTERS

Park's liberal attitude deserted him when he saw the "Dance of the Mumbo-Jumbo". A ritual whereby Mandingo men dressed up prior to resolving domestic disputes, Park thought it "an indecent and unmanly revel". On other matters he was broad-minded. When a group of intrigued women wanted to check whether a Christian man was circumcised, he joked that he would only show the prettiest.

THE MUMBO-JUMBO, BASED ON PARK'S DIARY DESCRIPTION OF THE DANCE

wherewithal to construct 50 ft (15 m) boats in situ on the Niger. Park was given a captain's commission and a generous grant toward the costs of the operation.

ILL-FATED MISSION

The expedition departed in January 1805, an injudicious time because they then arrived at the height of the hot season. Worse still, no Africans volunteered to join the group, fully aware of the weather conditions they would encounter. The convoy departed from Kaiai on April 27, 1805, retracing the route of Park's first expedition. From Bamako the journey to Sego was undertaken by canoe, but by August the

REAL KNOWLEDGE OF AFRICA
Park's diary, *Travels in the Interior of Africa*, remains in print as the first great anthropological work on Africa. The drawings were made by the English geographer James Rennell, working from Park's notes.

party was in disarray. Blighted by rains and fevers, matters had deteriorated still further by November, so that of the 44 Europeans who left the Gambia, there remained only Mungo Park and four others. The other men had died before they had even reached the Niger. Park and one of the surviving soldiers converted two canoes into one boat, which he named the *Joliba* (the Niger in Mandé). Park's letter to the Colonial Office reveals the desperate situation. He wrote: "Though all the Europeans who are with me should die, and though I were myself half dead, I would still persevere, and if I could not succeed in the object of my journey, I would at least die on the Niger." At Bussa Falls, the boat became lodged in the rocks, and, under attack by hostile locals, Park drowned as he attempted to swim to safety.

The details of Park's death were recounted in the journal of Amadi Fatouma, one of the guides who survived the expedition. This account was corroborated in 1825, when the Lander brothers (see pp. 200–01) reached Bussa Falls.

More than 200 years after his death, Park remains an inspirational figure. His diaries inspired Livingstone (see pp. 220–25) and the novelists Joseph Conrad and Ernest Hemingway. For his courage, open-mindedness, and modesty about all he saw, Park is held to be one of the first great explorers of Africa.

SIR JOSEPH BANKS
ENGLAND   1743–1820

The naturalist and explorer Joseph Banks was a leading figure in the late 18th and early 19th century scientific world.

Banks showed his extraordinary ability as a botanist on James Cook's first expedition to the Pacific Ocean. His passion for science in all its forms was to act as a catalyst for the transfer of scientific knowledge in Europe at that time. Along with close colleagues Carl Linnaeus and Daniel Solander, Banks was a key figure in the development of botany as a field of study. He was appointed president of London's Royal Society in 1778, and his position and reputation had a lasting impact on Mungo Park.

BANKS BECOMES A BUTTERFLY IN A CARTOON BY JAMES GILROY. THE OCCASION WAS BANKS'S KNIGHTHOOD IN 1797

MAJESTIC NIGER
This river island on the upper reaches of the Niger in Mali appears today as it did when Park saw it. The river runs for 4,025km (2,500 miles) eastwards from the hills of Sierra Leone to the Nigerian coast. Its breadth was a beautiful sight to Park as he followed its course through the great sub-Saharan Muslim empires of the area.

EXPERIENCING LIFE IN THE...

RAINFOREST AND JUNGLE

THE SPANISH CONQUISTADORS were the first Europeans to explore virgin jungle, venturing deep into the Amazon Rainforest in search of fabled cities of gold. Encountering true jungle, where towering trees gave way to dense, impenetrable vegetation, they took to waterways whenever possible. In this way, South America's greatest river—the Amazon—was charted, while in equatorial Africa, the Congo and Zambezi rivers were explored by Stanley and Livingstone to the same end in the 19th century.

LAW OF THE JUNGLE

The jungle is a hazardous arena for the explorer. Poison-dart frogs, tarantula spiders, anacondas, leeches, biting ants, killer hornets, and virile, waterborne diseases are only the mildest of the dangers. Other animals, such as crocodiles, include humans on their list of prey. Brushing against vegetation may embed barbs in human skin, which soon becomes infected in the humid conditions. Some dangers have vanished with time, although tribes practicing cannibalism—at whose hands the occasional missionary met his fate—persisted until the early 20th century in the jungles of Melanesia and some Pacific Islands. The indigenous peoples of the rainforest, however, have had good reason to fear the arrival of Europeans (see right).

The jungle allows no respite after dark. Hosts of bats and monkeys take the night shift, shrieking and hunting, attracted to the lights of the camp.

RAINFOREST RAFTERS
These New Guinea warriors, believed to be cannibals, were photographed in 1919.

LOST PEOPLES

Uncontacted jungle tribes have an enduring fascination in popular culture. Arthur Conan Doyle's *Lost World* (1912), for example, has engendered inumerable variations and movies. The human rights organization Survival International estimates that there are about 100 tribes worldwide, mainly in the Amazon Rainforest and the Malaysian archipelago, that remain uncontacted by civilization. To preserve their isolation, some have made contact dangerous or difficult. The Sentinelese of the Andaman Islands in the Indian Ocean habitually attack outsiders on sight. Those in Brazil are endangered by logging. Most lack immunity to common human diseases that explorers would carry with them.

DISCOVERED FROM THE AIR
An uncontacted Amazonian tribe was photographed from the air in May 2008. They tried to shoot arrows at the plane.

JUNGLE FEVER

Humidity can cause heat exhaustion and—more seriously—heatstroke, which can be fatal. The symptoms include nausea and dizziness, vomiting, diarrhea, and fatigue. Prickly heat, which occurs when sweat glands become blocked, results in an irritating rash, while damp conditions can lead to fungal infections of the feet and groin. Explorers have to put up with being constantly wet. Writing of the 16th-century Amazon Rainforest expedition of Gonzalo Pizarro, Peruvian historian Inca de la Vega observed that, "On account of the constant waters from above and below … their clothes rotted, so that they had to go naked."

SAFE SHELTER

Given the often waterlogged ground, and the snakes and bugs that lurk beneath the leaf litter on the jungle floor, the best shelters are those that are raised on a platform or suspended between trees. Mosquito nets are essential, as is a waterproof tarpaulin to keep out the rain—after spending the day soaked to the skin, it is important to sleep in a dry environment. Explorers of the past found it hard to make a camp in such conditions, where, even if a fire could be lit, it attracted swarms of biting insects. The conquistadors often used abandoned shelters, sometimes with fatal consequences. Once deserted by humans, shelters become havens for snakes, scorpions, the fungus that causes the lung condition histoplasmosis, and the assassin bug, which transmits the deadly Chagas disease.

AVOIDING CREEPY CRAWLIES
Jungle shelters are best located above ground level to deter insects, and should be sited away from rivers and rotting trees to avoid flash flooding and falling branches.

USING WATERWAYS

Jungle makes traveling overland very difficult. Not only must a path be hacked through tangled vegetation, but the ground may also be waterlogged or contain dangerous organisms, such as the parasitic guinea worm, known to 16th-century explorers as "the fiery serpent" for the pain it causes as it burrows into tissue.

Traveling jungle waterways is safer, but not without its share of hazards, including caymans, piranhas, and anacondas. Spanish conquistador Francisco de Orellana and his men built a brigantine—a two-masted vessel designed to be sailed and rowed—to travel down the Amazon River in the 16th century. For his exploration of the Congo River 400 years later, Henry Morton Stanley (see pp. 214–15) ordered the construction of a barge 30 ft (9 m) long in London. "When finished, it was to be separated into five sections, each of which should be 8 ft (2.5 m) long." These were shipped to Africa, ensuring that when Stanley began his journey of the Congo River, he had a large, soundly constructed vessel.

MESSING ABOUT ON THE RIVER
This boat is navigating a piranha-infested waterway in Guyana, in 1934. In such regions, traveling by canoe is inadvisable, given the danger of tipping over.

THE AFRICAN FEVER, HAVING FOUND MY FRAME WEAKENED, ATTACKED ME VIGOROUSLY

HENRY MORTON STANLEY, DESCRIBING A FEVER IN WHICH HE LOST 7 LB (3 KG)

JUNGLE FOOD

The jungle environment contains limited food and water and, for the uninitiated, using what little may be available locally could result in poisoning and death. Drinking untreated water can cause amebic dysentery, a dangerous and debilitating illness that was the cause of death for many of the conquistadors. In recent years, instances of water pollution from heavy metals, such as mercury—a by-product of the gold-mining industry—have become more common, particularly in the Amazon.

Early expeditions carried as much food as they could and relied upon bartering, buying, or stealing food from local people. When Francisco de Orellana's Amazon expedition exhausted its supplies, "they had nothing to eat but the skins that formed their girdles, and the leather of their shoes, boiled with a few herbs."

THE WORLD'S MOST DEADLY ANIMAL

In terms of the number of human deaths it causes each year, the tiny mosquito is the most dangerous animal in the world. The female carries viruses and parasites from person to person that result in diseases such as yellow fever, dengue fever, and malaria. Mosquitos bite and infect more than 700 million people annually in Africa, South America, Central America, and much of Asia, resulting in millions of deaths. In the humidity of jungles and rainforests, mosquitos breed in vast numbers, with females laying their eggs in marshy ground, ponds, and rivers. The link between mosquitos and malaria was discovered only in 1880 by Charles Louis Alphonse Laveran, a French army doctor in Algeria who observed parasites inside the blood cells of infected people. Before then, explorers of the tropics, such as René Caillié (see p. 201) were simply said to have died from a fever.

SNIFFY BITER
Mosquitos prefer some people to others. They sniff for sweat that smells sweetly of carbon dioxide and octenol.

RICHARD LANDER

MAPPER OF THE NIGER RIVER

ENGLAND   1804–34

TOGETHER WITH HIS BROTHER JOHN (1807–39), Richard Lander was credited with discovering the course of the Niger River in West Africa. Mapping the route of the river had been the great goal of British explorers since Mungo Park had first seen it in 1796. In 1832, Lander became the first winner of the Royal Geographical Society Founder's Medal, "for important services in determining the course and termination of the Niger." Two years later, while on a trade expedition, he died in an attack by Nigerian tribesmen.

ISLAMIC EMPIRE
Kano, in present-day Nigeria, appears today much as it did when Lander and Clapperton went there in 1825. Back then, the city was in the Islamic Empire of the Sokoto caliphate.

A LIFE'S WORK

- Traces the course of **the lower reaches of the Niger**, but is later killed when he returns to the area to open it up to European trade

- Is arrested for plotting against the king of Badagri and undergoes an **ordeal by poison**, proving his innocence by surviving the posion

- **Records local customs** such as body piercing, tattooing, and male and female circumcision

Richard Lander was born in Truro in Cornwall, England, in 1804, the son of an innkeeper. His brother John, who was to play a crucial role in his achievements, was born three years later. Richard showed early promise as an explorer, walking from his home town to London at only nine years old, before sailing to the West Indies at the age of 11. He later served as a manservant and assistant to English travelers in Europe and the Cape Colony, South Africa. Lander's great break came in 1825, when he accompanied Scotsman Captain Hugh Clapperton on his

second expedition to follow the course of the Niger River from the interior to its delta. This British expedition included two other Europeans: Doctors Dickson and Morrison. Both died from malaria shortly after their arrival in Africa. Close to Bussa Falls, where Mungo Park had died in 1806 (see pp. 194–97), some 200 miles (320 km) inland, Clapperton and Lander first sighted the Niger. From there, they traveled east to the city of Kano, then turned back to the west to reach Sokoto, a city on the banks of the Sokoto River, a tributary of the Niger. There, weakened by dysentery, Clapperton requested passage to the sea from Mohammed Bello, sultan of the city, by way of the Niger River. However, Clapperton's

THE NIGER DELTA
Richard Lander was the first European to reach the vast Niger Delta, an area of 30,000 sq miles (70,000 sq km), now home to 30 million people from more than 40 different ethnic groups.

illness was too much for him and he died on April 13, 1827, close to Sokoto. Suffering from a debilitating fever himself, Lander wisely traded equipment with Bello and gained permission to retrace his route overland to Badagri on the coast. His solo walk took him seven months. Having several times given up hope of returning alive, surviving arrest and brushes with Portuguese slave traders (although Lander had himself bought slaves for his journey), he expressed relief to be returning home.

BROTHERS TOGETHER

Lander returned to London, where Clapperton's papers were safely delivered and the full account of their joint achievement was published. He met with critical acclaim from the scientific and geographical communities and so impressed the British government that he was asked to return to the Niger to determine its lower course.

This time accompanied by his brother John, Richard set out from the coast on March 31, 1830, retracing the steps of the Clapperton expedition. After reaching Bussa Falls, they traveled up the treacherously rocky river by

Europeans in sight who might pay the fee, the Landers were handed over to a local trader, known as "King Boy," who paddled them to the Bight of Biafra in the Gulf of Guinea. There, the promise of a ransom was extorted from the unwilling captain of a British ship. Richard and John made their getaway on board this ship in the middle of a fierce storm, while the pirates waited eagerly onshore. The brothers finally returned to London, via Brazil, in June 1831. Fortune awaited them back home, where their journals were bought for 1,000 guineas ($75,000, today).

Richard Lander returned to Africa in 1832 as part of an expedition aiming to found a trading settlement on the Niger River. He was wounded in an attack and died from his injuries shortly afterward. Like so many of the early European explorers of Africa, a few years later his brother John succumbed to an illness he had contracted on the continent and died.

LANDER'S TELESCOPE
The Lander brothers surveyed the landscape that lay surrounding the Niger River. A Major W. M. G. Colebrooke gave Richard this wooden telescope for this purpose.

A contemporary of the Landers, René Caillié was the first European to reach the cities of Timbuktu and Djenné.

In 1827, he decided to make the first south to north crossing of the Sahara. He traveled through the West African cities of Djenné and Timbuktu in early 1828, before hiring a camel and crossing the desert with a caravan to arrive at Tangier, Morocco, in August.

canoe to the city of Yauri, where they were held hostage by the sultan for five weeks. On finally being allowed to leave, Richard and John were piloted back downriver by a local guide. The brothers noted a marked increase in river trade as they descended.

On November 5, near Kirree (present-day Asaba), the brothers' canoe came under attack from river pirates. They were taken prisoner and a ransom was sought. With no other

I STUPIDLY GAZED ON THE GHASTLY SPECTACLE BEFORE ME

RICHARD LANDER, ON WITNESSING HUMAN SACRIFICE IN BADAGRI

IN THEIR FOOTSTEPS

- **1825–27—Clapperton and Richard Lander explore the Niger**
  Clapperton dies of a fever, but Lander manages to return with Clapperton's papers

- **1827–28—Caillié crosses the Sahara**
  On the way, he visits Timbuktu, becoming the first European to enter the city and leave it alive, before crossing the Sahara to Tangier

- **1830–31—Brothers in West Africa**
  Richard and John Lander follow the Niger down to its delta in the Bight of Benin

- **1832—Richard Lander dies**
  He is killed on his third visit to Africa

○ Not shown on map

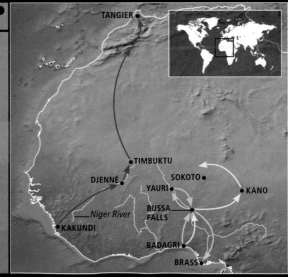

TANGIER

TIMBUKTU
DJENNÉ   SOKOTO
              YAURI   KANO
Niger River   BUSSA
              FALLS
KAKUNDI

BADAGRI
              BRASS

HEINRICH BARTH

A MODERN GEOGRAPHER IN WEST AFRICA

GERMAN CONFEDERATION   1821–65

HEINRICH BARTH WAS a German scholar, linguist, and explorer. His first taste of exploration came with a trip across the coast of north Africa, but it is for his travels in West Africa that Barth is remembered. In an era when it was normal for Europeans to consider other cultures inferior, Barth's sympathetic approach to the study of African peoples was ahead of its time. His meticulous account of his adventures remains a widely studied historical document.

In 1849, Barth joined the Mixed Scientific and Commercial Expedition to Central Africa, a British expedition under the command of a Captain James Richardson, which also included the noted German geologist and astronomer Adolf Overweg. The three men departed from Tripoli in spring 1850, but tensions within the party soon arose. Richardson's goal was to discourage the slave trade across the Sahara, while Barth and Overweg wished to conduct scientific study and to avoid local conflicts. The group reached the Tuareg town of Tin Tellust in early September, and stayed for two months before heading slowly south.

VILLAGE SCENE
Barth's account of his travels contains illustrations of scenes of West African life. This portrait is of the chief of the Musgu, a tribe living around the southern shores of Lake Chad.

SEAT OF LEARNING
Barth spent six months studying in Timbuktu. The city's university held unrivaled collections of ancient Arabic and Greek manuscripts.

GOING SOLO

In January 1851, the men reached Damergou on the southern edge of the Sahara, at which point Barth and Overweg parted ways with Richardson. They planned, however, to rendezvous at Kukawa on the shores of Lake Chad, but Barth sensed that Richardson, already ill, would not survive the journey. He wrote in his journal, "I did not feel sufficient confidence to entrust to his care a parcel for Europe."

After two days, Overweg and Barth also parted company. Barth set out for the city of Kano, meticulously recording the languages, customs, and histories of the peoples he encountered. He reached Kukawa in April 1851 to discover that Richardson had died. Overweg was also ill, and died in September 1852, just before fellow German Eduard Vogel arrived from Europe as a replacement for Richardson. It soon became clear that Vogel was a liability, refusing to learn Arabic, which was used as a second language by most people of the region. Undeterred, Barth departed for Timbuktu on his own on November 25, marking the dissolution of the official expedition.

UP THE NIGER

Barth spent the next year traveling along the Niger River, disguising himself in Arab dress to ensure a safe passage through Muslim lands hostile to Christian travelers. Throughout the

IN HIS FOOTSTEPS

➤ **1850–51—Across the Sahara**
The three explorers cross the Sahara Desert; they then split up, planning to rendezvouz at Lake Chad

➤ **1852–53—Along the Niger**
Traveling alone, Barth spends nearly a year making his way up the Niger River to Timbuktu; he stays in the city for six months

➤ **1854–55—Retracing his steps**
Despite rapidly failing health, Barth returns to Lake Chad and crosses the Sahara back to Tripoli

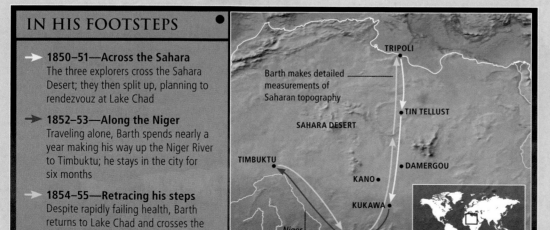

Barth makes detailed measurements of Saharan topography

TRIPOLI

TIN TELLUST

SAHARA DESERT

TIMBUKTU

DAMERGOU

KANO

KUKAWA

Niger River

wet season, he was severely weakened by bouts of fever, but he finally reached Timbuktu in September 1853. He stayed in the city for six months under the protection of his powerful friend Sheik El Bakay, an Arab who Barth described in a letter as "the Pope of Timbuktu." He made a detailed street plan of the city and notes on its potential for trade: "Small as it is, the city is tolerably well inhabited, and almost all the houses are in good repair. There are about 980 clay houses, and a couple of hundred conical huts made of matting."

Barth left Timbuktu in March 1854 and retraced his steps to Kukawa, suffering terrible rheumatism during another wet season. He pressed on across the Sahara, determined to reach home, "in order to give a full account of my labors and discoveries." By the time he reached Tripoli on August 28, 1855, he had traveled more than 10,000 miles (16,000 km) in just under six years. Barth's five-volume account of his travels provides a unique record of 19th-century west Africa, recording in minute detail the tribal vocabularies and places he visited. His observations enabled the first accurate maps of the region to be drawn, even though he had taken no astronomical readings. Barth's research was to form the foundation of all future geographical work in the Sahara, and he is regularly cited by historians today.

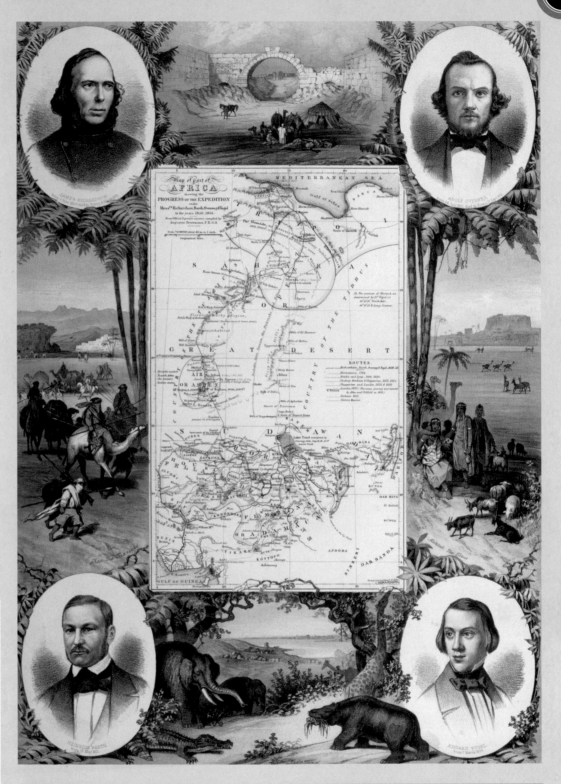

JAMES BRUCE
SCOTLAND   1730–94

James Bruce began life as an explorer after the death of his wife, funding himself with money inherited from his father.

Serving as British consul in Algiers from 1763, Bruce sought out Roman ruins and antiquities from Tunis to Tripoli. He survived a shipwreck off the coast of Libya to visit Crete, Rhodes, and Asia Minor. In 1768, he set out through Egypt dressed as a Turk, eventually reaching Gondar, the capital of Ethiopia, where he remained for two years. He then traveled to Lake Tana, the source of the Blue Nile, and in 1772 he became the first European to reach its confluence with the White Nile in Nubia.

[I AM] DETERMINED TO SET OUT TOWARD THE NIGER—TO NEW COUNTRIES AND NEW PEOPLE

HEINRICH BARTH

BURTON AND SPEKE

SEARCHERS FOR THE SOURCE OF THE NILE

ENGLAND   1821–90; 1827–64

RICHARD BURTON   **JOHN HANNING SPEKE**

THE EARLIEST MAP OF AFRICA, made by the Roman geographer Ptolemy, marked a mysterious land he called the "Mountains of the Moon," from which waters fed two parallel lakes. Although unconfirmed, these features were marked on all later maps for centuries. By the mid-19th century, speculation was rife about these lakes. Were they the source of the Nile River? In 1856, Britain's Royal Geographical Society decided to settle the question.

A LIFE'S WORK

- Burton undertakes a successful **hajj to Mecca** in 1853, disguised as an Arab and having had himself circumcised to reduce the risk of discovery

- Burton makes the first English translations of the *Kama Sutra* and *The Arabian Nights*

- During their first African expedition, Burton and Speke survive **horrific injuries**: Burton's cheeks are impaled by a javelin and Speke is repeatedly stabbed by spears

- Burton is the first European to set eyes on **Lake Tanganyika**, while Speke is the first European to see **Lake Victoria**

- Speke returns to Africa **with Grant**, and they identify **Ripon Falls** as the point at which the Nile River flows out of Lake Victoria

- Burton and Speke fall out over Speke's claims to have discovered **the source of the Nile**; Speke is proved correct after his death

- Speke **dies in a hunting accident** the day before he is due to debate publicly the source of the Nile with Burton

---

In London, the Royal Geographical Society (RGS) set up the East Africa Expedition and selected Richard Burton to lead it. Burton, a soldier, explorer, and distinguished Orientalist, chose British army officer John Hanning Speke as his companion. The men had traveled together on a British government expedition to Somaliland in 1854. Next, the RGS gave them the chance to renew their partnership on an expedition that could make history.

An unconventional but brilliant figure in strait-laced Victorian society, Burton was a free thinker who would go on to translate the *Kama Sutra* and *The Arabian Nights*. Famously, he had entered Mecca disguised as an Arab. His partner, Speke, had a more conventionally Victorian outlook, and a passion for big-game hunting. In short, the two shared little in common, and this was to contribute to a major disagreement over their "discoveries."

The pair set off to cross present-day Tanzania from the island of Zanzibar in June 1857, equipped with a map drawn by a J. J. Erhardt, a missionary recently returned to Britain from Africa. The map showed evidence of one vast inland sea, which eventually turned out to be lakes Victoria, Albert, and Tanganyika.

AN ARDUOUS JOURNEY

Even for such experienced explorers as Burton and Speke, the journey was difficult. Burton described how, when crossing the Rusugi River, they both had to be carried by their porters,

SKETCHBOOK PAGES
Speke's sketchbook is a remarkable record of his travels through Africa, with countless drawings of the flora and fauna he encountered.

AN "ARTIFICIAL HORIZON"
Speke navigated with the help of this instrument, which assisted in measuring the angle between celestial bodies and the horizon.

with "the upper part of the body supported by two men, and the feet resting upon the shoulders of a third—a posture somewhat similar to that affected by gentlemen who find themselves unable to pull off their own boots." Worse still, they contracted severe tropical infections: Speke lost the hearing in one ear due to a botched attempt to remove a beetle, while Burton was unable to walk for part of the journey. Both men were to suffer from temporary blindness brought on by fever. They had hoped to reach Unyanyembe, the capital of the "Mountains of the Moon," before the start of the wet season. During the final stage of the journey, they were exposed to monsoon conditions in open canoes. By the end of the expedition, their 30 asses had died, and many porters, refusing to deviate from the routes they knew, had left the party.

Reaching Lake Tanganyika in February 1858, Burton recorded the sighting of the lake, asking Sidi Mubarak Bombay, Speke's well-regarded African guide, "'What is that streak of light which lies below ...?' 'I am of the opinion,'

JOHN HANNING SPEKE
This oil painting of Speke, made after his death, portrays him standing in front of Lake Victoria, which he was convinced was the source of the Nile River. While out hunting on the day before he was due to debate the source of the Nile with Burton, Speke was killed by his own gun. He was an accomplished hunter, and some consider his death to have been suicide.

Unyanyembe - 4th October 1858 (J.H.S.)

SPEKE'S TANZANIA
In 1858, Speke recorded the landscapes through which he traveled on his way to Lake Victoria, such as this one at Unyanyembe. He later wrote about the region in his *Journal of the Discovery of the Source of the Nile* (1863).

ROUTE TO THE NILE
An 1863 map drawn by Grant and annotated by Speke shows their route from Zanzibar to Lake Victoria. The map also features lakes Albert and Tanganyika.

quoth Bombay, 'that that is the water.'" Burton's initial reaction was disappointment. "I gazed in dismay," he wrote. "The remains of my blindness … had shrunk its fair proportions … I began to lament my folly in having risked life and lost health for such a poor prize." But walking a few paces farther, "the whole scene suddenly burst upon my view … the shores … appeared doubly beautiful to me after the silent and spectral mangrove creeks on the East African seaboard. Truly it was a revel for me."

ON TO LAKE VICTORIA
By this time, Burton and Speke were physically weak and partially blinded, and their limited equipment had all been damaged, lost, or stolen. Speke recorded in his journal that their guide Said bin Salim, an Arab trader, proposed that they should head back to the nearest city, Tabora, where more money could be obtained to complete the exploration of the lake. The Englishmen agreed to return to the city to recuperate before undertaking further exploration. According to Speke, it was he who was most eager to continue. With Burton's agreement, he proposed that from Tabora they should then head north to reach Ukerewe, the great waterway described by Arab traders as being broader and longer than Lake Tanganyika. On returning to Tabora Burton was too ill to travel further, so Speke headed north with his own party.

Another Arab trader and friend, Mohinna, provided him with sufficient food and other supplies to make the journey possible.

In July 1858, Speke described his first impression of the new lake: "The caravan, after quitting Isamiro, began winding up a long but gradually inclined hill—which as it bears no native name, I shall call Somerset—until it reached its summit, when the vast expanse of the pale-blue waters of the N'yanza [the Bantu word for lake] burst suddenly upon my gaze." He named the lake "Victoria," in honor of his queen. In a later account, Speke was to record that, "I no longer felt any doubt that the lake at my feet gave birth to that interesting river, the source of which has been the subject of so much speculation."

RIVALRY AND ENMITY
Speke's theory was supported by Sheikh Snay, the Arab trader who had first described the lake to Speke and Burton. Speke was unwilling to travel along the south and east of the lake because the local people in those areas were described as "inhospitable," so further supporting evidence of the lake's role was not gathered. His assertion that he had discovered the Nile's source began the famous rift with Burton. On his return to Tabora, Speke "laughed over the matter, but expressed my regret that he [Burton] did not

SPEKE AND GRANT MEDAL
The Royal Geographical Society was so excited by the success of Speke and Grant's 1860–63 expedition that it struck this commemorative medal.

accompany me, as I felt quite certain in my mind that I had discovered the source of the Nile. This he naturally objected to, even after hearing all my reasons for saying so, and therefore the subject was dropped."

Notes from both explorers' field books had been read at RGS meetings during the expedition, but when he returned to London before Burton in May 1859, Speke was first to present his findings to the society, maintaining that Lake Victoria was the source of the Nile. Burton was furious: he had expected Speke at least to await his return before addressing the society. Burton asserted that Lake Tanganyika was the source of the Nile, believing that Lake Victoria was not one lake but a lake region of interconnecting waters. The enmity between the two was compounded by other factors, including disputes over personal payments made to porters.

SOURCE OF THE NILE

The RGS considered Speke's theory to have substance. In 1860, he was chosen to lead a new expedition to Lake Victoria. This time, he was traveling with James Augustus Grant (see box, right). His brief was to settle the debate and provide more detailed evidence of his claim. In July 1862, Speke correctly identified the Ripon Falls (in present-day Uganda) as the point at which the Nile flows from Lake Victoria, but as he and Grant did not then track the course of the river downstream, final proof was still required.

In 1864, on Speke's return to London, he and Burton were invited to appear before the British Association for the Advancement of Science to debate the issue at a meeting in Bath. On the day before the meeting, Speke was killed in a hunting accident. It would be the later expeditions mounted by Samuel Baker and David Livingstone (see pp. 220–25) that would confirm Speke's theory. However, Burton and Speke were both recognized for their parts in unlocking the secrets of the great African lakes.

JAMES AUGUSTUS GRANT
SCOTLAND   1827–92

Born in the Scottish Highlands, Grant (seated on the right, with Speke) started his career with the Indian British Army. Like Speke, he fought in the Sikh Wars of the 1840s. Illness prevented him from being with Speke when he found the Nile's source in 1862.

After the 1860–63 expedition, Grant published *A Walk across Africa*, as supplementary to Speke's account of their journey. In it he gave particular attention to "the ordinary life and pursuits, the habits and feelings of the natives" as well as to the economic resources of the regions he traveled through. He also made valuable botanical collections.

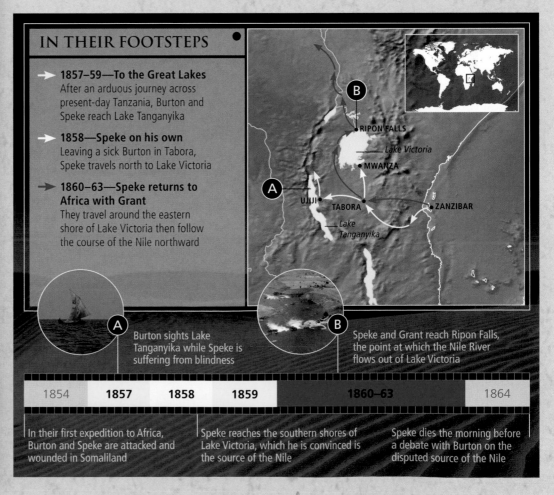

IN THEIR FOOTSTEPS

1857–59—To the Great Lakes
After an arduous journey across present-day Tanzania, Burton and Speke reach Lake Tanganyika

1858—Speke on his own
Leaving a sick Burton in Tabora, Speke travels north to Lake Victoria

1860–63—Speke returns to Africa with Grant
They travel around the eastern shore of Lake Victoria then follow the course of the Nile northward

A Burton sights Lake Tanganyika while Speke is suffering from blindness

B Speke and Grant reach Ripon Falls, the point at which the Nile River flows out of Lake Victoria

1854	**1857**	**1858**	**1859**	**1860–63**	1864

In their first expedition to Africa, Burton and Speke are attacked and wounded in Somaliland

Speke reaches the southern shores of Lake Victoria, which he is convinced is the source of the Nile

Speke dies the morning before a debate with Burton on the disputed source of the Nile

THOMAS BAINES

ARTIST TURNED EXPLORER

ENGLAND   1822–75

BORN IN KING'S LYNN, ENGLAND, to a seafaring family, Thomas Baines grew up dreaming of adventure. Unlike many of the privately funded "gentleman explorers" of the time, Baines had to earn his keep on the expeditions he joined. He did this by working as an artist, and produced a body of work that provides a unique pictorial record of northern Australia and southern Africa in the mid-19th century. Baines also became an accomplished naturalist in his own right, identifying and drawing new species of plant and insect.

ARTIST AT WORK

The young Baines learned his craft in England from the heraldic painter William Carr. In South Africa, he painted boats and portraits before joining the British army as a war artist during the Xhosa Wars. It was as the official artist on Gregory's northern Australia expedition (see below) that he began to record in detail the landscapes, flora, and fauna he saw. This sketch shows him working in a baobab tree by Lake Ngami, Botswana.

While serving an apprenticeship to a coach-builder, Baines would fill his sketchbooks with scenes of adventure. By the time he was 22, he had abandoned his trade and traveled to South Africa, where he worked as a sign-writer in Cape Town. Soon, however, he had ambitions to become a professional artist and from 1848 to 1851 he was employed as a war artist by the British army in the Cape. Baines next planned to undertake a journey for "artistic and geographic purposes into the African interior," with the main goal of locating the source of the Nile, but could not raise the necessary funds.

While on a visit to London in 1855, however, he was invited to join an expedition to northern Australia with the English explorer Augustus Gregory (1818–1905). The expedition's goal was to explore the northwest and Victoria River region and to assess its suitability for colonization. As an artist, Baines was the first European to make a visual record of the landscape and Aboriginal peoples of Australia's "top end." He completed a series of paintings that provide a unique pre-

MATABELE GOLD
In 1870, Baines joined the gold rush to Matabeleland. It proved to be one adventure too far, however, and he died of dysentery in Natal in 1875, at age 53.

photography record of mid-19th century Australia. He also began to record new species of plants and insects in his sketchbooks.

ALONG THE ZAMBEZI

As a result of the acclaim he received from the Australian expedition, Baines was appointed as artist to the "Zambezi Expedition" of Dr. David Livingstone in 1858 (see pp. 220–25). By character, Baines was a resourceful man, but Livingstone sought expedition members who would not interfere with or disrupt his plans. The expedition began without incident, and Baines was able to record the landscape of the Zambezi River and develop his skills as a naturalist. Disagreements between Baines and Livingstone started when the latter complained in his correspondence that Baines had "made away with [our] supplies of paper" (which may simply reflect the prodigious nature of Baines's output as an artist). Baines was accused of defrauding the expedition and forced to leave it in disgrace. Livingstone described

A LIFE'S WORK

- Works as a **war artist** during the Eighth and Ninth Xhosa wars in South Africa

- Becomes the first to make extensive **pictorial records of northern Australia**, discovering and drawing many new species

- Becomes one of the **first Europeans to see the Victoria Falls** during David Livingstone's Zambezi Expedition

- **Achieves fame** in Britain for his paintings and illustrations of his explorations

- **Travels solo** across southern Africa before becoming ill and dying in Durban

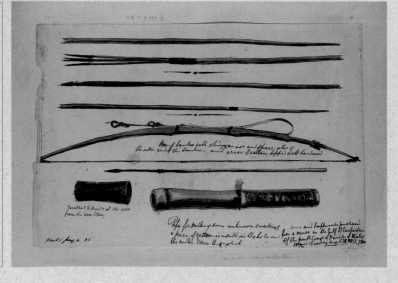

ARMS TO DRAW
Baines purchased these Aboriginal weapons in northern Australia. They include a bamboo bow, a pipe for smoking, and a gauntlet.

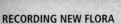

RECORDING NEW FLORA
Baines's curiosity as a naturalist led him to make prolific drawings of the new plants he found on his travels, including this one (above) of a bud and flower from a Gouty Stem tree, found by the Victoria River in Australia.

SCENES FROM THE MTWETWE SALT PAN
These two watercolors (left) were made by Baines on the same sheet and depict scenes from the Mtwetwe Salt Pan in present-day Botswana. The upper painting shows a group of wildebeest; the lower one depicts a clump of baobab trees.

Baines as a "lounger" and ensured that he would never again travel with an official expedition.

COMMERCIAL SUCCESS

Baines recovered from this setback and was soon able to continue his artist-explorer career. In 1861, he returned to Africa, joining James Chapman (1831–72), a South African cattle trader, on his expedition from the southwest coast to Lake Ngami and the Victoria Falls. He described how the water of the falls rushed forward with "so much violence as to break up the whole into a fleecy, snow white, irregularly seething torrent, with its lighter particles glittering and flashing like myriads of living diamonds in the sunlight."

The expedition surveyed the route and Baines gathered botanical samples, recording scenes in a series of artworks. Reproductions of his drawings of the falls were to grace many Victorian drawing rooms in Britain. Baines's expeditionary expertise and knowledge were of great interest to the British public. He contributed text and illustrations to various publications from which the armchair traveler could learn how to sketch while traveling, capture a hippopotamus, or build a bridge.

In 1868, Baines was appointed leader of an expedition to explore for gold in the Tati River region of northern South East Africa. His journey was hampered by a lack of funds, so he decided to forfeit a larger team and set out almost solo. He reached Durban in Natal, where he became ill and died from dysentery on May 8, 1875.

Later assessments of Baines's artistic output confirmed the views of Sir Henry Rawlinson, President of the Royal Geographical Society in London who, in 1876, stated that "perhaps none possessed greater courage and perseverance, or more untiring industry than Baines."

AN ARTIST IN AFRICA
With his taste for high adventure, Thomas Baines loved to capture scenes of action and drama against stunning natural backdrops. Here, a pair of European hunters are firing at a herd of stampeding buffalo on Garden Island, with the Victoria Falls in the distance. Baines paid particular attention to the detail of the flora and fauna, and the dress of the people he painted.

MARY KINGSLEY

INDEPENDENT FEMALE TRAVELER IN AFRICA

ENGLAND   1862–1900

NEW SPECIES
Kingsley brought back specimens of freshwater fish from the Gabon basin, including this snout fish. Three of the species she collected were subsequently named after her.

MARY KINGSLEY WAS BORN into a comfortable middle-class family in Victorian England and spent the first 30 years of her life as a dutiful daughter. Her father, George, was a doctor who had traveled widely, and Kingsley finally achieved her own ambition to explore following the death of her parents. Her primary motivation was to escape the restrictions placed on her by Victorian society, but to make her journeys appear more respectable, she carried out a commission for the British Museum to collect "fish and fetish."

A LIFE'S WORK

- A champion of **racial equality**, stating: "a black man is no more an undeveloped white man than a rabbit is an undeveloped hare"

- Almost uniquely for a woman of her time, she **travels independently**

- Becomes a witty, best-selling **travel writer**, not bound by social conventions

- **Survives cannibal traps** thanks to the protection afforded by her full Victorian dress

In common with most women of her class, Kingsley received no formal education. Instead, she spent as much time as she could in her father's library and avidly studied the papers he brought back from his travels. However, it was only following the deaths of both parents in 1892 that the 30-year-old gained the independence to explore. Her excitement as she planned her journey is conveyed in the foreword to *Travels in West Africa* (1897), where, when considering luggage for the trip, she "was too distracted to buy anything new in the way of baggage except for a long waterproof sack neatly closed at the top with a bar and handle." This first trip took her to Luanda in Angola. She spent time with the Fjort

tribe on the Congo River, traveled north through the Congo Free State, and crossed the river into French territory.

RIVER STEAMER
In October 1893, while on the Gabon River, she came upon the SS *Rochelle*, a steamer that she joined for the return journey to the coast. She describes the atmosphere on board: "At night just before the Sun goes down the whole air vibrates with the chirp of thousands of crickets and the bellowing of bullfrogs … the songs of the birds in the morning are delicious— soft long whistles and what not up to about 10 o'clock and then absolute and complete silence until about 5 when the cooler air wakes them into song." Kingsley returned to England in 1894 with a collection of fish samples and a determination to return to West Africa, and in particular to reach the Ogowé River in Gabon, about which very little was known in Britain.

By 1895, she was back on board ship heading for the coast of Africa. At Kangwe, near Lambaréné in Gabon, Kingsley stopped and

stayed with the Jacots (local French missionaries), before continuing her journey up river. During her canoe trip on the Ogowé River, Kingsley demonstrated her natural diplomacy and talent for entertainment. As the canoe met a strong current, she was advised to abandon ship. While the crew refloated the boat, she recalled, "I did my best to amuse the others by diving headlong from a large rock onto which I had elaborately climbed, into a thick clump of willow-leaved shrubs ... a display of art of this order should satisfy any African village for a year at least."

By the time she returned to Lambaréné and the Jacots, Kingsley had learned how to handle a canoe, studied the Igalwa tribe, and collected many more fish specimens. In July, she headed north to the Rembwe River. This area was inhabited by the Fan—a tribe rumored to practice cannibalism. But at Ncovi, a Fan village, Kingsley's party was welcomed, since one of her men was owed a favor by the chief. Potential tragedy was narrowly averted as they continued on into the forest, when Kingsley fell down a concealed pit. Her decision to travel in full Victorian women's clothing, ignoring advice to wear pants, saved her: "Here I was with the fullness of my skirt tucked under me, sitting on nine ebony spikes

some twelve inches [30 cm] long, in comparative comfort, howling lustily to be hauled out."

The party spent the night at the village of Efoua. It was here that Kingsley emptied one of the bags hanging from the roof of her hut into her hat to find that it contained "a hand, three big toes, four eyes, two ears, and other fragments of a cannibal feast." To avoid further danger, the group took a detour through swamps, landing at N'dorko. From there she traveled back down the Rembwe to Cameroon and climbed Africa's highest mountain on the west coast, Mungo Mah Lobeh (Mount Cameroon).

In October 1895, Kingsley returned home to celebrity status. She brought back impressive collections for the British Museum, with one brand-new species of fish, six "modifications of new forms which have to have proper scientific names given to them," a new snake, and eight new insects. In 1897, Kingsley published *Travels in West Africa*, followed by *West African Studies* in 1899. She returned to Africa in 1900, intending to collect fish in the Orange River, but became a nurse to Boer prisoners of war instead. She died of typhoid on June 3, 1900.

WEST AFRICAN VILLAGES
Kingsley stayed in villages of round adobe huts, similar to these in present-day Cameroon. The French authorities refused to sanction her journey, fearing for the safety of a woman alone among unknown tribes. Undaunted, Kingsley promised them that she would only go as far as science required.

IF WE DISTINGUISH OURSELVES, THE GREAT SOCIETIES WILL ADMIT WOMEN

MARY KINGSLEY

TRAVELING WITH THE LOCALS
Kingsley traveled up the Ogowé River with an entirely local crew. She was outspoken in her opposition to the racist theories of her time, regarding Africans as her equals.

IN HER FOOTSTEPS

1893—Kingsley's first visit to Africa
Spends time with the Fjort people in the Congo and travels along the Gabon River

1894—Uncertain itinerary
She travels overland from Matadi to Libreville at the estuary of the Gabon River

1895—Second visit to Africa
Kingsley returns to Africa and explores along the Ogowé River, staying with the Fan people

1900—Dies in South Africa
Kingsley travels to South Africa, where she nurses Boer prisoners of war and dies of typhoid

○ Not shown on map

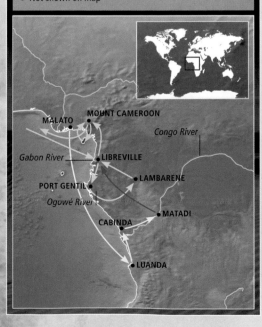

HENRY MORTON STANLEY

THE FIRST EXPLORER OF THE MEDIA AGE

WALES   1841–1904

A JOURNALIST, OPPORTUNIST, AND ADVENTURER, Henry Morton Stanley reinvented himself after an inauspicious start in life. Escaping an impoverished childhood in Wales for a new beginning in the United States, he rose to the prestigious position of international reporter for the *New York Herald* newspaper. His transition from journalist to one of the most famous explorers of the 19th century occurred after his near-legendary encounter in Africa with the great missionary-explorer, Dr. David Livingstone.

Born John Rowlands in Denbigh, Wales, Stanley was an illegitimate child who spent time in the local workhouse. At age 15, he left Wales for the port of Liverpool, where he found a passage to the United States. Heading for New Orleans, he took a job as a clerk with Henry Morton Stanley, a wealthy trader who all but adopted Rowlands and gave him his name.

Stanley traveled widely across the United States with the man he now called "father." At the outbreak of the Civil War in 1861, he was in Arkansas when he heard that New Orleans was being blockaded, cutting him off from his benefactor. Once more, he found himself "a strange boy in a strange land." Trapped, he enlisted with the Confederates, but switched sides to the Union after being taken prisoner.

A NEW CAREER

When the war ended in 1865, Stanley found employment reporting as a special correspondent on the "Peace Commission to the Indians" for the *Missouri Democrat,* and as a contributor to the *New York Herald.* His first experience of Africa came in 1867, when he reported on the British military's Abyssinian campaign for the *Herald.* From Abyssinia, Stanley traveled widely, filing reports for his American readers from various locations in Europe and the Middle East, including Athens, Alexandria, Beirut, and Barcelona. He was recalled to Paris from Spain in October 1869 to receive an unusual new commission: "Find Livingstone."

INTREPID ADVENTURER
Stanley adopts a characteristically imperious posture for this portrait. Accompanied by a large team of hired local porters, Stanley explored vast expanses of the African continent.

RAINFOREST RIVER
Stanley traced the Congo River from its headwaters to its mouth at the Atlantic Ocean. Also known as the Zaire, its overall length is 2,922 miles (4,700 km). The river and its tributaries flow through one of the largest rainforest regions in the world, second only in size to the Amazon Rainforest in South America.

AN HISTORIC MEETING

David Livingstone, the famed British missionary-explorer (see pp. 220–25), had returned to Africa in 1866 but had been out of touch with home ever since. James Gordon Bennett Jr., son of the proprietor of the *Herald*, scented a scoop and sent Stanley in search of Livingstone.

Stanley arrived at Ujiji in present-day Tanzania on November 10, 1871, reaching the last place Livingstone had been seen. He did not have to look much farther, since Livingstone had returned to Ujiji some 19 days earlier. The meeting of the two men provided one of the most famous newspaper headlines in history, although it is likely that Stanley's immortal words—"Dr. Livingstone, I presume?"—were made up after the event for the benefit of his best-selling memoir. Stanley accompanied Livingstone as far east as Unyanyembe before returning to Britain, where news of his success was to bring him fame and no small fortune.

DOWN THE CONGO RIVER

By 1874, Stanley was back in Africa on another expedition financed by newspapers. This time he was charged with tracing the Congo River from its headwaters to the ocean. After nearly three years, Stanley reached the Portuguese outpost of Boma at the mouth of the Congo. He had started his journey in Zanzibar with four Europeans and 350 Africans, but arrived at Boma the sole surviving European with just 114 African guides. Stanley was later criticized for incurring such

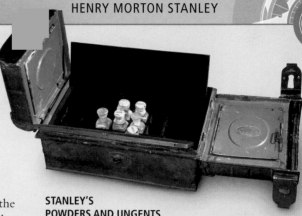

STANLEY'S POWDERS AND UNGENTS
Stanley compared traveling into the interior of Africa with embarking on a long sea voyage, in that it was necessary to take everything you needed with you, including medicine.

casualties. He was also criticized for the negotiations he conducted with the tribes living along the Congo on behalf of Belgian King Leopold II. With Stanley's help, Leopold established his authority over the Congo Free State, starting a 30-year period of colonial rule.

Stanley made a final visit to Africa in 1886 to rescue Emin Pasha, the beleaguered governor of Equatoria in southern Sudan. By 1890, he had achieved his mission, but the expedition was to severely tarnish his reputation. The Britons under his command had treated their guides with such extreme cruelty that one of the party, Major Edmund Barttelot, was shot dead by one of his own porters for his behavior.

"BREAKER OF ROCKS"

On his return to Britain, Stanley eventually faced down the criticism. He married and was elected a Member of Parliament. His gravestone is inscribed with the words *Bula Matari*, meaning "Breaker of Rocks" in the Kikongo language: the nickname given to him by his guides on the Congo expedition for both his severity and his willingness to help with the physical labor.

TROPICAL HEADGEAR
After Stanley appeared in publicity photographs wearing this sola topi, the design became the headgear of choice among colonialists in the tropics.

IN HIS FOOTSTEPS

→ **1871—The search for Livingstone**
Stanley travels to Ujiji to find the "lost" missionary Dr. David Livingstone; he finds Livingstone alive and well and travels with him along Lake Tanganyika before returning to Britain

→ **1874–77—Exploring the Great Lakes and the Congo**
Becomes the first European to travel all the way around lakes Victoria and Tanganyika, before following the Congo River

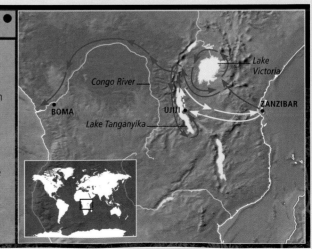

Lake Victoria
Congo River
BOMA
Lake Tanganyika
UJIJI
ZANZIBAR

SPREADING THE FAITH

F OR CENTURIES, BUDDHISTS, CHRISTIANS, AND MUSLIMS HAVE SENT OUT MISSIONARIES TO SPREAD THEIR FAITH. THE EXPANSION OF EUROPEAN-CONTROLLED TERRITORY AFTER THE AGE OF DISCOVERY GAVE CHRISTIANS VAST NEW AREAS OF THE WORLD IN WHICH TO EVANGELIZE.

DRAWING THE LINE
The Treaty of Tordesillas of 1494 established a demarcation in the Atlantic between Spanish and Portuguese interests, but no such division in the Pacific, which led to later disputes.

Missionaries had brought Buddhism to China in the 1st century CE and to Japan by 552, and had operated in Sri Lanka and Southeast Asia. By the 12th century, Muslim preachers were propagating their faith as far as the Indonesian archipelago. Christianity, too, had a long missionary history, from the journeys of St. Paul to the missions of men such as St. Boniface, whose efforts to convert the pagan Germans ended in his martyrdom in 754. There remained for Christian missions in Europe up until the conversion in 1368 of the last pagan ruler, Jagiello of Lithuania.

CHRISTIANITY SPREADS

Since the 11th century, the crusades had provided possibilities for evangelism with the (largely futile) attempts of clerics to win souls among the Muslims. However, with the Spanish and Portuguese discoveries of the 15th and 16th centuries, a promising new field for missions appeared. Priests accompanied the conquistadors to the New World and the voyages to Africa. In the Congo, a Portuguese mission resulted in the conversion of the son of the local king, who under the name Don Henrique became (in 1521) the "Vicar Apostolic" of West Africa, and the first indigenous bishop from sub–Saharan Africa.

Thereafter, the missions in Africa faded for several centuries, but in the Americas, evangelization

was pursued with great vigor, and the first diocese was established on Hispaniola in 1511. Thousands of native peoples were converted, but the *encomienda* system, which made them slaves to Spanish colonists, meant that many of the baptisms were effectively forced.

There were dissenting voices, and Dominican friar Antonio de Montesinos stood up for the indigenous people of Hispaniola. Bartolemeu de las Casas, a priest who came to the New World in 1502, wrote a thundering denunciation of the *encomienda*, which led to its curtailment in 1542.

LIMITED SUCCESS IN ASIA

In the East, Christian missions came across societies with well-established religions. The missionary effort was spearheaded by the Jesuits, priests of an order founded by Ignatius Loyola in 1534. That same year, a bishopric was established in the Indian city of Goa, from which Jesuit priests fanned out to Malacca and Macau. In 1549, the great Jesuit missionary Francis Xavier reached as far as Japan (see pp. 218–19).

In China, the efforts of the Jesuit Matteo Ricci won some respect—and a few

> Christian missionaries today lack the exploratory zeal of their 19th-century forbears but continue to offer medical or pastoral care. A radical form of Islam, however, has reached widely dispersed converts through the internet.

JESUIT SEAL
The seal of the Jesuit order was a symbol familiar to many Christian missions overseas until the suppression of the organization in 1793.

thousand converts—after his arrival there in 1583. From 1600, based at the court in Beijing, he gained imperial favor for his learning, but neither he, nor his missionary successors, were in any danger of supplanting Confucianism as the dominant creed in China.

PROTESTANT MISSIONS

The Protestant nations of Europe had not at first produced any notable missionary effort, but this changed in the late 18th century with the foundation of a number of missionary organizations, such as the Baptist Missionary Society (founded in 1792) and the Church Missionary Society (CMS, established in 1795). Initially, they concentrated their efforts in the South Seas, with mixed results since, through murder, desertion, or despair, the numbers of missionaries had dwindled to only seven in all the South Pacific by 1800. They moved on to Africa at the start of the 19th century.

INHUMAN TRAFFIC
Missionaries such as David Livingstone and Cardinal Lavigerie, Archbishop of Algiers, were prominent in the campaign to have the slave trade within Africa suppressed.

SNOW MOUNTAIN
When Ludwig Krapf first described Mount Kilimanjaro, he was derided by European critics, who thought a snow-covered mountain so close to the equator was impossible.

SETTING THE SCENE

- Christian **efforts to convert the Mongols** in the 13th century are generally unsuccessful. The Flemish Franciscan monk William of Rubruck's epic journey to Mongolia in 1253–55 (see pp. 54–55) results in just six converts.

- Pope Alexander VI issues **a Papal Bull in 1493** that heavily influences **the Treaty of Tordesillas** the following year. The treaty splits any new discoveries between Spain and Portugal. Spain is awarded all those west of a line some 1,100 miles (1,800 km) off the Azores, allowing the Portuguese to take Brazil when they find it in 1500.

- **The Jesuits are expelled from Japan** in 1587 and, despite tens of thousands of converts, Christianity largely disappears there amid widespread persecution by the new Tokugawa rulers after 1614.

- From their arrival in Quebec in 1625, **the Jesuits play a major role in exploration** and making contacts **among the Indian peoples**, most notably Father Jacques Marquette (see pp. 132–33), who finds an overland route to the Mississipi River in 1672–73.

- In 1853, **the Taiping rebellion** breaks out in China, nearly overthrowing the Qing dynasty. It is led by **a Christian convert, Hung Hsin-Chu'an,** who espouses the worship of *Shang-ti* ("the true God"), but who permits polygamy among his followers.

The CMS set up a college at Fourah Bay in Sierra Leone, whose alumnus Samuel Adjai Crowther became the first of a new generation of African missionaries when he traveled among the Yoruba people of Nigeria in the 1840s.

David Livingstone's great journey from Luanda in Angola to the east coast of Africa at Quelimane in 1854–56 (see pp. 220–23) was the most spectacular of a host of missionary journeys that crisscrossed the interior of Africa. German Ludwig Krapf crossed 200 miles (300 km) of arid scrub to reach the Ukambani and catch a first sight of Mount Kilimanjaro in 1851, and his compatriot Johann Erhardt sailed down the Kenyan coast as far as Kilwa. These missionary-adventurers contributed as much to the cause of African exploration as they did to the spread of Christianity.

NAGASAKI MARTYRS
As part of the Tokugawa suppression of Christianity, 26 missionaries and Japanese converts were put to death in Nagasaki in September 1622.

FRANCIS XAVIER

FIRST MISSIONARY EXPLORER IN JAPAN

SPAIN   1506–52

BORN IN NAVARRA, SPAIN, Francis Xavier was a pioneering missionary for the Catholic Church in the 16th century, noted for the fervor of his religious faith. He enjoyed limited success as a missionary in East Asia, finding many of the people resistant to Christianity, but in letters home he provided detailed accounts of the areas he visited. Xavier was one of the founding fathers of the Society of Jesus, a proselytizing religious order whose members are known as Jesuits. He was canonized in 1622.

A LIFE'S WORK

- **Travels extensively** around the islands of present-day Indonesia and Malaysia

- Spends two years in Japan, where he struggles to spread Christianity but is left with a favorable impression of **Japanese culture**

- Provides through his letters a **vivid account of Japan** and East Asia, areas little known in Europe at the time

- **Revered for his missionary zeal;** many **miracles** are attributed to Xavier following his death and he is declared a saint

HOLY RELIC
The humerus from Francis Xavier's right arm. This was the arm Xavier used at baptisms and can be seen at the Cathedral of St. Paul in Macao.

Xavier's first mission set sail from Lisbon in February 1542. He had instructions from Pope Paul III to minister to existing Catholic communities in Southeast India (where many Portuguese traders had abandoned their faith and adopted local customs), while also seeking new converts to Christianity. Before Xavier's departure, the pope made him an apostolic nuncio, or official envoy of the church.

FROM MALACCA TO JAPAN

He reached Goa in April, and traveled west around the coast of southern India, making his first mission to the pearl fishers of Paravas. Xavier found conditions harsh. "This country," he wrote, "always tries the strength to live in, either on account of the great heats of the summer or the excessive winds and rain of the winter." By 1547, he had traveled to Malacca, in present-day Malaysia, and to the Moluccas, or Spice Islands, at the eastern end of the Indonesian archipelago.

At the end of the year, Xavier returned to Malacca, where he met Yajiro, a Japanese man who had taken passage from Japan with a Portuguese trader. Xavier was fascinated by the young man's description of his homeland. He determined to spread the Christian message to Japan, departing from Goa in April 1549 on board a Chinese junk. He was aware of the risks this journey involved: "The voyage is exposed to very many dangers from tempests, shoals, and pirates … ship owners think it is a great thing if one ship out of two hold her course to Japan."

In addition to the difficulties presented by the voyage, the "idols" he saw being worshiped on board the vessel gave him a different problem. However, Xavier had the sense to recognize that he was dependent on the crew of the ship to provide him with safe passage and chose not to interfere with their traditions.

This voyage followed the trade route between Japan and India developed by the Portuguese.

DEATH OF A SAINT
This 19th-century Chinese colored engraving depicts the death of Francis Xavier on the island of San Chan, China.

Seven years earlier, the Portuguese adventurer Fernandez Pinto had been the first recorded European to land on the coast of Japan at Tanixooma, while in the early 1540s a Portuguese ship had been driven by a storm to the port of Cagoxima. These and other encounters set the scene for the beginning of the Nanban Period of prolific trade between Japan and the West, which lasted from 1543 until the exclusion of Europeans from Japan in 1641.

EXPLORING JAPAN

Shortly after his arrival in Japan, Xavier wrote that the people "are the best who have yet been discovered." He described how the Japanese were "… sparing and frugal in eating. The wine they drink is made of rice, for here there is no other." From their perspective, the Japanese viewed the incoming Europeans as crude: "They eat with their fingers instead of chopsticks as we use. They show their feelings without any self-control." Xavier crisscrossed Japan, at one point avoiding attack from bandits by disguising himself as the servant of a Japanese merchant, running alongside the merchant's horse with his bags.

The cultural traditions and all-powerful role of the Buddhist and Shinto religions made Xavier's mission difficult. After two years he returned to Malacca, taking with him two Japanese converts who had adopted the Christian names of Matthias and Bernard.

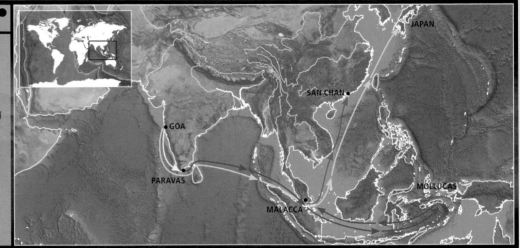

IN HIS FOOTSTEPS

1542–45—First mission in Asia
After arriving at Goa in May 1542, Xavier travels down the Indian coast to establish a mission at Paravas

1545–47—Journeys around Southeast Asia
Xavier travels east as far as the Moluccas before heading back west to Malacca

1549—Sails for Japan
After returning to Goa, he sails for Japan, where he lives for two years and travels widely

1552—Attempts to enter China
Xavier intends to set up a mission in China, but is turned back and dies of a fever on the island of San Chan

Matthias died on the journey but Bernard eventually arrived in Lisbon in May 1552, becoming the first Japanese person known to have set foot in Europe.

RETURN TO THE EAST

On the return voyage to Malacca, Xavier's ship was badly damaged during a severe storm and was forced to harbor at San Chan, an island off the coast of Canton, China. As he changed to another ship to continue his journey, Xavier learned of the enormous potential China offered for a mission: "An immense empire, enjoying peace, and, which as the Portuguese merchants tell us, is superior to all Christian states in the practice of justice."

Xavier returned from Malacca to San Chan in August 1552. The island lies 9 miles (14 km) off the coast and provided a trading point between Chinese merchants and Portuguese traders, who were prohibited from landing on the mainland. Xavier preached to the Portuguese on the island, living there in a rudimentary hut, since Europeans were forbidden to settle. His requests to be smuggled onto the mainland were refused by Portuguese and Chinese alike, fearful of the punishment the Canton governor would impose if they were caught. Indeed, once it became known that Xavier was on San Chan, food supplies to the island from Canton were restricted. Weakened by the blockade, Xavier finally succumbed to a fever and died there in December 1552.

During his lifetime, Francis Xavier's letters had been read out to congregations in Portugal eager to know more of his success as a missionary. When read today, Xavier's letters offer a unique insight into East Asia at a time of first contact with the European world.

THE MIRACLES OF FRANCIS XAVIER
During his final voyage, Xavier's ship, the *Santa Croce*, was becalmed for 14 days and supplies of fresh water ran out. According to church records relating to his canonization, Xavier was lowered overboard and the ocean around the ship miraculously turned to fresh water, which was then used to fill their storage barrels.

I DETERMINED NEVER TO STOP
UNTIL I HAD COME TO THE END
AND ACHIEVED MY PURPOSE

DR. DAVID LIVINGSTONE

THE EXPLORER'S CAP
As a British consul, Livingstone wore the Consul's Cap. He was wearing this distinctive cap on the day he met Stanley.

for miles around. Livingstone was the first European to witness this spectacular sight.

When Livingstone returned to Britain, it was clear that exploring had overtaken missionary work as his driving passion. He resigned from the LMS when they demanded that he do more evangelizing and less exploring, and returned to Africa in 1858 at the head of an expedition to open up the Zambezi River to navigation.

The expedition proved a disaster. Used to solitary exploration, he lost patience with his fellow Europeans, who were unable to match his disregard for bodily discomfort. He fell out with the expedition's artist, Thomas Baines (see pp. 208–11), who was expelled from the party. Then in 1863, Mary died of malaria and Livingstone was grief-stricken. To add further to his woes, their steam-launch, the *Ma Roberts,* kept breaking down. It turned out that the Zambezi could not be navigated for much of its length. Livingstone had shown himself to be a poor leader, and his reputation as an explorer was severely dented.

IN SEARCH OF THE NILE

Finding the source of the White Nile was one of the great quests of the Victorian period. In 1866, Livingstone was sent by the RGS to make his way along the Rovuma River to Lake Nyasa and then north to Lake Tanganyika. He wrongly believed that the Nile's source, if not Lake Tanganyika, was to be found to the west of the lake, and spent six years searching around Lake Tanganyika without any success. During this time, he lost contact with Europe for so long that Henry Morton Stanley (see pp. 214–15) was sent from Britain to find him. It was in the company of Stanley, in 1871, that he reached the Ruzizi River, finding that it flowed south and therefore was not the Nile. Livingstone then became convinced that the Lualaba River, which flowed to the west of the lake, was the Nile, but again he was wrong. Lake Tanganyika is, in fact, one of the sources of the Congo River.

When Stanley found Livingstone in 1871, he had already been seriously ill for two years, and Stanley tried to persuade him to return to Britain. Livingstone insisted that he had a mission to complete and returned to the swamps

of Lake Bangweulu. He died there in 1873 from malaria and internal bleeding. His trusted attendants, Chuma and Susi, carried his body on a remarkable 1,000 mile (1,600 km) journey on foot to the coast to be returned to Britain for burial. Attached to his body was a note from the people of Ilala, the area in which he had died, saying, "You can have his body, but his heart belongs to Africa." The heart had been cut from his body and buried where he had died.

Livingstone's explorations gained him fame in his lifetime, but his most enduring legacy was the close relationships he forged with local tribes and the role he played in ending slavery in the region which, as he wrote, "I shall regard that as a greater matter than the discovery of all the Nile sources together."

mission. He pressed on regardless and reached Loanda on the west coast in August 1855. Livingstone's health had broken down by this point and it took two months' convalescence for him to regain his strength.

On his return to Linyanti, Sekeletu, the ruler of the Makololo, gave him further provisions and men. He now determined to follow the Zambezi to the east coast of Africa, referring to the river as "God's highway." He left Linyanti in early November 1855, and by the middle of the month he had reached the greatest impediment to travel on the Zambezi—the Victoria Falls. The falls, called *Mosi-oa-tunya* ("smoke that thunders") by the Kololo, are 1 mile (1.6 km) wide and 300 ft (100 m) deep. The drop and the confinement within a gorge causes the water to bounce up in spray so high that it can be seen

JAMES CHUMA
A member of the Yao tribe, who lived along Lake Nyasa, Chuma was a former slave who accompanied Livingstone on his journeys from 1866 onward. He accompanied the explorer's body back to Britain in 1874.

MEETING STANLEY

Livingstone completely lost touch with the outside world after 1866, and in 1869 Henry Morton Stanley was despatched to find him by the *New York Herald* newspaper. The two men met in 1871 in the town of Ujiji on the shores of Lake Tanganyika, a moment immortalized by Stanley in his later writing. Stanley's articles rehabilitated Livingstone's reputation, which had suffered after the failure of his first Zambezi expedition.

"DR. LIVINGSTONE, I PRESUME"; STANLEY LATER WROTE THAT THIS IS HOW HE GREETED THE EXPLORER

IN HIS OWN WORDS

DAVID LIVINGSTONE

A **PROLIFIC LETTER WRITER** and journal keeper, Livingstone documented every aspect of his great expeditions across the African interior. He kept detailed accounts of his experiences and sent regular letters to his sponsors at the Royal Geographical Society in London. He also produced many sketches, maps, and watercolors, most notably of *Mosi-oa-Tunya* ("the smoke that thunders")—which he renamed Victoria Falls.

MISSIONARY TRAVELS

AND

RESEARCHES IN SOUTH AFRICA;

INCLUDING A SKETCH OF

SIXTEEN YEARS' RESIDENCE IN THE INTERIOR OF AFRICA,

AND A JOURNEY FROM THE CAPE OF GOOD HOPE TO LOANDA ON THE WEST COAST; THENCE ACROSS THE CONTINENT, DOWN THE RIVER ZAMBESI, TO THE EASTERN OCEAN.

BY DAVID LIVINGSTONE, LL.D., D.C.L.,

FELLOW OF THE FACULTY OF PHYSICIANS AND SURGEONS, GLASGOW; CORRESPONDING MEMBER OF THE GEOGRAPHICAL AND STATISTICAL SOCIETY OF NEW YORK; GOLD MEDALLIST AND CORRESPONDING MEMBER OF THE ROYAL GEOGRAPHICAL SOCIETIES OF LONDON AND PARIS, F.S.A., ETC. ETC.

Tsetse Fly.—Magnified—See p. 571.

WITH PORTRAIT; MAPS BY ARROWSMITH; AND NUMEROUS ILLUSTRATIONS.

LONDON:
JOHN MURRAY, ALBEMARLE STREET.
1857.

Ⓐ VICTORIA FALLS
This artwork of the Victoria Falls was first published in Livingstone's book *Missionary Travels and Researches in South Africa*. The columns of "smoke"—after which the falls were named by the local population—are clearly visible.

Ⓑ LION ATTACK
Livingstone was attacked by a lion and his arm left partially disabled during his first expedition in 1844. He was saved by a local teacher named Mebalwe, who was also badly injured by the animal.

Ⓒ BOOK FRONTISPIECE
The frontispiece of Livingstone's *Missionary Travels and Researches in South Africa*, first published in 1857. The book includes observations from his journey across Africa and down the Zambezi River.

Ⓓ DETAILED OBSERVATIONS
Livingstone documented his travels in a series of letters to the Royal Geographical Society, which formed the basis of his book manuscript. Dated January 25, 1856, an excerpt reads:
As we are now within a few days of the Portuguese station called Teté, I shall begin preparations for entering the world again by giving you a sketch of our progress thus far.

Ⓔ LIVINGSTONE'S PEN
The pen used by Livingstone to record his observations was brought back to Britain, along with many of his other personal effects, by E. D. Young in 1868.

Hill Changune, on the
banks of the Zambesi.
25th January 1856

15 Whitehall Pl

Sir,—
As we are now
few days of the Portuguese station
I shall begin preparations for
world again, while my men
in paddling each other across
rivers, by giving you a
gress thus far. No I.
visiting for rains at Li
chiefly to the country Nor
this No II. is inte

covered with trees

covered with trees

covered with trees

Dry

filled in Nitres

400 feet deep

sides perpendicular
neck so narrow

one can see across

from +
down to
the water

150 paces

Trees

F SKETCH OF VICTORIA FALLS
Livingstone produced several sketches and watercolors depicting scenes from the various African river systems along which he traveled. This artwork of the Victoria Falls in Zimbabwe—Livingstone was the first European to see them—dates from 1860.

G BOAT'S COMPASS
Dating from 1856, this is the compass that was used by David Livingstone on his first exploratory journey down the Zambezi River.

H MAP SKETCH
Livingstone's map of Lake Shirwa and the Shire River—meticulously handdrawn and colored on graph paper—shows his route through Malawi.

UNDERSTANDING OTHERS

THE WORLD'S GREAT DESERTS WERE AMONG THE LAST AREAS TO BE VISITED BY OUTSIDERS. TRAVEL THERE REQUIRED EXPLORERS TO ADAPT TO THE WAYS OF LIFE AND SURVIVAL TECHNIQUES OF LOCAL PEOPLES ON JOURNEYS THAT OFTEN CROSSED VAST, WATERLESS EXPANSES.

SLAVE TRADE
In the early 20th century, the Saharan lands still supported a robust slave trade, with transports heading north in convoys. Slavery was outlawed in Morocco only in 1930.

The desert fringes of advanced civilizations such as Egypt had long been regarded as inauspicious and dangerous places. In 525BCE, an army numbering tens of thousands was sent by Cambyses II of Persia to attack the Oracle of Zeus Ammon at Siwa, an oasis in western Egypt. The entire army was swallowed up by the desert sands and never seen again. Although a few Roman expeditions did cross the Sahara Desert, the vast expanse was left largely to local tribes. The domestication of the camel in the early 1st millennium BCE had provided a mode of transportation for goods and for people. This meant that, far from the arid wasteland of European imagining, the deserts of Central Asia, North Africa, and Arabia—or at least their fringes—came to host cultures of surprising tenacity and sophistication.

EXPLORING IN DISGUISE

Muslim travelers such as Ibn Battuta in the 14th century (see pp. 68–71) traversed the desert trade routes with comparative ease, but such facility was denied European explorers. The first to venture into Arabia since Roman times was an Italian, Ludovico di Varthema, who reached Aleppo in Syria in 1503. From there, he traveled in a pilgrim caravan disguised as a

DESERT ACCOUNT
Wilfred Thesiger, one of the last of the great European explorers of Arabia, kept meticulous records of his expenditure in the desert.

Muslim convert, and in this way, he was able to enter the cities of Medina and Mecca, both of which were strictly forbidden to Christians.

A few Europeans visited Arabia over the next century, mostly captives taken there by their masters. Gradually, however, journeys began to be mounted with the goal of cultural and scientific exploration. In 1761, the Dane Carsten Niebuhr and his Swedish companion Peter Forsskal (see pp. 270–71) left for Arabia armed with a 235-page list of questions that various scholars wished answered about the region. They traveled for two years down western Arabia as far as Yemen, collecting botanical specimens, and making astronomical observations, although only Niebuhr returned alive to Scandinavia.

In North Africa, it was the lure of the fabled city of Timbuktu, said to be host to unimaginable riches, that drew explorers. Frenchman René Caillie (see p. 201), set off from Sierra Leone in April 1827, reaching Timbuktu almost exactly a year later after enduring terrible

> By the start of World War II, roads and railroads crossed many of the world's desert regions and many of the old ways of life were dying out, but travel there still requires meticulous preparation, even today.

privations, including attacks of fever and scurvy. He had, in fact, been preceded two years earlier by the Scotsman Alexander Gordon Laing, who had been beaten to death as he began his return journey. Caillie managed to return alive. Although Timbuktu turned out to be a great disappointment in terms of gold, the exploration of the North African desert continued to bring in adventurers such as the German Heinrich Barth (see pp. 202–03), who extensively explored the deserts of southern Algeria and northern Chad in 1850–52, at one point surviving only by drinking his own blood. Fellow German Gustav Nachtigal traveled from Algiers in 1869 on a five-year journey that took him to the Tibesti Mountains, and on to the Sultan of Kanem-Bornu in present-day Chad.

INTO ARABIA

Explorers in Central Asia, such as Sven Hedin (see pp. 228–31) and Marc Aurel Stein (see pp. 234–37), were motivated by cultural concerns, such as the exploration of the ancient cities of the Silk Road. In Arabia, however, other matters came to dominate. A few mavericks continued to travel to Arabia, such as Richard Burton (see pp. 204–07), who disguised himself as "Sheikh Abdullah" on his 1853 journey to Mecca, and Charles Montagu Doughty (see pp. 246–47), whose travels in

MOUNTED WARRIORS
Arab tribesmen, such as these Saudi troops on an expedition against British-controlled Iraq in 1928, made extremely effective mounted warriors.

TEA TIME
The desert-dwelling Bedouin live by a strict code that demands the provision of hospitality to all travelers who come to them in peace.

SETTING THE SCENE

- So powerful in the imagination of Europeans is **the portrayal of Africa** by the **Greek historian Herodotus**, that Heinrich Barth travels with a copy of his *Histories* in his pocket.

- Timbuktu is not always impoverished. Its ruler **Mansa Musa undertakes a pilgrimage to Mecca** in 1325–27 during which his liberal expenditure of gold causes an inflationary spiral in North Africa, devastating the economy there for decades.

- When Italian traveler Ludovico di Varthema is thrown in prison in Yemen in 1503, he feigns madness by **trying to convert a donkey to Islam** and stabbing it when it fails to say the right prayers. He is released and returns home safely.

- **The armies of Ibn Saud** sweep through the Arabian peninsula, capturing Riyadh in 1902, and finally Mecca in 1925. His increased importance leads to a number of **attempts to enlist his support**, including by a British political agent named William Shakespear, who travels 2,000 miles (3,000 km) from Kuwait to Riyadh and then to Suez.

- When Wilfred Thesiger **crosses Arabia from the Hadhramaut to Abu Dhabi** in 1948, the local tribesmen in Laila refuse to accept his money before it has been publicly washed.

Arabia were made more arduous by his open admission of his Christianity. More common, however, were journeys such as that of William Gifford Palgrave, who was sent by the British government in 1862 to report on the Arabian kingdom of Riyadh.

OPENING UP THE DESERT

As travel in Arabia became more frequent, if not without its hardships, the range of travelers expanded. Dutchwoman Alexandrine Tinné had been traveling for 13 years in North Africa before her murder by Tuareg tribesmen near Muzraq in 1869. In Arabia, Lady Anne Blunt became the first western woman to cross the Nafud Desert in 1879. European influence in parts of the Middle East was consolidated after World War I, and British women Gertrude Bell (see pp. 252–53) and Freya Stark (see pp. 254–55) explored the Arabian deserts. The relations of explorers with the local Bedouin, and acceptance of the need to live like them, enabled some remarkable feats. Harry St. John Philby (see pp. 238–39) mapped huge areas of the Arabian peninsula, and in 1930–31, Bertram Thomas (see pp. 248–49) crossed the "Empty Quarter," the great South Arabian Desert that had been believed—at least by Europeans—to be impassable.

DESERT REST
The camel was a vital addition to desert journeys, and those Europeans who did not avail themselves of its use seldom survived for long. These Egyptian travelers have stopped for a moment to pray toward Mecca.

SVEN HEDIN

TRAILBLAZING EXPLORER OF CENTRAL ASIA

SWEDEN

1865–1952

SVEN HEDIN WAS A DARING EXPLORER who showed a ruthless, single-minded determination. In a career spanning 42 years, he led four major expeditions across Central Asia and Tibet, winning honors for geography and exploration from many countries. Hedin had studied under the distinguished German geographer von Richthofen and greatly admired Germany and its culture, a factor that later contributed to the severe tarnishing of his international reputation when he exhibited a naive support for Nazism.

A LIFE'S WORK

- Explores the **Takla Makan Desert,** reaching areas no European has been to before, and filling in many gaps in European maps in the process

- Crosses the **Pamir Mountains,** exploring the Taghdumbash, or "The Roof of the World"

- Explores many parts of Tibet previously unknown to Europeans and makes detailed **records of the culture and customs** of the Tibetan people

- Blazes a trail through the **Lop Nor Desert** that later explorers such as Marc Aurel Stein will follow

- Wins many awards for his contribution to the **geographical knowledge** of Central Asia

- His earlier accomplishments are overshadowed by his later **support for the Nazis.** During World War II, however, he saves many Danish Jews from the concentration camps

As a child, Hedin devoured tales of high adventure in the novels of Jules Verne and James Fenimore Cooper, and avidly followed the African exploration of Dr. David Livingstone (see pp. 220–25). At age 15, he witnessed the triumphant return of the Swedish explorer Nordenskiöld after his successful navigation of the Northwest Passage (see pp. 290–91). He was later to describe how, on that night, he was "prey to the greatest excitement. All my life I shall remember that day. It decided my career."

As a student he traveled through Russia, the Caucasus, and Persia to the borders of modern Pakistan. These were the travels of a young and

MUZTAGH ATA
Sheep graze at the foot of Muztagh Ata at the northern edge of the Tibetan plateau. In 1894, Hedin was the first European to attempt the 24,700-ft (7,500-m) climb, but he was forced to turn back before reaching the summit.

relatively inexperienced explorer. During his crossing of the Elburz Mountains in Persia, Hedin was caught out in a snowstorm: "I was not dressed for that kind of weather. I was literally held fast to my saddle by snow."

THE SKULL THIEF
Five years later, in 1890, Hedin returned to Persia, where he acted as interpreter for a Swedish diplomatic mission in Tehran. From there, he set off again on an adventure, following a caravan route north through Persia to Samarkand and Kashgar with a plan to travel 3,600 miles (5,800 km) on horseback, by sleigh, carriage, and train, estimating his costs at just under $1,000.

In northern Persia, he raided a Zoroastrian "Tower of Silence" (sacred burial mound) to retrieve samples of skulls. Exhibiting no respect for cultural or religious sensibilities, Hedin scaled the walls of the tower pretending that he planned to have a picnic, and swapped three melons in his travel bags for three of the skulls. Shrugging off the likely reaction of the local people, he wrote, "There might have been disturbances and riots, we might have been set upon and delivered up to the people. But everything went off well."

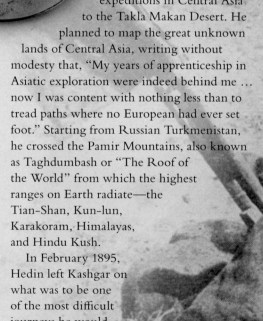

LEFT BY
DR SVEN HEDIN, MARCH 1901
NORTH OF LOP-NOR CENTRAL ASIA
FOUND DECEMBER 23. 1906
BY
DR M.A. STEIN

PRESENTED BY
DR SVEN HEDIN
TO THE ROYAL GEOGRAPHICAL SOCIETY
FEBRUARY 1909

MEASURE LOST
This metal tape measure was lost by Hedin north of Lop Nor Lake in 1901. Marc Aurel Stein found it in 1906 and returned it to its owner.

After his return to Stockholm in October 1893, Hedin set off on the first of his major expeditions in Central Asia to the Takla Makan Desert. He planned to map the great unknown lands of Central Asia, writing without modesty that, "My years of apprenticeship in Asiatic exploration were indeed behind me … now I was content with nothing less than to tread paths where no European had ever set foot." Starting from Russian Turkmenistan, he crossed the Pamir Mountains, also known as Taghdumbash or "The Roof of the World" from which the highest ranges on Earth radiate—the Tian-Shan, Kun-lun, Karakoram, Himalayas, and Hindu Kush.

In February 1895, Hedin left Kashgar on what was to be one of the most difficult journeys he would ever undertake. His goal was to find the lost city of Takla Makan, or Dandan-uilik. By

I WAS CONTENT WITH NOTHING LESS THAN TO TREAD PATHS WHERE NO EUROPEAN HAD EVER SET FOOT

SVEN HEDIN

PROGRESS AS A PILGRIM
Hedin is pictured here on the Tibetan plateau with companions Shagdur (left) and Shereb Lama (right). They are dressed as Buddhist pilgrims in an attempt to gain entry to Lhasa, the capital of Tibet, which was closed to foreigners. Their bid failed, however, and they were expelled from Tibet.

EXPELLED FROM TIBET

At the time of Sven Hedin's travels, much of Tibet was completely unknown to Europeans, and his explorations filled in some of the blanks on European maps. He was not a welcome visitor for long, however. He observed the Buddhist New Year celebrations, the Losar, at the monastic town of Tashi-limpo in 1907. The head of the monastery, the Tashi Lama, permitted him to photograph the area, but after six weeks, a message from Lhasa informed Hedin that he was no longer welcome in Tibet.

HEDIN DIRECTS THE LOADING OF PROVISIONS IN TIBET, FROM A MAGAZINE ILLUSTRATION OF 1909

April 25, his camel train was heading toward the Khotan-Daria River when he discovered a miscalculation in the volume of water taken at a waterhole. His men had filled their carriers with only enough water for two days, not 10.

FATEFUL DECISION

Two days out from their last supply, Hedin could have decided to return and refill, but instead chose to continue, rationing water to the extent that the men had only two cups per day and the camels none. Attempts to dig for water were to no avail, and by May 1, all supplies had been finished. In a desperate search for liquid, the men killed a sheep and drank its blood, then the urine of the camels, mixed with sugar and vinegar. Hedin wrote in his diary, "Halted on a high dune … we examined the east through the field-glasses; mountains of sand in all directions, not a straw, no life. All, men as well as camels, are extremely weak. God help us!" By May 3, Hedin and his guide, Kasim, were the only two able to continue. Two others, Mohammed Shah and Yolchi (who had been suspected of concealing and drinking their supplies), had both died at an encampment that Hedin

IMPRESSIONS OF TIBET
Here, Hedin has captured some of the strangeness of the closed country. The Tashi Lama, second only to the Dalai Lama, gave Hedin permission to take photographs in the town of Shigates—including this one of the Tashi's own family.

described grimly as "death camp." Islam Bai, the final member of the party, was close to death and remained at the camp as Hedin and Kasim set out unaided.

The two men began a tortuous crawl across the desert, burying themselves in the sand for coolness and sucking moisture from tamarisk plants. Coming upon tracks, Kasim realized with horror that they were his own: the men had crawled full circle in a day and night. On May 5, Hedin struck out on his own, reaching the bank of the Kohtan-Daria River. He drank his fill and carried water back to Kasim in his waterproof boots. Within hours, the two men were joined by a group of merchants who had found Islam Bai, along with Hedin's abandoned maps and diaries. They were saved, but Hedin's foolhardy behavior on this first exploration was to earn him stinging criticism back home.

Returning to his original mission, Hedin eventually found the lost city of Takla Makan and there collected hundreds of artifacts. He was elated by his success, writing that, "the ancient Chinese geographies … of the desert were now vindicated."

DESERT SANDSTORM
Hedin heroically leads his reluctant camels through a sandstorm. The event, depicted in a contemporary print, took place during his second expedition to Central Asia.

Hedin returned to the Takla Makan Desert three years later in 1899. This time well provisioned, he set off by boat, mapping the Yarkand and Tarim rivers before heading once again across the Takla Makan Desert with the goal of reaching the Lop Nor Desert. Marco Polo (see pp. 56–61) had traveled through this desert some 650 years earlier, but had not reached the Lop Nor Lake, a salt-encrusted lake bed known for centuries to the Chinese. During this expedition, Hedin came upon the 2,000-year-old city of Lou Lan, where he found Han dynasty manuscripts. Nevertheless, he did not stay long at Lou Lan, fearful of repeating the mistake of the water supplies. He headed onward, intending to cross the Tibetan plateau to Lhasa, the capital of Tibet. But he and his companions were apprehended by guards before reaching Lhasa, and escorted back to the border.

SUCCESS IN TIBET

Hedin carried out two more major expeditions, returning successfully to Tibet from 1906–08, mapping and recording significant new areas that had been blank on European maps of the time.

In 1926, at the age of 62, Hedin returned to China to reconnoître for a new air link between Beijing and Berlin. He planned to undertake aerial survey work, but the Chinese authorities forced him to abandon the plan, citing concerns over the security of archeological sites. By then, however, Hedin had made a monumental impact on the field of Central Asian exploration.

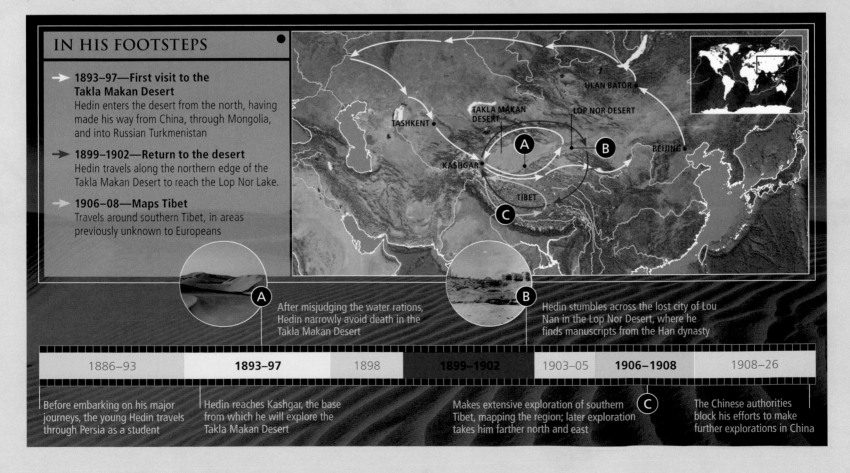

IN HIS FOOTSTEPS

1893–97—First visit to the Takla Makan Desert
Hedin enters the desert from the north, having made his way from China, through Mongolia, and into Russian Turkmenistan

1899–1902—Return to the desert
Hedin travels along the northern edge of the Takla Makan Desert to reach the Lop Nor Lake.

1906–08—Maps Tibet
Travels around southern Tibet, in areas previously unknown to Europeans

ULAN BATOR

TAKLA MAKAN DESERT

LOP NOR DESERT

TASHKENT

BEIJING

KASHGAR

A

B

TIBET

C

A After misjudging the water rations, Hedin narrowly avoid death in the Takla Makan Desert

B Hedin stumbles across the lost city of Lou Nan in the Lop Nor Desert, where he finds manuscripts from the Han dynasty

1886–93	**1893–97**	1898	**1899–1902**	1903–05	**1906–1908**	1908–26

Before embarking on his major journeys, the young Hedin travels through Persia as a student

Hedin reaches Kashgar, the base from which he will explore the Takla Makan Desert

Makes extensive exploration of southern Tibet, mapping the region; later exploration takes him farther north and east

C

The Chinese authorities block his efforts to make further explorations in China

TRANSPORTATION FOR THE SILK ROAD
Hedin's use of camels on his expeditions in Central Asia was a crucial factor in his success: able to withstand extremes of temperature and to survive many weeks without water, the Bactrian camel was a main mode of transportation for goods along the Silk Road. In addition, the camel's hair, gathered in the molting season, provided a rich source of fiber that was used by the Kirgiz people to make clothing and other textiles.

IT WAS A STRANGE SENSATION TO LOOK DOWN ON FIGURES WHICH BUT FOR THEIR PARCHED SKIN SEEMED LIKE THOSE OF MEN ASLEEP

MARC AUREL STEIN ON SEEING MUMMIES IN THE TURFAN REGION

MARC AUREL STEIN

THE "DISCOVERER" OF THE SILK ROAD

HUNGARY   1862–1943

MARC AUREL STEIN

HUNGARIAN-BORN ARCHEOLOGIST and explorer Marc Aurel Stein was inspired from an early age by tales of Alexander the Great's armies crossing Central Asia. After taking British citizenship, he was sponsored by British institutions to explore those very lands. Stein was to spend 30 years exploring. He uncovered evidence of a lost Buddhist civilization and brought to light manuscripts, frescoes, paintings, and relics. His most famous discovery, at Dunhuang, established how the routes of the Silk Road were connected.

Stein's first archeological exploration was along the Indian frontier, but Central Asia was always his goal. He much admired *On Asia,* by Swedish explorer Sven Hedin (see pp. 228–33), and, in 1900, set out on the first of his own expeditions to the deserts of Chinese Turkestan, taking with him a small team of dedicated assistants, as well as a pet dog—he was to own five over the years and called each of them Dash. Most were to accompany him on his explorations.

On his first expedition in 1900–01, Stein traveled over the Pamir Mountains to Kashgar in eastern China, and, heading via the town of Khotan, explored the southern edge of the Takla Makan Desert. There, he found evidence for early Indian, Chinese, and Hellenistic cultures among the ancient manuscripts and tablets he uncovered. Equally surprising, Stein also found that the desert had once sustained flourishing towns, abandoned over the centuries as the desert advanced.

By March 1907, during his second expedition, Stein had traveled more than 125 miles (200 km) east of Khotan, where he discovered the westernmost portion of the Great Wall of China, constructed 2,000 years earlier to protect China from attack by the Huns. There, he identified a fortified tower hidden in the sand dunes. Excavating the site, Stein's team found fragments of silk and inscribed wood dating from the Han period (206BCE– 220CE).

THE THOUSAND BUDDHAS

By 1907, Stein had traced the line of the Great Wall for a further 200 miles (300 km) east, until he came to Dunhuang. There, he made the discovery of his life, becoming the first European to enter the Mogao Caves, or the "Caves of the Thousand Buddhas." His excavations inside the caves revealed a host of important artifacts. He discovered more than 400 shrines and temples (originally decorated with wall paintings) constructed between the 4th and the 14th centuries. He also found manuscripts, silk paintings, and scrolls, including a copy of the Diamond Sutra, a work

VOTIVE PLAQUE
Stein found this 6th-century wooden panel in Dandan-olik in the Khotan oasis in the Takla Makan Desert.

TEMPLE OF ANCIENT SECRETS
Stein saw this sensational wall painting, dating from the 9th century, in the Mogao Caves, Dunhuang. After persuading one of the priests to allow him access he noted "… there appeared in the dim light of the priest's little lamp a solid mass of manuscript bundles rising to a height of nearly ten feet."

IN HIS FOOTSTEPS

→ **1900–01 and 1907–08—Stein's first expeditions into Central Asia**
Stein makes two journeys, exploring the routes along the southern edge of the Takla Makan Desert

→ **1913–15—Following the northern routes of the Silk Road**
Explores the Silk Road to the north of the Takla Makan Desert

⋯⋯ **The Silk Road**
The ancient trade routes first opened up during the Han dynasty 2,000 years ago, along which Stein travels

B Stein makes his greatest discovery at the Mogao Caves, where he finds the Diamond Sutra, the world's oldest surviving printed text

D While retracing his steps along the Silk Road in Pakistan, Stein documents his travels in a series of photographs

| 1862–99 | **1900–01** | 1902–06 | **1907–08** | 1909–12 | **1913–15** | 1916–43 |

A Stein makes his first major discovery at Niya, where he finds more than 100 wooden tablets dating from 105CE

Between journeys, Stein lives alone with his dog—pitching a tent in an alpine meadow

C Stein uncovers an ancient cemetery in the Turfan region; the bodies are wrapped in silks

E Exploring until the last, Stein dies shortly after arriving in Kabul

---

of Buddhist wisdom. When Stein's caravan left Dunhuang, it included 29 crates packed with manuscripts, paintings, and art. As an archeologist and scholar, his justification for removing vast amounts of material from this (and other) sites was to ensure their preservation and to enable detailed study. By late September 1907, Stein was surveying a route through the Kulun Mountains in western China, en route for Ladak with his guide, Lal Singh. After ascending a steep glacier to a height of nearly 20,000 ft (7,000 m), Stein described his physical condition: "I found that the toes of my feet had been severely injured by frostbite. This was bad luck, indeed, but I was glad all the same to know that our exploratory tasks had been carried through to their end." Stein was carried over the nine marches it took to reach the hospital at Leh, where the toes of his right foot had to be amputated.

DEPOSITING HIS FINDS

On his return to London in January 1908, Stein deposited his collections at various museums. Although an indefatigable scholar, the cataloging and research work on his finds, coupled with the production of maps from his topographical surveys, was an enormous undertaking. The surveying work alone created nearly 100 sheets of complete mapping. In addition, 8,000 manuscripts and documents required study. Stein was, however, eager to return to Central Asia once this initial work was published. His hope was to complete the next stage of the surveying work before the publicity surrounding his sensational finds at the Mogao Caves encouraged looters and treasure hunters.

Setting off again in 1913, Stein's third expedition, funded entirely by the Indian

NIKOLAI PRZHEVALSKY

RUSSIA   1839–88

Przhevalsky, a Russian army officer, explored Siberia in the 1860s. He also made four journeys into Central Asia.

His second expedition (1876–77) took him into the Takla Makan Desert, where he traveled through eastern Turkestan to Lop Nor, which it was believed had not been visited by any European since Marco Polo. Przhevalsky's third expedition (1879–80) took him over the Tian Shan Mountains to within 160 miles (250 km) of Lhasa, before the Tibetan authorities turned him back. He cataloged an enormous number of species of flora and fauna, including the only truly wild horse still known to exist—which is now called Przhevalsky's horse.

government, traveled from Srinigar in Kashmir, to Kashgar via the Karakoram, surveying the northwest fringes of the Takla Makan Desert.

Stein's goal this time was to explore the routes of the early Chinese Buddhist pilgrims. To this end, he traveled at a high altitude to avoid the summer heat in the Indus gorges. Although the route was hard, within the first two weeks more than 1,200 sq miles (3,000 sq km) had been mapped in a landscape "never surveyed or even seen before by European eyes." The route continued through the Darel and Tanjir valleys, where Stein recorded ancient fortress sites, evidence of early Buddhist settlement, and examples of Graeco-Buddhist designs woven into the wood carvings on houses, mosques, and gravestones. At the glacial pass of Darkot, he found evidence for his theory that 8th-century Chinese armies had used the natural gateway of the pass to stop the Tibetans.

RETRACING HIS STEPS

By September 1913, Stein was close to the border of Chinese Turkestan at the Mintaka Pass: "I now found myself on the ground familiar from two previous journeys. But the routes by which I had formerly reached it seemed quite 'lady-like' compared with our recent tracks. During the five weeks since our start from Kashmir we had crossed altogether fifteen passes, between 10,000 and 17,400 feet in height, and nearly four-fifths of the total distance

IMPRESSIVE PAGODAS
The network of shrines and temples Stein came across at Dunhuang varied from bare caves to elaborately decorated pagodas, such as this one at the Mogao Caves.

PICTURE DIARY
Stein made a photographic record of all his journeys. This 1926 picture shows a group of the local Gujar people on the mountain of Pir-Sar in Pakistan.

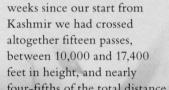

THE DIAMOND SUTRA

Among the manuscripts Stein found in the Mogao Caves was a copy of the Diamond Sutra, the oldest surviving printed book in the world. The manuscript dates from the 9th century, nearly 600 years before Gutenberg printed his first Bible in Europe. It is a Chinese translation of an earlier Sanskrit text, which recounts a conversation between the Buddha and a monk called Subhuti that was overheard in the city of Sravasti. The Diamond Sutra deals with many of Buddhism's most difficult themes, as the Buddha explains to Subhuti the elusive path to the enlightened "Buddha mind." Stein bought the 16-ft- (5-m-) long scroll from a monk who was guarding the caves. It is kept in the British Library in London.

A SECTION FROM THE DIAMOND SUTRA, A BUDDHIST TEXT STEIN TOOK FROM THE MOGAO CAVES IN 1907

BRONZE-AGE VESSEL
This 3,500-year-old tripod-footed ceramic vessel comes from the Rumishkan area of southern Luristan in Iran. It is one of many artifacts Stein donated to the British Museum.

covered, over 500 miles, had to be done on foot." Stein's work, and the sheer volume of material collected, had created new subject areas in Chinese archeology and art. However, by the 1920s, the Chinese authorities were becoming concerned about the flow of antiquities out of the country and began to restrict access at Silk Road sites. So Stein returned instead to his boyhood desire to explore Alexander the Great's routes through Afghanistan. In 1943, at the age of 81, Stein made his first visit to Kabul (where he gained permission to explore the ancient region of Bactria). Shortly after his arrival, however, he suffered from a stroke and died on October 26. His final words were: "I had a wonderful life, and it could not be concluded more happily than in Afghanistan, which I have wanted to visit for sixty years." Stein had provided some of the greatest insights into the civilizations of Central Asia and his collection has become the basis for extensive international research into these diverse cultures.

HARRY ST. JOHN PHILBY

TRUE EXPLORER OF THE "EMPTY QUARTER"

ENGLAND   1885–1960

HARRY ST. JOHN PHILBY, linguist, ornithologist, and Arabist, is one of the least known and most influential figures in the history of the Middle East. While working for British intelligence during World War I, he helped to ferment the Arab Revolt against Turkish rule, and in doing so developed a life-long love for Arabia. The British explorer Bertram Thomas beat him to become the first European to cross the Rub'al Khali, the "Empty Quarter" of the Arabian Desert, but it was Philby who explored the area more extensively.

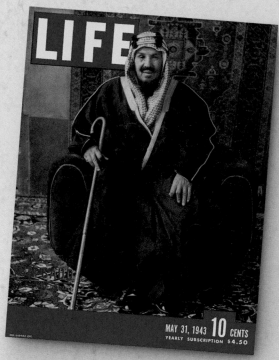

FIRST SAUDI
Abdul Aziz Ibn Saud (above) became the first king of the modern state of Saudi Arabia in 1926. Philby supported Ibn Saud's claim to the throne and became his close adviser.

In 1917, Philby was sent to make contact with a local Arabian ruler, Abdul Aziz Ibn Saud, a British ally during World War I. Philby had been warned by the Foreign Office that an overland route to Jeddah was too dangerous, since Ibn Saud had no control over the region's tribes, but Philby disproved this on his return, becoming the first European to complete an east–west crossing of Arabia in December 1917.

At the end of the war, he was named head of British Intelligence in Palestine, but found himself increasingly at odds with British policy in the region, which he felt was a betrayal of the wartime promise of a unified Arab nation. The

British wanted to make Sharif Hussein of Mecca king of liberated Arabia in preference to Ibn Saud, whom Philby considered the better candidate. Matters came to a head when Philby's secret communications with Ibn Saud were discovered and he was forced to resign in 1924 for his Arab sympathies. In any event, Ibn Saud ousted Hussein from the Hejaz (the western Arabian coast) and became king of Saudi Arabia.

In 1925, Philby settled in Jeddah and set up a trading company. He had huge influence in the new Saudi state, even arranging Ibn Saud's coronation. With the support of the king, he returned on camelback to survey the area to the south of Riyadh in 1928 and during this expedition began to formulate his long-term ambition to cross the Empty Quarter.

One of the least populated places on Earth, covering the southern half of the Arabian Peninsula, the Empty Quarter comprises towering sand dunes, some reaching 800 ft (250 m). Its western edge is marked by vast gravel plains. The climate is extremely harsh, with daytime temperatures commonly reaching 120°F (50°C) while at night often plummeting to freezing. Philby's ambition was initially thwarted by Thomas (see pp. 248–49), who crossed from south to north in 1931, a few months before Philby's planned departure.

PHILBY'S COFFEE POT
The appearance of the coffee pot signaled rest. Philby wrote, "the time draws nigh for a short halt, with coffee to cheer the heart of man."

A LIFE'S WORK

- Studies **Oriental languages** at Cambridge University, becoming fluent in Urdu, Punjabi, Persian, Baluchi, and Arabic

- Becomes a close adviser to the first king of Saudi Arabia, **Ibn Saud**

- Crosses the Empty Quarter from **north to south**, exploring the region extensively

- Carries out **survey work** in southern Arabia

- Names several **species of bird** after women he admires and has a species of partridge named after him (*Alectoris philbyi*)

I SHALL ALWAYS BE PROUD TO HAVE FOLLOWED IN PHILBY'S FOOTSTEPS

WILFRED THESIGER

Devastated by Thomas's success, Philby locked himself away for a week in despair. He had first planned the crossing back in 1924, but the fighting between Ibn Saud and Hussein had made conditions in the desert too dangerous.

NORTH TO SOUTH

Recovering from his disappointment, Philby determined to win the prize of crossing from north to south, with a wider exploration of the area between Hufuf and As Sulayyil, which he considered a far more ambitious undertaking. In January 1932, he set out from Hufuf with 14 men, 32 camels, and supplies to last for three months. He retraced Thomas's route southward as far as Shanna and the southern limit of the dunes before setting out to the west and heading toward As Sulayyil, a crossing of some 400 miles (650 km). Philby's attempt failed when, just 100 miles (160 km) into the journey, the camels began to suffer from exhaustion: the weight of the packs had been underestimated and proved too much for the animals to bear.

Philby set out on a second attempt later that spring, this time with a much smaller party. He reached As Sulayyil on March 14, having covered 1,700 miles (2,700 km). He described this journey in *The Empty Quarter*, published

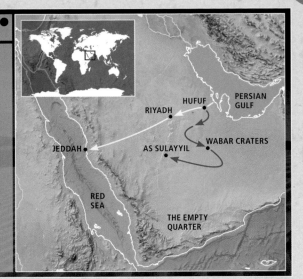

IN HIS FOOTSTEPS

→ **December 1917—departs Riyadh**
Philby safely crosses the Arabian Highlands to Jeddah, proving to the British that Ibn Saud has the loyalty of the tribes in the region; he is the first European to complete an east–west crossing of Arabia

→ **January 1932—departs Hufuf**
Philby and his party head toward the Wabar craters after hearing Bedouin legends about the lost city of Ubar (which is named in the Koran) and stories about lumps of iron the size of camels lying in the sand; when he finds the craters he believes them to be volcanoes

PERSIAN GULF
HUFUF
RIYADH
WABAR CRATERS
JEDDAH
AS SULAYYIL
RED SEA
THE EMPTY QUARTER

in 1933. He had explored the area extensively, discovering the eerie Wabar Craters (formed by meteorite impacts) while searching for the legendary lost city of Ubar.

Philby remained a vocal critic of British policy in Arab affairs to the extent that, en route to a book tour of the US in 1940, British authorities interned him in Britain under the Defense of the Realm Act, fearful of his rogue influence on oil-rich Arabia. An enigmatic

figure, Philby returned to Arabia in 1945, at age 60, and purchased his second wife, a 16-year-old girl from the slave market at Taif, near Mecca. His son, Kim, was by that time working in British intelligence as a spy for the Soviets.

SACRED HONOR
A convert to Islam, Philby made the hajj, or pilgrimage, to Mecca, in 1931. As a friend of Ibn Saud, Philby was invited to take part in the ritual cleaning of the sacred Kaaba (below).

JOHANN LUDWIG BURCKHARDT

THE FIRST EUROPEAN TO EXPLORE PETRA

SWITZERLAND   1784–1817

JOHANN LUDWIG BURCKHARDT was a Swiss explorer sponsored by the British African Association to explore the interior of North Africa. An intrepid character, he saw the importance of immersing himself in local culture to access places that were out-of-bounds to Europeans. Having turned himself into a knowledgeable scholar of Islam and passing himself off as a Syrian, Burckhardt visited the ruined city of Petra and the ancient Egyptian temple at Abu Simbel. He was also able to spend time in the holy city of Mecca.

Born in Switzerland and educated in Germany, Burckhardt moved to England in 1806 to pursue his dream of becoming an explorer. Bearing a letter of introduction from German naturalist Johann Friedrich Blumenbach (see p. 242), and with the support of Sir Joseph Banks (see p. 197), he persuaded the African Association in London to give its backing to a mission. Burckhardt lost no time in preparing for his vocation. He studied languages, the sciences, and surgery, until the Association gave him his brief in 1809: to explore the desert from Cairo to the Sudan. He was still only 25 years old.

SCHOLAR OF ISLAM
Burckhardt arrived in Aleppo, Syria, in September 1809. He was to spend the next three years there studying Koranic law and Arabic, adopting the disguise of a learned Arab and taking the name Ibrahim Ibn Abdallah. From a base at the

home of the British counsel in Aleppo—and later with a Turkish family—he made journeys to the surrounding areas. His approach was a modern one: in addition to assimilating the culture of the Arab people, he quickly learned about the traditions of the Bedouin and Wahabi tribes. Constantly testing and preparing himself for the hardships of expeditions, he took long journeys on foot and in great heat, eating a meager diet and sleeping on the ground. Meanwhile, he researched the accounts of Arab writers on the holy city of Mecca.

Throughout his travels, Burckhardt maintained a regular correspondence with Sir Joseph Banks. His letters show his inexperience during his first forays in Syria and, in one dating from 1810, his poor judgment in choosing a guide. He described in another letter how "we returned to town, to refit ourselves as well as possible, and then set out again the next night to rejoin our chief. The latter however having left the watering place, we were obliged to run after him in the desert for 36 hours …"

By May 1811, the young traveler had carried out three significant explorations of Syria, as far as Damascus, Palmyra, and Hauran. Confident that he was providing important new

SPANISH SILVER
Burckhardt kept meticulous accounts of his journeys. He carried with him silver Spanish dollars, but worked on the principle that the less money he took, the better the expedition would go.

A LIFE'S WORK

- Immerses himself in **Arab culture** and uses his **knowledge of Islam** to gain access to places previously barred to Europeans

- Is the **first European** to visit the ruined city of **Petra** in present-day Jordan

- Explores **Nubia** and describes the temples at **Abu Simbel** in great detail

- Spends time in **Mecca** and reports on the **religious ceremonies** he witnesses there

THIS VALLEY DESERVES TO BE THOROUGHLY KNOWN; ITS EXAMINATIONS WILL LEAD TO MANY INTERESTING DISCOVERIES

JOHANN LUDWIG BURCKHARDT ON SEEING PETRA

ANCIENT ROCK TEMPLES
In Nubia, southern Egypt, Burckhardt saw the rock temples at Abu Simbel. Carved during the 13th century BCE, the statues depict Ramesses II, a king known to scholars in Burckhardt's day only through the Bible. When Burckhardt saw them they were half submerged in sand, as in this photo from 1906.

information, the African Association had approved the extension of his plans by a further six months. Burckhardt was working hard: the contents of a package dispatched to Banks are listed as including "a classification of the principal Arab tribes near Syria; a treatise on Bedouin customs and manners; the journal of my tour in the Haouran; the journal of my tour of the Syrian mountains, and some geographical notices concerning the desert."

FINDING PETRA

In June 1812, Burckhardt set out on one of the greatest journeys of his life. Disguised as a Syrian, he crossed Palestine to the south of the Dead Sea. There, he found a guide to take him into the Valley of Ghor, where he described seeing "manna" being collected from the trees In the Bible, this was the food that sustained the Hebrews during their 40 years in the desert before their arrival in the Promised Land. As Burckhardt continued his journey, the guide then took him through a narrow valley, where he came upon the ruins of the Nabatean city of Petra. It must have presented an astonishing sight to the impressionable young man. To Banks he wrote of "the remains of an ancient city, which I conjecture to be Petra … a place which, as far as I know, no European traveler has ever visited."

Burckhardt's time for exploration of the ruins was limited, however, as he was wary of the local Bedouin who watched him constantly and who were suspicious of this European who had strayed so far from the coast.

After Petra, Burckhardt set a course for Suez and then to Cairo, which he reached in September 1812. Disappointed to find no

ROSE-RED CITY
Burckhardt described Petra, built in the 4th century BCE, as a "rose-red city, half as old as time." Seen here is Al-Dier, an unfinished tomb known as "the monastery."

caravans were heading along his intended route into the Western Desert, he changed his plan and traveled down the Nile. En route south he described the temple at Abu Simbel in great detail. He ventured deep into Nubia, where he found time to muse upon his prescription for successful traveling: "I put eight Spanish dollars into my purse, in conformity with the principle I have constantly acted upon during my travels, that the less the traveler spends while on his March, and the less money he carries with him, the less likely are his traveling projects to miscarry."

Burckhardt was one of the first Europeans to report on the economic practicalities of his expeditions. In *Travels in Nubia*, he breaks down expenditure in detail: he returned with three dollars, the rest spent on presents and fees for guides. His personal expenditure was limited to tobacco, bread, onions, and shoe repairs.

Still determined to see Mecca, he set out from Daraw in Egypt, in March 1814, traveling across the

Nubian Desert to Suakin, a port on the Sudanese coast of the Red Sea. There, he boarded a ship carrying pilgrims to Jeddah, and from there embarked on an arduous five-day caravan trek inland. He found company, however, in the form of the governor of Egypt, Muhammed Ali Pasha, who he met along the way. Pasha agreed to support Burckhardt's goal by professing him to be a worthy and devout Muslim. On joining the caravan, Burckhardt remarked on the importance of coffee. "Except coffee and water," he wrote, "nothing is to be procured in any of the huts on this road … whoever asks for it, has a small earthen pot of hot coffee set before him, containing from ten to fifteen cups: this quantity the traveler often drinks three or four times a day."

REACHING THE HOLY CITY

Burckhardt arrived in Mecca at about noon on September 9, 1814. He stayed for two months before returning to Cairo, by now suffering from malaria and malnutrition. He had been traveling for a little over two and a half years.

JOHANN FRIEDRICH BLUMENBACH

GERMAN CONFEDERATION   1752–1840

Blumenbach was a German naturalist and anthropologist who taught Burckhardt at the University of Göttingen in Germany.

He established one of the earliest anthropological divisions between human races, creating as subdivisions: American, Caucasian, African, Mongolian, and (later) Malay, based on physical geological evidence. For over 30 years, Blumenbach corresponded regularly with the English naturalist Sir Joseph Banks. Blumenbach regularly credited his English counterpart as the source of much of the data with which he developed his theories.

As he recovered from the hardships of his journey, Burckhardt occupied himself with preparing detailed reports on the ceremonies he witnessed at Mecca, while also considering where to explore next.

His plans were accelerated when, in April 1816, Cairo was struck by plague, and to avoid the illness he set out on an exploration of the Sinai Desert. Toward the end of this journey, at the Castle of Adjeroud, he and his party were forced, partly through thirst and partly due to the threat of ambush from robbers, to drink from a contaminated well: "the water we were thus obliged to drink was saline, putrid, and of a yellow green color, so that boiling produced no improvement in it, and our stomachs could not retain it."

Burckhardt returned to Cairo to await a caravan into the Sahara. Shortly before he joined it he was able to complete work on his journals and dispatch them to England. He had made his final journey, however. Burckhardt contracted dysentery and died in the city on October 15, 1817, at the age of 33.

IN THE FOOTSTEPS OF ABRAHAM
On his journey into Sinai, Burckhardt rested a while at the monastery of St. Catherine, built by early Christians in the 4th century. During his stay, he climbed Mount Sinai.

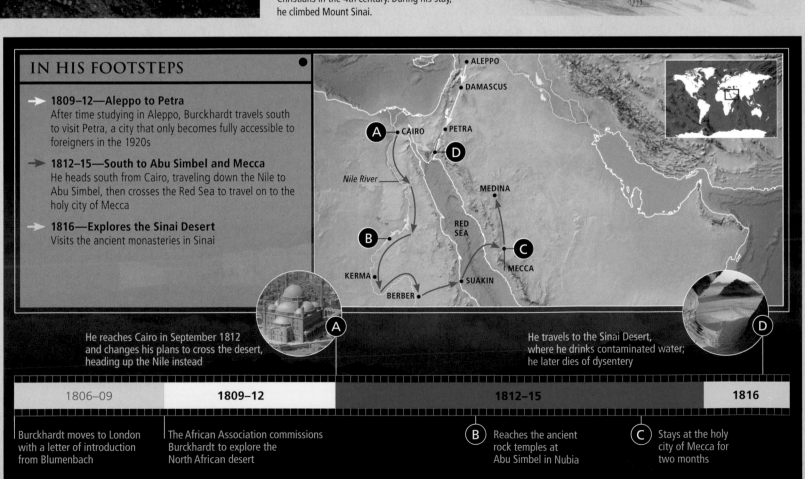

IN HIS FOOTSTEPS

1809–12—Aleppo to Petra
After time studying in Aleppo, Burckhardt travels south to visit Petra, a city that only becomes fully accessible to foreigners in the 1920s

1812–15—South to Abu Simbel and Mecca
He heads south from Cairo, traveling down the Nile to Abu Simbel, then crosses the Red Sea to travel on to the holy city of Mecca

1816—Explores the Sinai Desert
Visits the ancient monasteries in Sinai

ALEPPO
DAMASCUS
A · CAIRO PETRA
D
Nile River
MEDINA
RED SEA
B
C
MECCA
KERMA
SUAKIN
BERBER

A He reaches Cairo in September 1812 and changes his plans to cross the desert, heading up the Nile instead

D He travels to the Sinai Desert, where he drinks contaminated water; he later dies of dysentery

1806–09	**1809–12**	**1812–15**	**1816**

Burckhardt moves to London with a letter of introduction from Blumenbach

The African Association commissions Burckhardt to explore the North African desert

B Reaches the ancient rock temples at Abu Simbel in Nubia

C Stays at the holy city of Mecca for two months

CHARTING THE DEVELOPMENT OF...

EXPEDITION CLOTHING

WHATEVER THE ENVIRONMENT, expeditionary clothing has one common purpose: to protect the wearer from the weather, whether it is the intense heat of the Arabian Empty Quarter or the perishing cold of the Antarctic Peninsula. Over time, individuals have made personal refinements to suit particular conditions. As a signifier of "otherness," clothing has also had an important psychological role to play in identifying the explorer or, in some cases, concealing his or her identity.

CLOTHING AS DISGUISE

Early European travelers in the Middle East found that by adopting Arab dress they were able to travel with a measure of anonymity. The most successful, such as Johann Ludwig Burckhardt (see pp. 240–43), combined Arab dress with Arabic language skills. Richard Burton (see pp. 204–07), who, in 1853, was one of the first Europeans to enter Mecca, knew that he risked execution for his pilgrimage to the holy city, which was forbidden to non-Muslims. After months of studying Arab etiquette and manners, he finally made the hajj in Arab dress. Later passionate Arabists, including Bertram Thomas (see pp. 248–49) and Wilfred Thesiger (see pp. 250–51), understood the purely practical benefits of adopting local habits of dress: flowing Arab robes and the keffiyeh, or headdress, provided maximum comfort for the wearer by day and night.

1519—SEA CHEST
In the 15th century, maritime travelers keep suits of fine clothing in sea-going chests. The clothes are intended for ceremonial encounters in the New World and to depict the wearer's European status.

1608—FUR TRADERS
Quebec City is founded as a center of the fur trade, gradually fed by a demand from Europe, where pelt hats and coats are fashionable.

1823—TRUE WATERPROOF
Scottish chemist Charles Macintosh (1766–1843) patents his waterproof, rubberized clothing, just as European interest in exploration is beginning to grow.

CE | 1450 | 1500 | 1550 | 1600 | 1750 | 1775 | 1800

The escuapil, **a padded cotton tunic armor** worn by Aztec warriors, right, is a practical lightweight and flexible garment. It is adopted by the Spanish as an alternative to the heavier mail and armor suits brought over from Spain, which can weigh as much as 60 lb (27 kg). The escuapil provides **effective protection against the obsidian blades** of Aztec weapons, but not against Spanish bullets.

1520 AZTEC ARMOR

1634—CHINESE PUZZLE
French explorer Jean Nicolet becomes the first European to cross Lake Michigan in North America. He wears colorful Chinese robes, convinced he is about to reach China and meet Asian people.

The expeditions of **Lewis and Clark** (right) do much to **show the value of indigenous clothing.** The men take to wearing **leather deerskin "frocks,"** which are waterproof and durable. In addition, **deerskin leggings** offer protection to mid-thigh height, and they also adopt **moccasins,** the footwear of the American Indian tribes, keeping the leather supple by rubbing it with bear grease.

1804 LEWIS AND CLARK

THE AFRICAN "OUTFIT"

Victorian explorers Samuel Baker and Henry Morton Stanley (see pp. 214–15) realized that in the high humidity of sub-Saharan Africa, typical travel clothes were impractical. Baker was one of the first to design his own safari outfit: a loose-fitting cotton tunic and pants that protected him from the Sun and gave maximum flexibility of movement. Stanley developed the sola topi, or pith helmet, which he wore during his search for David Livingstone (see pp. 220–23). He adapted the helmet (which was later to become synonymous with colonial rule) by adding a band of Bombay fabric that protected the neck from the Sun. Livingstone, by comparison, wore the traditional Victorian garb of a black tailcoat, which would almost certainly have contributed to his many fevers when wet. His only concession to the conditions was his consul cap.

WOMEN TRAVELERS

For female travelers of the Victorian age, clothing presented different challenges. Both Mary Kingsley (see pp. 212–13) and Isabella Bird, for example, chose to keep to their late-Victorian styles of dress. Kingsley dismissed the concept of "rational" dress, and on one occasion her voluminous petticoats and stiff woolen costume protected her from impalement on the spikes of a hidden man-trap in West Africa. Bird would readily use her garments as cloths and for emergency purposes, finding herself reduced to one, overdarned travel outfit in 1876 as she traveled through Colorado, describing how: "It is singular that one can face the bitter winds with the mercury at zero and below it, in exactly the same clothing which I wore in the tropics!" As women gained independence, so an industry developed around their travel needs. In 1889, Lillias Campbell Davidson published *Hints to Lady Travelers At Home and Abroad*, which asserted that the days had passed when clothing made "the British female abroad an object of terror and avoidance to all beholders."

NEW AND OLD TECHNOLOGIES

Before World War I, clothing companies advertised their connections with the expeditions of Robert Scott (see pp. 312–15) and Ernest Shackleton (see pp. 318–19). Their polar clothing was made from cotton, wool, and silk, and Scott openly wondered whether fur-based clothing would have aided the progress of his final expedition. By comparison, American, Norwegian, and other explorers who had trained in the Arctic Circle adopted the millennia-old clothing techniques of the Inuit. Robert Peary (see pp. 308–09), Fridtjof Nansen (see pp. 296–97), and Roald Amundsen (see pp. 302–305) all chose to dress in furs and sealskin, noting their superior wind-proofing and quick-drying nature.

In 1924, George Mallory and Andrew Irvine set out on the final stage of their planned ascent of Mount Everest wearing clothing that would not have appeared out of place on a country ramble. Puttees and walking boots, combined with tweed suits, woolens, and cotton garments, offered limited protection. Edmund Hillary and Tenzing Norgay (see pp. 322–23) were both equipped with specially designed rubber-soled boots and down-filled jackets for their 1953 ascent. Today, porous, breathable fabrics such as Gore-Tex, invented in the 1970s, provide protection from the wind and rain while allowing perspiration to escape.

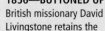

1856—BUTTONED UP
British missionary David Livingstone retains the heavy black tailcoat of a Victorian gentleman while in Africa.

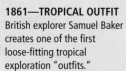

1861—TROPICAL OUTFIT
British explorer Samuel Baker creates one of the first loose-fitting tropical exploration "outfits."

1909—INUIT COMFORT
For his attempt on the North Pole, American explorer Robert E. Peary commissions fur suits from the Inuit and stuffs his boots with moss for insulation.

1961—US SPACESUIT
The two-layer suit is adapted from high-altitude jet aircraft pressure suits.

1980—NEW FABRIC
Breathable, waterproof Gore-Tex replaces older outdoor clothing fabrics.

| 1850 | 1875 | 1900 | 1925 | 1950 | 1975 | 2000 |

RICHARD BURTON

1853

Burton ensures safe passage on his **pilgrimage to Mecca** by adopting the identity and **dress of a Pashtun** (pictured). As he writes in his journal: "At Cairo I went to a Caravanserai. Here I became a Pathán [Pashtun]. I was born in India of Afghan parents, who had settled there, and I was educated at Rangoon, and was sent out, as is often the custom, to wander. I knew all the languages that I required to pass me, Persian, Hindostani, and Arabic."

1871—PITH HELMET
Welsh journalist and explorer Henry Morton Stanley popularizes the sola topi, or pith helmet.

With the advent of **new, hi-tech materials**, on their successful ascent of Mt. Everest, **Edmund Hillary and Tenzing Norgay wear the latest cotton-nylon mix fabrics**, silk inner gloves, and Swiss down mitts. Their boots are specially designed for use at very high altitude with thin, **microcellular rubber soles** and a double-vapor barrier. The total weight of the gear per man (as worn by Hillary, above) is estimated at 17 lb (8 kg).

EDMUND HILLARY

1953

CHARLES MONTAGU DOUGHTY

LAST OF THE ILLUSTRIOUS VICTORIAN EXPLORERS

ENGLAND   1843–1926

SCHOLAR AND EXPLORER Charles Montagu Doughty was a Victorian eccentric. Possessed of a wide-ranging intellect and a passion for archaic English, he spent the decade following his first degree in geology studying languages at universities across Europe. Later, he became a wandering scholar in Egypt and Palestine. He undertook his first major exploration of hidden Arabia in 1876. His book, *Travels in Arabia Deserta,* is one of the greatest firsthand accounts of Arabia of the 19th century.

Doughty's first journey of exploration, in 1876, was the result of a conversation overheard in an Arab coffee house. The eavesdropping Doughty learned of the existence of the rock carvings and tombs of Mada'in Salih, an ancient city in Saudi Arabia built in the first century by the Nabataeans, an ancient semitic people. He was determined to find them, and spent the next eight months in Damascus preparing for his expedition and learning Arabic. To cross the desert, Doughty needed to be accepted onto a camel train, and eventually he managed to find a place on the huge pilgrim caravan, consisting of 6,000 men and twice as many camels, heading to Mecca.

As a non-Muslim Doughty required a disguise and passed himself off as a "Syrian of middle fortune." Despite having no medical training, he carried a medicine chest, reasoning that a doctor would always receive a warm welcome. Yet he was reluctant to accept the customs and religion of his hosts, or to make any effort to conceal his Christian faith discreetly, so his Syrian disguise was soon seen through. In any event, this tall, red-headed, full-bearded man must have attracted notice. He was shunned by his fellow travelers, and only survived the journey through the kindness of the Bedouin people whose caravan he encountered. Doughty was left behind at Hejaz, and the caravan continued its journey to Medina and Mecca. He made his way independently to Teima, Jebel Shammar, and Ha'il. At Aneiza, he joined another caravan, this one carrying butter to Mecca, turning off just before the holy city to seek the protection of the sheriff at Taif.

CLASSIC ACCOUNT

Doughty finally reached Jeddah in the summer of 1878. In addition to visiting Mada'in Salih, he had observed and recorded the Arab world in

T. E. LAWRENCE
ENGLAND   1888–1935

"Lawrence of Arabia" was a British soldier known for his exploits as a liaison officer during the Arab Revolt of 1916–18. Long before his own Arabian adventures, he championed Doughty's writing.

Lawrence wrote in the introduction to the edition of *Travels in Arabia Deserta* published in the 1920s: "I have studied it for ten years, and have grown to consider it a book not like other books, but something particular, a bible of its kind. I do not think that any traveler in Arabia before or after Mr. Doughty has qualified himself to praise the book—much less to blame it."

detail, collecting a mass of information on the geology, hydrography, antiquities, and social customs of the Bedouin. He scrupulously charted each area he visited, and his chart of northwest central Arabia is still viewed today as a classic piece of cartography. He recorded the minutiae of his journey in his two-volume work *Travels in Arabia Deserta* (the first volume of which ran to more than 600,000 words and was first published in 1888). The books were not a commercial success. In addition to their excessive length, they were written in an idiosyncratic style consciously based on the English of the King James Bible from the 17th century. Gradually, however, the importance of Doughty's account came to be recognized, and it was republished just before his death with an introduction by T. E. Lawrence (see above). In addition to the more objective data regarding

the methods for pitching tents and loading camels, Doughty also recorded his feelings during his journeys, describing the sensations of extreme heat and fatigue he experienced in the desert landscape.

He was also witness to several natural events. Of a meteorite shower, he wrote, "An evening as the Arabs stood looking for the new moon, a little before the sun set, we heard a rushing sound in the heaven afar off. It was *nejm*, a star stone (said the Arabs) which had fallen they thought upon the mountains Rikb el-Héjr."

LATER RECOGNITION
Doughty's later career found him obsessively working on epic poetry as the achievements of his earlier exploration were largely ignored. In 1912, however, he was finally awarded the Royal Geographical Society's Gold Medal in recognition of his contribution to European understanding of the Arab world, and his forgotten book enjoyed a revival.

CITY OF THE NABATAEANS
Doughty was the first European to visit the rock carvings cut out of sandstone at Mada'in Salih. Dating from the first century CE, the city was the second most important of the ancient Nabotean kingdom, after Petra.

IN HIS FOOTSTEPS

→ 1876—Doughty's two-year journey around Arabia
After nearly a year spent in Damascus preparing for his trip and learning Arabic, Doughty embarks on his exploration of Arabia.

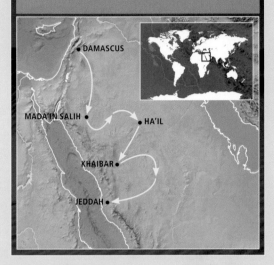

DAMASCUS

MADA'IN SALIH

HA'IL

KHAIBAR

JEDDAH

CAMEL CARAVAN
In the 19th century, huge caravans still crisscrossed the Arabian Desert carrying goods to trade, such as salt, or pilgrims to Mecca. Without the help of these caravans, Doughty's desert crossing would have been impossible.

BERTRAM THOMAS

THE DESERT DIPLOMAT

ENGLAND
1892–1950

BERTRAM THOMAS first visited the Middle East when he was posted to Mesopotamia (present-day Iraq) as a soldier during World War I. When the war ended, he stayed on as a civil servant, giving political advice to local leaders and developing a profound respect for the Arabs. By 1924, he had become the financial adviser to the sultan of Muscat. It was then that he began to plan his crossing of the Rub'al Khali: the notorious "Empty Quarter," consisting of some 250,000 sq miles (650,000 sq km) of uninhabited, shifting desert.

Thomas planned his expedition in secret, aware that Harry St. John Philby (see pp. 238–39) was also planning a crossing. To aid the success of his mission he was determined to win the respect of his guides from the outset: "I eschewed tobacco and alcohol to win a reputation for orthodoxy that would ultimately help me in the crossing of the Great Desert."

He set out in January 1930 on an initial exploratory journey into the Empty Quarter, accompanied by 28 Badu escorts and 48 camels. It soon became clear that the mountain-reared camels were a mistake, "useless in the soft sands of the desert." He therefore changed route and departed along the wadi (dry riverbed) system of Umm al Hait at the edge of the sands. As he traveled, Thomas experienced the hardships of the desert, lasting on little or no water for one or two days at a time. Arab clothing served him well: "one now appreciated the ample folds of the Arab head-dress for its protection by day and its warmth against the cold nights."

MAKING THE CROSSING

On the night of October 5, 1930, Thomas "quietly disappeared" by boat from Muscat. He had made plans to be met by a caravan at the city of Salalah, from where he would begin his

A LIFE'S WORK

- Proves that it is possible to **cross the Empty Quarter** of the Arabian Desert

- Is the first European to make contact with many of the peoples of Arabia, **leaving a favorable impression** that ensures future explorers will be given a warm reception

- **Uses local knowledge** to survive the extreme conditions of the desert

- Learns many of the local tongues, publishing a **study on the languages of the area**

- **Publishes a history** of the different peoples of Arabia

- After Arabia, he returns to Pill, Bristol, where he **dies in the house in which he was born**

IN HIS FOOTSTEPS

→ **First leg—departs Muscat**
In October 1930, Thomas makes a low-key departure by boat so as not to alert rival explorers to his plans

→ **Second leg—crosses Rub'al Khali**
Departs Salalah and enters the Empty Quarter, passing through the lands of tribes that permit him use of their springs; he reaches the Persian Gulf in January 1931, a journey of four months

PERSIAN GULF

BANAYYAN

MUSCAT

RUB'AL KHALI

THE EMPTY QUARTER

SALALAH

ARABIAN SEA

VALUE OF A BOTTLE

Thomas found water to be a valuable political commodity of the Empty Quarter, with tribes keeping secret their sources from enemies and outsiders.

crossing, but he found no camel train awaiting his arrival. To his frustration, he learned that warring between tribes had closed the routes out of the sands. Soon he had made alternative plans and set off with 30 men and 40 camels, telling only Salih bin Kalut (a sheik of the Rashid tribe) of his intention to cross. Salih agreed to take Thomas as far as the Murra tribal lands, from where he would continue his journey, assuming that the Murra would support it. He won the respect of the desert peoples, who permitted him use

of their precious watering places. Thomas learned how to read the desert, which he described as "a science known to every Badu. Every living creature— man, his camel, the wild animal, the reptile and the bird that alights … the sands have no recent secrets." On January 28, 1931, having survived sandstorms, water shortages, and blood-feuds, he reached the northern edge of the desert and days later saw the Persian Gulf, becoming the first European to cross the Empty Quarter: "I saw before me the sea … with the promise, after desert diet, of incomparable Arabian hospitality."

DESOLATE SPRING
The Kwar Hamidan Spring is the only permanent natural source of drinking water in the Empty Quarter. Thomas relied on his guides' knowledge to find other sources of water in the desert.

STUDENT OF ARABIA
Bertram Thomas is pictured with a group of warriors from the Shahari tribe in Oman. He gained the trust of the Shahari and other tribespeople by following their customs. He left such an impression that 22 years later, British explorer Wilfred Thesiger (see pp. 250–51) was welcomed by the Rashid, who remembered Thomas's tact and understanding for their way of life.

WILFRED THESIGER

A SELF-PROCLAIMED MAN APART

ENGLAND   1910–2003

A TRAVELER WHO SHUNNED the comforts of modern times, Wilfred Thesiger immersed himself in the cultures of the world's last untouched places. He traveled widely in Africa, Asia, and the Middle East, following "the lure of the unexplored, the compulsion to go where others have not been." Thesiger had a lifelong concern for the negative impact of progress on traditional societies, and his writings and photography provide an unembellished record of vanishing ways of life.

LIVING LIKE THE LOCALS
Thesiger embraced every aspect of the lives of the peoples he met. He learned Arabic and made use of local dress and items, such as this bronze dagger, for his travels in Arabia.

Born in Abyssinia—in present-day Ethiopia—in 1910, Thesiger was the son of a British diplomat and a close relative of an admiral, a general, and the viceroy of India. He later described, how, as a child, he simply "longed to be an explorer." Educated first at Eton, in England, his taste for travel was acquired during trips as an Oxford undergraduate, first to Constantinople (now Istanbul) aboard a tramp steamer, then to Iceland on an Atlantic trawler. In 1933, Thesiger embarked on the first of many journeys in Africa, tracing the course of the Awash River in his native Abyssinia. The following year, he joined the Sudan Political Service, relishing the challenge and hardship of overland trips to the little-known Tibesti Mountains in northern Chad and the Sudd wetlands of southern Sudan.

FIGHTING THE FASCISTS

During the Italian invasion of Abyssinia in 1935 and, later, at the outbreak of World War II, Thesiger took up arms in the Sudan Defense Force. Decorated for bravery in 1941, he was drafted into the SAS (British special forces) and served in North Africa and the Middle East, although he still found time to visit the spectacular rock-cut city of Petra.

Thesiger left the Army in 1943, returning to the country of his birth as adviser to Ethiopian Emperor Haile Selassie. At the end of the war in 1945, he took the opportunity to return to the wild on a UN study of desert locusts in Arabia. Thesiger spent the next five years crisscrossing the desert sands, exploring and mapping the landscape and coming to know its Bedouin peoples intimately. His sympathy for those he encountered was unmatched among explorers. He noted that, "To win respect [the stranger] must match their endurance, walking as far and riding as long, and bear heat, hunger, and cold with their uncomplaining indifference." He also understood the fine balance between the landscape and its people, noting that reading camel tracks was critical to survival. Thesiger was struck by the insularity of the desert: one clan he met, the Ruashid, knew little of the recent world war, but "had only heard of the war as between Christians." He always regretted parting from his Bedu companions who "were out of place among these soft townsmen … Lonely and apart I watched them drive in their camels and depart, back to the clean emptiness of the desert."

NOMADS OF EAST AFRICA
Thesiger encountered these Danakil nomads in present-day Djibouti and Eritrea during his 1933 expedition to follow the course of the Awash River.

MAN OF THE DESERT
Pictured here in Arabia's Empty Quarter in 1948, Thesiger preferred the company of local peoples to that of Westerners, a trait he described as a "life sentence of apartness."

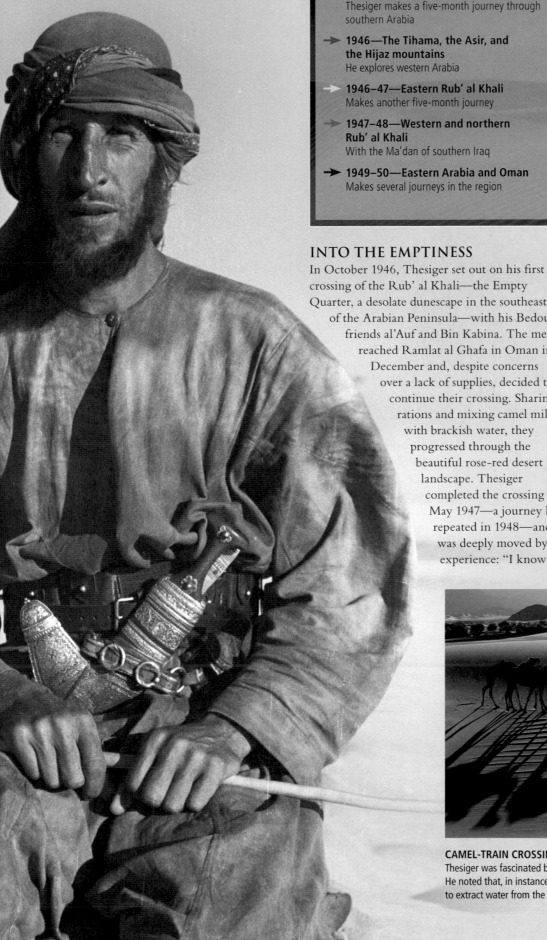

IN HIS FOOTSTEPS

→ **1945–46—Southern Rub' al Khali**
Thesiger makes a five-month journey through southern Arabia

→ **1946—The Tihama, the Asir, and the Hijaz mountains**
He explores western Arabia

→ **1946–47—Eastern Rub' al Khali**
Makes another five-month journey

→ **1947–48—Western and northern Rub' al Khali**
With the Ma'dan of southern Iraq

→ **1949–50—Eastern Arabia and Oman**
Makes several journeys in the region

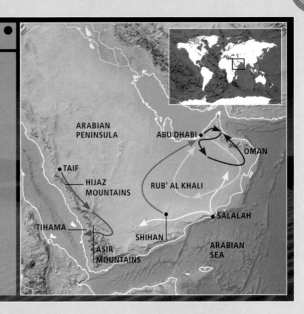

INTO THE EMPTINESS

In October 1946, Thesiger set out on his first crossing of the Rub' al Khali—the Empty Quarter, a desolate dunescape in the southeast of the Arabian Peninsula—with his Bedouin friends al'Auf and Bin Kabina. The men reached Ramlat al Ghafa in Oman in December and, despite concerns over a lack of supplies, decided to continue their crossing. Sharing rations and mixing camel milk with brackish water, they progressed through the beautiful rose-red desert landscape. Thesiger completed the crossing in May 1947—a journey he repeated in 1948—and was deeply moved by the experience: "I know that amongst them in the desert, I have found a freedom of the spirit which may not survive their passing." Several years later, he wrote of his travels in his widely acclaimed first book, *Arabian Sands* (1959), which has inspired future generations of travelers and writers alike.

Thesiger continued to travel for most of the rest of his life, spending seven years with the Ma'dan in the marshes of southern Iraq in the 1950s, living among the Bakhtiari nomads of Iran, and exploring such far-flung places as the Hindu Kush in Pakistan, Afghanistan, India, Kenya, and West Africa. His writings, botanical collections, rock, mineral, and insect specimens, maps, weather records, and photographs were to become a lasting legacy that richly enhanced the understanding of the people and places he visited. His works attest that he did indeed live his life "with savagery and color."

CAMEL-TRAIN CROSSING
Thesiger was fascinated by the role played by camels in desert life. He noted that, in instances of severe thirst, the Bedouin knew how to extract water from the stomach of a slaughtered camel.

GERTRUDE BELL

A WOMAN AT THE HEART OF THE ARAB WORLD

ENGLAND   1868–1926

An intrepid traveler, archeologist, and mountaineer, Gertrude Bell was a rare example of a woman living life to the full in a man's world. After graduating from Oxford University summa cum laude in history, she embarked on a series of adventures that led her to fall in love with the desert landscapes and cultures of Arabia. In addition to her passion for archeology, she was the only British female political officer operating during World War I, working tirelessly to lay the foundations for the modern state of Iraq.

ARCHEOLOGICAL EXPLORER
The medieval monuments of Hasankeyf, eastern Turkey, were among the sites Bell visited. She made detailed floorplans, measurements, and notes in English and Arabic. During these forays she would often stay as the guest of local chiefs.

A LIFE'S WORK

- Wins respect of local tribes throughout her travels in the Middle East, allowing **unparalleled access** that proves vital in future roles

- Masters **six foreign languages**: Arabic, Persian, French, German, Italian, and Turkish

- Opposes **women's suffrage**, believing women are not yet ready for political responsibility

Born into a wealthy family of industrialists, Bell made the most of her privileged background. Her first overseas trip came in 1892 with a visit to her uncle, the British ambassador in Tehran. Following a round-the-world steamship voyage in 1897, her love affair with the Arab world was sparked by a visit to Jerusalem in 1899. She learned Arabic and immersed herself in the culture of the Middle East, visiting Petra and Baalbek— now in Jordan and Lebanon, respectively— which awakened a fascination for archeology.

Returning to Europe, she proved herself an adept mountaineer, adding the Matterhorn to an impressive list of Alpine summits that already included Mont Blanc.

INTO THE DESERT

Following a second world cruise in 1902, Bell returned to Jerusalem in 1905 for a journey through Syria and Turkey, which she described in her 1907 book *The Desert and the Sown*. She ventured into Mesopotamia in 1909, crossing the

THE CAIRO CONFERENCE

After years spent among the many tribal groups of the Middle East, Bell was ideally placed to advise on the future administration of the British territories. Two new nations—Iraq and Transjordan, which later became Jordan—were created and rapidly granted self-rule when it became clear that British rule would be too costly. At the 1921 Cairo Conference, Bell and T. E. Lawrence succeeded in persuading Colonial Secretary Winston Churchill that the moderate, pan-Arab, pro-British Faisal was the man to lead the Iraqis as king.

GERTUDE BELL SEEN NEXT TO ABDULLAH, FAISAL'S BROTHER, WITH WINSTON CHURCHILL IN MARCH 1921. THE BRITISH PROCLAIMED FAISAL KING IN BAGHDAD ON AUGUST 21 OF THAT YEAR. ABDULLAH BECAME THE EMIR OF TRANSJORDAN.

THIS ... INCHOATE MASS OF TRIBES WHICH CAN'T ... BE REDUCED TO ANY SYSTEM

GERTRUDE BELL ON IRAQ

with Lawrence on intelligence to assist the British forces in Arabia, not to mention fomenting support for the Arab Revolt, before being posted to Basra in March 1916. There, she drew on her local knowledge to help compile accurate maps that assisted the British reclaim Baghdad in 1917, and continued to mix personal interest with high-level political machination—Bell cataloged the tribes to the north and northeast while making a treaty with a local sheikh to guard the western desert against the Turks and Germans.

FINAL ACHIEVEMENTS

When the Ottoman Empire collapsed in 1919, it fell to Bell to assess the options for the future of the region.

It was her report that led to Faisal I, former king of Syria, becoming king of Iraq in August 1921. Bell focused her other great passion into supervising excavations and examining finds for the opening of the Baghdad Archeological Museum. She defied the accepted wisdom that artifacts should be displayed in Europe and offered much of her own collection to the new museum, which opened in June 1926. It was to be the final achievement of her remarkable life—on July 12, she took an overdose of sleeping pills. Whether by accident or design it is not known, but more certain is her lasting contribution to the ancient and modern history of the Middle East, and to the founding of modern Iraq.

ARCHEOLOGICAL TROPHY
Bell received the Gill Memorial Award in 1913 for geographical and archeological exploits in the Middle East, requesting this miniature theodolite—a surveying tool—as her prize.

Syrian Desert, traveling down the Euphrates to Baghdad, then returning north up the Tigris. She stumbled upon Ukhaidir ("Little Green Place") an Abassid palace near Baghdad that she hoped would make her name as an archeologist. Sadly, Frenchman Louis Massignon had gotten there first, publishing his findings in April 1909.

Bell returned in 1911, and made for Carchemish in present-day Turkey. The ancient Hittite site was vital to the British military as a monitoring point of German construction of the Berlin–Baghdad railroad. It was there that Bell first met T. E. Lawrence (see p. 247), who was later immortalized as Lawrence of Arabia.

In 1913, Bell left Damascus for Ha'il, an oasis in northwestern Saudi Arabia, with 20 camels, three camel drivers, and two servants. Arriving in early 1914, she was placed under house arrest "like a story in the Arabian Nights," suspected of being a spy. The arrest did little to dim her enthusiasm for Arabia, and, once freed, she headed straight for Baghdad.

CLOUDS OF WAR

With the Ottoman Empire and much of the Middle East growing more unstable due to the outbreak of World War I, Bell joined the Arab Bureau in Cairo in November 1915. She worked

CAPTURING A LOST ERA
Bell was determined to be one of the first European women to explore the Arabian Desert, and set out for the oasis of Ha'il in 1913. She was an avid photographer and her photographs, such as this one of tribesmen, are a vital ethnographic record of a way of life now largely lost.

IN HER FOOTSTEPS

○ **1899–1900—First Middle East Journey** Visits Palestine and Syria; reaches the Jabal al-Druze and befriends Druze king Yahya Bey

○ **1905—Jerusalem, Syria, Asia Minor** As described in *The Desert and the Sown*, visits ruins across the region

→ **1909—Aleppo, Baghdad, Ukhaidir** Travels down the Euphrates to Baghdad and back up the Tigris to Asiatic Turkey

○ **1911—Ukhaidir, Najaf, Carchemish** Returns to Ukhaidir to map ruins and meets T. E. Lawrence at Carchemish

→ **1913–14—Into Arabia** To the oasis of Ha'il with mixed results; she is the second European female to visit the city

○ Not shown on map

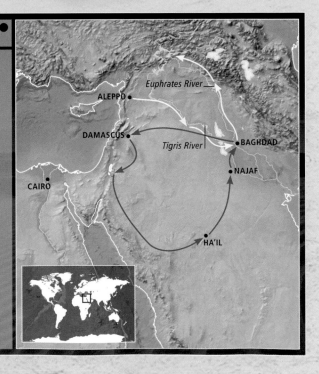

ALEPPO
Euphrates River
DAMASCUS
Tigris River
BAGHDAD
CAIRO
NAJAF
HA'IL

FREYA STARK

DOYENNE OF WOMEN TRAVELERS IN ARABIA

ENGLAND   1893–1993

A LIFE'S WORK

- Is the first Westerner to visit remote parts of western Iran, gathering much **topographical data** about the regions she visits

- Explores the remote **Valley of the Assassins** (the hashish-eaters) in Iran

- Travels widely around **southern Arabia**, visiting places previously unknown to Westerners

- Has no formal education but learns French, German, and Italian traveling with her parents

FREYA STARK WAS A TRAVEL WRITER and one of the first European women to explore the southern Arabian deserts, or Hadhramaut. A naturally curious and intrepid character, her most famous journeys took place in the 1930s, when she often went solo to areas few Europeans, let alone women, had ever been. She spoke fluent Arabic and Farsi, and was a fine cartographer. Over the century of her life, she published more than two dozen books about her travels and was still traveling well into her eighties.

PASSPORT TO ADVENTURE
Stark's stamp-covered, visa-filled passport from 1930 records her ceaseless wandering in the Middle East.

Stark's first journey took her to Baghdad in 1929. She described the city as "a wonderful place … for knowing other people and their businesses. The ramifications of the East must ever baffle us who have so much less time for sitting and talking and watching and listening." A mark of Stark's achievements in Arabia is the fact that she made great use of her gender to allow her to travel freely: "The almost only comfort about being a woman," she said, "is that one can always pretend to be more stupid than one is, and no one is surprised." In the early 1930s, Stark made four journeys: two into Luristan in Persia, and two into the mountains south of the Caspian Sea. She deliberately chose regions that were almost completely blank on the map, and made it her business to fill in the gaps as she explored the terrain. In addition to recording topography, Stark included as much detail on the local names of landmarks and villages. She also investigated ancient cemeteries, in one case making off with a Bronze Age skull wrapped in her handkerchief.

The major focus of her second Persian journey was a desire to visit the fabled Valley of Alamut, known as "The Valley of the Assassins," which held the headquarters of the Ismaili sect of the Shi'a. Stark mapped the valley and recorded the architecture and traditions of the

THE HADHRAMAUT
This town lies in the Wadi Doan Valley in the Hadhramaut, a remote desert area in Yemen. At the time of Stark's visit in 1934, the high plateau was part of the British-administered Aden Protectorate. Stark wrote about her time in the Yemeni highlands in her book *The Southern Gates of Arabia* (1936).

people with sharp observations. In particular, she noted with a certain scepticism the "Wolf and Ram" method of water supply in Shahristan, whereby water was allegedly delivered to the Assassins' Castle at Lambesar in skins tied to rams, which were then chased through tunnels up the hillside by wolves. Her resulting book, *The Valley of the Assassins* (1934), established her reputation as a travel writer.

THE HADHRAMAUT

In 1934, Stark traveled for two months in the Hadhramaut of southern Arabia, searching for Shabwa, a lost ancient city of 60 temples according to the Roman philosopher Pliny the Elder. Unfortunately, she contracted measles, and had to be airlifted back to Aden by the Royal Air Force, but not before she had recorded an intimate portrait of the people and landscape, commenting that: "I was the first woman to travel alone in the country, so they had no precedent to deal with me."

In 1937, she began a major exploration of the Hadhramaut, this time traveling with British archeologist Gertrude Caton-Thompson, and noted with sadness the changes brought by the encroaching modern world. She wrote, "The towns of the great Wadi, connected by a motor road with the coast and by a weekly airplane with Aden, were very different places from what I had known even four years ago on my first visit." She sensed change would be rapid and wanted to capture what she saw. However, her collaboration with Caton-Thompson was not a success. Stark preferred to travel alone, describing how, as she crossed the Wadi 'Amd,

"It was an incredible luxury to be alone. I settled in the thin shade of a samr tree and went to sleep, and woke after an hour or two to see a Se'ari tribesman sitting beside me, watching me quietly."

Following a period working for British Intelligence during World War II, Stark continued her travels in the 1950s. She indulged her fascination with Herodotus and Alexander the Great, retracing the routes of their travels in Asia Minor and published each account of her journeys in what was at the time an innovative style of travelogue.

IN HER FOOTSTEPS

1930–31—Luristan
At the start of the 1930s, Stark pays two visits to the remote region of Luristan in western Persia; she makes detailed maps of the area

1931—Valley of the Assassins
Stark maps the Valley of Alamut, also known as the Valley of the Assassins, in northern Persia; her book about the experience brings her fame

1934—The Hadhramaut, Yemen
Stark searches for the ancient city of Shabwa; she returns to the Hadhramaut three years later to find the region undergoing rapid change

ELBURZ MOUNTAINS
TEHRAN
PERSIA
ZAGROS MOUNTAINS
YEMEN
ADEN

BY DONKEY IN THE JABAL DRUZE
In 1928, during her first visit to Syria, Stark crossed the Jabal Druze, a volcanic region of Syria (above). Her account was published in her 1943 book, *Letters from Syria*.

CAMEL CROSSING
This camel train, photographed in 1925, is crossing the sand dunes of Tsagaan Nuur in central Mongolia. In the world's most remote deserts, such as the Rub' al Khali of Arabia, traveling by camel train is the safest method. Harry St. John Philby (see pp. 238–39) recorded how his camels lasted nine days without water, save for a daily sprinkling in their nostrils (known as "snuffing").

FERDINAND VON RICHTHOFEN

GROUNDBREAKING GEOGRAPHER

GERMAN CONFEDERATION 1833–1905

INSPIRED BY ACCOUNTS OF THE EXPEDITIONS of Alexander von Humboldt in Asia, the young geologist Ferdinand von Richthofen longed to explore. He visited East Asia as part of a Prussian mission, before formulating plans for a geological exploration of China, where he was the first to coin the phrase *Seidenstraße*, or "Silk Road," to describe the ancient trade route between East and West. Von Richthofen used groundbreaking new comparative techniques, and he is credited as one of the founders of modern geography.

EDGE OF CIVILIZATION
This fort in Jiayuguan, built in about 1372, guards the westernmost pass of the Great Wall of China and was once seen as marking the farthest edge of Chinese civilization. It was also a key waystation on the ancient Silk Road.

Von Richthofen studied geology at the University of Berlin and following graduation undertook geological research in the mountainous Tyrol region of Austria. In 1858, after publishing the results of his Alpine work with the German Geological Society, he was invited by the Prussian government to join a trade and diplomatic mission to East Asia.

The mission departed in May 1859 and visited Sri Lanka, Japan, Taiwan, the Philippines, Sulawesi, and Java. As a scientific observer, von Richthofen was given plenty of opportunity to spend time on his own research along with the naturalist Franz Wilhelm Junghuhn (1809–64).

On Java, the two men explored the interior of the island. Von Richthofen concentrated on gathering evidence of volcanic activity, recording in detail the volcanoes of the Preang region. They rejoined the main body of the mission at Bangkok in late 1861. Once the party of diplomats had departed by boat, von Richthofen undertook an overland journey through Thailand to Maulmain (present-day Moulmein in Myanmar) and finished his travels at Kolkata, India, in April 1862.

IN HIS FOOTSTEPS

➤ **1859–61—Travels with a trade and diplomacy mission**
As part of an official Prussian mission, von Richthofen travels extensively around Southeast Asia

➤ **1861—Overland to Kolkata**
Leaving the official mission at Bangkok, he travels on his own through Thailand and Burma to Kolkata (Calcutta)

➤ **1871–72—Explores China**
Von Richthofen travels extensively around China, identifying the ancient Silk Road trade routes through the Qilian Mountains

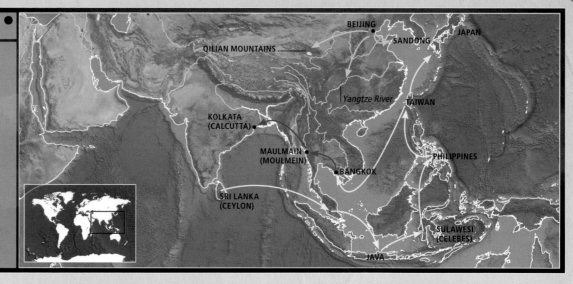

Although von Richthofen longed to visit China, foreign access to the country remained impossible due to the unrest caused by the Taiping Rebellion (1850–64). Instead, he set his sights on a new field of exploration and embarked on a geological survey of California's Sierra Nevada, discovering gold fields in the process. At the age of 30, he began pioneering studies of volcanic rocks and, supported by the American geologist Josiah Dwight Whitney (1819–96), developed his plans to carry out a geological survey of China as soon as it became safe to visit the country again.

CHINA AT LAST

Von Richthofen used Whitney's American contacts to secure funding for his trip to China from the Bank of California and the American Shanghai Chamber of Commerce. Later, recalling his discussions with Whitney, he

A CHAT WITH PRINCE GONG
An 1870 illustration shows von Richthofen enjoying a friendly smoke with Yixin, the First Prince Gong, who was in charge of governing China during the 1860s and '70s.

wrote: "We agreed that China is … the least-known [of] countries, and also in the highest degree is worth an investigation … here was a task of gigantic proportions."

He finally left for Beijing in the fall of 1871 and, during a year-long period, crisscrossed imperial China, gaining access to most provinces. No expedition was without danger, however. Shortly after arrival, en route to Chungkingfu on the Yangtze River, von Richthofen, his interpreter, and pack train were set upon in a murderous attack by a crowd demanding money. He wrote, "My interpreter, after knocking the first men down, had to run for his life from the overwhelming force … and narrowly escaped the poles and clubs swung upon him. He had the presence of mind to draw his revolver but not to fire it. My sudden appearance, in hurrying down the steep slope, with the same weapon in my hand, put an end to the attack." The fright the party received caused them to abandon this leg of the trip.

STUDENT OF CHINESE LIFE

In addition to geological survey work, von Richthofen recorded observations on all aspects of China—culture, climate, politics, the Chinese army, and the potential natural resources identified in his surveys, such as the coalfields at Shandong in northeastern China. He corresponded

with the Shanghai Chamber of Commerce to share his findings. In geographical terms, von Richthofen is best remembered for his identification of the Silk Road as an area that had seen the interplay of civilizations, goods, and people for thousands of years. His ideas about the impact of climate change on human settlement are still relevant to the study of the Silk Road today.

On his return to Germany in 1872, he compiled his findings, publishing a five-volume study of China between 1877 and 1912. In later life, von Richthofen's achievements, coupled with his position as professor of geography at the University of Berlin, would inspire generations of students. He also inspired the Swedish explorer Sven Hedin (see pp. 228–33), to continue his exploration of Central Asia. Von Richthofen's assessment of China sounds increasingly prescient: "[It] is materially one of the most richly endowed countries of the world, a country of vast resources, and of a future incalculably great and important."

RICHTHOFEN RANGE
The Qilian Mountains separate the Qinghai and Gansu provinces of northern China. They were formerly known as the Richthofen Range in honor of the explorer's achievements.

REACHING
FOR EXTREMES

REACHING FOR EXTREMES

▶ 1595
Willem Barentsz reaches the islands of Novaya Zemlya, where the pack-ice forces him to turn back from his search for a northeast passage to the Pacific (see pp. 288–89)

◀ 1611
English navigator **Henry Hudson**'s crew mutinies during a voyage in search of a northwest passage to the Pacific; they cast him adrift (see pp. 286–87)

1789
English captain **William Bligh** journeys to the South Pacific; his crew mutinies shortly after they leave Tahiti, claiming that he was treating them with undue cruelty

▼ 1799
Alexander von Humboldt begins a five-year journey of scientific discovery around South and Central America with botanist **Aimé Bonpland** (see pp. 266–69)

1801
Matthew Flinders leads a scientific expedition to Australia on board HMS *Investigator*

▲ 1831
Charles Darwin sets sail on the *Beagle*, taking this compass (see pp. 276–79)

◀ 1838
Charles Wilkes sets out for the Antarctic with a fleet of four ships on a US expedition to survey the south seas

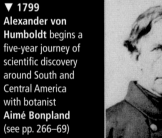

1845
John Franklin's expedition, sent by the British Royal Navy to find the Northwest Passage, vanishes off the coast of northern Canada (see pp. 292–93)

▲ 1854
Alfred Russel Wallace leaves for the Malay Archipelago, where he is the first European to describe birds of paradise; he formulates a theory of evolution independently of Darwin (see pp. 272–73)

1820
Russian **Fabian Gottlieb von Bellingshausen** first sights the Antarctic Peninsula

1864
US explorer **Charles Hall** leads an expedition in search of Franklin; he discovers the fate of Franklin and his crew after finding remains on King William Island (see pp. 306–07)

▼ 1893
Fridtjof Nansen's ship, the *Fram*, is trapped in the Arctic ice for three years in an unsuccessful attempt to drift to the North Pole (see pp. 296–99)

▲1875
The **British Arctic Expedition,** led by Sir George Strong Nares, fails to reach the North Pole but sets a new record for the farthest north yet reached

◀ 1879–80
Adolf Erik Nordenskiöld successfully navigates the Northeast Passage along the top of Eurasia; he returns to Europe via the Indian Ocean (see pp. 290–91)

▶ 1897–99
Adrien de Gerlache leads the *Belgica* expedition to Antarctica, with Roald Amundsen among the crew; Amundsen benefits from Inuit clothing

1901–04
Robert Scott leads the National Antarctic expedition, during which he surveys a route to the South Pole from a balloon (see pp. 312–15)

▲ 1906
With a crew of six, Norwegian **Roald Amundsen** completes a crossing of the Northwest Passage on his ship, *Gjøa* (see pp. 302–05)

▲ 1909
American **Robert Peary** claims to have reached the North Pole (see pp. 308–09)

By THE MID-19TH CENTURY, all of Europe and much of Asia, Africa, the Americas, and Australia had for many become familiar territory. Expeditions turned either to the acquisition of scientific knowledge in areas already known, such as Charles Darwin's great voyage on board the *Beagle*, or to the most extreme and remote parts of the globe. By the end of the 19th century, exploration of the Arctic and Antarctic had begun and, in 1911, Roald Amundsen stood at the South Pole. Attention also turned to the ocean depths, with the lowering of manned vessels and unmanned probes into the deepest ocean trenches. In the second half of the 20th century, exploration of the solar system began, as the United States and the Soviet Union competed with each other in the Space Race.

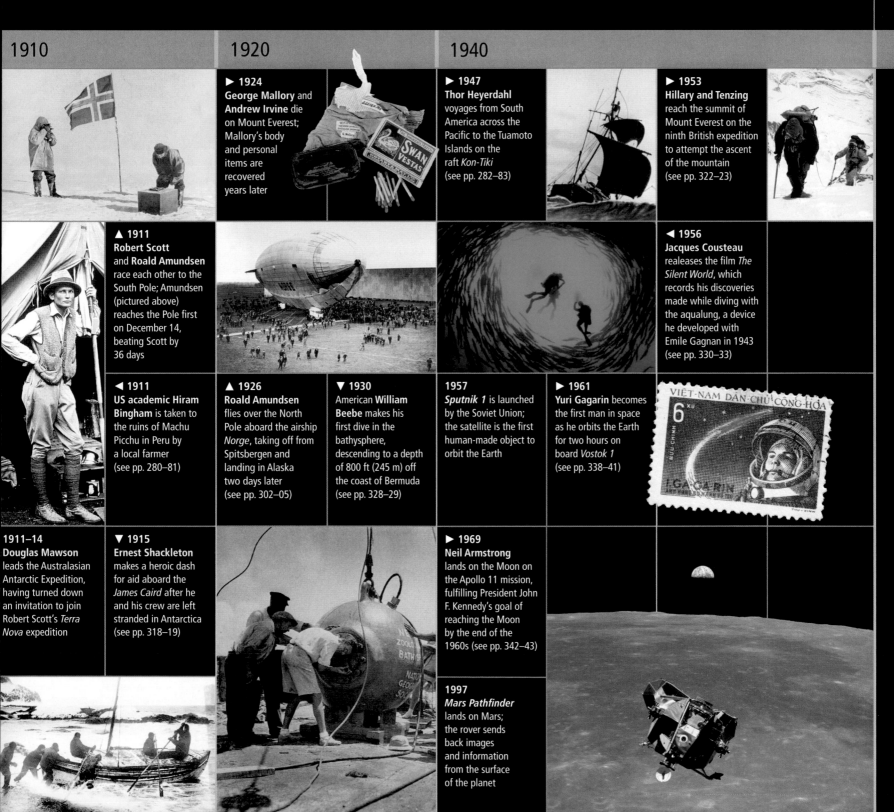

1910

▲ 1911
Robert Scott
and **Roald Amundsen**
race each other to the
South Pole; Amundsen
(pictured above)
reaches the Pole first
on December 14,
beating Scott by
36 days

◀ 1911
**US academic Hiram
Bingham** is taken to
the ruins of Machu
Picchu in Peru by
a local farmer
(see pp. 280–81)

1911–14
Douglas Mawson
leads the Australasian
Antarctic Expedition,
having turned down
an invitation to join
Robert Scott's *Terra
Nova* expedition

1920

▶ 1924
George Mallory and
Andrew Irvine die
on Mount Everest;
Mallory's body
and personal
items are
recovered
years later

▲ 1926
Roald Amundsen
flies over the North
Pole aboard the airship
Norge, taking off from
Spitsbergen and
landing in Alaska
two days later
(see pp. 302–05)

▼ 1930
American **William
Beebe** makes his
first dive in the
bathysphere,
descending to a depth
of 800 ft (245 m) off
the coast of Bermuda
(see pp. 328–29)

▼ 1915
Ernest Shackleton
makes a heroic dash
for aid aboard the
James Caird after he
and his crew are left
stranded in Antarctica
(see pp. 318–19)

1940

▶ 1947
Thor Heyerdahl
voyages from South
America across the
Pacific to the Tuamoto
Islands on the
raft *Kon-Tiki*
(see pp. 282–83)

1957
Sputnik 1 is launched
by the Soviet Union;
the satellite is the first
human-made object to
orbit the Earth

▶ 1969
Neil Armstrong
lands on the Moon on
the Apollo 11 mission,
fulfilling President John
F. Kennedy's goal of
reaching the Moon
by the end of the
1960s (see pp. 342–43)

1997
Mars Pathfinder
lands on Mars;
the rover sends
back images
and information
from the surface
of the planet

▶ 1953
Hillary and Tenzing
reach the summit of
Mount Everest on the
ninth British expedition
to attempt the ascent
of the mountain
(see pp. 322–23)

◀ 1956
Jacques Cousteau
realeases the film *The
Silent World*, which
records his discoveries
made while diving with
the aqualung, a device
he developed with
Emile Gagnan in 1943
(see pp. 330–33)

▶ 1961
Yuri Gagarin becomes
the first man in space
as he orbits the Earth
for two hours on
board *Vostok 1*
(see pp. 338–41)

VIÊT-NAM DÂN-CHU CÔNG-HOA
6 xu
I. GAGARIN

EXPLORING FOR SCIENCE

THE PURSUIT OF SCIENTIFIC KNOWLEDGE WAS AMONG THE LAST OF THE MOTIVES TO EMERGE FOR EXPLORATION, BUT ONCE THE WORLD'S MAJOR LANDMASSES HAD BEEN DISCOVERED, IT BECAME ONE OF THE DRIVING FORCES BEHIND CHARTING THE NEW-FOUND LANDS.

ARCHEOLOGICAL SENSATION
In 1911, US explorer Hiram Bingham was the first scientist to see Machu Picchu—a lost Inca city in the Andes. It proved one of the most significant archeological finds of the century.

The great scientific discoveries of the 17th century promoted the idea that exploration should not simply be a means of acquiring new territory, but should be in itself a scientific discipline in pursuit of knowledge about the world. Among the earliest exponents was Maria Sibylla Merian, a Dutchwoman who was the first to describe scientifically the transformation of caterpillars into butterflies, and whose travels in Dutch-controlled Surinam in 1699–1701 prefigured those of many later scientific travelers.

> After World War II, when modern aviation and satellites enabled the mapping of the globe to be completed, scientists turned to the exploration of the last frontiers—the ocean depths and the Solar System.

NEW METHODS

The work of the Swedish botanist Carl Linnaeus, who in the 1730s devised a scientific system for naming and classifying organisms, gave a framework within which botanical travelers could operate.

The first fruits of this came with two of the great voyages of 18th-century exploration, both of which were accompanied by botanists. Louis de Bougainville (see pp. 150–51) brought with him another Frenchman on his circumnavigation of 1766–69, Philibert de Commerson, who during the course of the voyage collected 3,000 new species and identified 60 new genera. On the 1768–71 voyage of Captain Cook's *Endeavour*, Joseph Banks (see pp. 156–59) came along as the expedition's naturalist. During their seven weeks ashore while the *Endeavour* was being repaired

after striking the Great Barrier Reef, Banks made the first significant collection of Australian flora and cataloged some 800 species. On his return to Britain, he became the guiding force behind a number of other exploratory expeditions, including William Bligh's 1809 voyage to the South Pacific in search of breadfruit, which ended in a notorious mutiny on board his ship, the *Bounty*.

Banks was also instrumental in having the English navigator Matthew Flinders appointed as commander of the circumnavigation of Australia by the *Investigator* in 1801-03. Among the members of her crew were the naturalist Robert Brown, landscape artist William Westall, and mineralogist John Allen, a sign that expeditions now regarded scientific research as among their priorities.

At the end of the voyage, Brown stayed in Australia until 1805, collecting specimens from New South Wales and Tasmania. Although his best examples were lost when the ship in which he was returning home was wrecked, he still described more than 1,700 previously unknown species.

GLOBAL PICTURE

The opening up of vast new areas to exploration in the 19th century gave impetus to scientific discussions about how species had spread across the globe and how they might have changed over time. Charles Darwin's voyage in the *Beagle* in 1831–36 (see pp. 276–79), during which his observation of the slightly different species of finch on each of the Galápagos Islands helped him to formulate his theory of evolution, was but the most famous. English naturalists Alfred Russel Wallace and Henry Walter Bates (see pp.272–73) traveled along the Amazon River for eight years from 1844, and this and Wallace's subsequent eight-year expedition to the Malay Archipelago helped him to formulate an evolutionary theory parallel to, but separate from, Darwin's.

Carrying with him the proofs of Darwin's *Voyage of the Beagle*, the English botanist Joseph Dalton Hooker, who accompanied the *Erebus* expedition to the Antarctic in 1839–43, was typical of the new traveler-scientists. His work on the voyage resulted in six large volumes on the flora of Antarctica, New Zealand, and Tasmania. As social opportunities widened in the late 19th century, so some

BUG BOOK
During his Amazonian expedition, Bates cataloged nearly 15,000 species of insect, more than half of which were new to science.

CURRENT EXPLORER
German explorer Alexander von Humboldt's expedition to South America in 1799–1804 observed the ocean current that is named after him and recorded a transit of the planet Mercury.

BIRD EXTINCT
English naturalist Charles Darwin began his research into the origin of species at a time when the dodo had been extinct for 150 years, prey to overhunting in the Indian Ocean.

SETTING THE SCENE

- Alexander von Humboldt and his botanist companion Aimé Bonpland (see pp. 266–69) had intended to join French naturalist **Nicolas Baudin's circumnavigation of the globe** in 1800. But when they arrive in Ecuador, they find that Baudin has changed his plans and has sailed via South Africa instead.

- Among the many plant-hunters Joseph Banks sends abroad is the Scottish botanist **Francis Basson**, who visits South Africa, Madeira, the Canaries, and the West Indies in search of new species, before **freezing to death** in North America in 1805.

- One of the species that Banks encounters and sketches in Australia is a **kangaroo**, the first time that Europeans have seen the species.

- In 1838, Captain Charles Wilkes sets out for the Antarctic on a US expedition to survey the South Seas, in part motivated by a theory that the **Antarctic might be "hollow,"** with a sea in the middle. Although unable to validate or disprove this theory, he does sight the vast **Shackleton Ice Shelf** for the first time.

- In 1947, the Norwegian ethnographer Thor Heyerdahl sails 5,000 miles (8,000 km) in a **balsa-wood raft** from Peru to the Tuamotus in the Pacific Ocean in an effort to prove that there could have been contacts in ancient times **between Polynesia and South America.**

women began to take advantage of the opportunity to travel and to contribute to the phenomenon of exploration for science. Among them the redoubtable Englishwoman Isabella Bird spent a year in Japan in 1878–79 before visiting Singapore, Malaya, and then, ten years later, investigating remote parts of Kashmir and Ladakh. In the mid-1890s, Mary Kingsley (see pp. 212–13), herself the daughter of explorer George Henry Kingsley, set out for Africa in search of natural history specimens. Exploring remote reaches of Senegal, Gabon, and Angola, she visited regions that few outsiders had ventured into, collecting large quantities of fish, three species of which were previously unknown to science.

RIVER HAZARDS
A break for turtle fishing during Henry Walter Bates's travels down the Amazon River results in a hazardous encounter with a crocodile.

ALEXANDER VON HUMBOLDT

THE WORLD'S LAST GREAT RENAISSANCE MAN

PRUSSIA   1769–1859

A **PIONEER OF A STRICTLY** evidence-based approach to scientific study, Alexander von Humboldt was not only a great naturalist, but also contributed to a diverse range of disciplines, including astronomy, meteorology, and geology. From 1799–1804, he explored Latin America and was one of the first Europeans to record what he saw from a scientific perspective. His rigorous approach to study was a forerunner to the modern scientific method, and he laid the foundations for the modern discipline of geography.

Von Humboldt was initially destined for the sober upper-middle-class career of a politician, studying finance and political science at the universities of Frankfurt and Göttingen (in present-day Germany). During a summer vacation from his studies in 1789, he undertook his first scientific excursion, traveling up the Rhine Valley and recording mineral data during the trip. This led to his first publication in 1790 and cemented his passion for combining travel with exploration. His friends at university also encouraged him to consider a calling as a scientific explorer. One such friend was Georg Forster, the naturalist who had traveled with Captain James Cook (see pp. 156–59) on his second voyage on board HMS *Resolution*.

To equip himself for a career as a geographer, von Humboldt broadened his studies to include foreign languages, geology, astronomy, anatomy, and the use of scientific instruments. He had already published widely on associated subjects when, in 1795, he made his first geological and botanical tours of Switzerland and Italy. Following the death of his mother in 1796, and his subsequent inheritance of significant family wealth, von Humboldt felt able to abandon his official duties as Assessor of Mines in Berlin and embark on the first of his expeditions.

Originally, von Humboldt planned to join a French Navy South Seas voyage in 1798, but was frustrated when the expedition funds were withdrawn by the French government. He soon overcame his dismay, however, when he, along with French botanist Aimé Bonpland (see p. 269), were invited to travel with a Swedish party to Egypt by way of Algiers, embarking on their sea voyage at Marseille. These plans, too, were thwarted when the Swedish ship was damaged in a storm off Portugal and delayed for many months of refit at Cadiz in Spain.

CHANCE DESTINATION

With characteristic energy, von Humboldt and Bonpland traveled to Madrid, hoping to rejoin the Swedish ship later. During the journey, the naturalist took astronomical measurements, studied the magnetic forces at play and recorded, for the first time, the true physical geography of the Spanish plains. In Madrid, he was granted an audience with King Carlos II and offered passports to travel in the Spanish New World. For the first time, von Humboldt set his sights on South America.

HOWLER MONKEY
Von Humboldt made many detailed drawings in Latin America, including this one of a howler monkey.

A LIFE'S WORK

- Explores the **Amazon River** and traces the Orinoco River to its source with the Amazon
- Is the first to propose that **South America** was once joined to Africa
- Argues that the **intensive deforestation** of rainforest could lead to climate problems
- Discovers that **volcanoes** lie along geological fault lines
- Finds **60,000 plants** unknown in Europe (doubling the number of known plants)
- **Treats his typhoid** with a bitter mixture later made famous by Angostura
- Formulates a law governing **atmospheric disturbances** and the Earth's magnetism
- Conducts the first census of **indigenous peoples** in New Spain (much of present-day Central America and the western United States)

ALONG THE ORINOCO
In addition to discovering the source of the Amazon, von Humboldt and the botanist Aimé Bonpland journeyed through the wild jungle interior of Venezuela to map the course of the Orinoco River (shown here). The explorers were the first Europeans to establish the existence of the Casiquiare River, a natural canal that links the Amazon and Orinoco river systems. This section of the expedition alone took more than four months to complete and covered a distance of approximately 1,725 miles (2,776 km).

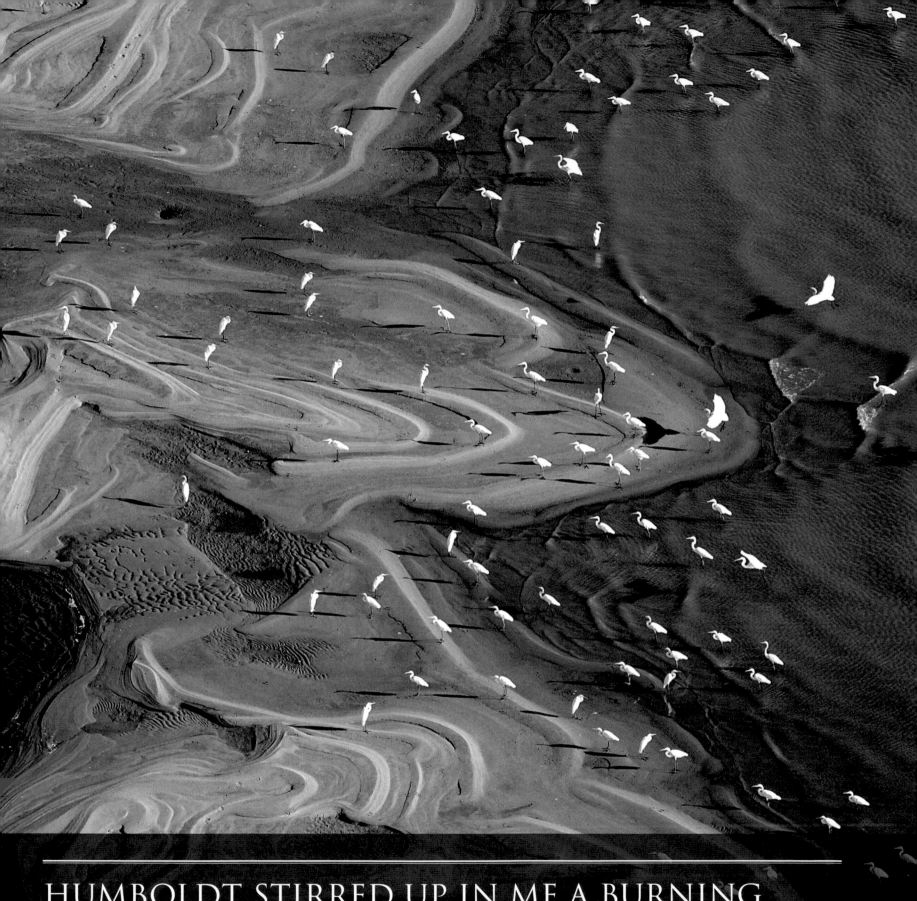

HUMBOLDT STIRRED UP IN ME A BURNING
ZEAL TO ADD EVEN THE MOST HUMBLE
CONTRIBUTION TO THE NOBLE
STRUCTURE OF NATURAL SCIENCE

CHARLES DARWIN

DATA COLLECTOR

For von Humboldt, all scientific observation had to be based on observed data, without appeal to supernatural forces. To this end, he carried with him on his journeys the most accurate and sophisticated scientific instruments of his day, each kept in its own velvet-lined box. His strict methodology was to become known as Humboldtian Science.

VON HUMBOLDT IN LATIN AMERICA,
PAINTED BY F. G. WEITSCH IN 1806

LATIN AMERICAN EXPEDITION

With his companion Bonpland, von Humboldt sailed on June 5, 1799, from La Coruña. During the voyage, he recorded the flow of currents and measured water temperature and the effects of wind patterns, formulating his theory that the rotation of the Earth did not affect the direction of currents. The ship arrived at Cumaná, Venezuela, five weeks later, and he enthusiastically described his impressions of the landscape: "We beheld a verdant coast, of picturesque aspect. The mountains of New Andalusia, half-veiled by mists, bounded the horizon to the south. The city of Cumaná and its castle appeared between groups of cocoa-trees. We anchored in the port about nine in the morning; the sick dragged themselves on deck to enjoy the sight of a land, which was to put an end to their sufferings. Our eyes were fixed on the groups of cocoa-trees that border the river: their trunks, more than sixty feet high, towered over every object in the landscape. The plain was covered with those arborescent mimosas, which, like the pine of Italy, spread their branches in the form of an umbrella. The pinnated leaves of the palms were conspicuous on the azure sky, the clearness of which was unsullied by any trace of vapor."

From his base at Cumaná, where he and Bonpland collected specimens and took detailed measurements of the coast, von Humboldt was witness to a spectacular meteor shower (the Leonids). He also witnessed volcanic eruptions around the city, which he attempted to compare to past eruptions, but found the city's records of events mostly destroyed by termites.

THE INTERIOR AND BEYOND

In the early part of 1800, von Humboldt and Bonpland left the coast to undertake their first major expedition inland, exploring and mapping the course of the Orinoco River. The expedition lasted more than four months and covered more than 1,725 miles (2,776 km) in a largely uninhabited, rugged, jungle country. On this expedition, they discovered the link between the water systems of the Orinoco and Amazon rivers, and von Humboldt's exact pinpointing of the bifurcation (where the river forks into its tributaries).

On November 24, 1800, the two explorers sailed for Cuba, where von Humboldt collected data on the island's population, agriculture, technology, and trade. After a stay of some months they returned to South America at Cartagena, Colombia. Ascending the swollen waters of the Magdalena River and crossing the frozen passes of the Andes, they reached Quito, Ecuador, on January 6, 1802. During their stay in the city, they scaled the volcanic peaks of

IN HIS FOOTSTEPS

- ○ **1789—First scientific expedition**
  Travels along the Rhine River

- ● **1795—Tours Switzerland and Italy**
  Makes geographical and botanical recordings

- → **1799—1800—Travels to Latin America**
  Accompanied by botanist Aimé Bonpland, von Humboldt sets sail for the New World

- → **1801—04—Cuba to Lima**
  They travel across the Andes as far south as Lima before setting sail for Mexico

- → **1804—Back to Europe via Washington**
  The two travelers spend six weeks with US President Jefferson before sailing for Bordeaux

- ● **1829—Russian exploration**
  Crosses the Central Asian Plateau

- ○ Not shown on map

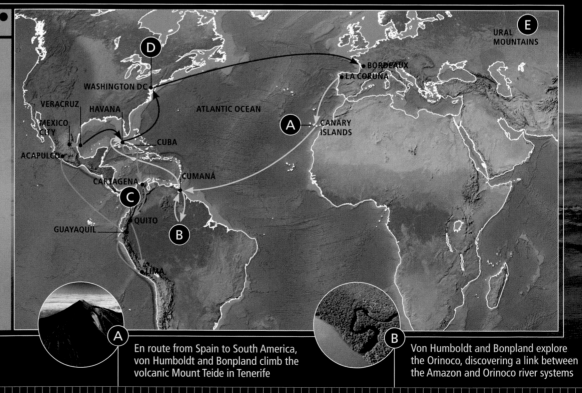

A En route from Spain to South America, von Humboldt and Bonpland climb the volcanic Mount Teide in Tenerife

B Von Humboldt and Bonpland explore the Orinoco, discovering a link between the Amazon and Orinoco river systems

| 1759–88 | **1789** | 1790–94 | **1795** | 1796–98 | **1799–1800** | **1801–04** |

As a child, von Humboldt is known as "the little apothecary" for his love of collecting plants and insects

Von Humboldt is inspired by his friend Georg Forster, who had traveled with his father on Cook's second Pacific voyage

The two explorers land at Cumaná, in present-day Venezuela, on July 16, 1799; on the night of November 11–12 that year, they witness a spectacular meteor shower known as the Leonids

Pichincha—von Humboldt and his party reached an altitude of 19,286 ft (5,878 m), a world record at the time. The journey concluded with an expedition to the sources of the Amazon River en route for Lima, Peru. At Callao, Peru, on November 9, he observed the transit of Mercury. There, he also studied the fertilizing qualities of guano, which was later introduced into Europe as a result of his writings. A rough sea voyage took the companions to Mexico, where they remained for a year, before heading north to Washington, D.C. They stayed for six weeks as guests of President Jefferson, himself a scientist, who was eager to hear about von Humboldt's discoveries.

ACROSS RUSSIA

Following his return to Europe, von Humboldt spent many years writing up his scientific theories. He was to make one more journey of exploration, a 25-week crossing of the Russian Empire in 1829, a journey of more than 9,500 miles (15,000 km). On his Russian trip, he corrected the estimated height of the Central Asian Plateau and accurately predicted the presence of diamonds in the Ural Mountains.

Von Humbolt spent his final years engaged in diplomatic work. His last great scientific work was a five-volume treatise called *Kosmos* (Volume One published in 1845), in which he attempted to unify the natural and geographical sciences. His thinking had always been underpinned by a belief in an underlying unity to the universe, and *Kosmos* was an attempt to provide a comprehensive overview of the world, drawing together geology, meteorology, geography, and biology into a systematic whole. Von Humboldt was the first truly modern scientist of the natural world, using observation and measurement to guide his theories. He was probably also the last person to have contributed to so many different fields of knowledge.

TOPOGRAPHICAL MAP
Von Humboldt used a shading system to show slopes on this 1803 map of New Spain. Before this, mountains had been represented on maps in profile.

AIMÉ BONPLAND
FRANCE   1773–1858

Born at La Rochelle, France, in 1773, Bonpland's early years were taken up with military duty and the study of medicine, a not unusual combination of careers for a man of that time.

Bonpland was invited by Alexander von Humboldt to accompany him on his expedition to Latin America, and it was the explorer's wealth that supported the younger botanist's expenses. The five-year adventure was to catapult von Humboldt to a position of great celebrity. Bonpland, who oversaw the expedition's botanical collections, received a state pension. Interest in science extended to the highest levels of French society at the time, and Bonpland was given the directorship of the Empress Josephine's botanical gardens at Malmaison. Over the next 10 years, he researched and refined his collections to publish what were to become several classic works both under his own name and as co-author with von Humboldt.

RETURN TO ADVENTURE
In 1816, Bonpland left France to take a teaching position in Buenos Aires, Argentina, where he remained for a year before setting off again to explore South America. While journeying to Bolivia, he was arrested as a spy and incarcerated by the dictator of Paraguay, who detained him for 10 years. On regaining his liberty, he settled in Corrientes, Argentina, where the government of the province presented him with an estate. In 1853, he moved to Santa Ana, Argentina, where he cultivated the orange tree, and kept on with his scientific research.

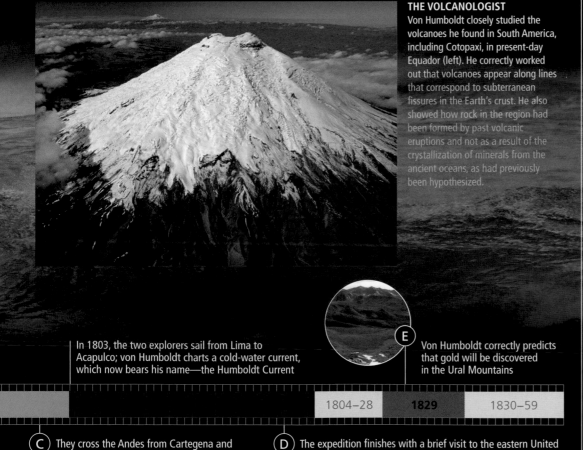

THE VOLCANOLOGIST
Von Humboldt closely studied the volcanoes he found in South America, including Cotopaxi, in present-day Equador (left). He correctly worked out that volcanoes appear along lines that correspond to subterranean fissures in the Earth's crust. He also showed how rock in the region had been formed by past volcanic eruptions and not as a result of the crystallization of minerals from the ancient oceans, as had previously been hypothesized.

In 1803, the two explorers sail from Lima to Acapulco; von Humboldt charts a cold-water current, which now bears his name—the Humboldt Current

E

Von Humboldt correctly predicts that gold will be discovered in the Ural Mountains

| 1804–28 | **1829** | 1830–59 |

C   They cross the Andes from Cartegena and arrive in Quito, where von Humboldt studies several prominent volcanoes

D   The expedition finishes with a brief visit to the eastern United States and a meeting with Thomas Jefferson, the country's third president; they depart for France in June 1804

HIBISCUS CALYPHYLLUS,
COLLECTED IN VENEZUELA

CARSTEN NIEBUHR

AN ENLIGHTENED EXPLORER

HANOVER   1733–1815

A MATHEMATICIAN AND CARTOGRAPHER with a hunger for knowledge, Carsten Niebuhr epitomized the rational ideals of the European Enlightenment. His achievements in recording and mapping the Middle East are all the more remarkable for the fact that he was entirely self-taught. Niebuhr's four-volume *Travels through Arabia and Other Countries* (1778), which featured his observations of the people, geography, and artifacts of the region, became a classic in its field that remained in print long after his death.

Unlike many explorers of his era, who generally had independent means, Niebuhr came from an impoverished background. His parents died when he was very young, leaving him to eke out a living as a peasant farmer. Undaunted, he eventually qualified as a surveyor and joined a scientific expedition under the patronage of Frederick V of Denmark. The expedition was made up of two Danes—a linguist named Friedrich von Haven, and Christian Kramer, a noted doctor and zoologist—plus two Swedes: the botanist Peter Forrskal and an ex-soldier named Lars Berggren, who was the party's servant. Niebuhr and Georg Baurenfeind, a German artist, completed the party. By early 1761, the team was ready to set off. Leaving Copenhagen in January 1761, the expedition traveled to Marseille, Malta, Constantinople (Istanbul), and Rhodes. On September 6, they arrived at Alexandria in Egypt. By now, relations between the six men had descended into fractious arguments.

GOING NATIVE

One point of consensus, however, had been to adopt eastern-style Turkish dress on leaving Constantinople to avoid being identified as Europeans. This plan was effective: the Danish Consul at Rhodes was reported to be terrified by the appearance of the group—believing them to be Turkish sailors, he refused them entry to the consulate. Despite their disputes, the expedition continued.

ARABIC TABLET
Niebuhr reproduced many inscriptions he copied down during the expedition in his book.

IN HIS FOOTSTEPS

→ **1761—Exploring Egypt**
The expedition journeys to Alexandria and travels up the Nile to visit the Great Pyramids before crossing to Suez

→ **1762–63—Across Arabia**
They sail down the Red Sea as far as Jeddah, then continue overland to Mocha

→ **1764–67—Overland return**
After sailing to Bombay, Niebuhr is the last surviving member of the expedition; he recovers his health in India before embarking on an extensive solo exploration of Persia, Palestine, and Turkey

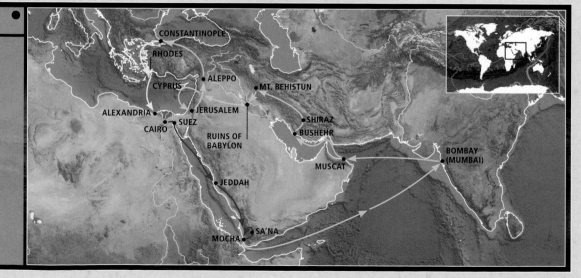

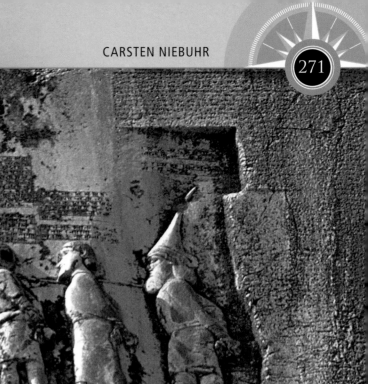

The party remained in Egypt for a year, traveling up the Nile from Alexandria. On first seeing the Great Pyramids, Niebuhr reported how "the traveler is astonished, and feels his imagination in some measure expanded, when he arrives at the foot of those prodigious masses."

From Egypt, the party sailed down the Red Sea as far as Jeddah, making regular landings at points along the coast. During the voyage they found themselves at the mercy of a drunken ship's helmsman. Niebuhr recounted that "we incurred considerable danger; in doubling a cape surrounded with banks of coral, because our pilot was drunk. He had frequently asked us for brandy, on pretence that he could not see the hills, or the outline of the coast, unless his sight was cleared by drinking a little liquor."

INTO ARABIA

From Jeddah, the party continued south overland. As the expedition progressed, they gradually adopted Arabic customs. In Niebuhr's words, "a traveler will always do well therefore to take an early opportunity of securing the friendship of a guide by a meal." During this period both Niebuhr and von Haven contracted

NIEBUHR'S PATRON
Impressed by Niebuhr's potential, Frederick V of Denmark (right) invited the young surveyor to join the scientific expedition.

malaria, so Forrskal explored the hills in northern Yemen alone. Unfortunately, Forrskal's plant specimens were confiscated and destroyed by the authorities when the team reached Mocha. Von Haven's illness had also worsened and he died shortly after their arrival there. The remaining group ventured farther inland, all suffering from ill-health: at Tarim, Forrskal's infection from malaria worsened and he died in July 1763.

The four survivors traveled onward to Sa'na, the capital city of Yemen. Here the group was granted an audience with the Imam, who surprised Niebuhr with his scientific and mathematical knowledge learned from Turkish, Persian, and Indian merchants. Niebuhr gave the Imam "some pieces of mechanism," including watches, gifts that were very favorably received. In return, the Imam procured camels for the group's return journey to Mocha, along with a letter of credit granting them extra funds. The return leg of the trip was beset by storms, locust clouds, and putrid water supplies.

THE SOLE SURVIVOR

On reaching Mocha in August 1863, all were suffering from severe malarial infection or dysentery. Berggren died in Mocha, shortly before Baurenfeind, Kramer, and Niebuhr sailed for Bombay.

THE VICTORY OF DARIUS
On his travels, Niebuhr visited the mountain of Behistun in present-day Iran. Carved into the rock, he saw an impressive inscription depicting the battles and victories of the legendary Persian king, Darius the Great (c. 550–486BCE).

Baurenfeind died during the voyage, Kramer shortly after arriving, leaving Niebuhr the sole survivor of the expedition. He stayed in Bombay for 14 months as he recovered slowly from his illness before setting out to explore on his own.

Niebuhr traveled from Bombay back to Europe overland. He explored Persia, Cyprus, Jerusalem, and Turkey on the way, visiting the ruins of Persepolis and Babylon and traveling extensively through Palestine. He reached Copenhagen in November 1767. His detailed observations led to the publication of *Travels through Arabia and Other Countries* in 1772. The maps featured in this book were still in use 100 years after Niebuhr's groundbreaking travels.

A TALENTED SURVEYOR

Niebuhr earned his place on the expedition for his skills as a surveyor, mostly learned in an 18-month crash course before they set out. A talented mathematician, he quickly mastered the formulae required to carry out triangulation. This is the technique of measuring angles to determine the relative horizontal and vertical positions of distant points. Of equal importance was Niebuhr's ability to plot these measurements accurately on a map, understanding how the projection of the globe onto a flat surface distorts its representation.

ALFRED RUSSEL WALLACE

THE "OTHER" EVOLUTIONARY THINKER

ENGLAND   1823–1913

NATURALIST, ANTHROPOLOGIST, and botanist, Alfred Russel Wallace conducted extensive field work in the Amazon basin and in the Malay Archipelago. Tragically, he lost his entire specimen collection on the voyage back from the Amazon, but he went on to build another huge collection in East Asia, where he formulated his own theory of natural selection independently of Charles Darwin. It was Wallace's proposed theory that spurred Darwin on to publish his *Origin of Species,* 20 years after he had begun work on it.

HENRY WALTER BATES
ENGLAND   1825–92

Shunning a planned career at his father's hosiery factory in Leicester, the amateur entomologist Henry Bates instead took off to the Amazon with his friend Wallace.

Bates was to spend 11 years in South America, covering more than 1,800 miles (2,900 km) and collecting 14,000 species of insect, more than half of them new species. On his return to London, he was persuaded by Charles Darwin to publish *Naturalist on the Amazon River* (1863).

Wallace's first taste of the natural world came as he helped his elder brother in land survey work. However, the younger Wallace was more interested in flora and fauna than the contours of the land. Later, while he was teaching in Leicester, he met Henry Walter Bates (see right), an entomologist who shared his enthusiasm for the collection and study of insects. Both men had been inspired by Charles Darwin's account of his voyage on the *Beagle* (see pp. 276–79), and together they planned a joint expedition to the Amazon.

BIRDWING BUTTERFLY
This is one of thousands of butterfly specimens that Wallace brought back from Asia. His extensive collection is kept at the Natural History Museum in London.

THE LOST COLLECTION
In 1848, Wallace and Bates set sail for Pará, Brazil, where Wallace was to spend four years exploring the rainforest. He was particularly delighted by his exploration of the Uaupés River, in the Rio Negro region. As he recounted 60 years later, "no collector had stayed at any time … or passed through it."

On the return journey in 1852, Wallace's ship, the *Helen,* caught fire, and all his specimens were destroyed. He and the other survivors were cast adrift in a small open boat for 10 days before

they were rescued. As he later wrote, "When the danger appeared past I began to feel the greatness of my loss. With what pleasure I had looked upon every rare and curious insect!" Wallace used his remaining notes to publish his study as *Narrative of Travels in the Amazon and Rio Negro* (1853). In it he gave a passionate description of the rainforest: "Delight is a weak term to express the feelings of a naturalist, who, for the first time, has wandered in a Brazilian forest."

HEADING EAST
In 1854, Wallace traveled to the Malay Archipelago to study the relationship between geological changes and the degrees of difference between animals of adjacent districts. He expounded on this in a paper called "On the law that has regulated the

A LIFE'S WORK

- Explores the **Amazon Rainforest,** but his specimens are lost in a shipwreck

- Travels around the **Malay Archipelago,** collecting thousands of specimens and identifying the Wallace Line

- Formulates a theory of **natural selection** independently of Charles Darwin

- Champions his **colleague and friend Darwin**'s theory of evolution

- Often described as the **Father of Biogeography**, Wallace shows the impact of human activity on the natural world

TRUTH IS BORN INTO THIS WORLD ONLY WITH PANGS AND TRIBULATIONS "

ALFRED RUSSEL WALLACE

KEEPING NOTES

Wallace kept several notebooks at any one time on his travels, making sketches and notes for papers. He also kept separate journals to record day-to-day events.

introduction of new species," in 1855. With his assistant Charles Allen, he was to collect more than 125,000 specimens and make more than 60 journeys through the Malay Archipelago. Wallace was thrilled at the sight of butterflies: "It is one thing," he said, "to see such beauty in a cabinet, and quite another to feel it struggling between one's fingers and to gaze upon its fresh and living beauty."

"SURVIVAL OF THE FITTEST"

While lying low with malarial fever in 1858, Wallace was first inspired to think of the idea of the "survival of the fittest." Once recovered, he wrote to Charles Darwin about his idea. Both men had independently drawn the same conclusions on the origin of species, but it was to be Darwin, publishing one year later, who would go down in history as the Father of Evolution. Darwin always fully acknowledged Wallace, while Wallace would concede that Darwin had elaborated on the theory in greater detail. In 1862, having returned from travels through New Guinea, Wallace published his account with a map showing what was to become known as the "Wallace Line," which splits Indonesia into two parts: with flora and fauna of Australian origin on one side, and of Asian origin on the other. He continued with his scientific research, along with campaigning for social reform, right up to his death, at age 91.

BIRDS OF PARADISE

Wallace was the first Briton to see the many species of Bird of Paradise in their natural habitat in the Malay Archipelago. This species, Wallace's Standard Wing (scientific name *Semioptera Wallacei*), was collected by him on Bacan Island, Indonesia.

IN HIS FOOTSTEPS

→ **1848—Voyage to Brazil**
Wallace and Bates sail to Pará at the mouth of the Amazon River; Wallace spends the next four years exploring the Amazon Rainforest

→ **1852—Return to Britain**
Wallace sails back to Britain; on his return, he publishes *Narrative of Travels in the Amazon and Rio Negro*

‖‖ **1854–62—Explores the Malay Archipelago**
He travels widely around the region, identifying the "Wallace Line"; he develops his theory of natural selection during his stay

LIVERPOOL

PARÁ

RIO NEGRO

On the voyage back to Britain, Wallace's ship catches fire and he loses all his specimens from South America

BUG FINDER
These insects were collected by Wallace in the Malay Archipelago in
1854–62. Of the largest beetle on the next page, he wrote that it is
"never captured except when it comes to drink the sap of the sugar palms."

FIVE WEATHER-BEATEN FISTS GRASPED THE POLE AND PLANTED IT AS THE FIRST AT THE GEOGRAPHICAL SOUTH POLE

ROALD AMUNDSEN

ship from San Francisco was sighted—the *Gjøa* had passed into navigated waters, meaning that the Northwest Passage had been crossed. However, in early September the ship became ice-bound once again, and the crew was forced to overwinter at King Point, close to Herschel Island, some 60 miles (100 km) from the Alaska border. Undeterred, Amundsen made an 800-mile (1,300-km) journey by dog-sled inland to the nearest telegraph station at Fort Egbert in Eagle City, Alaska. The news broke early to the world's press on December 5, 1905, when the content of his telegram was intercepted. Returning to the *Gjøa*, Amundsen completed the final stage of the journey to San Francisco in October 1906.

SMALL LUXURIES
On the *Fram*, pipes, such as this one belonging to Amundsen, usually appeared after dinner.

PLANS UP-ENDED

Back in Norway, Amundsen—now enjoying considerable financial backing thanks to his success—set his sights upon the geographic North Pole. He planned to use the *Fram*, the specially designed polar-exploration vessel built for Nansen in 1893, to drift over the Pole while frozen into

the winter pack-ice. Everything was in place when, in 1909, news arrived that first Frederick Cook and then Robert Peary (see pp. 308–09)—both of whose claims would be contested—had gotten there first. Ever the pragmatist, Amundsen swiftly turned to the South Pole, but kept his plans secret for fear of losing funding. He was also mindful that Robert Scott (see pp. 312–15) had announced an expedition, so wished to gain the upper hand over his British rival. Amundsen only made public his actual destination while en route to Antarctica in August 1910. From the island of Madeira he sent letters to Nansen and the Norwegian king, Haakan VII, and telegrammed Scott with the simple message "BEG TO INFORM YOU FRAM PROCEEDING ANTARCTIC." Given his desire for "firsts," there can be little doubt that Amundsen deliberately sought an advantage, and Scott would have been well aware of the implications for his expedition. Before they proceeded, Amundsen gave his crew the chance to go home, but none did.

The *Fram* crossed the Antarctic Circle in January 1911 and dropped anchor at the Bay of Whales in the Ross Sea. The ship then sailed for Buenos Aires, leaving a nine-man wintering party to set up depots at intervals toward the Pole. Amundsen's closest depot to the Pole was at 82°S, 170 miles (275 km) closer than Scott's closest, which was at 79°29'S.

RECORDING THE CONQUEST
Reaching the South Pole on December 14, 1911, Amundsen took readings with a sextant and artificial horizon as evidence. Notes were also left in a tent in case the party failed to reach the *Fram*.

IN HIS FOOTSTEPS

→ **1903–06—Northwest Passage**
Amundsen and six crew navigate the Northwest Passage for the first time

→ **1910–12—South Pole**
After a last-minute change of destination, Amundsen leads four companions to reach the South Pole for the first time

○ **1918–25—North Pole aboard the *Maud***
Returning to his first love, Amundsen attempts to drift over the North Pole aboard a ship stuck in the Arctic ice. The *Maud* drifts back and forth for seven years, during which time Amundsen considers flying instead

→ **1926—North Pole aboard the *Norge***
Amundsen and 15 crew fly over the North Pole on the airship *Norge*

○ Not shown on map

TELBOR

BARROW — D

A — KING POINT

NORTH POLE

SPITSBERGEN

E — BARENTS SEA

CHRISTIANIA

ANTARCTIC PLATEAU — C

They reach the South Pole on December 14

The previous "farthest south," set by Shackleton

Amundsen's party reach the Axel Heiberg Glacier on November 21

B

ROSS ICE SHELF

A On the death of his mother, Amundsen abandons his medical studies to join a sealing expedition to the Arctic

A The *Gjøa* is iced in at King Point; Amundsen takes a sled to the nearest telegraph station 800 miles (1,300 km) away

Changing plans at the last minute, Amundsen heads south for an attempt at the South Pole, reaching the Ross Ice Shelf on September 8, 1911

B

Amundsen serves as a first mate on the failed Antarctic expedition

News reaches Amundsen that Peary has beaten him in the

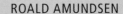

AIRBORNE FIRST
After an abortive attempt to reach the North Pole by
seaplane in 1925, Amundsen achieved his goal in May
1926 aboard the airship *Norge*.

By September 1911, Amundsen judged his men
sufficiently fit, and on October 19, five men and
four light sleds, each pulled by 13 dogs, set
out across the crevasse-ridden Ross Ice Shelf.
They reached the Queen Maud Mountains, the
biggest obstacle between them and the Pole, on
November 11 and spent four hard days crossing
them. After reaching the polar plateau via the
Axel Heiberg Glacier, onward progress was
relatively straightforward. On December 8,
they passed the farthest point south reached
by Shackleton (see pp. 318–19), then pressed
on to reach the South Pole on December 14,
1911. Amundsen had achieved another "first"
through careful planning and good practice, a
method that would see him continue to push the
limits of exploration in later expeditions until
his untimely death (see box, below) in 1928.

INUIT KNOW-HOW
The knowledge gained from
the Inuit during the 1903–06
exploration of the Northwest
Passage helped to shape
Amundsen into a hardened,
resourceful polar explorer.
Skills such as making clothing
from furs and skins were vital
to the success of future trips,
but just as critical was careful
planning. Amundsen wrote:
"Victory awaits him who has
everything in order—luck,
people call it."

A HERO'S DEATH

Amundsen retired from exploration in 1926, having
fulfilled all his ambitions. British accusations of
dishonor over the secrecy of his Antarctic plans in
1910 were said to have hurt him, but no one would
question the honor of the manner of his death. In
1928, at almost 60 years of age, Amundsen joined a
rescue flight in the search for his friend, Italian
airshipman Umberto Nobile, with whom he had
flown over the North Pole on his final expedition.
Nobile's airship had come down near Spitsbergen,
and Amundsen's plane is also thought to have
crashed in the fog over the Barents Sea. The
wreckage was never recovered, despite recent
searches using unmanned submarines.

C They push across the high
Antarctic plateau, 10,000 ft
(3,000 m) above sea level

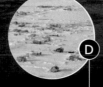

D The *Norge* lands at Barrow
in Alaska after flying over
the North Pole

1912–25	**1926**	1926–28

Reaches the
South Pole in
December 1911

Amundsen and his team sail north to
Hobart, Tasmania, where his success is
announced on March 17, 1912

With co-pilot Oskar Omdal, Amundsen
makes a failed attempt to fly from Alaska
to Spitsbergen across the North Pole

Amundsen's plane is lost in foggy
conditions over the Barents Sea;
the wreckage is never found **E**

CHARLES HALL

UNLIKELY LEADER OF AMERICA'S FIRST POLAR PARTY

UNITED STATES   1821–71

A PUBLISHER BY TRADE, Charles Hall was driven to the Arctic by a conviction that survivors from Franklin's "lost" expedition of 1845 were still to be found. As publisher of the *Cincinnati Occasional* and *The Daily Press*, he was well aware of the sensation Franklin's disappearance had caused. The knowledge of Arctic survival techniques that Hall acquired on his two expeditions in search of Franklin led not only to US-government backing for an attempt on the North Pole, but also proved essential to future polar explorers.

A LIFE'S WORK

- Thrives while **exploring solo, embedded with the Inuit** during his first and second expeditions, becoming the first American to learn Inuit ways

- Sails **further into the Arctic Circle** than anyone before him

- Writes a detailed two-volume account of his time among the Inuit between 1860 and 1863, which becomes an **essential work of commentary and reference** on all aspects of Inuit life, and a valuable resource for later polar explorers

- Fails to show the necessary **leadership skills** to effectively head the more organized third expedition, possibly provoking a resentful crew to **poison** him

Hall was born in Vermont in 1821 and received little formal education. He was a blacksmith's apprentice as a boy, but possessed an inquiring mind that would take him far in life. Fascinated by the searches for the "lost" expedition of John Franklin (see pp. 292–93), Hall spent nine years studying the findings of Francis McClintock, a British Royal Navy officer who had led several searches for Franklin between 1849 and 1859. Hall concluded that there could still be survivors. Despite having no experience of polar

exploration, he managed to raise funds for a search expedition of his own. He set out in May 1860 aboard the whaler *George Henry*, which was captained by Sidney Budington, a veteran of the Arctic. Also on board was Kudlago, an Inuit with whom Hall had struck up a friendly rapport. On sighting his first iceberg, Hall noted: "all my conceptions of its grandeur were more than realized." He later landed on an iceberg and reached its summit "using a boat-hook as a sort of alpenstock to aid me."

GRIM DISCOVERY
Here, Hall discovers the remains of Franklin's men on King William Island. Any hope that members of Franklin's crew had survived to tell the tale were dashed.

Hall planned to hire Inuit helpers and to navigate his way northwest to King William Island, where traces of Franklin's party had been found. However, the ice proved too thick for travel beyond Baffin Island, so Hall remained there a while to study Inuit culture. He took to wearing a *tuktoo* (caribou-skin) jacket and pants, and slept head-to-toe with nine others as a guest of his guide, Keyezhune. He especially enjoyed Inuit feasts, eating warm seal's liver and entrails and endearing himself to his hosts by asking for a second helping.

In the summer of 1862, Hall—guided by English-speaking Inuit couple Ebierbing and Tookoolito—explored the nearby islands. Spotting pieces of brick among the possessions of an Inuit woman, Hall realized that here were artifacts from English explorer Martin Frobisher's expedition of 1557–58. "There in my hand was undoubtedly a relic of that expedition which had visited the place only eighty-six years after the discovery of America by Columbus."

MISSION ACCOMPLISHED

After returning without evidence of Franklin in 1863, Hall failed to raise sufficient funds for a full-scale expedition, partly because the Civil War had broken out. In 1864, he sailed north aboard the whaler *Monticello*, again piloted by Captain Budington, and accompanied by Ebierbing and Tookoolito. The trip was to last five years. He traveled north through Hudson Bay, overwintering at Fort Hope on Repulse Bay, just inside the Arctic Circle. By 1869, he had traveled the remaining 300 miles (500 km) to the coast of King William Island. There he located the graves of several of Franklin's men, recovering human remains and several artifacts. Having proven beyond doubt that none of Franklin's expedition had survived, Hall spent the remainder of the trip living with the Inuit. He was one of the first Americans to show that by following Inuit ways, it was possible to survive in harsh polar regions.

SHARING FRANKLIN'S FATE

Hall returned to the Arctic in 1871 with a very different mission. His nine years of experience in the polar field had brought official recognition, and soon after his return to the US in 1869, he was commissioned to lead the first government-funded expedition. With an ultimate goal of reaching the North Pole, $50,000 was spent equipping and preparing his ship, the *Polaris*.

The expedition left New York in late June 1871, sailing via Baffin Bay into Smith Sound, the strait separating Canada from Greenland. By August 29, Hall had set a new northerly record for shipping in the Arctic Circle, reaching a latitude of 82°11'N. Turned back by thick ice soon after, the ship put into a bay on

LIFE IN THE EXTREMES
An image from Hall's *Arctic Researches Among the Esquimaux* (1865) shows an Inuit village near Frobisher Bay. Hall was fascinated by their customs and survival techniques.

the northwest coast of Greenland to overwinter. Although his friend Budington was captain of the ship, Hall struggled to assert his command over the large team, and the expedition soon split into factions. Confident that the position of the ship had ideally placed them for a spring attempt on the Pole, Hall made an initial sledding sortie northward. On his return to the *Polaris* on October 24, he reported stomach cramps. His condition rapidly deteriorated, and he died on November 8, 1871. The expedition suffered a similarly dire fate: the factions separated in the winter of 1872 when the *Polaris* became trapped in ice, and the two groups were fortunate to be rescued in the spring of 1873.

Hall had complained of feeling unwell after drinking oversweetened coffee, and in 1968 a further clue was found to his macabre end. His exhumed body was shown to contain high doses of arsenic in the hair and nails. Had onboard rivalry spilled over into treachery, or did Hall unwittingly self-administer the poison, a common ingredient in medicines at the time? Hall's death bears enough mystery to match that of the object of his fascination—John Franklin.

ADOPTING INUIT WAYS
Hall was one of the first American explorers to adopt Inuit ways and tools, such as these wooden snow goggles.

PERMAFROST FUNERAL
This image appeared in a newspaper of 1873. The solemn burial of Hall by a grieving crew is a fanciful depiction for the newspaper's readers. His habit of micromanaging the expedition was resented by some of the men and at least one of the mourners may have been responsible for poisoning Hall.

IN HIS FOOTSTEPS

1864–69—Searching for Franklin
Hall explores the Melville Peninsula, Gulf of Boothia, and King William Island in search of Franklin

1871—To the North Pole
Sails along the west coast of Greenland in the *Polaris*, hoping to reach the North Pole

1872–73—The survivors drift south
Following the death of Hall, his crew drifts southward in the ice and is rescued in the spring of 1873

Hall dies at Thank God Harbor in November 1871

GREENLAND

MELVILLE PENINSULA

BAFFIN BAY

DAVIS STRAIT

KING WILLIAM ISLAND

ROBERT E. PEARY

CONTROVERSIAL ARCTIC EXPLORER

UNITED STATES   1856–1920

A CENTURY AFTER Robert E. Peary claimed to have reached the North Pole, controversy still rages over the veracity of his story. Some have even accused him of fraud, arguing that he could not have made his dash for the Pole in the time he said it took him. Others have set out to prove that his claims were entirely reasonable. Whatever the truth, Peary remains an important figure in polar exploration for his earlier pioneering work in the Arctic, mapping the northern shores of Greenland and Ellesmere Island.

A MIXED WELCOME HOME
Peary returned to the US in 1909 to a mixed reception. While some were sceptical of his claims, the people of Bangor, Maine, awarded him with the Loving Cup in a public ceremony.

A commander in the US Navy, Peary made the first of several expeditions to Greenland and the Canadian Arctic in 1886. In the course of these first explorations, he lost eight of his toes to frostbite. In 1906, he claimed to have reached a latitude of 87°06'N, a new record for the farthest north yet reached. This was doubted later, since it meant he must have traveled at least 80 miles (130 km) without making camp. The speed at which Peary claimed to travel was to come under even greater scrutiny three years later.

THE PEARY SYSTEM
On February 27, 1909, Peary led an expedition party of 24 men and 133 dogs from Cape Columbia, located 413 miles (665 km) from the Pole. The expedition departed with Captain

INUIT METALWORK
Peary was surprised to find that the Inuit had metal tools. Their only source of metal was iron from meteorites.

Bob Bartlett blazing a trail, using a pioneering method known as the "Peary System," in which one man skied ahead of the main party to warn of hazardous pressure ridges and open-water channels. The agility and rapidity of the front man allowed him to set a course for the main party with as few detours as possible. The party also comprised support explorers, whose job was to lay depots along the way for the return journey and to carry essential equipment. In this way, the men earmarked for the final assault kept fresh by carrying a lighter load. One by one, the support parties turned back, leaving six men to make the dash to the North Pole.

PERFECT POLAR CONDITIONS
In the early hours of April 2, 1909, along with his trusted fellow explorer Matthew Henson (see pp. 310–11), and his best Inuit dog drivers, Ootah, Ooqueah, Seegloo, and Egingwah, Peary set off under clear skies for the final leg of the journey. After five long marches in perfect conditions, he took readings and was satisfied that they had reached the ultimate north. He wrote in his journal: "The Pole at last!!! ... my dream and ambition for 23 years. Mine at last."

The six men hurried back from the Pole with such ease that Ootah remarked to Henson: "The devil is asleep or having trouble with his wife,

or we should never have come back so easily." But Peary's troubles were just beginning as he returned to face a world that did not believe he had reached the Pole. Not only that, but he discovered that it was widely accepted that his former colleague turned archrival, fellow American Frederick Cook, had beaten him to the prize a year earlier. It is now thought that Cook, in fact, fabricated his evidence and did not reach the Pole, but experts remain divided over Peary's claim.

RETRACING PEARY'S STEPS
In 2005, British explorer Tom Avery set out from Cape Columbia to recreate Peary's dash to the Pole. Avery's intention was to test Peary's claim that the journey could be made in 37 days. Using replica sleds and similar equipment—including a steering contraption called an *amituk* (Inuit for "thingamajig"), Avery beat Peary to the Pole with five hours to spare. However, the exploration establishment was not convinced by Avery's achievement, claiming that ice conditions were different. Nonetheless,

POSING AT THE POLE
Peary took this photograph of his companions at the North Pole. Henson is standing in the middle carrying the US flag.

A LIFE'S WORK

- Claims to have discovered **a large island he names "Crocker Island"** in the Arctic; it is later shown to have been a mirage

- Believes he has reached the North Pole in 1909, but others believe that **Frederick Cook may have beaten him to it**

- Cook's claim is quickly discredited, but now **Peary's claim has been cast into doubt**

- **His measurements of the ocean depths**, which could prove he made it, remain disputed

Avery stood up to the barrage of criticism by stating that he had proved that it was possible for a man to walk the distance Peary had claimed in the time he had claimed. In the process, Avery had himself set a new record for the fastest surface journey to the North Pole.

Others, however, remain unconvinced. The great British polar veteran Sir Wally Herbert—who definitely did reach the North Pole on foot on April 6, 1969—had put an end to widespread sympathy for Peary's claim, which had been supported by the National Geographic Society. Herbert's book, *The Noose of Laurels* (1989), offers compelling evidence that Peary had neither the technical expertise nor the time available to carry out the dash to the Pole as he had claimed. If Herbert is right, then the first person to have arrived at the

IN THEIR FOOTSTEPS

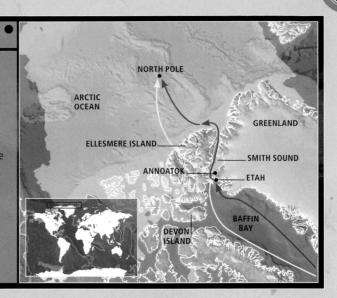

→ **1908—Cook's route**
Frederick Cook claims to have reached the North Pole, but the evidence he produces to back up his claim is later discredited

→ **1909—Peary's route**
A year after Cook, Peary claims to have reached the Pole; to this day, his claim remains disputed

○ **1969—Herbert reaches the Pole**
Herbert leads a team to the Pole, the first undisputed journey there on foot

○ Not shown on map

ARCHRIVALRY
A French magazine depicts Peary and Cook in a fist fight at the North Pole. We can at least know for sure that there are no penguins in the Arctic!

Pole was Alexandr Kuznetsov—by plane on April 23, 1948—and Herbert himself was the first to reach the Pole by a surface route. Experts from the Scott Polar Research Institute, at the University of Cambridge in the UK, think Peary may have failed to reach his goal by as much as 100 miles (160 km). They do not doubt that Peary himself believed he had made it, but the controversy over his claims remains.

SIR WALLY HERBERT
ENGLAND   1934–2007

In a career that lasted more than 50 years, Herbert traveled a total of 23,000 miles (40,000 km) through the wastelands of the polar regions.

His greatest feat came in 1968–69, when he led the British Trans-Arctic Expedition. They completed a 3,800-mile (6,100-km) surface crossing of the Arctic Ocean from Alaska to Spitsbergen, passing over the North Pole on the way. The journey convinced Herbert that Robert Peary could not have reached the North Pole.

MATTHEW HENSON

AFRICAN-AMERICAN EXPLORER OF THE ARCTIC

UNITED STATES   1866–1955

MATTHEW HENSON was an African-American Arctic explorer from Charles County, Maryland. Orphaned at the age of 11, he made his way to Baltimore, where he was hired as a cabin boy, spending six years traveling across the Pacific, the Atlantic, the South China Sea, and the Baltic. Henson's resourcefulness, coupled with his practical skills and ability to learn the ways and language of the Inuit, won him a key role in Robert Peary's explorations of the Arctic and his attempts to reach the geographical North Pole.

INUIT PROTECTIVE CLOTHING
Henson oversaw the making of clothing from Arctic hare, seal, caribou, and—most prized of all—Polar bear. Garments were made by the Inuit women, who chewed the hides until pliable.

Henson gained invaluable practical skills during his six years sailing the oceans, including navigation, carpentry, and mechanical know-how. But it was a chance encounter with Robert Peary (see pp. 308–09) in a fur store in Washington, D.C., that eventually led to his adventures in the Arctic. Impressed by what he saw, Peary, then a young civil engineer, hired Henson as a valet for a canal-building survey of Nicaragua in 1887. The young man showed great aptitude in the challenging conditions of the jungle, and his reliability so impressed Peary that he was invited to join an as-yet unfunded expedition to Greenland and the polar ice cap.

FIRST-NATION TECHNOLOGY
The Inuit wore snowshoes such as these to walk on deep, powdery snow. Henson used them on Peary's expedition.

By 1891, with the necessary funds secured, the North Greenland expedition became headline news, and Peary was besieged by applicants. But it was a small team of just six explorers that set out from New York aboard the *Kite* in June 1891, surviving a battering voyage through pack-ice before arriving at McCormick Bay on the northwest coast of Greenland in late July.

EXPLORING THE INTERIOR
The objective of the expedition was to explore Greenland's ice cap and gather information to help with planning future attempts on the Pole, but Henson's first task was of a more practical nature. He was responsible—almost single-handedly—for the construction of Red Cliff House, the wooden hut that would serve as the expedition headquarters. It was during this task that Henson first worked alongside the Inuit, who welcomed him as one of their own. Their help and advice enabled him to master the Inuit language and to gain sledding skills that would be critical to his future success.

Returning to Greenland in 1893, Henson was frustrated by Peary's refusal to include him on a sledding expedition. Peary later wrote that Henson was "a hard worker and apt at anything; [he] showed himself, in powers of endurance and ability to withstand cold, the equal of others in the party," but nevertheless obliged him to carry out menial duties. However, Henson was not one to bear a grudge, so he made the most of the opportunity to spend more time with the Inuit, becoming accepted when he adopted an orphaned boy named Kudlooktoo.

When Peary returned to the camp, determined to overwinter while most of the party returned home, Henson was the only man to support him until another man, Hugh Lee, followed his example. It was a winter that almost ended in disaster. While traveling in the small whaleboat *General Wistar*, Peary and Henson were battered by a violent storm—named *Anoahtaksoah* ("Demon of the Great Ice") by the Inuit—that nearly drowned them. In 1895, Peary, Henson, and Lee undertook a long

FRIEND OF THE NORTH
Carried to the Arctic by a spirit of adventure, Henson took to the ways of the people he found there like no other before him. They were vital to his success.

A LIFE'S WORK

- Is welcomed by the Inuit, who roll up his sleeve with great humor and fascination to reveal a **skin color** virtually identical to their own

- Masters the art of dog-sledding with the use of a 30 ft (9 m) whip, which eventually leaves him with a **deformed right thumb** from cracking the whip over the head of the lead, or "king," dog

- Earns the Inuit name **Miy Paluk**, which means "Matthew, kind one," or "dear little Matthew"

journey across 450 miles (725 km) of the ice cap in northeastern Greenland. They were left alone with three sleds and 37 dogs after their Inuit helpers had abandoned them, fearing the god Kokoyah would kill them all. The three men made it back in June, reporting that "the condition of the country did not allow much exploration." Having shot and eaten all but one of their dogs to survive, Henson vowed not to return to the Arctic "with the strongest resolution … never again! No more! For Ever!"

But Henson did return to the Arctic on several expeditions as Peary's "assistant." During an 1898 expedition to explore the ice north of Greenland further, Peary found himself so badly frostbitten—he was to lose all but one of his toes—that Henson, having nursed his companion and strapped him to a sled, led the return journey, covering more than 250 miles (400 km) in 11 marches. Peary asserted that Henson "is a better dog driver and can handle a sled better than any man living, except some of the best Eskimo hunters."

TO THE POLE

Henson accompanied Peary on several attempts on the Pole itself, reaching 174 miles (280 km) from their goal—the nearest yet—in 1906. Their eighth and final chance came in 1909, by which time Henson was 42 and Peary 10 years his senior. By now, Henson was fluent in the language of the Inuit and had become the vital link-man between Peary and the Inuit helpers. He was responsible for selecting sled-drivers and their dogs and hand-built more than 20 sleds of Peary's own design. He also tutored less-experienced members of the party, patiently explaining how best to stand to avoid heat loss and how to build an igloo. Henson set out on March 1 with Peary and a team of five, each of whom was in command of their own sled and two others—piloted by Inuit drivers—in order to carry enough supplies to reach the Pole. Their five companions dropped back one-by-one after caching supplies for the Pole party.

TREACHEROUS TERRAIN
The windswept ice of Ellesmere Island in Canada—base camp on the 1909 expedition—was a dangerous landscape, at times the sea-ice became buckled and uneven, while leads—areas of open water between the ice—posed a constant threat.

Henson, Peary, and four Inuit drivers reached a point that they thought to be the North Pole on April 6, 1909. Henson later wrote, "As I stood there at the top of the world and thought of the hundreds of men who had lost their lives in the effort to reach it, I felt profoundly grateful that I had the honor of representing my race in the historic achievement." Completely exhausted, Peary was unable to lead the return journey, and it was Henson's determination that led to their successful return to Cape Columbia on April 23, 1909, having covered more than 500 miles (800 km) in 16 arduous days.

HI-TECH STOVE
The 1909 party used this oil stove built by Henson and designed by Peary. It could melt ice and boil water far quicker than other stoves.

DELAYED RECOGNITION

Despite being Peary's right-hand man and preferred choice of companion to reach the Pole, Henson's achievement on the the expedition went unrecognized. In fact, Henson never met Peary again, although the two did correspond over his autobiography *A Negro Explorer at the North Pole*. While Peary received awards and a Navy pension, Henson took a job in a Brooklyn garage until he was given a government position as a mail carrier at US Customs and only received official recognition in the later years of his life. In 1950, he was honored in a military ceremony at the Pentagon, and in 1954 received a presidential citation from President Eisenhower.

"FOR ARCTIC EXPLORATION" THIS MEDAL WAS AWARDED TO PEARY BY THE RGS IN LONDON

ROBERT SCOTT

TRAGIC HERO OF ANTARCTICA

ENGLAND   1868–1912

BRITISH NAVAL OFFICER Captain Robert Falcon Scott was "bitten by the pole mania" when he tried, and failed, to reach the South Pole in 1902. He finally made it 10 years later, only to find that he had been beaten there by Norwegian Roald Amundsen. Unlike Amundsen, who had learned from the Inuit how to use dogs in the Arctic, Scott relied too heavily on poorly selected ponies and man-hauled sleds. Partly as a result, he and his four companions all died in the terrible weather conditions of the return journey from the Pole.

Scott's first experience of the Antarctic came when he led the National Antarctic Expedition of 1901–04, which included Ernest Shackleton (see pp. 318–19) as Third Officer. Scott's ship, the specially built research vessel *Discovery,* landed at Cape Adare on January 9, 1902. During that first Antarctic summer, he made the continent's first balloon ascent from the Bay of Whales to observe a possible route to the South Pole.

After sheltering for the winter, two expeditions were undertaken. One party headed west in search of the Magnetic South Pole, while Scott set out on November 2 with Shackleton and physician Edward Wilson and headed for the Geographical South Pole. They turned back after setting a new record for the farthest point south yet reached, but still 500 miles (850 km) short of the Pole. Scott recorded that they returned to base camp at Hut Point because they were "as near spent as any three persons can be." It was a harrowing return journey and Shackleton, in particular, suffered extreme exhaustion. After that experience, Scott had no illusions about the unforgiving conditions of the Antarctic.

On his return to Britain, Scott found himself proclaimed a hero and fêted by royalty, but his eyes were still firmly fixed on the South Pole. Within two years, he was planning a return to Antarctica to make another attempt. By 1906, however, Scott and Shackleton had had a falling out, and Shackleton led his own expedition, setting another new record for the farthest south yet traveled, but narrowly missing the Pole. Scott knew that he had to act quickly if he were to win the prize himself.

By 1910, preparations were complete, and he sailed for Antarctica on board the *Terra Nova* with a crew of 65 men, including six veterans of the *Discovery.* Scott took with him new motor-sleds, which he had tested in France and Norway. He also took dogs and ponies as part of a complex transportation strategy that would rely ultimately on a great deal of brute manpower. His distaste for the use of dogs as transportation was to result in a fatal misjudgment.

THE RACE BEGINS

In October 1910, Scott received news that the Norwegian explorer Roald Amundsen (see pp. 302–05) was also heading for Antarctica. Amundsen himself had been beaten to the North Pole by Robert Peary (see pp. 308–09). Unlike Scott, he was only interested in "firsts" and so the race to the South Pole was on.

WRITING BY CANDLELIGHT
On the return from the Pole, Scott wrote his journal by candlelight, using the matches to light his pipe, up to his final hours, when he wrote, "I do not think I can write more."

A LIFE'S WORK

- Heads the 1901–04 *Discovery* expedition, on which he **works out a route** to the South Pole from a hot-air balloon

- Reaches the South Pole just **36 days after his rival**, Norwegian explorer Roald Amundsen

- Pioneers the use of **motorized sleds**, but fails to recognize the importance of dogs

- Along with his four comrades, **dies on the return journey** from the Pole, just short of safety, as they encounter particularly atrocious weather

DEPARTURE OF THE *JAMES CAIRD*
Five men set off with Shackleton on the *James Caird*: Captain
Frank Worsley, seasoned explorer Tom Crean, sailors John
Vincent and Timothy McCarthy, and carpenter Harry McNish.

out on this journey on April 24, with supplies
for just one month. The crew sailed through
complete darkness for up to 13 hours a day. On
the 16th day, they landed at King Haakon Bay
on South Georgia, having run out of water.

Leaving behind three men, McNish,
McCarthy, and Vincent, on May 19 Shackleton
set out with Crean and Worsley to reach the
whaling station at Stormness, 22 miles (35 km)
away. They crossed glaciers and mountains over
3,900 ft (1,200 m) high, attaching screws to
their boots to form crampons. After failing to
descend a high ridge known as the Trident, the
men were forced to jump down an immense
crest while attached to a small coil of rope, and
narrowly avoided being dashed on the rocks.
They finally reached Stormness Bay after
traveling nonstop for 36 hours. Worsley boarded
a whaler to rescue McNish, McCarthy, and
Vincent. Shackleton made three attempts to
rescue the crew from Elephant Island, but was
foiled by the ice. The 22 remaining crew
members were finally rescued on August 30
with the help of a small Chilean navy tug.

Elation at their miraculous escape was
short-lived, however, as the crew returned home
to discover the horrors of World War I. They
put their survival down to the leadership of the
man they called "Boss," and many of them
signed up for Shackleton's final expedition to
Antarctica, on which he died of a heart attack.

"THE END" FOR THE *ENDURANCE*
In a photograph by expedition photographer Frank Hurley,
Shackleton (far right) can be seen leaning over the side of
the *Endurance* a week before the crew abandoned the ship.

DIFFICULTIES ARE JUST THINGS TO OVERCOME, AFTER ALL "

ERNEST SHACKLETON

LEGENDARY VESSEL OF A HEROIC EXPLORER

THE *ENDURANCE*

ON JANUARY 18, 1915, THE *ENDURANCE,* Ernest Shackleton's ship for his Trans-Antarctic expedition, was trapped by ice in the Weddell Sea, close to Antarctica. By the end of February, the vessel was being squeezed by extreme pressures, locked in an ice floe that was moving southwest. "The Boss," as the men nicknamed Shackleton, described a sound that "resembles the roar of heavy, distant surf. Standing on the stirring ice one can imagine it is disturbed by the breathing and tossing of a mighty giant below." By November 21, the men watched from an ice floe as the ship sank. So began the remarkable story of Shackleton's leadership and survival on the ice.

▲ **FIRESIDE TALES**
The nightwatchman on duty tells the team a fireside story in "The Ritz," as the ship's wardroom was nicknamed.

▲ **EXERCISING THE DOGS**
When the ship became firmly trapped in the ice in February 1915, the dogs were transferred from the ship to ice kennels or "dogloos."

▲ **ICE-BOUND SHIP**
This haunting image of the *Endurance* trapped in the ice was taken by Frank Hurley, the expedition's official photographer.

▲ **RELAXING OFF DUTY**
Frank Hurley (left) and surgeon Alexander Macklin at home on the *Endurance* surrounded by mementos, including Australian Hurley's boomerang mounted on the wood panel.

▼ **PASSING THE TIME**
Meteorologist Leonard Hussey (left) and Frank Hurley occupy themselves during the days of darkness by playing chess.

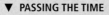

▲ **MESS DINNER**
The crew celebrates midwinter with a hearty dinner on June 22, 1915. A year later, on Elephant Island, the men would toast the date with a drink of hot water mixed with ginger, sugar, and a dash of methylated spirits.

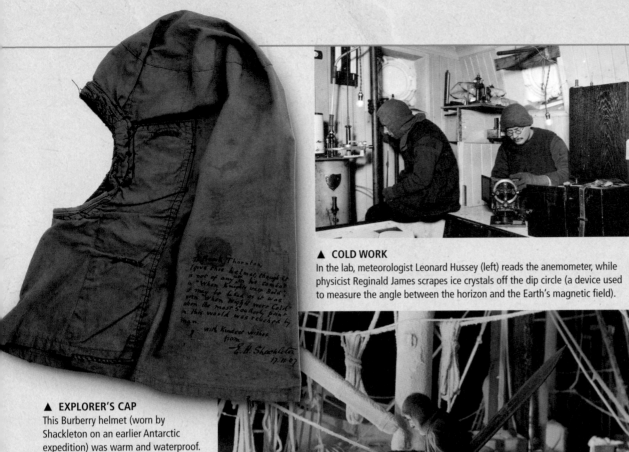

▲ **COLD WORK**
In the lab, meteorologist Leonard Hussey (left) reads the anemometer, while physicist Reginald James scrapes ice crystals off the dip circle (a device used to measure the angle between the horizon and the Earth's magnetic field).

▲ **THE LABORATORY**
Robert Clark, the expedition's biologist, studies microbes by the light of an oil lamp. All his painstakingly collected specimens would be lost in the destruction of the ship.

▲ **EXPLORER'S CAP**
This Burberry helmet (worn by Shackleton on an earlier Antarctic expedition) was warm and waterproof.

▲ **AN EXPLORER'S STUDY**
Shackleton's study on board the *Endurance* contained a small library of reference works, a typewriter, and a stove pipe connected to the kitchen for warmth.

▲ **ICE WATCH**
The nightwatchman returns to report after making an inspection of the ice closing in on the ship.

◄ **ESSENTIAL PROVISIONS**
The crew unpacks provisions as the ship enters the Weddell Sea.

▼ **SETTING UP OCEAN CAMP**
The team sets up camp on the ice after the demise of the ship. Shackleton and Frank Wild stand in the foreground, left.

▲ **SHIP'S CHORES**
The expedition's geologist, James Wordie, Third Officer Alfred Cheetham, and ship's surgeon Alexander Macklin (left to right) wash the galley floor of the *Endurance*. No one was exempt from such duties, however menial.

HILLARY AND TENZING

CONQUERORS OF MOUNT EVEREST

NEW ZEALAND
NEPAL

1919–2008
1914–86

EDMUND HILLARY

TENZING NORGAY

MANY HAD TRIED AND FAILED before Edmund Hillary and Tenzing Norgay finally conquered the world's highest mountain, Everest, in the Himalayas of Central Asia, in 1953. Their achievement brought them worldwide fame, which did not always sit easily on their shoulders. The mountain has been scaled many times since, but remains a formidable challenge, and more than 200 climbers have lost their lives on its slopes.

TENZING AT THE TOP
Hillary took this iconic shot of Tenzing, but there are no pictures of Hillary at the summit. He had forgotten to show Tenzing how to use the camera before the ascent.

11:30 a.m., May 29, 1953: the precise time at which Hillary and Tenzing became the first recorded humans ever to stand on the summit of Mount Everest. The peak, also called Mount Chomolungma, straddles the border between Nepal and Tibet in the Himalayas mountain range. The mountain's peak is one of the most hostile environments on Earth. It is 29,029 ft (8,848 m) above sea level, and the atmosphere at this altitude contains only one-third of the oxygen found at sea level, and this has a

dangerous effect on a climber's body. It can cause a fatal cerebral edema to strike at any time, for instance, and nonessential body functions close down, making digestion and sleep impossible.

INITIAL FAILURE

In the face of such extreme conditions, many previous attempts to scale the mountain had failed. The British climber George Mallory took part in three unsuccessful expeditions to climb the mountain. When asked why, he famously replied "because it's there." Mallory and his partner, Andrew Irvine, died on the mountain in 1924, and it is not known for certain if they reached the summit.

The 1953 expedition also looked at first like it would end in failure. Hillary and Tensing had not been the first choice to try for the summit. Expedition leader John Hunt chose fellow Britons Tom Bourdillon and Charles Evans to be the first pair to try on May 26. They ran into difficulties 1,000 ft (300 m) from the top and turned back.

Three days later, however, Hillary and Tenzing made their successful bid for the top. The Nepalese Sherpa Tenzing was a formidable mountaineer, but Hillary, by his own admission, was no "hot shot rock climber." What the bee-keeping New Zealander lacked in

technique, however, he made up for in huge reserves of determination. Hillary maintained that "strong motivation is the most important factor in getting you to the top." Another factor was the use of bottled oxygen to help combat the effects of extreme altitude, something that Mallory had declared to be "unsportsmanlike."

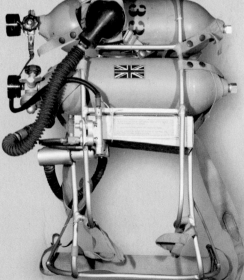

OXYGEN SUPPLY
Hillary and Tenzing both carried oxygen tanks on their backs. The air is particularly short of oxygen above 26,000 ft (8,000 m).

A LIFE'S WORK

- **Probably the first men** to reach the summit of Everest, but definitely the first to do so and **return alive**

- They **refuse for many years** to say who stepped onto the top first, preferring to share the honor and the fame that goes with it

- Hillary goes on to reach both **the North and South poles**, flying over the North Pole in 1985 in the company of Neil Armstrong, the first man on the Moon

- Hillary dedicates much of the rest of his life to **improving the lives** of the people of the Himalayas, while Tenzing returns to **a quiet, private life**

THE ROOF OF THE WORLD

Standing on top of the world, Hillary and Tenzing paused briefly to admire the view over Nepal and Tibet, plant their summit flags, and take photographs. The media attention that was heaped on the two climbers upon their descent took both men completely by surprise, but their newfound fame came at a price. Speculation developed as to which man was the first actually to set foot on the top. The expedition team leader made the decision to avoid the issue by saying that the men had arrived at the summit at "almost the same time." But the spirit of the achievement was blighted by rumors that Tenzing had been virtually dragged to the top by Hillary. Later in life, both men wrote in their memoirs that Hillary reached the rounded snowy dome first, with Tenzing five or six paces behind.

After Everest, Hillary had further successes as an expeditioner, most notably in 1958, when he became the first to reach the South Pole overland

since Robert Scott in 1912 (see pp. 312–17), and the first ever to reach it by motorized transportation. Yet Hillary most wanted to be remembered for his work with the people of Nepal, helping to build much-needed schools, hospitals, airstrips, and bridges. Tenzing led a quiet life after Everest, working as director of field training for the Himalayan Mountaineering Institute in Darjeeling, India.

VIEW FROM THE SUMMIT
Hillary took this picture looking west from the summit over the Himalayas. Everest is one of 14 mountains higher than 26,000 ft (8,000 m), all of which are in Asia.

RANULPH FIENNES
ENGLAND   B.1944

Born into an aristocratic family, Fiennes spent eight years in the army before beginning his remarkable career as an adventurer.

Fiennes was the first person to reach both the North and South Poles by a surface route, and the first to cross Antarctica on foot. In 2000, he suffered severe frostbite in an unsuccessful attempt to be the first to reach the North Pole solo and unsupported. He later amputated several of his necrotic fingers himself using a saw in his garden shed. Despite subsequently undergoing major heart bypass surgery, Fiennes showed no signs of slowing down and, in 2009, aged 65, he became the oldest person ever to climb Everest.

NOBODY CLIMBS FOR SCIENTIFIC REASONS ... YOU REALLY CLIMB FOR THE HELL OF IT

EDMUND HILLARY

THE DAY BEFORE THE ASCENT OF EVEREST
Hillary and Tenzing are pictured here on the Southeast Ridge, preparing to leave to establish the final camp below the summit, Camp IX, from where they made their ascent.

HIGH ALTITUDE

WHEN ASKED WHY he wanted to climb Everest, British climber George Mallory retorted "Because it's there!" He was probably exasperated at being asked to justify why climbers risk their lives in what the French mountaineer Lionel Terray called the conquest of the useless. Climbing mountains purely for the sake of it probably began with the 1786 ascent of Mont Blanc by Jacques Balmat and Horace-Bénédict de Saussure. Almost a century later, Edward Whymper scaled the Matterhorn, the last of the great Alpine peaks, after which attention moved to the high mountains of the Himalayas.

WHITE HELL

Avalanches are an ever-present danger in the high mountains. The 1922 British Everest Expedition was abandoned after seven sherpas were killed by an avalanche, while on a German expedition to Nanga Parbat, in the Himalayas, in 1937, seven climbers and nine sherpas were killed when their camp was buried beneath an avalanche. Most victims, if not killed outright, die through lack of oxygen. The recent invention of the "avalung," a breathing apparatus worn on the chest, reduces this risk.

EARLY OXYGEN PACK
Oxygen was first used on Mt Everest by chemist George Finch during the 1922 British attempt.

MAKING CAMP ON HIGH GROUND

Since the chances of finding shelter at high altitude are slim, one of the most essential items of equipment for any climbing expedition is a tent. A high-altitude tent must provide shelter from the extremely strong winds and heavy snowfall encountered on high slopes. Without shelter from the elements a climber risks exposure and death.

EVEREST BASE CAMP
Heavy-duty tents are essential even at the comparatively safe Everest Base Camp, which sits at an elevation of 17,087 ft (5,208 m).

Edward Whymper summed up the requirements of a mountaineering tent as being "sufficiently portable to be taken over the most difficult ground, while combining lightness with stability." For Alpine climbing, Whymper used a tent that consisted of four poles, a length of cord, a large sheet of muslin for the roof, and a large piece of plaid rubberized cotton for the floor and internal walls.

Maurice Herzog and three fellow climbers lost their tent during a nightmare descent from Annapurna, Nepal, in 1950.

They eventually found shelter at the bottom of a 15-ft (5-m) crevasse after fellow-summiteer Louis Lachenal had fallen into it. The climbing team found it more comfortable than the prospect of hacking a cave out of the ice, but had only one sleeping bag between four, so placed their feet inside it in the hope of preventing further frostbite. Herzog's condition worsened until he was unable to walk—he owed his life to a Sherpa named Pandi who carried the 200-lb (90 kg) Frenchman on his back.

THE TRICKS OF THIN AIR

High altitude can have a debilitating effect on the human body, ranging from fatigue and strokes to cerebral and pulmonary edema—an accumulation of water in the brain or lungs—which can be fatal. Snow reflects 80 percent of UV light compared to just 20 percent for sand, so snow blindness is a risk. The mind can become confused due to low oxygen. High altitude also brings intense cold and the added risk of hypothermia and frostbite.

BLINDNESS RISK
A porter on the 1924 British Everest expedition wears improvised goggles.

TOUGH TRANSPORTATION

Reaching a high summit is often dependent on knowledge of previous climbs. If attempting an unexplored peak, a reconnaissance trip is vital. The successful 1953 Everest expedition utilized photographic data from previous attempts and information from a 1951 reconnaissance expedition.

BEASTS OF BURDEN

The best high-altitude pack animals are those native to the locality. In the Andes, llamas boast padded hooves that give greater traction over mountain terrain. In the Himalayas, yaks can haul loads to 20,000 ft (6,000 m). Once beyond the range for animals, manpower is essential. None of the Everest expeditions would have succeeded without sherpa porters and climbers.

HIGH WIRE
Crossing crevasses is very dangerous. They can widen or collapse without warning. The Khumbu Icefall, Mt. Everest, (shown here) is impassable without rope and ladder.

HAULING FOOD

Edible flora and fauna is scarce at high altitude, so rations were carried by pack animals or porters. Despite this, in 1868 George Hayward was forced to eat his yak after reaching the source of the Yarkand River in the Karakorum Mountains. For the successful ascent of Everest in 1953, food supplies were organized with military precision. Basic "compo" (composite) rations fed 14 men for a day on oatmeal biscuits, sausages, butter, jam, cheese, chocolate, meat, baked beans, and canned fruit. Assault rations contained oats, powdered milk, sugar, jam, cookies, banana bars, cheese, salt, cocoa, tea, and soup. Luxury items included canned fruit, coffee, sardines, and rum.

COPING WITH EXTREMES

At high altitude, both the terrain and the weather can be treacherous. Equipment failure or a missed footing can result in a fall of hundreds of yards, which—even if not immediately fatal—can result in death due to the impossibility of hospital treatment. With the ever-present danger of frostbite, the properties of the climbing boots used are of great importance. For the 1953 Everest expedition, boots were specially made with a layer of insulation that protected the foot from exterior moisture and from perspiration. The boots were also fitted with an outer covering of a rubber-coated stockinette. Making the boots tested the capacity of the manufacturers to the full, especially since Edmund Hillary wore size 12 boots, while some of the sherpas wore only size 6. Both the climbers' outer clothing and the expedition tents were made of a cotton-nylon mix, treated with a waterproof coating. The tents were of the two-man Meade design that had remained unchanged since the 1920s, while larger domed tents were also used for communal sleeping and as mess tents at lower altitudes.

PEOPLE DO NOT DECIDE TO BECOME EXTRAORDINARY. THEY DECIDE TO ACCOMPLISH EXTRAORDINARY THINGS

EDMUND HILLARY

EXPLORING THE DEEP

F OOD, TREASURE, AND WARFARE WERE THE EARLIEST MOTIVATIONS FOR UNDERWATER EXPLORATION. DIVING FOR EDIBLE MOLLUSKS OCCURRED AS EARLY AS 4500BCE, WHILE TODAY, ROBOTIC SUBMERSIBLES EXPLORE THE EARTH'S LAST FRONTIERS—THE DEEP OCEAN FLOORS.

DIVING IN MYTH AND LEGEND
A 15th-century French manuscript depicts Alexander the Great in a glass diving bell. Aristotle's *Problemata* described Alexander's underwater activity at the Siege of Tyre (332BCE).

Some of the earliest evidence of undersea exploring comes from about 3200BCE, when decorative objects made from mother-of-pearl appeared in Thebes, Greece, in quantities that could not have been sourced from beachcombing alone. Sponges, pearl oysters, red coral, and murex shells—yielding purple dye—were also of high value at the time. The 17th-century English physicist Edmond Halley later explained how these early free divers harvested their quarry: sponge divers were "accustomed to take down in their mouths a piece of sponge soaked in oil, by which they were able to dive for a longer period than without it."

TALES OF EARLY DIVING

In the 5th century BCE, the Greek writer Herodotus wrote of the skill and daring of Scyllias and his daughter Cyane in his *Histories*. This pair of divers were employed by the Persian king Xerxes to gather treasure from his sunken galleys. In revenge for a broken promise by Xerxes, the pair dived to sever the anchors of his ships before swimming 9 miles (14 km) underwater. Human physiognomy makes this an unlikely tale, but some have suggested that the pair's escape was aided by the use of hollow reeds as breathing tubes. According to a description in the *Technica Curiosa* by 17th-century German physicist Gaspar Schott, a demonstration took

> The limitation of free diving—the strength and lung capacity of the diver—was surmounted by the diving bell, which was known of from the time of Aristotle in the 4th century BCE. It kept the same basic form until the 16th century.

place in 1538 before Emperor Charles V at Toledo by "two Greeks [who] let themselves down under water in a large inverted kettle with a burning light and rose up again without being wet." Schott also described *Lorica aquaticus* ("aquatic armor") illustrated by a man walking into water wearing a small diving bell reaching to his feet.

DIVING BELL

In 1691, Halley patented a revolutionary design for a diving bell. A truncated wooden cone measuring 3 ft (1 m) in diameter at the top and 5 ft (1.5 m) at the base, it contained 60 cubic ft (1,700 liters) of air supplied from barrels weighted with lead. Leather pipes fed air to a diver outside the bell, while a companion sat on wooden staging within the bell. During descent, the bell paused at 12 ft (3.5 m) to allow water to be expelled by air from one of the barrels, while a stop-cock at the top of the bell could be adjusted to release stale air.

During experimental dives, Halley sent messages to the surface in the empty air barrels. He remained underwater at a depth of 60 ft (18 m) for up to 90 minutes. Describing the

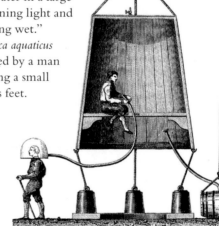

BENEATH THE SURFACE
Halley's diving bell was fitted with a window for observation and could remain submerged for extended periods of time, eventually clocking a record four hours underwater.

revolutionary nature of his patent, he wrote, "This I believe to be an invention applicable to various uses, such as fishing for pearls, diving for corals, sponges, and the like in far greater depths than has hitherto been thought possible." In 1790, engineer John Smeaton further improved the design by introducing a continuous supply of air, which was pumped into the bell from a cable on board ship.

FROM BELL TO HELMET

Although Halley's bell enabled divers to remain underwater for considerable periods of time, it offered little flexibility to the diver or scope for exploration. German inventor Augustus Siebe was the first to attempt individual diving equipment. In 1819, he designed a metal helmet that was attached to a waterproof canvas jacket, forming an "open" suit that was supplied with air by a hose from the surface. However, the jacket could fill with water if the diver fell or lost his footing—a potentially fatal design flaw. In 1837, Siebe designed a "closed" underwater suit. It weighed

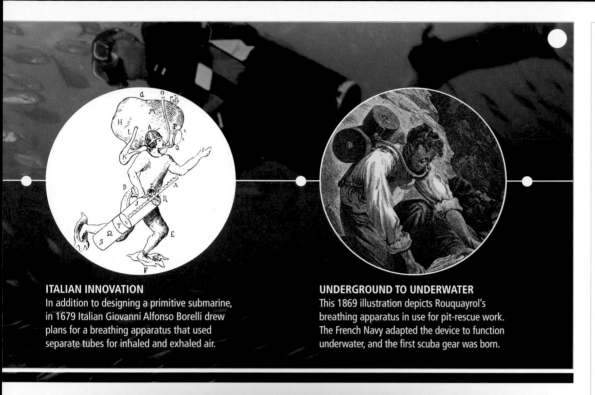

ITALIAN INNOVATION
In addition to designing a primitive submarine, in 1679 Italian Giovanni Alfonso Borelli drew plans for a breathing apparatus that used separate tubes for inhaled and exhaled air.

UNDERGROUND TO UNDERWATER
This 1869 illustration depicts Rouquayrol's breathing apparatus in use for pit-rescue work. The French Navy adapted the device to function underwater, and the first scuba gear was born.

DIVING INTO THE DEPTHS
Present-day submersible craft can reach depths that were utterly unattainable to the ancient explorers. The vessel DeepSee can take a pilot and two passengers to a depth of 1,500 ft (450 m) or 250 fathoms.

SETTING THE SCENE

- Herodotus describes a diver named Colas in the 5th century BCE **whose skills were so extraordinary** that he was nicknamed "Pesce" ("Fish"). The historian wrote that, "It was said of him, that without coming at all to land, **he could live for several days in the water**; that he could even walk across the straits at the bottom of the sea. One of their kings had the cruelty to propose his diving near the Gulph of Charybdis, and to tempt him threw in a golden cup. In a third attempt to gain this, **it is supposed that he was caught by the whirlpool**, for he appeared no more…"

- In his medieval accounts, Marco Polo (see pp.56–59) describes how "the pearl oysters are taken by men who go down in water as much as fifteen or twenty sailors arms." This unit of measurement—or fathom—dates back to the ancient Greeks, consisting of **the length of a mariner's outstretched arms**.

- In order to improve visibility and the duration of dives, 14th-century pearl divers in the Persian Gulf adopt **rudimentary goggles with lenses made from ground and polished tortoiseshell**.

- During visits to the coast of Japan in 1584, Dutch traders observe **female divers capable of diving to eight fathoms** and spending **the best part of 15 or 20 minutes beneath the water**. They were recognizable as divers by their eyes, which were "red as blood."

nearly 200 lb (91 kg) and comprised a canvas outer suit that was weighted with lead shoes and a leather weight belt. With some modification, this form of underwater dress remained in use for a century or more. However, although the suit allowed flexible movement of the diver, the cable that supplied air from the ship on the surface restricted how far the diver could travel to the length of the cable itself. In 1860, however, two French inventors, Benoît Rouquayrol and Auguste Denayrouze, patented an invention named the *aérophore*—a compressed air device attached to the back of the diver. Rouquayrol, a mining engineer, originally created the device for pit-rescue work but with Denayrouze, a French naval officer, adapted the equipment for underwater use. Initially, the *aérophore* was an uncomfortable system, but by 1865, the two men patented a new version that was worn with *Le Groin*—a glassed helmet—the precursor of the modern diving mask. Finally, in 1943, Jacques Cousteau (see pp.330–33) invented his revolutionary aqualung, which led to the complete independence of the modern diver.

WILLIAM BEEBE

DEEP-SEA EXPLORER AND OCEANOGRAPHIC PIONEER

UNITED STATES   1877–1962

NATURALIST AND UNDERSEA EXPLORER William Beebe pioneered the use of technology to study undiscovered deep-sea life-forms in the 1930s. Already an acclaimed ornithologist, he used the newly invented bathysphere to uncover the world beneath the waves in a series of deep-sea dives off the Bahamas, coming face-to-face with marine specimens that had never been seen before. Beebe's prolific writing, coupled with his enthusiasm for the natural world, greatly boosted public interest in the marine environment.

STUFF OF ADVENTURE
The bathysphere was an international sensation that appealed to an audience of all ages, such as the youthful readership of this 1937 UK monthly publication.

Born in Brooklyn, New York, and educated at Columbia University, Beebe's early career as a naturalist began as Assistant Curator of Birds at the Bronx Zoo. He undertook research expeditions to Singapore, Mexico, the Galápagos Islands, and the jungles of South America, conducting birdlife surveys and collecting specimens for the New York Zoological Society's collection. He went on to establish a reputation as an ornithologist of

international renown and achieved critical acclaim for *A Monograph of the Pheasants*, a major illustrated study of pheasants in Asia.

PLUMBING NEW DEPTHS

By the age of 51, Beebe's interest in oceanography was becoming more than just a passing diversion. Following initial expeditions above the waves aboard the *Arcturus*, he shared his desire for a way to examine deep-sea subjects at close quarters with his friend, former US President Theodore Roosevelt, an avid naturalist. At the time, the farthest depth for safe diving was just 200 ft (60 m), below which the pressure caused physical problems for the diver. Many of the fragile undersea life-forms would also be crushed or disfigured by the changes in pressure if brought back to the surface. Beebe consulted various engineers and diving specialists before being introduced in 1928 to Otis Barton, a wealthy industrialist who had invented the bathysphere, a submersible craft that he described as a "hollow steel sphere on the end of a cable." The interior

INTO THE BLUE
On August 15, 1934, the bathysphere was lowered into the waters off Bermuda for its record half-mile dive.

DEEP-SEA MACHINE
Beebe and Barton pose with the bathysphere during the 1934 *National Geographic* expedition. The circular entrance hatch, which weighed 400 lb (180 kg), was bolted shut after entry to seal the occupants safely inside.

it was agreed to that more than five seconds' radio silence would signal to the surface crew that the divers were in trouble. When they reached a depth of 2,000 ft (600 m), the final traces of light from the surface disappeared and they were surrounded by pitch blackness. Beebe later commented, "It is only a psychological mile-post, but it is a very real one. We had no realization of the outside pressure but the blackness itself seemed to close in on us."

The pair became overnight media sensations, with front-page headlines in the *New York Times* and an enthralled readership. In 1932, Beebe made a radio broadcast from the bathysphere to an audience of millions across the US. Their craft was buffeted by swells and both men were injured, before Beebe signed off from the depths: "Otis Barton and I bid you farewell from a depth of 670 meters [2,200ft] beneath the surface of the Atlantic Ocean, off Bermuda."

RECORD-BREAKERS

Barton and Beebe's final expedition together came in 1934 in a *National Geographic*-sponsored dive. The pair broke the half-mile barrier to

reach a record depth of 3,028 ft (923 m). However, Beebe's interest did not lie in simply breaking records. His motivation was to be able to see and record the marine life that lived at these previously unexplored ocean depths.

Beebe's explorations were among the first to be accessible to the wider public—US audiences were thrilled by the adventurous tales recounted in *National Geographic* magazine—but the breathless prose of his accounts veiled the serious scientific endeavors of his work. Lacking modern cameras, Beebe noted the details of his discoveries and later described them to an artist, whose drawings would often become the subject of criticism and debate among fellow scientists.

Beebe was at the forefront of oceanographic study in the 1930s, and the legacy of his unlocking of the secrets of the oceans was a public captivated by the wonders of the deep. He remained active well into his eighties, returning to his first love of ornithology. From the veranda of his home in rural Trinidad, he observed nesting birds through a pair of custom-built giant binoculars mounted on a tripod.

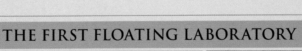

BALL OF STEEL
The bathysphere was a simple sphere 4¾ ft (1.5 m) in diameter, made from cast steel 1 in (2.5 cm) in thickness. Oxygen was supplied from a pressurized cylinder, while fans circulated the air over pans of soda lime to absorb exhaled carbon dioxide.

pressure was maintained at sea-level rates, while at a depth of 1,400 ft (425 m) the pressure on the hull would be 1,000 times greater. Strengthened quartz glass was used for two port-holes, while a third held a powerful searchlight. A solid rubber cable carried oxygen, electricity, and a telephone line from the surface-ship down to the chamber.

FIRST DIVES

The first dives in the bathysphere took place off the coast of Bermuda in June 1930. Attached by cable to a barge, the *Ready*, Beebe and Barton made several test-dives in the sphere. Beebe wrote of their findings in his best-selling account, *Half Mile Down*: the light changed to "this indefinable blue … It seemed to me that it must be like the last terrific upflare of a flame before it is quenched."

As the dives went deeper, Beebe noted the bioluminescence of several of the sea creatures, many of whom emitted their own light. During the dives, Beebe kept in constant telephone contact with his assistant, Gloria Hollister. Such were the potential dangers of the dive,

DEEP-SEA MACHINE
At 2,000 ft (600 m), Beebe and Barton witnessed deep ocean creatures, such as this anglerfish, that had never before been seen alive in their natural habitat.

THE FIRST FLOATING LABORATORY

The modern science of oceanography effectively began with the great voyages of HMS *Challenger* between 1872–76. The ship covered nearly 69,000 nautical miles (208,000 miles or 130,000 km) as a team of scientists took samples and measured the depths of the oceans. The expedition was organized by the Royal Society of London and led by Professor Charles Wyville Thomson, who removed the warship's guns to make room for two fully equipped laboratories. Upon their return, Thomson's assistant, John Murray, supervised the production of a mammoth 50-volume report on their findings.

HMS *CHALLENGER*, DURING WHOSE FOUR-YEAR VOYAGE NEARLY 5,000 NEW SPECIES OF MARINE LIFE WERE DISCOVERED

MAN CARRIES THE WEIGHT OF GRAVITY ON HIS SHOULDERS ... BUT HE HAS ONLY TO SINK BENEATH THE SURFACE AND HE IS FREE

JACQUES COUSTEAU

DIVING CAGE
From the safety of a cage, a scientist watches the behavior of a Great White, one of the largest and most aggressive sharks.

DANGERS OF THE DEEP

Scuba-diving has revolutionized underwater exploration by giving divers the freedom of having their own air supply. The activity is extremely dangerous, however. Each year the sea claims the lives of divers who have run out of air, been struck by a vessel, become tangled or trapped, or even attacked by a dangerous animal. International safety codes apply to all categories of diver. Scuba divers follow strict predive routines to ensure maximum safety. On a boat dive, predeparture tide times and Èup-to-date weather reports for the dive area are essential. Scuba equipment is checked for malfunction, and the air-gas mix and average air consumption aÈre calculated in advance, with a reserve to allow for an emergency. In cold water, the protection level of exposure suits is also assessed to ensure that the dive time is possible without risk to the diver.

DIVE BUDDIES

The buddy system is vital to scuba-diving safety. Divers operate in pairs of "buddies" and are expected to monitor each other during a dive and ensure that the other does not get into trouble. Buddies stay close to each other throughout the dive so that they can help in an emergency, if necessary, sharing their air supply until they can return to the surface. Buddies use a system of internationally recognized hand signals to "speak" underwater. Some divers may make solo dives without a buddy, particularly when they want to focus on activities such as underwater photography rather than their buddy's welfare. Only divers with hundreds of hours of experience are allowed to dive solo.

THE SEA, ONCE IT CASTS ITS SPELL, HOLDS ONE IN ITS NET OF WONDER FOREVER

JACQUES COUSTEAU

THE ALIEN OCEAN FLOOR

In 1977, scientists from the Scripps Institution of Oceanography in California made a discovery that would overturn one of the most fundamental beliefs about the nature of life on Earth. Sending the submersible ALVIN 6,900 ft (2,100 m) to the East Pacific Ocean floor, they discovered bizarre, chimneylike structures, belching out superheated water and minerals from the planet's crust. Surrounding these hydrothermal vents were large communities of fauna, including giant tube worms and scaly-footed gastropods, which subsist by converting the heat and minerals from the vents into food—a process known as chemosynthesis. In other words, life was thriving in places where sunlight—thought until then to be the source of all food, energy, and, therefore, life—had never penetrated. Huge fields of vents have since been found.

BEYOND THE BOIL

The vents can reach temperatures of 752°F (400°C), but do not boil due to the pressures at such a depth. The vents are clustered around unstable areas of the Earth's crust.

INTO THE SOLAR SYSTEM

OVER A PERIOD OF JUST 43 YEARS, SPACE FLIGHT TECHNOLOGY DEVELOPED FROM A RUDIMENTARY, LIQUID-FUELED ROCKET TO THE ENORMOUS SATURN V CRAFT THAT TOOK HUMANS TO THE MOON. RESEARCH WAS RAPIDLY ADVANCED BY THE SUPERPOWER COMPETITION OF THE COLD WAR.

STUDYING THE SOLAR SYSTEM
The cosmological system of Copernicus, credited as the father of modern astronomy, was the first to put the Sun at the center of the solar system, as seen in this 17th century depiction.

The first people known to have studied the solar system were the ancient Babylonian, Egyptian, and Assyrian astronomers. Their observations were preserved from distant antiquity by later Greek scholars. In 150BCE, Hipparchus—and later, Ptolemy in his *Almagest*—used the evidence of Egyptian astronomers to interpret celestial events, proposing that the Earth was a stationary, fixed plane at the heart of a heavenly vault, on which the Sun, Moon, and stars were "fixed" in a series of outer spheres.

ASTRONOMICAL ADVANCES

It was not until the revolutionary work of Polish astronomer Nicolaus Copernicus in the 16th century that our understanding of the Earth's position in relation to the Moon and stars was radically transformed. Copernicus made the crucial realization that the Sun was at the center of the solar system, which later influenced the work of German mathematician Johannes Kepler and Italian scholar Galileo Galilei. Kepler's rules of planetary motion, formulated in 1605, would inform the theory of universal gravitation proposed by

WATCHING THE STARS
Isaac Newton designed the first reflecting telescope in 1668, using it to observe astronomical phenomena, such as a comet in 1680. His theory of universal gravitation proved vital to the science of space travel.

the English physicist Isaac Newton. This in turn was later used for the calculation of how much rocket power was needed to break free of planet Earth's gravitational pull.

ROCKET POWER

From the 13th century, rockets began to be developed for use in warfare. A crude form of short-range weapon capable of causing alarm and surprise was developed in medieval China. By the late 18th century, the English inventor William Congreve had refined military rockets, demonstrating his first solid-fuel-powered model in 1805. Metal-cased and with much greater targeting accuracy, his invention laid the foundation for the development of the modern rocket.

SCIENCE FICTION

In the 19th century, writers such as Jules Verne and H. G. Wells wrote stories of space travel that inspired the future scientists of 20th-century travel. Verne described a fantastical journey to the Moon in *De la Terre a La Lune* ("From the Earth to the Moon," 1865) while Wells described an invasion from Mars in *The War of the Worlds* (1898). The feats of their space-traveling heroes

> The earliest recorded astronomers were the Babylonians, who composed star catalogs as early as 1200BCE. They observed the planets, stars, and constellations, and philosophized on the nature of the universe.

were impossible with the technology of the time. Without a continuous source of oxygen to enable combustion, a rocket could not operate in the vacuum of outer space.

In 1903, the Russian writer Konstantin Tsiolkovsky proposed that rockets could be propelled into space in his avant-garde work *The Investigation of Space with Reactive Devices*, which combined mathematical theory with ambitious futuristic plans for space stations, satellites, and interstellar transportation.

TURNING FICTION INTO FACT

The invention of a rocket-fueled propulsion system in the early 20th century by US scientist Robert H. Goddard allowed the first guided-rocket research to take place. Inspired by Wells's writings as a boy, Goddard registered 214 patents for a host of inventions relating to rockets while working for the US Department of War at Clark University from 1914. By 1920, his reports described the potential for an unmanned rocket to reach the Moon and signal its arrival by detonating a flare device. Ridiculed in the press, Goddard moved to New Mexico to continue his research, building models and conducting test flights with support from the Smithsonian Institution. He soon proved his critics wrong, successfully launching the first liquid-fueled rocket in 1926. Reports of Goddard's work spread throughout the scientific

◄ **1969 MODULE**
The Apollo X command module launched in May 1969, carrying astronauts Thomas Stafford, John Young, and Eugene Cernan. It is now at the Science Museum, London, England.

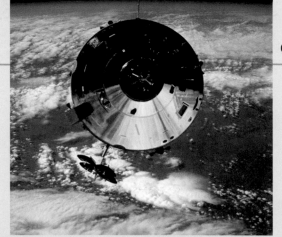

◄ **EARTH ORBIT**
The Apollo IX command module in orbit above the Earth, as seen from the lunar module, March 1969.

▼ **IMPROVISATION**
Aboard the Apollo XIII, on April 17, 1970, astronaut John Swigert holds the "mailbox," an improvised device designed to purge carbon monoxide from the lunar module.

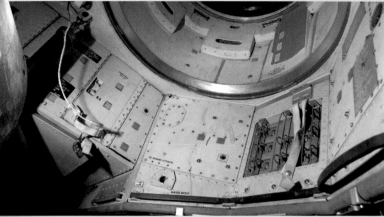

▲ **REHEARSAL MODULE**
This is the interior of the Apollo X module, which orbited the Moon in May 1969 as a rehearsal for the Apollo XII Moon landing.

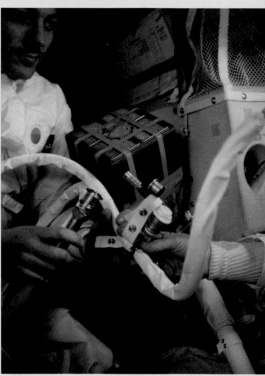

▶ **OCEAN TOUCHDOWN**
This is the Apollo XI command module shortly after touchdown in the Pacific Recovery Area, with US Navy pararescue personnel in attendance.

▲ **APOLLO IX MISSION**
Astronaut Dave Scott stands in the open hatch of the module, testing the docking procedures that made the lunar landings possible. Apollo IX included the first crewed flight of the lunar module.

◄ **TECHNICAL CHECKS**
Working in the Apollo Mission Simulator at the Kennedy Space Center, Florida, Apollo XII astronaut Michael Collins follows checks on technical material on June 20, 1969.

POST-APOLLO EXPLORATION

THE NEW FRONTIERS

Just eight years after the first manned space flight of Soviet cosmonaut Yuri Gagarin, the United States successfully landed a man on the Moon as part of its Apollo program. Optimism over the possibilities for future exploration proved unfounded, however, as the enormous cost of space programs became prohibitive.

Following the success of Apollo 11, public interest in the remainder of the Apollo missions diminished. The annual cost of the program was some $3 billion, and such high levels of spending had become politically unjustifiable for the US government. Apollo 17 returned to Earth on December 19, 1972, and humans have not been back to the Moon since.

SCIENCE IN SPACE

From the early 1970s, the focus of the US space missions switched to the development of a reusable orbital program. Skylab, the first experimental space station, orbited at a height of 270 miles (430 km) above the Earth's surface and proved that humans could live and work in space. Skylab's first three-man crew took off on May 14, 1973, for a 28-day mission at zero gravity. Over three missions, scientists carried out the first detailed study of the Earth from an orbiting spacecraft. The operation was truly international, and scientists from 28 nations

took part in the experiments and research. By the end of its third mission in 1974, Skylab had orbited 3,900 times, passing over 75 percent of the Earth's surface. It used solar panels to generate its electricity, affording the astronauts such comforts as solid foods and a collapsible shower enclosure.

THE SPACE SHUTTLE

NASA embarked on the next stage in the development of its manned space program in 1981, with the launch of the first space

shuttle, *Columbia*, from the Kennedy Space Center in Florida. The shuttle was a reusable craft, capable of docking with the International Space Station. Its flight controls were completely computerized, using "fly-by-wire" technology originally developed for fighter pilots, which reduces the risk of mechanical error. The part

MARS EXPLORER
The first NASA Mars Rover was successfully landed on Mars in 1997. As of 2010, two Rovers are sending back images and analyzing samples from the surface of the planet.

SPACEWALK
Astronaut Owen Garriott performs a spacewalk outside the Skylab space station to adjust one of the station's solar panels, which provided Skylab with all of its electricity.

> I THINK HUMANS WILL REACH MARS ... I WOULD LIKE TO SEE IT IN MY LIFETIME
>
> **BUZZ ALDRIN**

EARTH'S SPACE STATION
The International Space Station, which is nearing the end of its construction, is clearly visible in the night sky to the naked eye.

The completed station will comprise 16 pressurized modules, which have been sent into orbit and docked with the previously docked sections of the station. The ISS is a collaborative project between Russia, the United States, Japan, and Europe, and as of 2010, is the largest artificial satellite ever to be sent into space. It has been continuously staffed since November 2000 and is expected to remain operational until 2020. One of the ISS's main scientific goals is the assessment of systems that could be used on future manned flights to the Moon or Mars. After a 40-year hiatus, the project to transport human beings to other parts of the solar system could soon be taken up again in earnest.

of the shuttle that returns to Earth, the Orbiter, carries between five and seven crew, and its payload can accommodate large satellites, such as the Hubble Space Telescope, which was carried into orbit in April 1990 (see right). To date, there have been 114 missions, with the loss of two shuttles. The *Challenger* exploded in January 1986, 73 seconds after liftoff, while the *Columbia* was destroyed during reentry to the Earth's atmosphere on February 1, 2003. In both cases, the entire crews were lost. NASA plans to retire the three remaining space shuttles in 2010. Eventually, they will be replaced by the new generation Orion craft.

SPACE STATION
Construction of the International Space Station (ISS) began in 1998, and is scheduled for completion in 2011.

SPACE TELESCOPE

The Hubble Space Telescope has been sending back images of deep space from its orbit around the Earth since 1993. Away from the distorting effects of the Earth's atmosphere, it has given us views of galaxies so distant that their light is billions of years old. It is scheduled to be replaced in 2014 by the infrared James Webb Space Telescope.

THE HUBBLE ULTRA DEEP FIELD, AN IMAGE OF DISTANT GALAXIES UP TO 13 BILLION LIGHT-YEARS AWAY

SHUTTLE SERVICE
The first space shuttle, *Columbia*, took off from the Kennedy Space Center in Florida on April 12, 1981, 20 years to the day after Yuri Gagarin made the first manned space flight in *Vostok 1*. The shuttle completed 37 orbits in a successful 55-hour mission before returning safely to Earth, making an unpowered landing at the Edwards Air Force Base in California.

FUTURE SCIENCE EXPLORATION

DISCOVERING THE FUTURE OF HUMANKIND

MUCH OF TODAY'S scientific research and exploration centers on the need to understand human impact on the Earth. Multidisciplinary teams comprising geographers, geologists, microbiologists, and others, work on international projects using the latest in high-technology equipment, often remotely from space, to observe and model changes in the world around us.

WORK IN PROGRESS

- The latest computer models predict that **the Earth will warm by at least 4°F (2°C)** in the coming decades; scientists face the dual challenge of slowing down global warming and mitigating the effects of warming

- The ongoing **deforestation** of the world is an active area of research, as scientists learn more about the role forests play in climate change

- In 2008, for the first time in history, **more than half the world's population**—3.3 billion people—was living in **urban areas**; by 2030, that number is expected to increase to 5 billion; such rapid urbanization requires scientific research to understand how best to manage finite resources in the fast-growing cities

WINDS OF CHANGE

Officially the dustiest place on Earth, the Bodélé Desert Depression in Northern Chad is an unforgiving landscape. Howling winds whip up millions of tons of white dust, which in turn are blown as far away as the Amazon Rainforest. But the region was not always so inhospitable. Six thousand years ago, North Africa was wetter, and the area contained one of the largest freshwater lakes in the world— about the same size as the Caspian Sea—filled by rainfall draining from Central Africa and what is now the central Saharan Desert. Scientific research has shown that the lake extended as far as Nigeria and Niger. It is now a chalky-white lake bed, and the dust is made not of sand, but nutrient-rich diatomite, the remains of microscopic organisms that once lived in the lake. International teams of scientists have established the age of the fossil lakes and have discovered how the dust brings added fertility to the soils in the Amazon region and contributes nutrients to the Atlantic Ocean, which in turn help to increase algal growth.

The algae help to absorb carbon dioxide from the Earth's atmosphere. These discoveries enable us to understand the impact of the dust in a future, drier world, as well as revealing precisely how the climate has changed in the recent past—vital information that allows the modeling of future climate change.

BENEATH THE OCEANS

Scientists from the United States Woods Hole Oceanographic Institution (WHOI) are expanding our knowledge of the deepest places on Earth. The scientists use high-tech equipment such as the robotic submersible *Nereus* to monitor the movement of the Earth's tectonic plates, and

DEEP DIVER
In May 2009, *Nereus* made the deepest dive ever achieved, reaching a depth of 6.8 miles (10,902 m) to the Mariana Trench on the Pacific Ocean floor, the deepest point on Earth.

a remote monitoring unit called REMUS, which uses sonar techniques to map areas of the seabed in lanes of overlapping widths—a technique that is known as "mowing the lawn." Data is enhanced using high-resolution cameras built into the submersibles, providing new insights into the composition of the Earth's crust and mantle at ocean floor level. This assists scientists who predict natural disasters such as volcanoes, earthquakes, and tsunamis. The WHOI also records, maps, and finds samples of hitherto unknown seafloor communities of flora and fauna, which in turn inform research into the possibilities of life elsewhere in the solar system.

GLACIAL WATERS

The glaciers that drain the Greenland Ice Sheet, calving fleets of icebergs into the Arctic Ocean, are now thinning and retreating at a dramatic rate. Scientists are exploring the effects of distinct phenomena affecting the vulnerability of melting ice sheets to warming.

Every single quart of glacial melt water contains up to one million microbial cells, which are released each spring and summer when the ice thaws. Teams from Russia, Norway, and the UK have collaborated to study

DESERT DUST
During field research in the Bodélé Depression, scientists endure choking dust and viciously high temperatures.

EQUIPPED WITH HIS FIVE SENSES, MAN EXPLORES THE UNIVERSE ... AND CALLS THE ADVENTURE SCIENCE

EDWIN HUBBLE

glaciers at varying stages of melt. In addition, the research has revealed that glaciers are thriving ecosystems and that the microbes that colonize them may actually be accelerating their melting. DNA tests have enabled scientists to see how cryoconite (which comprises microorganisms, dead organic matter, and mineral debris) forms and influences the ice environment, and how its presence can increase the absorption of solar radiation by up to 30 percent. Glaciologists are now trying to understand how this will affect the future movement of ice sheets, and how increased melt water will impact on salinity levels in the Arctic Ocean.

POLAR ADVANCES

Rapid developments are also taking place in the field of polar science. The study of subglacial lakes first began in the late 1960s with Russian radar data from Lake Sovetskaya in the Eastern Antarctic. From the 17 known subglacial lakes in the 1970s, satellite imagery has shown that the number today stands at 145 and is increasing, indicating that the polar ice sheets are melting at an alarming rate. Analysis of these interconnected lakes is showing their dynamic role in the system of ice flow and balance in Antarctica.

In addition to the study of the way climate affects the poles, scientists are also using innovative techniques to explore more fundamental scientific questions. By drilling holes in the Antarctic ice sheet, which have a high degree of transparency, it has been possible to capture neutrinos, a form of subatomic particle, which, when captured, shed light on the nature of stars, black holes, and dark matter in the universe.

PARTICLE SMASHER

One of the most ambitious scientific projects ever conceived is taking place more than 300 ft (100 m) under the ground at CERN, a research center in Switzerland. The Large Hadron Collider is a circular tunnel 17 miles (27 km) long, through which tiny protons are accelerated to nearly the speed of light and crashed into each other. By analyzing the fallout from these high-speed collisions, scientists are hoping to explore some fundamental questions about the universe, such as why objects have mass and what dark matter may be. If we can discover what happened when the universe was born, we will have a better understanding of its future.

LARGE HADRON COLLIDER, A RING OF SUPERCONDUCTING MAGNETS COOLED TO JUST ABOVE 0°K BY LIQUID HELIUM

ICE CAVE
Scientists may spend weeks at a time under a layer of ice over half a mile thick, living in and studying ice caves that form under glaciers. The scientists monitor the microbial life thriving in glaciers and the rate at which the ice is melting.

INDEX

Main entries for explorers are in **bold**.

ACKNOWLEDGMENTS

The **Royal Geographical Society** (with **IBG**) would like to thank Jamie Owen and Joy Wheeler in the picture library; Julie Carrington, Jools Cole, Susanna James, David McNeill, Nick Smith, Catherine Souch, Sarah Strong, Janet Turner, and Samuel Vale.

Dorling Kindersley would like to thank the following people for their help with the preparation of this book: Sharon Spencer and Joanne Clark for design, Jenny Baskaya for picture research, and Ed Merritt for the maps.

Tall Tree Ltd would like to thank: Debra Wolter for proofreading and Chris Bernstein for the index.

The publisher would like to thank the following for their kind permission to reproduce their photographs:

Key:
a-above; b-below/bottom; c-center; f-far; l-left; r-right; t-top; bkg-background.
AA - **The Art Archive**; BAL - **The Bridgeman Art Library**; DK - **Dorling Kindersley**; NHM - **The Natural History Museum, London**; RGS - **© Royal Geographical Society.**

1 RGS. 2–3 RGS. 4–5 RGS. 6 RGS: (bl) (bc) (br). **Corbis:** Bettmann (tl). **Getty Images:** Banco Nacional Ultramarino/ BAL (tr); Bibliothèque Nationale, Paris/ Imagno (tc). **6–7 Getty Images:** BAL (c). **7 RGS:** (bl) (bc). **Corbis:** Bettmann (tc) (br); The Gallery Collection (tl). **Getty Images:** National Library of Australia, Canberra/BAL (tr). **8 RGS:** (b/3) (b/1) (t/4) (t/5). **Corbis:** Bettmann (t/2); The Gallery Collection (t/3); Sandro Vannini (t/1). **Getty Images:** (b/5); Hulton Archive (b/6); Imagno (b/2); National Library of Australia, Canberra/BAL (t/6); Popperfoto/Bob Thomas (b/4). **8–9 Getty Images:** Photographer's Choice/Jochen Schlenker (c) (b/4). **9 RGS:** (t/6) (b/2) (b/5). **Corbis:** Bettmann (b/1); Sean Sexton Collection (b/3); Stapleton Collection (t/1). **Getty Images:** BAL (t/2); Hulton Archive/Stringer (t/5). **NASA:** (b/6). **courtesy of the National Park Service:** (t/4). **Marinemuseum, St Petersburg:** (t/3). **10–11 Corbis:** Richard T. Nowitz. **12 Alamy Images:** WoodyStock (fclb). **Corbis:** Bettmann (tr); Araldo de Luca (tc); Gianni Dagli Orti (tl) (cla); Guenter Rossenbach (ca). **Getty Images:** Axiom Photographic Agency/ Chris Caldicott (fbr); De Agostini Picture Library/W. Buss (crb); Photodisc/ Medioimages (bl). **13 Alamy Images:** David Paterson (bc). **Corbis:** Robert Harding World Imagery/Sybil Sassoon (clb); Royal Ontario Museum (cl); SABA/

Shepard Sherbell (tr); Gustavo Tomsich (tl). **Getty Images:** Apic (c); Stone/Russell Kaye/Sandra-Lee Phipps (br). **14 Corbis:** Stapleton Collection (b). **DK:** The British Museum, London (tr). **14–15 Corbis:** Gianni Dagli Orti (t/bkg). **15 RGS:** (tc). **Corbis:** The Gallery Collection (cl). **Getty Images:** Stock Montage (tl). **16 akg-images:** Hervé Champollion (cla). **Corbis:** AA (cra). **DK:** The British Museum, London/Peter Hayman (crb). **17 Corbis:** Brooklyn Museum (tc); Gianni Dagli Orti (tr) (b). **18 Alamy Images:** Paul Almasy (br). **Getty Images:** National Geographic/Michael Nichols (cr). **19 Alamy Images:** Mary Evans Picture Library. **20 AA:** Museo Naval, Madrid/ Gianni Dagli Orti (br). **Corbis:** Roger Tidman (cra). **Rvalette:** (cla). **21 Corbis:** Science Faction/Fred Hirschmann (r). **Hannes Grobe:** (tl). **22 Corbis:** The Gallery Collection (cla). **Getty Images:** DK/Gary Ombler (crb). **23 Corbis:** Sandro Vannini. **24 Corbis:** Kazuyoshi Nomachi (bc). **Getty Images:** BAL (ca); The Image Bank/Andrea Pistolesi (cra). **25 Corbis:** Robert Harding World Imagery/ Nico Tondini (cra). **Getty Images:** BAL (tl); Time & Life Pictures/Mansell (b). **26 Corbis:** Frans Lemmens (c). **26–27 Corbis:** Science Faction/Louie Psihoyos (b). **Getty Images:** Aurora/Ted Wood (bkg). **27 Corbis:** Hulton-Deutsch Collection (tr). **Getty Images:** Three Lions (clb). **28 Corbis:** Burstein Collection (bl); The Gallery Collection (tr). **28–29 Corbis:** Jose Fuste Raga (t/bkg). **29 Getty Images:** Photographer's Choice/Michele Falzone (tc); Win Initiative (tl). **30 The British Museum, London:** (cr). **31 Corbis:** Edifice (t). **Mogao Caves:** (br); **ZazaPress:** (bl). **32 DK:** National Maritime Museum, London/Tina Chambers (cl). **Getty Images:** AFP/Carl de Souza (b). **33 Getty Images:** Tin Graham (cla). Illustration by Al-Biruni (973-1048) of different phases of the moon from *Kitab al-tafhim* (cr). **34 Corbis:** Homer Sykes (tr). **DK:** Danish National Museum/Peter Anderson (bc). **34–35 Corbis:** Wolfgang Kaehler (t/bkg). **35 RGS:** (tl) (b). **Getty Images:** Jeff J. Mitchell (tc). **36 Corbis:** Werner Forman (bc). **Getty Images:** Hulton Archive (cla). **37 Corbis:** Bettmann. **38 Corbis:** Robert Harding World Imagery/Yadid Levy (c). **Getty Images:** BAL (b); National Geographic/Peter V. Bianchi (tc). **39 Corbis:** Tom Bean (cra); Bettmann (crb); Wolfgang Kaehler (cla). **Getty Images:** First Light/Yves Marcoux (bl). **40 Alamy Images:** Alex Ramsay (br). **The Viking Ship Museum, Roskilde, Denmark:** (cl) (bl) (c). **41 BAL:** Viking Ship Museum, Oslo (bc). **Corbis:** Werner Forman (tc). **DK:** Roskilde Viking Ship Museum, Denmark/Peter Anderson (cr). **Getty

Images:** Robert Harding World Imagery/ David Lomax (tl). **The Viking Ship Museum, Roskilde, Denmark:** (bl) (br). **Werner Forman Archive:** Viking Ship Museum, Bygdoy (tr). **42 Alamy Images:** The Art Gallery Collection (br). **Rolf Müller:** (tr). **42–43 Corbis:** Angelo Hornak (t/bkg). **43 Corbis:** Lindsay Hebberd (b); Jose Fuste Raga (tl); Alison Wright (tc). **44 RGS:** (tr). **AA:** The British Museum, London (tr). **Private Collection:** (cr). **45 Corbis:** Robert Harding World Imagery. **46 Alamy Images:** ArkReligion.com (cla); The Art Gallery Collection (cr). **46–47 The Trustees of the British Museum:** (b). **47 Alamy Images:** AA (c). **Corbis:** Asian Art & Archaeology, Inc. (cr); Richard T. Nowitz (tl). **48–49 Getty Images:** BAL. **50 akg-images:** (clb). **Corbis:** The Gallery Collection (tr). **DK:** National Maritime Museum, London/Tina Chambers (cl). **Getty Images:** BAL (cla) (bc) (tc); Panoramic Images (cra); Workbook Stock/Eitan Simanor (c). **Private Collection:** (crb). **51 Corbis:** (clb); Bettmann (cb) (crb); Chris Hellier (tl); Angelo Hornak (br); Frans Lanting (tr); Francesc Muntada (tc); Stapleton Collection (bl). **Getty Images:** Photographer's Choice/Christopher Thomas (ca). **Library of Congress, Washington, D.C.:** (cr). **52 AA:** Museo Correr, Venice/Dagli Orti (cr). **Corbis:** The Gallery Collection (tr). **52–53 Corbis:** Barry Lewis (b); Michel Setboun (t/bkg). **53 Corbis:** Bettmann (tc); Nik Wheeler (tl). **54 akg-images:** (cla). **Alamy Images:** The Print Collector (tr). **Getty Images:** Photographer's Choice/Massimo Pizzotti (bc). **55 Corbis:** Nik Wheeler (b). **Photolibrary:** John Warburton-Lee Photography/Antonia Tozer (c). **56 Corbis:** Bettmann (cla). **57 Getty Images:** Bibliothèque Nationale, Paris/ Imagno. **58 Corbis:** Zhuoming Liang (bl). **Getty Images:** Altrendo (bl). **58–59 Getty Images:** Roger Viollet Collection (tc). **59 RGS:** (br). **Alamy Images:** Mary Evans Picture Library (cra). **Corbis:** Fadil (bl). **Getty Images:** China Span/Keren Su (clb). **60–61 AA:** Bibliothèque Nationale, Paris. **62 Getty Images:** AFP/Frederic J. Brown. **63 Alamy Images:** Chris Hellier (cla). **DK:** National Maritime Museum, London (br). **64 Corbis:** Martin Puddy (clb). **Getty Images:** The Image Bank/ Ashok Sinha (crb). **National Palace Museum, Taiwan:** (cla). **65 Alamy Images:** Stuart Forster (tr). **Corbis:** Asian Art & Archaeology, Inc. (c); JAI/Michele Falzone (bl). **Getty Images:** The Image Bank/Christopher Pillitz (bc). **Private Collection:** (clb). **66 Getty Images:** BAL (bl); Popperfoto (bl). **66–67 Getty Images:** Photographer's Choice/Travelpix Ltd (t/bkg). **67 Alamy Images:** AA (tc). **DK:** National Maritime Museum, London/James Stevenson (br). **Getty Images:** BAL (tl). **68 Corbis:** Bojan

Brecelj (bc). **69 Getty Images:** Apic. **70 Corbis:** EPA/Namir Noor-Eldeen (bc). **Getty Images:** Photographer's Choice/ Travelpix Ltd (t). **71 Corbis:** Burstein Collection (cr). **Getty Images:** AFP/ Yasser Al-Zayyat (cb); Gallo Images/ Thomas Dressler (bc). **Private Collection:** (bl). **72 Getty Images:** Apic. **73 Getty Images:** Apic. **74 Getty Images:** BAL (tr). Calicut from Georg Braun and Franz Hogenber's atlas *Civitates orbis Terrarum*, 1572 (b). **74–75 Corbis:** (t/ bkg). **75 Corbis:** Bettmann (cr); Bojan Brecelj (tc); Michael Freeman (tl). **76 Alamy Images:** Mary Evans Picture Library (cr). **BAL:** Private Collection/ Ancient Art and Architecture Collection Ltd. (cla). **77 Getty Images:** Biblioteca Estense, Modena/BAL (tr); Tobias Titz (b). **78 AA:** Marine Museum, Lisbon/Dagli Orti (br). **Photo Scala, Florence:** Museu Nacional de Arte Antiga, Lisbon (bl). **Alvesgaspar:** (cla). **79 Getty Images:** Gallo Images/Anthony Bannister (cra). **Alvesgaspar:** (tl). **80 Corbis:** The Gallery Collection (cla). **Getty Images:** Kean Collection (cr). **Carlos Luis M C da Cruz:** (bl). **81 Getty Images:** Banco Nacional Ultramarino/BAL. **82 RGS:** (cl) (cb) (cr) (cfc). **Corbis:** Werner Forman (bc). **DK:** National Maritime Museum, London/James Stevenson (c). **Getty Images:** National Geographic/Walter Meayers Edwards (bl). **83 RGS:** (br). **DK:** National Maritime Museum, London/ James Stevenson (bc). **Getty Images:** Aurora Open/Peter Dennen (cr); SSPL (cl) (clb). **84 Corbis:** Danny Lehman (bl). **Getty Images:** Digital Vision/John Wang (tr). **84–85 Corbis:** Frans Lanting (t/bkg). **85 Corbis:** Bettmann (tl) (tc). **Getty Images:** AFP/Philippe Desmazes (b). **86 Corbis:** The Gallery Collection. **87 AA:** Museo Navale, Pegli/Dagli Orti (bl). **Corbis:** The Gallery Collection (ca). **88 Corbis:** Reuters (b). **Getty Images:** Roger Viollet Collection (tr). **89 Alamy Images:** Mary Evans Picture Library (clb). **AA:** General Archive of the Indies, Seville/Dagli Orti (br). **Corbis:** Yann Arthus-Bertrand (cra). **Getty Images:** Tribaleye Images/Jamie Marshall (cla). **90 Nau Santa Maria de Colombo:** (c) (bl) (br) (cb) (clb). **90–91 Alamy Images:** Mikael Utterstrom (tc). **91 Nau Santa Maria de Colombo:** (tl) (bl) (br) (c) (cr) (tc) (tr). **92 BAL:** Bristol City Museum and Art Gallery (bl). **Corbis:** Bettmann (cla); Hans Strand (tr). **93 AA:** Bibliothèque Nationale, Paris/Harper Collins Publishers. **94 akg-images:** The British Library, London (cra). **Getty Images:** National Library of Australia, Canberra/ BAL (cla); Time Life Pictures/James Whitmore (tl). **95 AA:** General Archive of the Indies, Seville/Dagli Orti (tl). **Getty Images:** Hulton Archive (br). **Photo Scala, Florence:** The British Library, London (tr). **96 Alamy Images:** The Art Gallery Collection (tr). **Corbis:** (cla). **97**